P9-CNF-917

PALACE POLITICS

PALACE
POLITICS

AN INSIDE ACCOUNT OF THE FORD YEARS

★★★★★★★★★★★★★★★★★★★★★★★★★★★★★★★★★

ROBERT T. HARTMANN

McGraw-Hill Book Company

NEW YORK   ST. LOUIS   SAN FRANCISCO
DÜSSELDORF   MEXICO   TORONTO

Copyright © 1980 by Robert T. Hartmann.
All rights reserved.

Printed in the United States of America.
No part of this publication may be reproduced,
stored in a retrieval system, or transmitted, in any form
or by any means, electronic, mechanical, photocopying,
recording, or otherwise, without the prior
written permission of the publisher.

2 3 4 5 6 7 8 9 D O D O 8 7 6 5 4 3 2 1 0

LIBRARY OF CONGRESS CATALOGING IN PUBLICATION DATA

Hartmann, Robert Trowbridge,
    Palace politics
    Bibliography: p.
    1.   United States—Politics and government—
1974–1977.   2.   Ford, Gerald R., 1913–
3.   Hartmann, Robert Trowbridge, 1917–
I.   Title.
E865.H37   973.925   80-11237
ISBN 0-07-026951-3

Book design by Roberta Rezk.

TO ROBERTA

Niente senza te

ACKNOWLEDGMENTS

This study might never have been undertaken without the generous support of the Hoover Institution on War, Revolution and Peace at Stanford University.

For encouragement and assistance, great or small, I am especially indebted to Gwen Anderson, Bill Baroody, Joe Bartlett, Benton Becker, Carl Brandt, Arthur Burns, Dick Burress, Jack Calkins, Glenn Campbell, Jim Cannon, Liz Carpenter, Bill Casselman, Thad Cochrane, Tom Corcoran, Louise Doying, Milorad Drachkovitch, Alex Dreier, Jerome Dreyer, Gerald Ford, Milt Friedman, Lois Gibson, Bob Griffin, Bryce Harlow, Rob Hartmann, Charles Hawes, Grace Hawes, Gail Raiman Helms, Bob Hynes, Bruce Lee, Kristina Lindbergh, Virginia Lipscomb, Bill Markert, Jack Marsh, John McGoff, Neta Messersmith, Bob Michel, Bill Middendorf, Hugh Morrow, Rogers Morton, Bob Orben, Willis Player, John Rhodes, Nelson Rockefeller, Rick Sardo, Hugh Scott, Doug Smith, Jerry terHorst, Paul Theis, Bill Timmons, Win Weitzel, Don Wiggins, John Williams and Joann Lynott Wilson.

To scores of friends not on this limited list I apologize and thank them also. None of the above is at all to blame for my opinions, conclusions, inadvertent errors or advertent biases.

We had no tapes in the Ford White House. I had no time to keep an elaborate diary. I rely on a journeyman reporter's eyes and ears, scattered notes and the corroboration of colleagues and contemporary documents. I would not swear that all my reconstructed dialogue is verbatim. When direct quotes are used, they are a matter of record or my best understanding of the speaker's meaning. When in doubt, or for brevity, I have paraphrased.

The principal reference books I have consulted are listed in the bibliography, regardless of their merit. Periodicals are cited in the text.

President Ford's own memoirs, published when mine were almost finished, required adding a few footnotes. I was extensively interviewed by his autobiographical associate but deliberately refrained from consulting my former boss with respect to my own recollections. History would not be well served by our comparing notes.

Washington, January 20, 1980   R.T.H.

CONTENTS

★★────────────────────★★

INTRODUCTION

★★─────────────★★

ABOUT THOSE PRAETORIANS

Throughout this volume the reader will encounter frequent references to "Nixon's Praetorians," "the Praetorian Guard" or "the little Praetorians." The significance of these terms may require some elaboration.

The early Romans, jealous of their republican traditions, did not permit armed soldiers within the city walls, where they might intimidate the Senate and People of Rome. Later, when all of Italy acquired Roman citizenship, the Legions were forbidden south of the Rubicon River.

Julius Caesar, at the beginning of the rather rapid dissolution of the republic, was the first to defy the Rubicon taboo. Augustus went a step further by introducing his own elite palace guard, called Praetorians, *within* the walls of Rome.

Edward Gibbon, in his *Decline and Fall of the Roman Empire,* described the consequences: "By thus introducing the Praetorian guards . . . into the palace and the Senate, the emperors taught them to perceive their own strength, and the weakness of the civil government; to view the vices of their masters with familiar contempt, and . . . their pride was nourished by the sense of their irresistible weight."

The Praetorians were selected among the sons of the noblest Roman families, and their original mission was the protection of the person of the Emperor. In addition, they were highly privileged hostages for the good conduct of their kin against subversion or revolution. Their commander, neither born to the purple nor elected by the Senate and People, was more powerful than Caesar himself. In the end, the Praetorians chose and deposed Emperors at their pleasure.

There is nothing about the eternal struggle of men (and women) for pre-eminence, power and place in political life that is not exhaustively examined by Gibbon. Nothing has really changed but the names and the severity of punishment for failure.

To condense the consequences of Praetorian power, Gibbon goes on to describe history's most sordid succession.

PALACE POLITICS

On March 28, A.D. 193, the Praetorian Guards marched boldly at noon to the Imperial Palace and assassinated Pertinax, who in three months had displeased them by his stern discipline and return to the old Roman law. They much preferred the bloodthirsty excesses of his mad predecessor, Commodus, the gladiator tyrant.

Bearing Pertinax's head on a pike, the Praetorians proclaimed from the ramparts of their fort that the Roman world was to be auctioned off to the highest bidder. The winner was Didius Julianus, an elderly Senator distinguished only by his wealth. He promised 200 pounds sterling (by Gibbon's calculation) to each Praetorian and was promptly hailed as Caesar.

Julian enjoyed his succession to the mantle of the great Julius only until June 2, as long as it took the fierce Pannonian legions of Septimus Severus to reach Rome by forced marches from the Danube to the Tiber. Julian lost his head in turn.

And that, according to Gibbon, was the beginning of the end of the Roman Empire.

I must freely acknowledge that "little Praetorians" was not the way the more obnoxious of the Nixon palace guards were commonly characterized. In Congressional cloakrooms they were known variously as "Katzenjammer Kids," "California Mafia" or "those little jerks in the White House," to mention only the mentionable. Some Rockefeller aides dismissed them as "those Munchkins."

The classical Roman analogy came to me from George Reedy* as a shorthand term for the close-knit group of Haldeman–Haig subordinates that Ford, as Vice President, scathingly branded "an arrogant, elite guard of political adolescents" who nearly wrecked the Republican Party. "Praetorian" is both elegant and apt.

As in all categorizations, however, some injustice may be done by lumping all these former campaign hustlers and self-anointed experts together. Some of my best friends were then and still are Nixon loyalists whose dedication to the national interest and to Ford cannot be questioned.

Because I believe in the doctrine of redemption, and youth is the only completely curable affliction, most of the little Praetorians whose palace politicking hastened the end of the Ford Presidency are not individually named. This is not to spare their feelings—they will recognize themselves—but to preserve their future usefulness to the Re-

---

* *The Twilight of the Presidency*, New York: New American Library, 1970.

2

public. Some day they may return to the White House as mature citizens.

Nor were the principal Praetorians, who *are* identifiable, inherently wicked and evil. They were merely small.

The bedrock disagreement between the Praetorians and the handful of us who stubbornly resisted them was that they wanted to make Jerry Ford into somebody quite different from what he was. Their constant cry was for him to be "more Presidential." Presumably their model was President Nixon—but *which* Nixon? Sometimes their model seemed a creation of a pollster's computer, sometimes a gilded image graven in the wilderness of their sharp but unseasoned minds.

To those who knew the real Jerry Ford, this was not only blasphemous in principle but impossible in practice. The man we knew was what we had as President, and what we had was not bad. What we had to "sell" to the electorate was not a packaging problem but a clearer appreciation of the genuine article.

Ford's integrity, which had carried him this far, was all that could carry him further. Long before television, Lincoln grew a beard to enhance his "image." But it was not the chin whiskers that won him a second term and a unique place in the hearts of his countrymen. It was integrity, warts and all.

There are as many ways of being "Presidential" as we have Presidents. The way for a President to be Presidential is to be himself. We have had some superb actors in the White House, but acting was a part of their nature long before they got there. When Teddy or Franklin Roosevelt went into their theatrics, they were simply being themselves. We have had some brilliant wits, but when John F. Kennedy tossed off a fast comeback he was being himself. When LBJ tried to be FDR, or when Nixon attempted a JFK joke, they bombed.

Jerry Ford was incapable of playing any role except that of Jerry Ford. Whenever, under the prodding of the Praetorians, he appeared out of character, it severely eroded his integrity. When his actions seemed contrived, calculating or cute, his credibility suffered.

In the beginning, before the Praetorian encirclement was complete, the new and unknown President was seen in refreshing contrast to his predecessor—a natural, friendly, sincere and modest man who told the truth and tried his best. At the end, he was seen as a genial but generally less competent extension of his predecessor, locked in Nixon's legacy and proud of perpetuating Nixon's policies.

Had he changed?

PALACE POLITICS

When I was in the White House I was asked this question maybe once or twice a week, and I always answered: not fundamentally. He had to ration his time more carefully, deal with matters of greater moment, make hard decisions himself which previously he could have compromised. But he hadn't become a totally different man.

There is a canard that the Presidency changes people, that the pressures of the office either bring out the best or the worst—sometimes both—in the ordinary mortals who briefly occupy the Oval Office.

What happened to Ford is what always happens to those in high places: The public becomes much more interested in their character and habits after they are elevated where everyone can get a look at them. We change our ideas about them more than they themselves change.

But it is indisputable that every President is surrounded by those who want to change him. Every President, like the later Caesars, has his Praetorian Guard. And whether he can command them, or they command him, is a measure of the President's effectiveness and the confidence that will be given him by the American people.

1

Instant Vice President

The 895-day Presidency of Gerald R. Ford was unique and unprecedented. No two words in the lexicon of political journalism are more frequently abused. There is really very little new under the sun. But consider:

No President except Ford ever held office without having been elected by a majority of Presidential electors to be either President or Vice President, or, in the early instances of Thomas Jefferson and John Quincy Adams, having been declared the winner by the House of Representatives as the result of an electoral tie.

No Vice President except Ford ever succeeded to the Presidency on any basis other than the death of an incumbent President. No President, prior to Nixon, ever resigned.

No President, prior to Nixon, ever faced criminal prosecution after leaving office.

No Vice President, prior to Ford, was ever chosen by the untried process of the Twenty-fifth Amendment, ratified in 1967. (Subsequently, of course, Nelson A. Rockefeller was similarly chosen and confirmed.)

Nobody except Gerald R. Ford has ever become President through the deliberate and voluntary act of his predecessor. (Had Nixon been removed from office, Ford would have become President through the impeachment votes of a majority of Representatives and the convicting votes of two-thirds of Senators. Had Nixon declared himself disabled or had the Vice President and a majority of the Cabinet certified his inability under the Twenty-fifth Amendment, Ford would only have become Acting President.*)

* Until the Twenty-fifth Amendment, the Constitution was unclear as to whether a succeeding Vice President was actually President or Acting President. John Tyler insisted he was "The President" over strenuous objections, among them that of John Adams. All others followed Tyler's precedent, but it was not written into the Constitution until 1967.

5

PALACE POLITICS

Nobody, not even George Washington, has ever become *both* Vice President and President without having publicly sought and striven for either office, without the citizens of every state considering his candidacy and passing judgment on his fitness, either directly or through elected representatives.

All these exceptions to the normal rules of Presidential and Vice Presidential selection and succession converged on a sixty-year-old Congressman from Michigan—a state that had never produced either a President or a Vice President—in somewhat less than one year.

On August 8, 1973, Vice President Spiro T. Agnew held a televised news conference and denied as "damned lies" charges in several newspapers that he took kickbacks and systematic payoffs while Governor of Maryland. Two months later he copped a plea, resigned, and on December 6 Ford became Vice President.

On August 8, 1974, President Nixon told the American people, over national television networks, that he intended to resign the following day. Thus, Gerald R. Ford became our thirty-eighth President.

★

The first time Richard Nixon mentioned Spiro Agnew as a potential Vice President, Jerry Ford let out a loud horse laugh. That was an earlier August, at Miami Beach in 1968. Jerry Ford, the Minority Leader in the House, was Permanent Chairman of the Republican national convention. The previous night, cheering delegates had acclaimed Richard Nixon, the party's 1960 standard-bearer, for a second try. Then they went off to drink and party. Nixon summoned the real power brokers of the GOP and his Praetorian Guard to his headquarters suite in the Hilton Plaza at the north end of the Gold Coast.

Ford slept soundly at the Fontainebleau. His feelings were not hurt for not having been invited to help the candidate choose a running mate, possibly because he nursed a long-shot hope of being chosen. He is, anyhow, an instant sleeper.

Richard Nixon and his companions didn't get much sleep. They were well aware that his 1960 defeat may have been due to his hasty selection of Henry Cabot Lodge after Nelson Rockefeller refused the number-two spot on the ticket. Despite his move to Manhattan, Nixon was still a Californian to most voters and he still needed an authentic Eastern type a little more liberal than his own image, one who might take urban and ethnic voters away from the Democrats.

Nixon narrowed the field down to the Governors of Massachusetts and Maryland, John A. Volpe and Spiro T. Agnew, and in the end tilted southward. Massachusetts had never done much for him. So

6

now, after a quick catnap, Nixon had to placate all the party Pooh-Bahs who hadn't been invited to the real running-mate deliberation. There were Senator Everett Dirksen, whose son-in-law, Howard Baker, was a long shot; Nixon's former campaign manager Bob Finch, who led a lot of lists; National Chairman Ray Bliss; and the two Congressional campaign chairmen, Representative Bob Wilson and Senator George Murphy. And, of course, good old Jerry Ford.

In 1960 Ford had, in his own words, "gingerly entertained the flattering notion of friends that a Nixon–Ford ticket would be a winner." Unfortunately, he recalled, "that draft diminished to a flat calm."

It was not Nixon's way to come directly to the point. First, he'd try to make everybody a little less unhappy about the decision he had already made. "I've been weighing a long list of very fine possibilities," Nixon began. Then he looked straight at Ford. Too bad, he said, that Jerry had plainly announced his only ambition was to be Speaker, otherwise he'd make a wonderful running mate. Then, for the benefit of the other Minority Leader present, he told Dirksen how highly he regarded Senator Baker and what a great future Howard had in the Senate. He praised his loyal longtime aide, Bob Finch, who had a great future in California. Now, if anybody had any candidates they'd like to mention, he'd be happy to hear them.

Ford, seconded by Bob Wilson, startled the gathering by proposing Mayor John V. Lindsay of New York. Lindsay was the very model of effete Eastern liberalism to the Nixon Praetorians. He was hardly an ideological soul mate for Ford and Wilson. But they had served together in the House, and, pragmatically, it was in New York and its neighboring states that Republicans had failed to recoup their Congressional losses of 1964.

Unhappily, as Nixon went around the table and other potential running mates were discussed, nobody so much as mentioned his secret choice. His darting eyes took on a slightly desperate cast and finally he coughed and interrupted: "There's ... ah ... another very popular ... ah ... Republican Governor I've been hearing a lot of good things about ... ah ... Ted Agnew."

Ford's raucous whinny shattered the silence. His nervous, high-pitched laugh had been known to penetrate the sandstone walls of the Capitol and was a sure sign of inner tension. Dirksen and Ray Bliss betrayed theirs by simultaneously trying to bum cigarettes from each other. Haldeman and the rest of Nixon's Praetorians stared at Ford as if he had farted.

Nixon was startled off his stride only for a moment, then plunged on with his eulogy of Agnew, who had declared for Rockefeller earlier in the campaign and was not even at the convention. Nixon thanked everybody, said he would think the names over and announce his decision soon.

Before Ford got back to the Fontainebleau, the word was out. Nixon and Agnew. Tricky Dick and Spiro Who?

Ford and some others were appalled but lauded the Nixon choice like good soldiers. Representative Charles Goodell (R–New York) was so mad he led a futile floor rebellion for Lindsay and was promptly marked for oblivion by Nixon and his Praetorians.

I was somewhat chagrined myself. Ford was Permanent Chairman of the convention, and I was Ford's assistant. As such, one of my chores was to keep the Secret Service advised of the most likely nominees of the convention. Under the so-called "Bobby Kennedy Law," in effect for the first time, protection was provided for Presidential and Vice Presidential candidates of major parties as soon as they could be identified.

Nixon had been the odds-on Republican favorite all along, but now the agents wanted to know who else they should be ready to watch over. That very morning I had huddled with Ford and Dirksen and then given the Secret Service a list of their three best guesses— none of them Agnew. (As I recall, they were John Volpe, Charles Percy and John Lindsay, but nothing was ever written down.)

Agnew's protective detail had a little trouble locating him, but he arrived in Miami Beach in time for his acclamation. Who could have guessed that this handsome Greek immigrant's son and the poor Quaker boy from Whittier, California, soon to join him on millions of television screens, would twice win and then renounce the two highest elective offices of the Republic?

Who could have foreseen that the United States of America, on our two hundredth celebration of repudiating unelected rulers, would have an unelected President and an unelected Vice President as well?

★

When the Founding Fathers sat down in Independence Hall to draft a Constitution, they were torn between their fears of an arbitrary, too powerful ruler and their experience of the chaos caused by having no central authority at all.

Ever since tribes of human beings started to settle within fixed territories and to subordinate themselves to a chief warrior in order to

8

defend their lands and arbitrate their quarrels, the most vexing of political problems has been the transfer of leadership. From the Roman Co-Consuls to the Russian Presidium, it is the immutable testimony of history that two or more human beings cannot share power equally. Fortunately the framers of the Constitution overcame their king-shy feelings and settled for a single President, trusting that Washington would establish the necessary republican precedents of modesty and restraint. Furthermore, they provided an orderly means of removing a President—or other officials who might abuse their powers—through impeachment by the House and trial by the Senate. And if a President were unable to perform his duties, through death, disability, resignation or removal, his place would immediately be taken by a Vice President.

They did not even mention the office of Vice President during the first three months of the Convention. It first appears in the rather complicated proposal for choosing the President indirectly by the votes of "electors" from each state. Electors would vote for two persons, the one getting a majority to be President and the runner-up to be Vice President and President of the Senate. Some delegates grumbled that there wouldn't be enough for a Vice President to do. Benjamin Franklin wisecracked that he should be addressed as "Your Superfluous Excellency."

The method of choosing a Vice President was changed by the Twelfth Amendment, after the Jefferson–Burr tie in 1800, so that future Presidents and Vice Presidents would be selected separately and would normally be of the same party rather than rival winner and loser for the Presidency. But the Constitutional duties of a Vice President were unchanged until the Twenty-fifth Amendment made a slight but significant addition.

Under the Twenty-fifth Amendment, the Vice President and a majority of the Cabinet may declare a President to be unable to discharge his powers and duties if the President will not or cannot do so himself. In effect, this means a President cannot be involuntarily relieved of his authority (except via the impeachment route) without the concurrence of the Vice President. Unless the Vice President goes along, the Cabinet could be unanimous and still unable to oust a President.

But what happens when both the President and the Vice President cannot function? Fortunately the situation has never arisen. The Constitution leaves further succession to the Congress. In 1792 Congress decided that the President pro tempore of the Senate and then the Speaker of the House should be next in line. From 1886 until 1947 they were replaced by the Cabinet, starting with the Secretary of State. President Harry S Truman, who served nearly a full term without any Vice President, persuaded Congress to put the Speaker first, the President pro tempore second and then the Cabinet—which is how it stands now. As a practical matter, it would seem difficult to go beyond the Speaker (except in a nuclear holocaust) because immediately after he became President the House would elect another Speaker.

Like the original framers in Philadelphia, the drafters of the Twenty-fifth Amendment were most economical in their language. Section 2, which applies to filling a Vice Presidential vacancy, is one sentence of thirty-four words, reading: "Whenever there is a vacancy in the office of the Vice President, the President shall nominate a Vice President who shall take office upon confirmation by a majority vote of both Houses of Congress."

That is one reason the Constitution is so durable; it leaves a multiplicity of details to be worked out as necessary—by legislation, by judicial rulings, even by Executive assertion, such as the doctrine of "executive privilege."

The same procedure Congress devised for Ford was followed, less than a year later, for Nelson Rockefeller. Two times sets a fairly solid precedent, but one or one hundred years hence other Congresses can change the method if they please.

The deliberations of the original Constitutional Convention are fairly fully preserved. Section 2 of the Twenty-fifth Amendment, however, remains something of a mystery. A diligent search of subcommittee and committee reports, and of the public Senate and House debates in the *Congressional Record,* fails to turn up much enlightenment as to the genesis of this single sentence which made Gerald R. Ford first Vice President and then President of the United States. But it is clear that the main preoccupation of the drafters was the disability—temporary or permanent—of the President, not the Vice President.

Prior to Agnew's resignation, the office of Vice President had been vacant during sixteen intervals for a total of thirty-seven years. When a Vice President died in office (as seven have), resigned or succeeded to the Presidency, the Republic survived without one. The Senate always elected a substitute presiding officer from its own number, who was in the chair most of the time anyway. And a kind fate preserved every

President who served without a Vice President for the balance of his term.

Then, in 1955, President Dwight D. Eisenhower suffered a severe heart attack while vacationing in Colorado. Ike was then sixty-five, our oldest President since James Buchanan. His Vice President was Richard M. Nixon, then only forty-two years old. Eisenhower was never in a coma, as some of his predecessors had been, but he was totally immobilized for weeks.

In this nuclear age, much concern was expressed as to whether the ailing President would be able to react quickly should an emergency arise. Nixon was extremely circumspect, wanting to give no indication of grabbing power.

Although the government's business went forward on its own momentum until Ike was back in the Oval Office, Congress buzzed with disability proposals, but no legislation came of them. Eisenhower and Nixon made public a written agreement that would cover any future health crisis. It was intended to apply only to themselves, but President John F. Kennedy made a similar pact with Vice President Lyndon B. Johnson, as did Johnson with Hubert H. Humphrey.

These informal understandings were the genesis of the Twenty-fifth Amendment. Eisenhower subsequently suffered a minor stroke, which only temporarily affected his speech, but the frightening possibility of mental disability arose.

Senator Estes Kefauver (D–Tennessee), often a bridesmaid in the Presidential and Vice Presidential lists, seems to have authored the first Constitutional Amendment resolutions in 1963. They never got beyond subcommittee consideration. In 1964 the nation was again without a Vice President. Senator Birch Bayh (D–Indiana), chairman of the Constitutional Amendments Subcommittee of the Senate Judiciary Committee, put together a new resolution that incorporated elements of the Eisenhower–Nixon agreement, Kefauver's and other proposals. It was substantially identical to the Twenty-fifth Amendment, as far as it went. However, it would have permitted the Acting President, supported by a majority of the Cabinet, to prevent the President from reclaiming his office merely by informing Congress in writing that the Presidential inability continued.

It is somewhat frightening to recall that this clear invitation to Vice Presidential intriguing to depose a President was approved by sixty-five Senators and opposed by none. Happily, the House took no action.

PALACE POLITICS

On January 28, 1965—the same month Jerry Ford was elected Minority Leader of the House—President Johnson endorsed Senator Bayh's resolution, which had been greatly improved in the House Judiciary Committee by Chairman Emanuel Celler (D–New York). In case of conflict over continuing inability between a President and a Vice President serving as Acting President, Congress would decide by a two-thirds vote in each body. A twenty-day limit for Congressional action was agreed to. The final Bayh–Celler version was adopted 72–0 in the Senate, and the House approved it by 368–29, Representative Ford voting "Aye."

Senator Bayh conceded in 1973 that although his committee anticipated a great many eventualities during its 1965 deliberations on Presidential succession, it failed to foresee what the situation would be when the Twenty-fifth Amendment was first put to the test.

"Who could have imagined the possibility of a Vice President resigning—for the second time, but this time because of charges of criminal misconduct?" Bayh said. "Who could have imagined that at the same time we were trying to fill a Vice Presidential vacancy, the future of the Presidency itself was being questioned by a number of people and a number of news sources throughout the country?"

Bayh and others during the Ford hearings and debates made it plain that they felt they were passing on the qualifications of the next President rather than the next Vice President. And that if they did not have a Vice President, the next President might be Speaker Carl Albert.

Albert himself led the list of those who, for various reasons, were unenthusiastic about his elevation. For one thing, the constant companionship of Secret Service agents cramped his life-style, and, more importantly, it would be unthinkable politics for a Democratic House to impeach a Republican President in order to propel the Speaker to the White House.

Yet, to go back only a few weeks, it was Speaker Albert's decision that made Vice President Agnew's resignation all but inevitable.

On September 25, still protesting his innocence, Agnew went to the Speaker's office to hand him a formal letter requesting that the House initiate impeachment action against him. His lawyers took the position that a President or Vice President could not be indicted or tried on criminal charges while holding office. Agnew argued that he could therefore not defend himself against the leaks of charges from the U.S. Attorney's office for Maryland in court or be vindicated in

12

any forum other than the House. He cited the case of an early predecessor, ironically the only Vice President who ever resigned—John Calhoun.

This South Carolinian precedent failed to move the Speaker from Bug Tussle, Oklahoma. Nor did the pleas of Gerald Ford and Les Arends, the Minority Whip, who at the Vice President's request agreed to urge Albert to entertain the unusual plea, succeed.*

The relationship between Agnew and Ford had been friendly but essentially partisan. They campaigned for each other's election—Agnew was a great hit in Grand Rapids—and had a brief but significant alliance at the 1972 Republican convention—which is, I believe, a hitherto untold tale.

Ford was again chosen Permanent Chairman, but there was a vast change from 1968. This time the Praetorian Guard from the White House was really running the show. Literally. The entire convention proceedings were scripted in advance by professional television people and put on the TelePrompTer. Everyone appeared on a stopwatched cue and spoke what had been prepared for him to build up to the second coming of Richard Nixon.

Good old Jerry was somewhat annoyed but mostly amused by this puerile puppetry, but every now and then he would deliberately mess up the careful orchestration. Then, on the final day of the convention, I picked up some astonishing news.

"You won't believe it," a friend began, "but they are worrying themselves sick about Agnew getting a bigger ovation tonight than Nixon."

"Who's 'they'?" I asked. Agnew was an accomplished crowd-pleaser. Convention delegates want raw meat, and Spiro would chew up radic-libs and nattering nabobs and spit them out still bleeding.

"I don't know exactly," he admitted, "but I know what they're going to do about it. At the end of Agnew's acceptance speech, instead of standing there for the cheers, the Vice President will go right on and introduce the President. Nixon comes on stage and they'll both take the applause together, so you can't tell who's yelling for whom."

"But what's Jerry doing? Dammit, the Permanent Chairman is

---

* Agnew resigned before his constitutional claim of immunity was resolved—and it has never been adjudicated. Vice President Aaron Burr was indicted for murder by the state of New Jersey after his 1804 duel with Alexander Hamilton but was not impeached or even arrested.

introducing President Nixon just like he did four years ago," I spluttered.

"He won't have any choice. They're already rewriting the tail end of Agnew's speech. The Vice President will be so surprised he'll just stammer through it before he figures out why."

"We'll see about that," I muttered.

When I unraveled this dark plot to Ford in his air-conditioned house trailer behind the convention hall, he just chuckled. "But I have the gavel," he said.

He hugely enjoyed being Permanent Chairman. It was almost like being Speaker. It takes a special kind of authority and inner calm to control a very large roomful of egocentrics. You have an overkill plenitude of power, but you exercise it disarmingly so neither friends nor foes resent it. Ford was more adept with a gavel than with the thunderbolts emblazoned on the Presidential seal.

Regardless of how his speech was rewritten, Agnew confided, Ford would present the President to the convention.

"Just keep that gavel in your hands," I said. "The only gavel in the hall, I guarantee you, will be the one in your hand. When Agnew starts his speech, don't leave it at the podium, but take it with you. When he finishes, you will be the only one who can get order and present the President."

Agnew kept his bargain. Ignoring the TelePrompTer, he finished his acceptance speech with a tribute to, but not an introduction of, the President. When Nixon came striding onto the platform, flanked by his attractive family, it was Gerald Ford who gaveled the audience to order and proclaimed, "Ladies and gentlemen, the President of the United States."

Nobody among the millions of viewers knew it wasn't supposed to be that way, but the Praetorians never forgive or forget.

When the Agnew story broke in the August 7, 1973, *Wall Street Journal,* the Vice President denied everything. He also went to Ford's office to assure him privately that he had done no wrong. Agnew left the impression that someone was out to get him, a very credible assumption for anyone in politics. Someone usually is. Ford had no reason to doubt his word.

But Ford was careful. He never again saw the Vice President alone. He also did a little discreet checking on his own. Speculation was rife that the White House wanted Agnew to resign so that John Connally could be groomed as Nixon's heir in 1976. Although Watergate was not yet recognized as the millstone it would later become, it was plain enough that the last thing the Republican Party needed was another scandal in high places.

The Minority Leader was at his place on the House floor when the House convened at noon on October 10, 1973. I was in his Capitol office watching the UPI news ticker, which I had insisted upon installing when I went to work for Ford in 1966. As often as not, this is how you find out what is going on a few steps down the hall.

The ticker was chattering about the Yom Kippur War and Anwar Sadat's surprising successes east of Suez. Suddenly the dispatch broke off and the bell rang for a "bulletin"—a hot news item.

"WASHINGTON: VICE PRESIDENT AGNEW RESIGNED HIS OFFICE AT 2:05 P.M. TODAY."

I waited for a few more details, then ripped them off the machine and ran for the House floor, down the aisle and slipped into the row behind Ford's seat, passing them to him.

"Agnew quit," I whispered.

Ford shook his head and gave a low whistle. "You're kidding!" he said. Like most of us, he thought Agnew would fight to the end.

Sam Garrison, a lawyer on Agnew's staff, delivered a personal letter to Ford minutes after the Vice President's single sentence of resignation was delivered to Secretary of State Henry Kissinger. He showed it to me later that night.

Dear JERRY,
Today I have resigned as Vice President of the United States. After an extremely difficult weighing of all the factors, my deep concern for the country required this decision.
You have been a staunch friend. I shall always count your friendship as a personal treasure.
My gratitude and affection will always be yours.
Sincerely,
TED

If Ford ever answered this letter, I never saw it.

Now things really began to happen fast. The White House called. Would Mr. Ford be able to come down at 4:00 P.M. to meet with the President? About the way we should go about filling the vacancy under the Twenty-fifth Amendment. Of course he'd be there.

Ford worked his way over to Carl Albert and they huddled briefly. He was getting the Speaker's agreement to hold off a roll-call vote until he got back from the White House. It was important to Ford to be recorded on this D.C. Home Rule bill.

Carl Albert, I suddenly realized, was now the *de facto* Vice President of the United States. A phalanx of Capitol policemen was already arrayed outside his office and at every entrance to the House chamber and the public galleries. They would shortly be augmented by Secret Service agents on round-the-clock details. Except on the House and Senate floors, where they are never knowingly permitted, the security men would be with Albert for almost two months (and would appear next year for the duration of Rockefeller's confirmation).

While Ford went to see the President, I started digging out of our files everything I could find on the Twenty-fifth Amendment. I also began to get the gnawing feeling that Jerry Ford just might be the man to be the next Vice President.

I checked the ticker again. Speculation centered on John Connally, Nelson Rockefeller, Ronald Reagan and Elliot Richardson. A balloon was floated for Chuck Percy, probably by his own people, since Nixon had vowed him eternal enmity. Barry Goldwater was mentioned, along with Mel Laird, Anne Armstrong and Chief Justice Warren Burger. But nobody from the House. No Ford.

I mentioned this to Paul Miltich, Ford's press secretary. Mightn't it be a good idea if we drifted up to the press galleries and dropped the boss's name into the ears of a few reporter friends?

Paul readily agreed. "Can't do any harm," he said. "But Nixon will never do it." I knew Nixon a lot better than Paul, whose contacts had been largely limited to Michigan politicians. I knew Nixon had an extremely logical and orderly mind and relished surprises. He desperately needed a "Mr. Clean" to reverse the shock of Agnew's sordid downfall and shore up his own precarious position. Somebody who was widely acceptable to the Republican Party regulars (who had just lost their hero) and also to the Democratic Congress. Nixon would want a proven loyalist, a middle-of-the-roader and an Eisenhower internationalist in foreign affairs. Why not Jerry Ford?

Nixon's made all the wrong decisions lately, I told myself. It's about time for him to make a right one.

When Ford got back from meeting with the President, he and Hugh Scott had already briefed the White House press at Nixon's request. He filled me in quickly.

First, the President had told the Republican leaders more details of the case against Agnew. Then he turned briskly and dispassionately to the business at hand. As he understood the Twenty-fifth Amend-

16

ment, Nixon said, the Constitution would brook no unnecessary delay in filling the Vice Presidential vacancy. There was no specific deadline, but the language *"Whenever* there is a vacancy . . . the President *shall* nominate" was mandatory.

Nixon said that naturally he had given some thought to the matter since he first heard of Agnew's difficulties but that he still had a completely open mind. He wanted to hear from as broad and representative a spectrum of the Republican Party as possible in the time at hand.

The President asked Scott and Ford to pass along to their respective colleagues, all Republicans in the House and Senate, his request to send him in sealed envelopes their first, second and third choices for the nomination, ranked in order. He suggested that the two Minority Leaders gather up the sealed Congressional ballots and deliver them to his personal secretary, Rose Mary Woods, by 6:00 P.M. the next evening, Thursday, October 11. Similar instructions were given to National Chairman George Bush to poll the Republican National Committee. GOP Governors and others would also be queried, Nixon said.

"The President told us there are three criteria he would go by," Ford related. "First and foremost, it should be a strong person capable of becoming President if need be. Second, he or she should generally share his views on policy, particularly on national security and foreign affairs. And third, he or she could be confirmed by this Congress without long-drawn-out controversy."

"That sounds to me like Jerry Ford," I said.

"It could apply to a lot of people," he said, grinning, and hurried off to the House floor while I began getting out a rush notice to be on the desks of all our Members first thing next morning.

Neta Messersmith, my superefficient secretary, was going over her calendar to remind me of the things I had to do the next day. That was our final routine of the day, though whenever the House was in session I stayed around until Ford departed.

"Aren't you going to the Press Club tonight?" she asked.

It was the National Press Club's annual Congressional Night, a stand-up booze-and-buffet party to which each member was supposed to bring one or more Senators or Congressmen. There were skits by home-grown talent, and a spokesman for each party would make a burlesque political speech, the champion Congressional humorist being Mo Udall of Arizona.

I thanked Neta for her reminder and rushed up to the House

17

floor. It was 7:00 P.M. and they were voting on final passage of the bill which gave Home Rule to Washington by 343–74.

After Ford voted "Aye" and saw what the outcome would be, we walked together back to his office. Everybody had gone, and it was a good chance to talk with him a little as he unwound and packed his battered briefcase for home.

"It's really sad about Agnew," he reflected. "Why do these guys think they can get away with it? If I wanted to be a thief, I'd get in any other business but politics. And what did he get? Peanuts, really. He's a very smart guy. He could have made twice that much honestly— well, legally anyhow—practicing law. I just wonder how much more of this the country can take."

I had Ford, not Agnew, on my mind. "This is Congressional Night at the Press Club," I reminded him. "You ought to make an appearance—especially tonight. You don't need to stay long, and it's right on the way home."

"What do you mean—'especially tonight'?"

"Well, I think you're going to be the next Vice President," I said, "and if so, it'll do you no harm to be one of the boys there tonight. They're always short of interesting Republicans."

"O.K.," he said, "but I have to be home by eight-thirty."

We headed for his official limousine, waiting at the Capitol door. The evening was fun, but when I looked around for Ford to tell him it was 8:15, he had already gone.

Thursday the name of Gerald Ford began to appear on more and more lists, generally as a long shot. There were more "authoritative sources" at the White House than Checkers had fleas.

It was reported from Texas that Connally had asked Nixon not to consider him, but this evoked neither confirmation nor denial. Don Rumsfeld was reported flying home from his NATO post in Brussels, and it was noted that Nixon had favored him with three key assignments and Cabinet rank. Unidentified persons close to Rockefeller reportedly let it be known that the Governor would not necessarily refuse Nixon as he had in 1960. Reagan was also said by "associates" to be receptive.

Dick Burress, the former staff director of the Republican Policy Committee in the House who had joined the first Nixon staff as Deputy Counsel, was in town doing a little lobbying for the Hoover Institution at Stanford, which he had just joined as associate director. Over lunch, Dick agreed with me that Ford would be a logical dark horse.

"The President will never pick an eager beaver who is going to overshadow him, either deliberately or because it just comes naturally," he said. "Big John Connally only has to walk into a room to eclipse everybody there. Rocky is too secure and Reagan too smooth for Nixon to have around. He'd be comfortable with Jerry, and Jerry isn't running like crazy for the job."

We speculated whether Nixon had already made his choice, as he had with Agnew, and was just going through the exercise of flattering Republican Party wheels by soliciting their advice. Nobody could be sure. The President was holding his cards close, and his Praetorians were obviously orchestrating a lot of contradictory White House leaks to confuse the media.

If the ballots were to influence the outcome, however, sheer numbers would favor Ford. Political animals being what they are, the Republicans in the House could be expected to put their leader either first or second on their lists. So would a lot of Republican Senators and Governors whom Ford had obliged. In his tireless crisscrossing of the country for GOP candidates, as well as presiding over two national conventions, he was on cordial terms with most party officials.

Ford himself pretended not to be interested and discounted his own chances. He said he expected John Connally to be the winner. He knew Nixon regarded him as the toughest contender for the Presidency in 1976, and that was the reason the Texan formally became a Republican.

This would have been a great scenario if it had not been for the gathering storm of Watergate. Nobody said it out loud as yet, but Nixon already and imperceptibly had lost the clout it takes for a lame-duck President to dictate his successor to the party—especially when his choice had been a lifelong Democrat only recently repented.

If Republicans found Big John a come-lately convert, many Democrats saw him as a renegade. The nominee had to be quickly confirmable by the heavily Democratic Congress. Connally was not.

Making sure nobody missed this point, Speaker Albert told reporters at his daily session just before the House convened that he was sure the President would want to consider Jerry Ford. Mike Reed, his able assistant, phoned to tell me about it.

"That's very kind of him, and I know Jerry will appreciate it," I said.

"It was no casual compliment," Mike said. "The word we passed directly to the President was much blunter. The Speaker said in his opinion Ford is probably the *only* Republican we would confirm."

Unbeknown to me at the time, Nixon was getting similar counsel

19

from people like Mel Laird and Bryce Harlow, who could also qualify as experts on how Congress might respond.

The House Members' ballots began coming in—most in sealed envelopes as requested, but many not even folded and handed to Mildred Leonard in Ford's front office or to me with the transparent hope that the Minority Leader would know he led their lists. It was a far from scientific sample but, aside from showing that Ford would get a respectable number of votes, indicated that Reagan and Rockefeller would also run strong and that Connally had virtually no support.

Shortly before the 6:00 P.M. deadline we packed the envelopes up in a stationery box and Jerry, beaming at the near unanimous return on our checkoff list, tucked it protectively under his arm and took off for the White House, early for him.

I went home early for me, too, and tried to convince my wife, Roberta, that my hunch was right. On the 11:00 P.M. news we learned that the President had gone by chopper to Camp David, where, according to Ron Ziegler, he would study the recommendations and make his decision.

"Does Jerry really want to be Vice President?" Roberta asked. "What does Betty think about it?"

"I don't know," I said, answering both questions at once. "It would be a nice way to cap his career, since it's not likely he'll ever be Speaker now. And you know every President since the war, except Ike and Kennedy, got there by being Vice President first. It's not something a politician turns down without thinking twice."

"But does Jerry want to be President?" she persisted.

"They all do," I said. "Let's go to bed."

★

As Nixon recalls it, he quickly reduced his candidate list to Ford, Connally, Reagan, Rockefeller and Richardson. Attorney General Richardson had asked the President not to consider him because of his role in Agnew's removal. Connally was still Nixon's favorite, but he, predictably, was controversial and had also asked to be taken off the list. Nixon obliged both. That left Rockefeller, Reagan and Ford.

Nixon in his memoirs makes his decision simplicity itself, a matter of party unity. Either Rockefeller or Reagan would divide Republicans, as both subsequently did. Ford would be acceptable to both wings. This is not too flattering to Ford but, one must admit, not much different from the way most running mates have been chosen over the years—or the way Ford himself chose Robert Dole in 1976.

20

Nixon came down from the mountaintop at 8:30 A.M. Friday morning, October 12, 1973. According to *Time* magazine, he confided his choice only to Alexander Haig and Ron Ziegler.

"Loving surprises the way most politicians love parades, he would unveil his nominee with the same kind of full-dress performance in the East Room that he had played effectively when he sprung the nomination of Warren Burger as his Chief Justice," *Time* reported.

Ziegler told newsmen that the President would announce his decision over all the networks that evening at 9:00 P.M. before a select guest list of government and party leaders.

Ford and Scott were summoned to the White House, ostensibly to discuss how the nomination should be formally conveyed to Senate and House under the untried Twenty-fifth Amendment.

I made several calls to close friends at the White House—Bill Timmons, Max Friedersdorf, Rose Mary Woods. Nobody gave me a clue. Then the invaluable UPI ticker told me that Nixon was conferring with Ford now, and Scott was on his way back to the Hill after refusing to talk with White House reporters. Why was he seeing them separately? Always before they'd gone into the Oval Office together, and why wouldn't they if the subject was really Congressional procedures? Why wouldn't they if he was going to confide his choice to them ahead of schedule?

Unless one of them was it. Both had been mentioned, but I had long ago ruled Scott out because Pennsylvania had a Democratic Governor and Nixon couldn't risk losing another vote in the Senate. Then why Scott first and Ford second?

Of course. Because he wanted to let Hugh down gently first. But no. He could have let them both down gently, one at a time, with the same explanation.

I gave up. No man living can outguess Richard Nixon when it comes to figuring things out to the third, fourth and fifth degree of indirection.

Scott was on his way back to his Capitol office. If he had refused to talk to the White House reporters, it must be that he wanted first to talk to his reporter friends who regularly covered the Senate.

I lit out for Scott's office on a dead run. The Senate Minority Leader was already back, surrounded by two-score reporters outside his office door. I shoved my way into the circle to try to hear what he was saying. No, he would not be Nixon's nominee. He was not exactly ecstatic but taking it like an old pro.

"What about Jerry Ford?" somebody shouted.

"Well, Mr. Ford was on top of my list of three," Scott began. "But I don't think I'm at liberty to answer that. . . ."

My heart rose as the Senator paused and pointedly looked around at all the tape-recorder microphones stuck in his face. Then he gave a great big stage wink and silently shook his head in the negative. I slunk away on leaden feet.

But when Jerry returned from the White House he was walking on cloud nine. He insisted that the President had told him nothing.*

I hated to tell him what Scott had said, but I did. He didn't seem to care. He had slipped out the basement side door of the White House and avoided reporters there. Now he told Miltich he wouldn't talk to any newsmen from the Congressional press galleries, either.

When Miltich left I closed the door.

"Tell me exactly what happened, please," I begged. "Step by step."

"Well, the President got up to greet me and as we were sitting down, here comes Ollie Atkins to take our picture. And I wondered about this and the President said, kind of jokingly, to Ollie: 'This better be good, because it might be an historic photograph.'"

"Don't you think he was telling you something?" I asked.

"Well, I figured he was just teasing," Ford replied. "He did the same to Hugh. Ollie shoots everything, you know."

"That would be a pretty cruel joke if he didn't mean it," I said. "Whatever his faults may be, he really isn't a sadist. He has a soft heart for old friends. I don't think he'd do that to you."

"Well, we talked about tonight and who was invited, and he said he'd send an official nomination message up tomorrow, even though it's Saturday.

"Then he asked me where I expected to be about seven-thirty tonight, because he was going to telephone the person he had picked so he or she would be sure and be at the White House on time. I said I'd be home having dinner. The President said I should stay near the phone, because I was one of the finalists on his list. He said he wished he had as many friends across the country as I have."

I was now 99 percent convinced, despite Scott's report. Ford was philosophical, saying he would wait and see; it wouldn't be long now. The real clincher came, though, almost by accident.

---

* Nixon had, in fact, told him everything—and Ford had pledged that he would not run for President in 1976, according to Ford's memoirs.

"I sure wish I could be down there to see the announcement," I said.

"I wish you could too, Bob," Jerry commiserated. "But they don't even have room for all our Republican Members. So they're only inviting the upper half of each delegation by seniority. I told him a lot of our people would be awful mad, but that's the way it is."

Given the dimensions of the East Room, the largest hall in the White House, this was understandable. But then, a few minutes later, Bill Timmons called and invited me.

Me, the Minority Sergeant-at-Arms? But not half of the Republican Congressmen who had votes? It had to be because I was Ford's number-one man. It had to be because Ford was Nixon's choice.

The Praetorians were at pains to make my presence not too obvious a giveaway, however. They had also invited Joe Bartlett, the Minority Clerk.

When I reported this to Jerry, he smiled noncommittally and said he was going home. His devoted staff followed his example; incredibly, Miltich maintained his initial skepticism and disappeared for the remainder of that momentous evening.

I had plenty of time to kill before 9:00 P.M., and I found myself thinking about the first time I ever went to the White House.

In November of 1938, two months after the Munich conferees hailed "peace in our time," I turned up at the end of the tourist line after walking down from the Capitol. I had been an exchange student that summer in Japan and was bumming my way home the long way. At twenty-one, I had to find a job at the tag end of the Depression, after witnessing the ugliness of war and famine in China as well as the delicate beauty of prewar Japan; the last days of the White Man's Burden from Singapore to Cairo; the posturings of Mussolini's *Fascisti* and the chilling arrogance of Hitler's Nazis; the drowsy indifference of Paris and London.

Being broke, I walked all over Washington that day and fell in love with it sixteen years before it became home. Now, three decades later, the White House policeman checked my name and waved my little blue Volkswagen through the southwest gate between the black Lincolns and Cadillacs.

It wasn't the first time Joe Bartlett and I had been to White House affairs, of course, but it was certainly the first time the military aides escorted us to seats right up front, in the third row, underneath the larger-than-life portrait of George Washington. Then we knew we were right.

23

"Look, there's Richardson," I whispered to Joe.

"And here comes Hugh Scott," he whispered back.

"Whoever it is, he's probably upstairs having a drink with the President."

I had hardly said this when Jerry and Betty came in without fanfare and took their places among the House hierarchy. Neither Connally, Rockefeller nor Reagan were anywhere in evidence. My spirits sagged.

Then the ever-exhilarating moment came when a voice intoned: "The President of the United States . . . and Mrs. Nixon."

As the Nixons passed the Fords there was the usual warm recognition but nothing special, it seemed to me. Pat took her seat with Tricia Cox and Julie and David Eisenhower to the left of the temporary raised platform, and the President stepped up and stood alone behind a single microphone.

Like the practiced pro he is, Nixon worked the suspense for all it was worth. People sat around the dinner table in homes all over the country making family bets.

The evening network news commentators had given them little help. Most hedged their last-minute guesses with a list of finalists. Only one, ABC's veteran Congressional expert Bob Clark, got it right. Citing a definite tip from "extremely high authority" in the Senate, Clark flatly picked Ford on the 6:00 P.M. show.

Bob, with whom I worked the White House beat in the Eisenhower–Kennedy years, is one of the most conscientious reporters I've ever encountered. Clark had witnessed—and duly reported—Hugh Scott's silent headshake eliminating Ford. I wondered at the time if Scott were playing the White House game of confusing the media but really knew and saved the real scoop for Clark. Much later I asked the Senator.

"I just might have done that, if I'd known," Scott said. "I don't blame you for suspecting me, especially since I didn't want my answer on tape. But this is what really happened.

"The President didn't tell me that morning who it would be. What he told me was that it wouldn't be me. He'd given it a lot of thought, and all that, but we just couldn't trade my seat on the Senate aisle for the powerless one up on the podium. Nobody in the party deserved it more, but he was sure I'd understand," Scott recalled.

"Well, I said the right things, and waited to see if he was going to tell me any more, but he obviously wasn't going to let me in on his secret. But I figured if I asked him flat out, is it Ford, he would just say he couldn't tell anybody his decision. So I worked around it by saying, 'Mr. President, will it be anybody else from the Congress?'

"And Nixon said no, it wouldn't be anybody from the Hill. So help me, he just lied. That was the first time, though he later misled me into sticking my neck out for him again about the tapes. I still wonder why he did it, because in a few hours I'd know the truth anyway. I suppose he'd have said he thought I was talking about the Senate."

One of the vast unseen audience watching ABC that evening in a suburb of Boston was Mike Ford, a student at Gordon Theological Seminary. Mike, twenty-three, was the eldest of the Fords' four children and the only one married. After he heard Clark's confident forecast that his father would get the nod, Mike picked up the telephone and called home. Betty answered and said she knew nothing for certain. Yes, there had been a lot of rumors, but they were about to get dressed to go to the White House and find out.

Gerald Ford himself told the rest of the story as follows:

"Then, at seven-thirty, the upstairs phone rang. It has no extensions and is an unlisted number. Our daughter, Susan—she apparently has listed it with certain favorites of hers—dashed upstairs thinking it was going to be one of them.

"It turned out to be for me and she yells downstairs, 'Dad, the President wants to talk to you.' So I dash upstairs—pretty fast. The President came on the line and said, 'Jerry, I've got some good news for you, but maybe you'd better get Betty on the line so she can hear it too.'

"So there I am, on the phone with no extensions and Betty is talking to Mike on the phone that has five extensions. Well, I try to explain all that to the President but finally I give up and say, 'Mr. President, would you mind hanging up and calling back on the other line?'

"Well, he did, and I went downstairs and got Betty off the phone and he, the President, fortunately didn't change his mind in the meantime."

Jerry wowed at least a hundred audiences with that story during the 1974 campaign, but it didn't happen exactly that way. As hand-tailored slightly by Bob Orben, enlisted to help invigorate Ford's Vice Presidential speeches, it made a good-humored but subtle point about Ford's independence.

The way Jerry Ford actually got the word from the White House differed from Orben's edited versions primarily in the fact that President Nixon curiously opened the conversation by saying, "Jerry, General Haig has some good news to tell you." Then he put Haig on, and Haig broke the news officially that the President had decided to nominate Ford to be Vice President.

I often wondered—as did Ford—why Nixon at this magic moment let Haig do the talking. The President, we knew, preferred to handle everything through subordinates. Haig often listened, for Nixon's protection, to at least one end of important telephone conversations. Even though Mel Laird had sounded Ford out previously and was assured he would not refuse the nomination, Nixon was always on guard. He may have wanted Haig to fend off any eleventh-hour reservations or conditions Ford might have.

But perhaps there was another, more basic explanation. Was Nixon telling Ford, right off the bat, that in the future the Vice President of the United States would normally be expected to communicate with the President through his chief of staff? In his elation, Ford took it with equanimity. But he soon dropped Haig when recounting the tale.

The nation was waiting, and President Nixon, in the East Room, was visibly wallowing in his stellar role. For what seemed to be an eternity, he talked about all the good things he had done for the country, as indeed he had. He did not mention Agnew but appealed to Americans to turn away "from the obsessions of the past" and begin anew to use the basic strengths with which the nation had been abundantly blessed.

Then, as the audience wriggled in their wretched seats, he tossed off the first clue. His choice was "a man who has served for twenty-five years in the House of Representatives with great distinction." All eyes turned to Jerry Ford. Nixon paused dramatically, and the audience jumped to its feet and burst into sustained applause.

"Ladies and gentlemen," he said sternly, "please don't be premature. There are several here who have been in the House twenty-five years."

He rambled on, prolonging the suspense. Finally: "I proudly present to you the man whose name I will present to the Congress of the United States for confirmation as the Vice President of the United States—Congressman Gerald Ford of Michigan."

The crowd went berserk at the anticlimax, me included. The sedate premises resounded with whoops, whistles and Rebel yells.

Ford bounded to the platform and the two men locked arms.

"They like *you*," Nixon whispered to the beaming Ford.

For a moment words seemed not to come out. But Nixon obligingly backed away, leaving Ford alone at the mike, and he haltingly began: "Mr. President, I'm deeply honored and I'm extremely grateful and I'm terribly humble. But I pledge to you, and I pledge to my colleagues in the Congress, and I pledge to the American people, that to the best of my ability—if confirmed by my colleagues in the Congress—that I will do my utmost to the best of my ability to serve this country well and to perform those duties that will be my new assignment as effectively and as efficiently and with as much accomplishment as possible."

He concluded simply: "Thank you very much."

Obviously no speech writer crafted that for him. For it was authentic Jerry Ford, and Americans across the land saw something they hadn't seen from Washington in years—a real person, speaking from his heart. Someone who didn't think he was God, or God's vicar, or the victim of unnamed evildoers among the citizenry. It was, in a curious way, reminiscent of Harry Truman's assumption of the Presidency in 1945. The moon and the stars and the planets had fallen on him, but he would do his best. Americans like that.

Nixon motioned for Pat and Betty Ford to join them on the platform. Aides released the photographic pool from the rear of the room, and flashbulbs popped like Roman candles. Nixon turned to offer congratulations to Betty. She replied in a stage whisper: "Congratulations or condolences?" Nixon smiled but had no answer.

At the President's bidding, everybody filed into the Blue Room for formal handshakings. The knowing ones went first to the State Dining Room buffet before drifting back to the end of the receiving line. I was wondering which to do when a military aide tugged at my elbow.

"There's a phone call for Mr. Ford," he said. "Would you like to handle it?"

It was Senator Hubert Humphrey, one of the three living former Vice Presidents. I quickly pulled the boss temporarily out of the receiving line to accept Humphrey's warm good wishes and to chat briefly. (Later that evening, Agnew got through to the Ford residence and added his own.)

Dick Frazier, who had been driving official House limousines for many years, had brought Jerry and Betty to the White House and was waiting to take them home. As they started to enter the car, a Secret Service agent intervened.

"I'm afraid you'll have to ride with us," he told Ford politely but firmly. "But you'll have to tell us how to get there."

It was the beginning of a new way of life, not only for the Fords but for all of us. I have never seen anyone's high elation collapse so suddenly as Frazier's, and I kept him company as we led the armored limousine across the Potomac to Crown View Drive in Alexandria.

The Praetorians wouldn't get to me until tomorrow.

2

TRUTH IS THE GLUE

★★————————————————————★★

While the prospect of Jerry Ford being nominated for Vice President of the United States was about the only thing on my mind throughout Friday, October 12, 1973, quite a lot of other things were happening.

Three hours before President Nixon disclosed his surprise choice, the U.S. Circuit Court of Appeals dropped a bombshell of its own. In a landmark 5–2 decision that was four hundred pages long, the appellate court ordered President Nixon to turn over White House tapes subpoenaed by Special Prosecutor Archibald Cox to U.S. District Judge John J. Sirica. Though this stunning setback would be appealed to (and unanimously affirmed by) the Supreme Court, it was in fact the beginning of the end for President Nixon.

It made it virtually certain that Jerry Ford would be the next President of the United States. A gutsy President can simultaneously stand off the media and the Legislative Branch or the media and the Judicial Branch, but he cannot survive the determined opposition of all three.

If we did not grasp this in a blinding flash of clarity on the morning of October 13, neither did anybody else. Americans had never deposed a President, save by an assassin's bullet. Our traditions are not long, but they are very strong. We do not like new, different and deeply disturbing circumstances. We hope they will go away, and usually they have.

There were still more momentous portents on October 12, 1973. It was the kind of day that gives news editors ulcers. The House of Representatives gave final approval to a War Powers Act sharply limiting the President's traditionally unrestricted powers as Commander-in-Chief to send U.S. forces into combat without Congressional assent.

The White House imposed nationwide rationing of heating oil, jet and Diesel fuel and kerosene, the first controls since World War II, as an initial response to the Arab oil embargo. The eventual gasoline shortage and increase of all energy costs triggered the worst economic recession since the Great Depression, darkening Ford's election prospects for 1976.

Henry Kissinger held his first news conference as Secretary of State after successfully shoving Bill Rogers out of the Cabinet. The Israelis were within eighteen miles of Damascus. Egyptian and Syrian defenders began firing Soviet-supplied SAM missiles into Israeli jets. Henry warned the Kremlin that détente was being jeopardized by the escalating Middle East war.

The difficulties facing the United States and whoever might be its President were obvious enough, but the priority item on Jerry Ford's agenda was the annual Red Flannel Day Parade in Cedar Springs, Michigan. He hadn't missed it in twenty-five years, and a little thing like being nominated for Vice President wasn't going to stop him this time.

No sooner had we settled down in his Capitol office Saturday morning, however, than the White House called, summoning him to a session with the President.

"I wonder what's up," I said.

"Come along and we'll see," he replied, equally puzzled.

In the big black Secret Service limousine Ford lit his pipe and puffed contentedly.

"Did I ever tell you about the time Lyndon Johnson called me down to the White House on a Saturday morning like this?"

He hadn't.

"Well, I was puttering around the house, and I figured there must be some international crisis about to blow up the world for him to send a car for the Republican leader. So I pulled on some decent clothes, and when we got to the front portico, an usher took me up the elevator to the family floor.

"There was old LBJ, sitting in the Lincoln bedroom all by himself. I sat down and the President leaned over and put his hand on my knee.

"'I'm going to leave here in a couple of days,' he said, 'and I've been thinking about it. I don't want to leave any enemies if I can help it. Now you know when you first took over, I said some pretty mean things about you.'"

(LBJ was, in fact, the source of two savage wisecracks that have plagued Ford to this day—one that "Jerry's a nice guy, but he played football too long without a helmet" and, worse, that "Ford's the only man I ever knew who can't chew gum and fart at the same time." The

New York *Times* laundered the Presidential quote before everlastingly repeating it.)

"The President said he had me pegged wrong and he was sorry he said those things and that they'd gotten into print. He said he couldn't have asked for any more loyal support when the country's national interests were at stake. He just wished he'd gotten as much from his own party."

"He might have said it in public," I said. "Those cracks were as devastating as Alice Longworth's branding Dewey 'the little man on the wedding cake.' "

"Well, it was about as close as a proud man like Lyndon could ever come to apologizing," Ford said. "I said he could forget it and wished him all the best."

The White House car pulled into East Executive Avenue and stopped at the "basement" business entrance. The Vice President-designate was whisked into the Oval Office by General Haig. Meanwhile, I was taken in tow by Bill Timmons, Nixon's assistant for Congressional liaison. We had worked closely since 1969. Bill had neatly listed on a yellow foolscap pad what Ford should be doing for the next few days.

First of all, Timmons said, the President was having a Sunday worship service at the White House next morning and wanted the Fords to be there. And Roberta and I were invited.

I explained that Ford had a long-standing date at the Red Flannel Day Parade in a town near Grand Rapids, and after that he was going to fly to Utah to see his college-age son, Jack. Then Monday he'd make two speeches in Portland, Oregon. And if we didn't start soon, he'd miss the last commercial flight.

"Don't worry, Bob," Bill said with the serenity of a senior Praetorian. "The Secret Service won't let him take that plane anyway. We'll lay on a small jet to take him up to Michigan. Then we'll bring him back tonight so he can make church in the morning."

He turned to his foolscap program. "Monday: Courtesy calls on House Judiciary and Senate Rules members. Clean up office affairs. Plan answers to Hearing questions. Work on new House GOP leader."

"That's *all* we have to do on Monday?" I asked.

"We can put those things off until Wednesday," he continued. "We'll get him out to Utah after the worship here Sunday morning, and he can overnight there with the boy or go on to Portland. The jet can get him back here Monday night in time for the farewell dinner for Bill Rogers. Now on Tuesday . . ." Timmons raced on. "Jerry should meet first thing in the morning with Al Haig."

"Don't you think Al Haig ought to meet with the Vice President?" I interjected. I was not really sore at Bill, but he *had* been around the Praetorian Guard too long.

"Well, it'll be more convenient down here, because afterward he'll get a briefing from the National Security Council, the Domestic Council and the economic advisers. He and Haig should talk about personnel, payroll and budget. I think you ought to sit in on this too, Bob. And, oh yes, Mrs. Ford ought to see our social secretary, Lucy Winchester, about upcoming social events and her responsibilities."

I resisted another protocol crack.

About this time the Oval Office meeting broke up. The press and photographers were ushered in to find the President surrounded by Ford, Kissinger and Haig. Nixon waved a supersecret intelligence folder at them and announced, "Starting immediately the Congressman [Ford] will receive the daily intelligence briefings and will participate in meetings of the National Security Council, the Cabinet and other meetings that the Vice President would participate in once he is confirmed."

He went on to say arrangements were being made for Ford to have an office in the Executive Office Building ". . . so he can get his work prepared for the day when he moves from the House down here—and, of course, over in the Senate they give you an office, too."

The President chuckled at his own idea of a small joke, reminding everyone that he'd once been a Vice President, too. He explained that Kissinger had been briefing them both on the Mideast situation, because ". . . the Congressman is leaving for previous out-of-town engagements."

Obviously, I thought, Bill's little agenda had been well worked out with Haig and the other Praetorian Guard long before we got there. On the way back I showed Ford Timmons' notes.

"Since they're giving us a plane," he said, "why don't you come along? It looks like we've got a lot to talk over. But you'll have to wear something red in Cedar Springs or you'll be arrested and fined."

The more enterprising Capitol reporters were camping in the Minority Leader's outer office awaiting his return from the White House. The questions were a foretaste of what was to come before his confirmation.

What had Nixon talked about before telling Ford he was tapped? Nothing much except to inquire about my health, Ford said. Not even after the Agnew thing? Well, *are* there any skeletons in your closet? Everybody laughed. None that he knew of, Ford replied.

"I think the President wants me to spend a lot of time on the Hill," he said. "It's where my background is and where I can help most."

I pricked up my ears at that. Nixon had just finished telling reporters at the White House that he was fixing up an EOB office where the Vice President-designate could work. Now, Ford was telling the President what *he* wanted to do and what he *was going* to do. His roots were still deep in the Hill.

Before the press questions ended, he had promised to make a full financial disclosure, turn his income-tax returns over to the Senate and House committees, sell the only stock he owned and resign from one corporate board in Grand Rapids. Then came the whammer.

"Will you be a candidate in nineteen seventy-six?"

He replied that he had no intention of being a candidate in 1976 for any national office. "I say that as forcefully as I can," he added. At the time, I suspected this disclaimer was designed to make his confirmation easier.

Neither the Democrats nor a good many Republicans* were anxious to build him up as a frontrunner in 1976. What they all wanted—and what in the end they got—was a conscientious caretaker of the Constitution. They wanted 1976 to be wide-open.

The buzzer sounded, calling the House into session. The reporters had their story. As Ford entered the chamber, the handful of colleagues present gave him a standing ovation. When we left the Capitol by the Speaker's entrance to head for Michigan, a small crowd of weekend tourists was waiting to wave and shout friendly congratulations.

Gone forever were Jerry Ford's virtually incognito comings and goings, the restorative solitude of solo travel.

It wouldn't have done him much good to go home in triumph to Grand Rapids. This was the Saturday of the Michigan–Michigan State football game. As we drove through the nearly deserted city, I reminded Ford it was the first time I'd been to Grand Rapids in all the years I'd worked for him.

---

* Including President Nixon. I learned for the first time from Ford's memoirs that Nixon had already elicited his pledge not to be a 1976 candidate.

PALACE POLITICS

His Washington staff was mostly recruited from Michigan. Frank Meyer, administrative assistant until his death in 1972, handled the Grand Rapids constituents. I didn't know beans about Michigan.

★

It was a clear, crisp autumn day in Cedar Springs, the leaves just starting to turn to vivid reds and yellows. Ford donned a bright-red flannel vest. It seemed that everyone in town shook his hand and he called each by name, enjoying every minute of the boisterous march.

When we came to the head of the picnic line the future Vice President and guest of honor fumbled and pulled out a $10 bill to pay for our heaping paper plates of home-fried chicken, which came to about 75 cents each.

On the flight back he turned serious. "Bob, I want you to be my chief of staff," he said. "We've got a lot to do to get ready for the hearings. We'll have to pull together some volunteers—people we know we can depend on who'll really work, not just be along for the ride. I don't have any more money to hire staff and won't have until I'm confirmed, so we have to depend on the best brains we can borrow, right away, so think about it. You'll be in charge of the whole team, and I'll back you up."

This took me by surprise. As long as I had known him he had never delegated authority to a single subordinate. He liked to deal with two or three approximately equal aides, never defining their exclusive territory or precise pecking order.

After the usual modesties about being deeply honored and hoping I would justify his confidence, I gingerly voiced some of my misgivings. I could do the job as to looking out faithfully for his interests, but insofar as others had to be involved, he would have to make it plain that I was, indeed, his deputy rather than merely an aide.

Then, quite inconsistently, I grumbled about the title of "chief of staff." Sounded too much like Haldeman, I said.

Ford grinned. "I knew you'd say that. But it isn't something I just made up. I've thought about it. You were in the Navy. Isn't the role of a chief of staff exactly what you've been scolding me about? He deals with other chiefs of staff and even, when it suits his admiral, with other admirals. Isn't a chief of staff what I want now?"

"Sweet Old Bob, that's what they'll call me—SOB," I came back. "O.K., you're the admiral."

34

So, high in the sky somewhere over Indiana or Ohio, it was settled between us, and from that moment until his inauguration as the thirty-eighth President of the United States, when he named me a member of his Cabinet, he kept the bargain.

And so did I. I was his SOB and his chief of staff, not the only SOB but the only official chief of staff Jerry Ford ever had.

Nixon created that title for Haldeman and passed it on to General Haig. Ford never referred to Haig as *his* chief of staff, following the advice of his transition team. Don Rumsfeld and his successor, Dick Cheney, were formally Assistants to the President with the added function of "staff coordinator."

But I was right in my initial instincts. "Chief of staff" is a Prussian concept foreign to our Constitutional Presidency. Generals and admirals may have them, even Vice Presidents, but there is only one Chief Executive, one Chief to hail and one to blame.

On that homeward flight we came to several practical and basic decisions that brooked no delay. First, Ford would continue to operate from his Minority Leader's office off the Rotunda of the Capitol.* We would say "thanks but no thanks" to the President's effort to move us down to the Executive Office Building even one minute before final confirmation. It would be presumptuous, and politically calamitous, to move into Agnew's downtown digs prematurely. We wondered why the Nixon Praetorians, brilliant politicians as they imagined themselves, couldn't see this.

Second, Jerry Ford would go right ahead, insofar as possible, being Minority Leader of the House. He would give nobody the impression that he was Vice President already, as Nixon had that morning. And from his own well-entrenched position, he would run his own show during Senate and House deliberations on his nomination.

Finally, there was the dilemma of what to do about Agnew's people. By and large, they were good people who had done a good job for their boss, only to be suddenly left adrift. Ford never hesitated on this one. "I want my own team," he said in words that were to flash back

---

* It had been the original location of the Library of Congress, when the young government in Washington acquired the private collection of Thomas Jefferson. Next it was the Speaker's office for long years. According to tradition, the last time Sam Rayburn and Joe Martin had to trade offices (in the 80th and 83rd Congresses), Mr. Sam said he liked it where he was and Joe could keep H-230 with its sweeping vista past the Washington Monument to the Lincoln Memorial.

grotesquely two years later when, as President, he fired Jim Schlesinger and Bill Colby, elevated Don Rumsfeld and George Bush, rehabilitated Elliot Richardson and pointed Nelson Rockefeller and Rogers Morton toward the exit door. "I feel sorry for them, but we can't have anything to do with them."

"They're just sitting around with nothing to do," I said. "You know that breeds mischief. We could use some helping hands."

Ford said he would speak to Mike Mansfield and Hugh Scott so that Agnew's Senate staff could remain on the payroll until the vacancy was filled. I should urge the White House personnel office to find places for the former Vice President's people on the executive payroll. Nobody should be led to expect, however, that they would automatically be picked up by the new Vice President.

As it turned out, all but one of Agnew's aides, aside from his Senate and military staffs, found other jobs by the time Ford took over. Al Haig gave the project a high priority.

The nub of all this is that a new broom must sweep completely clean. Cruel as it may be, the only moment this is possible is right at the outset. Ford's initial judgment was right, and he was wrong to shade it when he became history's first unelected President.

So in mid-October 1973 my immediate task was to assemble in a few days a volunteer team of total Ford loyalists to handle a huge and unprecedented test, his confirmation as Vice President under the Twenty-fifth Amendment.

Ordinarily, he would have been confirmed for a Cabinet or judicial nomination by voice vote after a couple of days of courteous questioning. But for all the "buddy system" that prevails in Congress, and for all of Ford's deserved reputation as a good and honorable guy, this was not going to be an ordinary joy ride.

Time magazine's cover, over a Janus-like juxtaposition of Nixon's and Agnew's grim faces, solemnly asked "Can Trust Be Restored?"

Sam Ervin's gavel had just banged down on thirty-seven days and two million words of testimony, conflicting and unfocused but profoundly disturbing, about Watergate. Americans watching their television screens had seen and heard the top law-enforcement and security officials of the federal government, the Attorney General of the United States, the heads of the FBI and the CIA admit or alibi being manipulated by the White House in the investigation of what had originally been called "a two-bit burglary." They learned that the President of the United States for many months had secretly tape-recorded every conversation he had had in his office or on the telephone and that most of his top aides had bugged their own talks as well as those of suspected "enemies," either by official taps or through illegal plumbers. Sweeping invasions of privacy, whether justified on the pretense of national security or simply for political advantage, had been approved at the White House and the Committee to Re-elect the President (CREEP). Hundreds of thousands of campaign dollars, of uncertain origin, showered down on these repugnant projects in bewildering abundance. Records and evidence had been wantonly destroyed.

The mood of Americans was sullen and cynical, that of their elected representatives scared and savage. The Democratic leaders of Congress were acutely aware that public opinion would not tolerate ducking their duty, nor too obvious partisanship in the doing. Speaker Albert and Senator Mansfield, with their lieutenants, moved swiftly. They squelched talk of a joint committee investigation or of the creation of special confirmation bodies.

Following the regular rules of the two chambers, Albert assigned jurisdiction to the House Committee on the Judiciary and Mansfield to the Senate Committee on Rules and Administration. The Senate, with its established procedures for probing Presidential appointments, would probably go first. Anything unresolved by Rules would be taken up by the Judiciary Committee of the House.

The Judiciary chairmanship had just passed from the aging but acute dean of the House, Emanuel Celler (D–New York), to Pete Rodino (D–New Jersey), who had come to Congress in the same freshman class as Ford. Its ranks had become even more loaded with liberal anti-Nixon Democrats.

The Senate Committee on Rules and Administration was headed by two courtly and complete politicians, Chairman Howard Cannon (D–Nevada) and Marlow Cook (R–Kentucky). If there was such a thing as a blue-ribbon panel of inner-circle Senate powerhouses, Rules was it.*

---

* Divided equally, except for the Democratic chairman, Rules on the majority side consisted of Claiborne Pell (Rhode Island); Robert Byrd (West Virginia), then the Democratic Whip and now Majority Leader; James B. Allen (Alabama); and Harrison Williams, Jr. (New Jersey). Minority members besides Cook were the Republican leader Hugh Scott (Pennsylvania); Bob Griffin (Michigan), the Republican Whip and a steadfast Ford ally; and Mark Hatfield, former Governor of Oregon and a moderate-liberal in GOP terms.

PALACE POLITICS

On the same Saturday that President Nixon's formal nomination of Ford was received by Senate and House, Chairman Cannon called his committee together.

The Senators agreed:

To ask the FBI for a complete field investigation of Gerald Ford, expected to consume at least a fortnight.

To ask the Library of Congress for all the information it had on his life and public career, including an analysis of his legislative positions and voting record during twenty-five years.

To request the loan of staff experts from the General Accounting Office and of investigators from the Government Operations Permanent Investigations Subcommittee.

To request the American Bar Association and local bar associations for a report on Ford's standing as a lawyer.

To allow live television coverage of the open hearings.

To guard against leaks during the investigation.*

Obviously, this was going to be a real investigation.

On Tuesday morning, wondering if maybe we hadn't already wasted too much time in the luxury of Air Force II, Ford and I showed up at the White House for the "briefing" by General Haig that Timmons had insisted on.

In his "corner pocket" office inherited from H. R. Haldeman, with Williamsburg green woodwork and a bewildering array of electronic gadgets, the general was all genial host. He introduced his assistant, John C. Bennett, a retired Army major general and a West Pointer, like so many of Haig's personal aides. (We were learning the Praetorian ways; it's always good to have a witness when you can't have a tape.)

After some chitchat about Ford's hectic weekend, Haig got down to business. "STA will be vacating the office next week," he said coldly, using the White House shorthand for the former Vice President. "He'll have a place up the street to sort out his papers."

"I think," Ford said firmly, "I'll be better off to stay right where I am until I'm actually confirmed. But, of course, I appreciate what Agnew's staff people are doing, and Bob will be in touch with them."

Haig never blinked. He was an old hand at this.

"Well, of course, the President will be expecting you at the Cab-

* This is the standard politician's alibi-in-advance suggesting that leaks invariably come from the staff. The fact is that 99 percent of all significant secrets are spilled by the principals or at their direction. Miraculously, however, the Senate hearings on Ford were virtually leakproof.

38

inet meeting. That's day after tomorrow, isn't it, John? Yes, at ten. And one of your staff people will be welcome—Bob, I assume, *or* your chief political adviser."

Touché. Haig knew very well no Congressman likes to admit he needs any *political* advice, least of all Jerry Ford. With a disarming smile he turned to me.

"And you're welcome to attend our senior staff meeting, too. That's at eight-thirty every morning* for about thirty to forty-five minutes—and, of course, whenever the President meets with the joint leadership of Congress."

I thanked the general, and he moved on. "The President will want you to chair the Domestic Council meetings when he can't be there," he said to Ford. "The Vice President is a member by statute, but the Council hasn't actually met for a long time. Ken Cole runs the staff, and I'll arrange for him to bring you up to date. And, of course, there'll be a lot of appearances around the country. I suppose you have quite a few of your own already."

Ford said yes, but he was going to have to cancel a good many of them to concentrate on the confirmation hearings. The two generals seemed a little taken aback that he was expecting anything but swift approval. What could they possibly drag up?

"Nothing really new. But I assume they'll go over all the stuff in that Winter-Berger book [*The Washington Pay-Off*] with a fine-tooth comb and want to know everything about my family finances and campaign expenditures. And, of course, some of 'em are still sore about the Douglas impeachment," Ford replied, pretty accurately forecasting the thrust of the next two months.

"Well, I can tell you this much," Haig said. "The President will have you out in front a lot more than you'll want to be." Haig, too, was a fair prophet. "You'll want an advance man—and we'll be glad to lend you one of our best, young fellow named Dewey Clower. He'll tie in closely with the Secret Service. And probably some help in the speech-writing department; we can do that, too. I'll have Dave Gergen call on you. Let's see, have you a good scheduler? John, let's see what Dave Parker can do there. And, of course, you'll need a foreign-policy guy and a political guy . . ."

* I never picked up this invitation while Nixon was President. It was not a boycott, as some whispered, simply the fact that during those hours I was busy as a bird dog doing Ford business. I wish now I had attended. It would have been fascinating to watch what I later read.

PALACE POLITICS

Hey, wait a minute! I wanted to scream. What do you think you're doing, picking the Vice President's new staff? But I looked at Ford and he had on his Sphinx face, so I kept still.

"About that Secret Service detail," Ford interjected, as if he hadn't been listening any further. "Who has the say about picking them? Do I have or do you?"

Anyone who thinks Jerry Ford is so open, so wholesome, so nice a guy that he doesn't know how to put down or turn off a presumptuous intrusion hasn't ever really tried it. Just to nail down the point, Ford went blandly on: "You know, what we really need most is some more good secretarial help."

"Of course. Mike Dunn can help there, and there's our White House typing pool." Haig recovered fast and raced on to finish.

We rose, smiling and saying "thanks."

That very afternoon Jim Rowley, director of the Secret Service, and two assistants came up to Ford's Capitol office to brief him on security. (A "briefing" is when a specialist who knows more about his narrow field than his victim tells a captive senior what he thinks the ignoramus needs to know. The common denominator of all "briefings" is that they are never brief.)

Rowley and I greeted each other warmly. In my White House reporting days Jim was one of the good guys. Secret Service agents and the "newsies" couldn't live without one another. The Service uses the surrounding crush of photographers and reporters to reinforce their protective screen around the President's person. The reporters in turn pick up considerable useful gossip from these omnipresent bodyguards, who do blabber in their off-duty hours.

Ford told Rowley of his forthcoming travel plans and asked about protection for his family as well as himself. Rowley explained that, strictly speaking the law provided Secret Service protection only for the President's family. The Vice President's family's protection depended on any known threats or a specific request.

"Have there been any threats?" Ford asked anxiously. Here was a negative component of his new glory.

There had been thirteen in the past, mostly connected with Ford's image as a Vietnam "hawk," Rowley said. None aimed at his family, none serious, none yet related to the Vice Presidency. (This was ironic, considering he was later to set a record of two overt assassination attempts by women with handguns.)

Finally, to get to Ford's question to General Haig, of course he would have his say.

(Most of the agents drawn from Agnew's detail were discreet, courteous and thoroughgoing professionals. Jerry Bechtel, Jim Taylor and others were a great help to me and the other neophytes in Ford's entourage. Inexorable Secret Service rules compelled Ford to bequeath most of them to Rockefeller and take over Nixon's "first team." In my book, his Vice Presidential protectors were second to none.)

As soon as the three agents left, taking advantage of Ford's admission that we needed more secretarial help, I hit him again for some reinforcements for myself.

His own staff—Mildred Leonard, Dorothy Hessler (now Downton), Anne Kamstra, Ruth Kilmer, George Willis, Esther Dukov, Dottie Cavanaugh and others—were stretched to the utmost. I'd been bugging Ford for some time to let me hire another secretary, someone of my own choosing like Neta or her predecessor, Helen Schroeder, someone I could depend on in a pinch. Well, the pinch was here.

Ford finally agreed but, typically, proposed a compromise. There was a very bright girl in Grand Rapids from a fine family who had quit postgraduate studies to get involved in helping his constituents. She was young but a fast learner, and he thought she'd be just what I needed. Her name was Gail Raiman.

I wasn't what you'd call wildly enthusiastic, having learned that letting your boss pick your subordinates is usually a fatal error. I stalled and then came back with a countercompromise. We'd need at least *two* more trustworthy secretaries to handle the confirmation work, separate and apart from his regular House business. Why not get Gail on the next plane from Grand Rapids and I'd also try to shanghai my former Girl Friday, Joann Lynott Wilson? Ford agreed—and I even got Neta a well-deserved raise.

When I came to Washington in 1954 to head the Los Angeles *Times* bureau, I hired Joann, and we worked happily together for nine years. Joann and Gail both answered my SOS with alacrity. Three more dissimilar ladies would be hard to find. For all her Washington sophistication, Joann was a novice on Capitol Hill. Gail was straight out of Kalamazoo College, infatuated with Washington and possessed of a driving ambition to succeed. Ford was right: She was not only smart but quick to recognize and recover her mistakes. Gail never walked when she could run, though sometimes she ran roughshod over others. She was decisive and a terrific organizer.

Neta, the serene and sympathetic veteran of Congressional office politics, kept the show running and never for a moment relinquished her position as my No. 1 assistant—though she was proud of and preferred the title of personal secretary. We were bound together by long association and dedication to Jerry Ford—and her discretion and ability to keep confidences were unparalleled.

Lest I forget to do so in every chapter, let me say now that all three of my personal aides served me with loving understanding and unselfish loyalty. They all willingly sacrificed personal leisure and risked their health to help the President carry out his staggering responsibilities. That their ultimate purpose was to serve our country does not diminish my personal gratitude and affection.

The press, while generally according Nixon's choice of Ford such faint praise as "safe and unimaginative" and "a low-profile team player of little color, less humor and no pronounced eccentricities," supplied some early storm warnings.

Some sorehead, never identified, warmed over the suggestion that Ford had profited unscrupulously through a ghost-written book and *Life* magazine article about his service on the Warren Commission investigating President Kennedy's assassination. The Washington *Star* revived a 1969 campaign story that Ford performed financial sleight-of-hand by funneling some Washington fat-cat contributions to the GOP Congressional committee, which then gave substantially the same amount to Ford's campaign in Michigan. In its only new revelation, the *Star* alleged that $38,216 flowed into Ford's 1971 kitty from a D.C. fund-raising party for lobbyists where, quite lawfully, donors did not have to be identified.

The FBI, still smarting over the disclosure that its director, J. Patrick Gray, had destroyed Watergate evidence in his possession, assigned more than 350 field agents to the Ford inquiry. This was more than had ever been put on the tail of any citizen not suspected or accused of any violation of law.

In addition to this small army of G-men, there were scores of Internal Revenue auditors poring over Ford's tax returns and financial records, double-tracked by the suspicious experts of the Joint Congressional Committee on Taxation.

Experienced investigators of the Senate and House committees were sifting the files of every Washington bureaucracy that deals in contract awards and political appointments for evidence of any impropriety or pressure from the Congressman from Grand Rapids. All of his thirteen campaign reports on contributions and expenditures were critically re-examined.

What neither Constitution nor custom provided, however, was

any mechanism for the object of all this attention to protect himself. In the normal testing of a national candidate's record and fitness, he has a seasoned campaign organization and ample funds to deal with the charges raised by his opponents, by vindictive enemies and by the zealous media. An accused criminal is entitled to court-appointed legal assistance or a public defender to plead his innocence.

As Minority Leader, Ford had a staff of seventeen, a few more than most House Members but smaller than any Senator's. Within the week of Ford's nomination, we put together a remarkable defense team for the confirmation, mostly from volunteers. Usually volunteers are worth about what you pay them. This time we got a gifted group of solid Ford enthusiasts who somehow put aside personal convenience, pecking order, prima-donna tendencies and considerations of public or private reward.

Alphabetically, the key members of the team were:

Benton L. Becker, a thirty-two-year old attorney born and bred in Washington, with an incisive legal mind and an even blend of political realism and idealism. Now Professor of Law at the University of Miami, he first came to Ford's attention as one of the Department of Justice lawyers investigating the pecadilloes of Representative Adam Clayton Powell (D–New York). He was recruited from private practice by Representative Joe Waggoner (D–Louisiana) in 1970 to help investigate charges against Supreme Court Justice William O. Douglas. Benton developed a strong bond of mutual trust and admiration with Ford during that association, which I shared.

Kenneth L. Belieu, fifty-nine, had just closed out a long Federal career starting as an infantry second lieutenant in 1940. He survived the Battle of the Bulge, only to lose his lower left leg in Korea. Retiring in 1955 as a colonel, he became a professional staff member of the Senate Armed Services Committee. President Kennedy named him Assistant Secretary of the Navy, and President Johnson promoted him to Under Secretary, but Belieu returned to private life in 1965. At the outset of the Nixon Administration, Bryce Harlow brought Ken back as his White House deputy for the Senate. In 1971 Nixon sent him to the Pentagon as Under Secretary of the Army, making him the first person ever to hold both jobs. Belieu's forte was lobbying Senators of both parties.

Philip W. Buchen, at fifty-eight, was not quite the oldest member of the team but had known Ford the longest. They had been fraternity brothers (DKE) at the University of Michigan in the 1930s and on the eve of Pearl Harbor formed a law partnership in Grand Rapids. In his pre-Salk childhood Phil had been crippled in one leg by polio. While Ford went off to the Navy, Buchen pursued his legal career, which by 1973 had brought him to the top rank of corporate lawyers in Michigan's second city. Buchen and Ford remained fast friends as well as attorney and client. Phil knew almost everything about the Grand Rapids side of Ford's affairs.

(Also performing Herculean labors, though not actually part of Ford's Washington team, was his Grand Rapids accountant Robert J. McBain. Bob came up with incredibly complete and precise documentation of all Ford's financial transactions and tax returns.)

Richard T. Burress, fifty-one, had barely begun a challenging new job as Associate Director of the Hoover Institution on War, Revolution and Peace at Stanford University. He had been an FBI agent and a Marine in World War II. After practicing law and labor relations he learned Congressional politics as minority counsel of the House Labor and Education Committee. Representative John Rhodes (R–Arizona) next made Dick staff director of his Republican Policy Committee. Later, he reported to Ford as Minority Sergeant-at-Arms of the House, and I succeeded him in this job when he became Deputy Counsel to President Nixon. His first White House boss was Dr. Arthur Burns, a wise and mellow veteran of both Washington and Wall Street, the Republican Bernard Baruch with pipe instead of a park bench.

In 1969 we all assumed that, with seasoned pros like Harlow, Laird, Burns, Timmons, Burress and others joining the new Administration, Nixon's rapport with Congress would be peaches and cream.*

Bill Cramer, fifty-one, former Florida Congressman, first established a beachhead in the House for Southern Republicans during the Eisenhower years. Ford, as Minority Leader, gave enormous impetus to this two-party trend by forcing senior Democrats leftward with their party or into retirement. He helped Cramer up the ladder of House

---

* We didn't reckon with the Praetorian Guard, commanded by H. R. Haldeman and John Ehrlichman, largely composed of former Nixon advance men like themselves. Intoxicated by power, fiercely possessive of the President, ambitious, arrogant, tough, tireless, invincibly ignorant, the little Praetorians stormed into the White House much like Andy Jackson's mud-booted backwoodsmen to gorge on the sweet fruits of victory.

There is, as all Presidents eventually learn, a vast difference between running a campaign and running a country. Haldeman's Praetorians were political illiterates who thought themselves past masters. Washington's ways were not their ways, and they would make Washington conform.

leadership, sought his counsel, and Bill became a loyal Ford ally. But Cramer came a cropper when he ran for a vacant Senate seat in 1970. He opened a Washington law office with his former House assistant, Dick Haber, and retained his influential role as Florida's GOP National Committeeman.

Cramer was a bulldog-tough and battle-tested operator. His tongue was as razor-sharp as his mind, his Washington contacts were legion, and he had a deep affection for Ford. It was mutual; Ford once remarked that if he were in trouble and was innocent, he'd get Buchen to defend him, but, if guilty, he'd want Bill Cramer. Now he had both.

(Haber ran the law office while Cramer and Becker devoted full- and overtime to Ford. We considered Dick very much part of the team, along with Paul Yates, minority counsel of the House Public Works Committee, whom Cramer also dragooned.)

Hartmann comes next alphabetically. I was fifty-six and had been with Ford for seven years. My current titles were Minority Sergeant-at-Arms of the House and Legislative Assistant to the Minority Leader. I was responsible for almost everything unrelated to Ford's role as Representative of the Fifth District of Michigan. I did the staff work connected with his role as Minority Leader. When the House was in session I was usually within beckoning range, sometimes acted as lookout when he was off the floor. I carried confidential messages to and from other Republican members and their aides, with my Democratic counterparts in the Speaker's and Majority Leader's offices. People got to me when they couldn't get to Ford, or didn't want to bother him, to relay their concerns. Some of my best friends, of both parties, were and are in the House of Representatives.

I was go-between with the Senate leadership, the Republican National Committee, Governors' Association and Congressional campaign staffs. When Nixon was nominated I was at Permanent Chairman Ford's side on the convention podium. I represented him in the Inaugural arrangements and became his liaison with the White House and Executive departments. I pushed Ford's requests and helped Nixon's lobbyists—Harlow, Timmons and others—push Administration programs in the House.

I didn't see much of President Nixon beyond formal occasions, but he always greeted me warmly. I had known and supported him since he first ran for Senator in California. While chief of the Los Angeles *Times* bureau in Washington from 1954 to 1963, I covered his Vice Presidency from the mob scene in Caracas and the Kitchen Debate in Moscow to the cliffhanger climax of the 1960 campaign in Los Angeles. I suspect he was among those who recommended me to Jerry Ford in 1965. I had known Ford only socially through mutual California friends in Congress such as Glen Lipscomb, Pat Hillings, Craig Hosmer and Oakley Hunter, all strong Nixon men.

Elated as I was at Nixon's comeback in 1968, I was by then a thoroughly committed Ford man. I had no premonition that my boss would ever wind up in the White House or even as Vice President. But I firmly believe that no man can serve two masters and that undivided loyalty is the touchstone not only of politics but of every human endeavor. I do not say unquestioning, but undivided.

I had observed for a long time that Nixon, and the more fanatic followers he attracted, expected 100 percent fealty or nothing at all. This exacting measure was applied to all Republicans and even to the news media. Let me cite just two examples.

I was the beneficiary of numerous Vice Presidential news tips (including an advance copy of the "Yalta papers" that spoiled a John Foster Dulles–James Reston deal for a New York *Times* exclusive), and I reported Nixon's doings with a benevolent objectivity in vivid contrast to the venomous undertone of some of my Washington colleagues. Early in the 1960 Presidential campaign I did a series of in-depth interviews and lengthy profiles of the leading prospects. Jack Kennedy, Adlai Stevenson, Stuart Symington and Hubert Humphrey were all delighted with my fairness and accuracy (LBJ refused to see me and Nelson Rockefeller bowed out), but Nixon had his nose out of joint for weeks. Why? Because I started off my analysis of the Republican forerunner with the observation that "The trouble with Richard Nixon is, he's an egghead."

In 1968 President Johnson went on all the networks for an unusually partisan attack on Republican obstructionists in Congress. Ford, Laird & Co., the aging "Young Turks" of the House, cried "foul" and demanded equal time for rebuttal. When somewhat to our surprise we got it, Candidate Nixon stepped front and center and volunteered to utilize this free half hour for the GOP. It was well before the convention, and National Chairman Ray Bliss ruled that the Republican response would be delivered by Minority Leaders Dirksen and Ford.

Nixon's little Praetorians were livid. Bliss had delivered Ohio in 1960 (Kennedy, in victory, called this his greatest disappointment) and masterminded the Republican resurgence of 1966 and 1968. But this small transgression doomed him, like Lucifer, to be cast into outer darkness when the Praetorians settled old scores.

Since Jerry Ford was an active combatant in Washington and popular personally, his attacks on LBJ frequently got better press treatment than Nixon's, which surely smarted. And the Praetorians were visibly unhappy in 1968 when Ford and the other House leaders, unwilling (with good reason) to rely much on Nixon's coattails, mounted their own independent national campaign for House candidates by crying alarm that George Wallace's votes might throw the election into the House of Representatives. Thus, when Nixon's Praetorians came to Washington they were not really grateful to those who took them by hand around Capitol Hill—the men's rooms and the committee rooms—and told them the difference.

But Ford was a solid party team player. If he had a major flaw it was excessive deference to the President. Other Republican members began to gripe openly that he could not effectively carry their complaints to the man in the White House, that he would not lay the law down to Nixon on legislative realities. Politics is a trading game, and Senators and Congressmen get what they want from Presidents by being a little difficult. Ford was a wheel who seldom squeaked.

Americans like an independent streak in the officials they elect and re-elect. Even—or especially—in Vice Presidents, where the forces of nature usually bring it out. Presidents and their sycophants inevitably deplore it. I had watched Nixon, Johnson, Humphrey and Agnew writhing with this dilemma, and it was very much on my mind as Ford set off down the Vice Presidential road.

Robert O. Hynes, thirty-six, was another volunteer who took leave for a new career to join Ford's confirmation team—took it without pay to avoid any hint of conflict of interest. Bob was the minority counsel and right-hand man of Representative H. Allen Smith (R–California) during Smith's long tenure as ranking Republican on the House Rules Committee. After Smith retired, Bob made a soft landing as a Washington vice-president of NBC. They both volunteered to help Ford, but Smith found the tension too much for his health. Hynes carried on.

Bob was enthusiastic, savvy and well liked. He did his homework fast and well. He was used to working with the other House people on our team, and his contributions were legion.

Paul Miltich, fifty-four, was, like me, a Ford regular rather than a volunteer. He had been press secretary since 1966, a few months my junior in Ford's service. Paul covered Capitol Hill for the Booth Newspapers of Michigan, including the Grand Rapids *Press.*

At first, Miltich and I did not hit it off very well. For a newsman,

PALACE POLITICS

Paul was not a particularly gregarious type. I was hired neither as speech writer nor press secretary but primarily as an idea man. Paul's focus was essentially Michigan, while mine was Washington, political and national. Neither of us was subordinate to the other, but we often collided, and the primary fault was Ford's.

Ford liked giving us duplicating assignments, which we only belatedly discovered. We both protested, whereupon he made things worse by giving me only his major speeches to write and Miltich all the boilerplate. This was a recognition of the facts of life, since I worried for weeks over an important address while Paul had the knack of turning out texts like a baloney machine.

When Miltich, watching his home television, saw my prediction confirmed that Nixon would choose Ford we temporarily buried the hatchet and worked in reasonable, if not rapturous, harmony throughout Ford's Vice Presidency. Paul was doggedly devoted to Ford. When he was first demoted and then promoted out of the White House, I was sad.

Ford's marching orders to the team, when we assembled around his desk that bright October morning, were at first startling and unsettling. "Hold nothing back," he said. "Anything they want, if we have it, give it to them. I don't want any papers from the files destroyed, or hidden, or doctored up. We are not going to cover up anything and we are not going to stonewall."

He looked around at our somewhat bemused faces and added: "I'm not just saying that for the record. Nothing can possibly hurt us more than for somebody to remove something that looks embarrassing from my files and have it turn up somewhere else. If it looks like a problem, there's a reasonable explanation, and we'll give it to them. My conscience is clear.

"I told them that even in advance of any formal requests, I would authorize Bob McBain to turn over to proper investigators all pertinent information about my income-tax returns and financial affairs, ask Pat Jennings [Clerk of the House] and the Ethics Committee to make my records available and request Dr. Carey [Attending Physician of the Congress] and any other doctors who've treated me to do likewise," Ford added. "Of course, we'll want to go over all this stuff at the same time; you can't remember everything."

So the course was set. We seven would try to match the efforts of hundreds of skilled investigators with our own probe of everything there was to learn about Jerry Ford's past. We would try to anticipate anything they might dig up and have a ready answer with evidence to back it. Outnumbered as we were, we had one decided advantage: We had Jerry Ford.

As if to demonstrate our task was not entirely hopeless, he pulled open the right-hand drawer of his desk and produced, tidily bound in rotting rubber bands, all of his check stubs from his Congressional campaign and personal accounts for the past ten years; all of his pocket diaries showing his travels and expenses incurred; all of his daily appointment memos; and carbon copies of his state and Federal tax returns, election campaign filings and confidential reports to the House Ethics Committee on his investments and interests.

"This will do for a start," he said, shoving them across the desk. "Anything looks funny, ask me about it."

It was a disarming demonstration of exactly how well organized Jerry Ford had been over the years. In all our office safes, in the long rows of locked file cabinets, in his own bank box, there was nothing that proved more vital to his confirmation than the contents of that open drawer he kept beside him.

"Well, let's get to work," Ford said. "We haven't got a whole lot of time. Cannon thinks they'll start the hearings November 1, with live television."

When we reconvened in my office next door to divide up our Herculean labors, I added a charge that those parting words triggered. "Gentlemen, before we get down to cases, I'd like to make a point the boss didn't make and maybe would have difficulty making. We really have two jobs to do at the same time. One, obviously, is to prepare him and supply him with the facts and figures, the evidence and the endorsements, the legal and Constitutional briefs he needs to get confirmed. The other important thing we have to do in the process is make Jerry Ford better known and more favorably known to the American people.*

"A lot of people will be out there digging up stuff to make him look bad," I continued. "We can't just be on the defensive, proving he isn't a heel. We've got to use the same television time to show he's really a hero."

* A quickie poll by Dr. Gallup for the New York *Times* confirmed this. Two-thirds of the national sample approved of Ford's selection and only 7 percent disapproved, but a massive 27 percent had no opinion. When asked what kind of a President he might be, 55 percent of the total and exactly half the Republicans said they had no idea.

"What are you trying to do, Bob, run him for President already?" someone wisecracked. But they all agreed.

Two priority projects faced the confirmation team. The first was defensive—an "Answer Book" that was Benton Becker's baby. This evolved into a loose-leaf folder indexed to provide Ford at the witness table with facts, figures and explanatory documents covering every question we could anticipate. The documentary material could be slipped out of its plastic page and entered into the hearing record.

The other project took the offensive: Ford's opening statement at the start of the public hearings. This was my baby. I had helped him compose some pretty good speeches before, but this would be Ford's all-important, make-or-break opportunity to get his licks in first.

Burress and Hynes put together a second loose-leaf volume of Ford's legislative and political policy record. Over twenty-five years nobody who has to state his position a hundred times a week and eventually vote "Yea" or "Nay" on ingeniously worded resolutions is going to be perfectly consistent. Convictions and circumstances do change. But it all had to be researched and plausibly explained.

Partly to instruct ourselves, partly to refute the notion that Ford had no scholarly or intellectual dimension, an impressive roster of professors of American history and political science were asked for their views on the scope and function of the Vice Presidency in the current context. Their responses were greatly helpful. One, especially appreciated, was from Ford's law professor at Yale, Eugene V. Rostow, brother of Walt and LBJ's Undersecretary of State.

Professor Rostow, now emeritus, wrote his former pupil: "Constitutionally and politically, the first important requirement for the post, I should say, is that the Vice President be capable of discharging the duties of the Presidency, should fate call him to that office. The basic question to ask about a prospective Vice President is whether he has the character and insight to do what Teddy Roosevelt and Harry Truman did when they were called to the Presidency."

Another whose counsel was especially solicited by Ford was his own favorite among the three living former Vice Presidents, Senator Hubert H. Humphrey. Humphrey responded to his probable 1976 rival with generous and trusting candor for one whose future Presidential ambitions were then far from foreclosed. "The office of the Vice Presidency," Humphrey wrote, "has been described in many ways, but one accurate characterization is to say that it is an awkward office at best. The man who occupies it will have many responsibilities and no authority. . . . The power and authority that you have as Vice President will be determined by the measure of the power and authority that the President is willing to share with you or delegate to you. . . . Likewise, he can remove the authority and power at his will. I used to call this Humphrey's Law—'He who giveth can taketh away and often does.'

"Finally, it is important for a Vice President to remember that he is not the President and, therefore, can only speak for the government when he is authorized to do so."

He concluded: "I believe that it is important for the Vice President to be loyal to the President's policies and at the same time to speak candidly, in private, with the President in any disagreements in policy so that the President may have the benefit of the Vice President's advice and counsel. . . . I emphasize the direct and personal relationship. It isn't good enough to convey one's observations to the President's subordinates."

Humphrey for once stopped too soon. Never good enough—and sometimes fatal.

3

OLD GHOSTS RETURN

★★————————————★★

Washington is never a one-ring circus. Ford's problems in gaining the No. 2 job were suddenly shoved onto a back burner by a dramatic escalation of the problems of No. 1. On the day Nixon nominated Ford, the Circuit Court of Appeals had ordered the President to turn over the nine tapes subpoenaed by Special Prosecutor Archibald Cox to U.S. District Judge John J. Sirica.

It was at first assumed that the 5–2 split decision would be carried to the Supreme Court, but the deadline came and no appeal. Nixon instead publicly proposed a compromise. The President knew that Sam Ervin's Watergate Committee also wanted the tapes—that there was bad blood between the seasoned Senate investigators and Cox's army of zealous young Harvard prosecutors. On Wednesday, Judge Sirica had quashed Ervin's effort to subpoena the tapes.

Nixon was a Senator for only two years, but as Vice President he presided over that body for eight. He had seen how reluctantly Senators censure even a prodigal (Joe McCarthy) and how readily they rise up to hail the virtue of an inner-club member. Of such pillars, none was more revered than John Stennis, a conservative Mississippi Democrat.

The President, therefore, proposed that he himself would make a summary of what the controversial tapes contained. He would permit Senator Stennis to listen to the actual tapes and attest that nothing pertinent to Watergate had been distorted or omitted from Nixon's summary. The President would then hand the summary over, not only to the Special Prosecutor, whose right to the security-sanitized evidence on the tapes had already been affirmed by the Court of Appeals, but also—generously and gratuitously—to the Senate Watergate committee which had just been judicially denied it.

Chairman Ervin and the ranking Republican, Senator Howard Baker of Tennessee, quickly endorsed it. Stennis, then seventy-two and recovering from a near fatal gunshot wound, agreed as readily.

52

Simultaneously, Nixon was immersed in one of the greatest foreign-policy gambles of his Presidency. The same Saturday morning that Nixon's nomination of Ford went to the Congress, the President had made the fateful decision to strip down the U.S. defense arsenal and airlift critical arms to save Israel from being pushed into the sea. The Friday of his Stennis compromise, he dispatched Kissinger to Moscow. He was properly concerned lest a showdown with Cox or the courts be read in the Kremlin as a sign of weakness in Washington.

Richardson was the key to the situation, obviously the President's subordinate, nominally Cox's superior in the chain of command. But what is "special" about a Special Prosecutor is that he really has no boss.

Richardson had picked Cox and pledged that he would not fire him except for "extraordinary improprieties." Richardson had been preoccupied negotiating Agnew's resignation and plea-copping, but he agreed to put the Stennis compromise to his former Harvard professor and fellow Bostonian. He seems to have clung to the hope that Cox would get him off his conscientious hook by resigning first. But Cox, flatly rejecting the President's proposal, went a step further by asserting that Nixon couldn't fire him; only the Attorney General could do that.

The Saturday Night Massacre actually began shortly after noon, when Cox called a news conference at the National Press Club. Ford had just put out a press release praising the Stennis compromise. Cox told the President of the United States on nationwide television that he intended to press for the tapes—and more, if need be. He was not going to quit.

General Haig, ever Nixon's accommodating hangman, telephoned Richardson almost as soon as Cox finished his public defiance to relay the President's explicit order to fire Cox. Richardson demanded to see the President and tender his resignation in person. When the Attorney General arrived at the Oval Office, Nixon worked Elliot over again, pulling out all the stops. Richardson refused. There was an exchange of muted snarls, and the ex-Attorney General left.

Haig started down the line. Deputy Attorney General William Ruckelshaus was now in charge. Would he, as Acting Attorney General of the United States, carry out the orders of the President of the United States? Ruckelshaus, who knew what was coming, would not.

Next in succession came Solicitor General Robert H. Bork. At about 6:00 P.M. he signed a brief letter drafted at the White House that summarily fired Cox.

PALACE POLITICS

General Haig ordered the FBI to move in force through the nearly deserted corridors of the Justice Department and, as darkness fell, to seal the files and offices of Richardson, Ruckelshaus and the Special Prosecutor. Then, almost as if by command, the White House Praetorians began to spread the slander that Richardson had a long-standing drinking problem. It was one of their favorite tactics.

Ford was aghast when he learned of all this. It was the first time, I think, that he began to wonder a little. The matter of a Democratic Harvard professor and longtime Kennedy family friend losing a clear test of will to the President of the United States was one thing. But the echoes of jackbooted secret police barring purged officials from their own desks in the dark of the night was bloodcurdling. Not here, not in Washington, D.C.

How would this incredible stupidity, at this moment, affect his own fate? After all, Elliot Richardson had been Nixon's original "Mr. Clean." Nixon had nominated Richardson to the top or second spot in three of the four most sensitive Cabinet departments. Richardson certainly had burning political ambition. For him to quit, for Nixon to permit it, for ambitious Bill Ruckelshaus to follow suit, there must be something terribly wrong somewhere.

"How can he be so dumb?" Ford asked me the next morning. "If the tapes will clear him, why doesn't he just turn them over and put an end to all this?"

I didn't have an answer, and neither did he.

"I guess the reason is the same one we've talked about before," I said lamely. "When the time comes for Nixon to choose between the men and the boys, he always chooses the boys."

The Saturday Night Massacre, which set off what Haig colorfully termed a "firestorm" of enraged public opinion, had one beneficial effect for us. It set the House liberals, and particularly those on the Judiciary Committee, aflame with impeachment fever.

In the avant-garde was black-haired, brooding Representative Jerome Waldie (D–California), who, curiously, resembled nothing more than the obverse image of the young Richard Nixon relentlessly pursuing Red devils in the House a generation earlier. If Father Drinan, the militant priest-politician from Massachusetts, would gladly have applied the faggot to the President's burning pyre, he would probably have heard the heretic's last confession before the flames consumed him. Waldie's was a more primitive, visceral hate. He seemed ready personally to pinion Nixon for a public drawing and quartering.

The most implacable of Ford's tormentors, for reasons that continue to escape me, was Representative Elizabeth Holtzman (D–New York), who had upset the venerable Manny Celler in a Democratic primary. Ms. Holtzman had a taut legally trained mind, a bite like a moray eel and a heart as soft as tungsten steel. Led by the likes of these, a movement gained momentum to hold Ford's nomination hostage while the House brought Nixon to book. Eleven Democratic Members joined in a proposed resolution to shelve the Vice Presidential vacancy "until such time as the President has complied with the final decision of the court system as it regards the White House tapes."

The Democratic elders were cautious but sensed the sudden shift in their rank-and-file. Speaker Albert called a Democratic caucus to vent the steam. Chairman Rodino, anxiously eying his New Jersey district, which was slowly turning from Italian to black, postponed the Ford hearings for at least three weeks. This finally insured that Ford's first inquisitors would be Senators, and that was the way we wanted it. The Senate would be exacting but within certain fixed rules. There were no scatterbrains on the Rules Committee. There was, furthermore, Ford's staunchest of Senatorial friends, Bob Griffin (R–Michigan).*

All of the Republican Senators were eager to offer Ford helpful hints, but Bob Griffin had the pragmatic sense to spend hours coaching Jerry's confirmation staff as well. Our strategy was to bring out all the worst things that could be charged against Ford in the Senate round, thoroughly air them and dispose of them, leaving the House hotheads little to chew but their own ideological cud. Public and press would be getting bored for the second time around.

The success of this plan depended on our not allowing the House investigators to hold any bombshells back. Here the historic rivalry between the two bodies worked to our advantage. No Senator, even the most critical of Democrats, wanted to pass judgment on Ford and

---

* Griffin and Ford quite literally owed their jobs to each other. Griffin was first elected to the House after Ford was already a fixture. But it was Griffin and Charlie Goodell (R–New York) who spearheaded the "young Turks" revolt against Minority Leader Charles Halleck (R–Indiana) in 1965 which put Ford atop the pyramid in a 73–67 vote-squeaker.

The next year, Senator Pat McNamara died. Michigan Governor George Romney had a vacancy to fill and his own candidate in mind. But he could hardly risk bypassing Ford. Ford had by then clearly decided his goal was the Speaker's gavel. He declined but insisted that Romney appoint Griffin. The Governor agreed, and Bob went on to win two Senate terms.

later learn that the Senate probers had missed an important bit of evidence.

As the FBI, IRS and committee investigators swarmed like locusts over the Fifth District of Michigan and fanned out across the country, most of the friendly witnesses would telephone and tell us the questions they'd been asked. We admonished them to tell the whole truth and nothing but the truth, but in the process we accumulated a fair idea of the areas the investigators were concentrating on.

The first surprise that popped up, which somebody leaked to the press, was that Ford had got a job at the Treasury Department for G. Gordon Liddy of Watergate fame. We could find nothing in our files under either "Liddy" or "Treasury." I had pretty much handled job-seekers for Ford after Nixon's 1968 victory and had no recollection that Liddy was ever on our list of recommendations.

So we asked Ford about it. "Sure," he recalled instantly. "You know Liddy tried to run for Congress in the Republican primary in upstate New York that year. But Ham Fish [the incumbent Republican] won handily and I went up to Dutchess County to campaign for him. Liddy was at the rally. Afterward, Ham confided to me he was worried that this guy Liddy might be building himself up to run as a Conservative Party candidate. If Nixon won, couldn't I help fix Liddy up with some kind of a job in Washington and get him out of the way? I said sure, I'd see what we could do."

After the election, Ford continued, Liddy had come to see him with a stack of endorsement letters from Fish and other GOP leaders in New York. He left a résumé that Ford passed along to Treasury, and in due course they took Liddy on.

The next salvo of torpedoes was more serious. Robert Norman Winter-Berger surfaced again. About a year earlier a mini-sensational book (*The Washington Pay-Off*) by Winter-Berger had been published. The author represented himself as a big-shot New York lobbyist who was welcome in most Washington politicians' company and was the recipient of their most incredible self-incriminating confidences. He had, he said, enjoyed the virtual run of Speaker John McCormack's office through friendship with Nathan Voloshen, a shadowy Capitol fixer who later pleaded guilty to influence-peddling and got a suspended sentence because of failing health.

The book's index was a virtual Who's Who of prominent politicians. Winter-Berger claimed to have witnessed a hysterical and profane President Johnson, in McCormack's office, offer to pay Bobby Baker one million dollars to take the rap (for alleged improprieties as

56

Senate Secretary) in silence. Voloshen was to pass the message; the book did not say whether it was either passed or paid.

This was not the wildest of Winter-Berger's scattershot charges. Senator Pell (D–Rhode Island), a member of the committee that was investigating Ford, was subjected to scurrilous insinuations, not the least of which was a supposed plot in which he employed the author to knife Bobby Kennedy so that he, Pell, could be LBJ's running mate in 1964. Winter-Berger's early targets were Democrats, but in 1966, so he claimed, he paid a mutual friend $1,000 for an introduction to Gerald Ford, the new House Minority Leader.

Ford actually came off somewhat better in the book than most of the victims of the author's spite. Winter-Berger portrayed himself as a very intimate companion and counselor of Ford's. He conceded that Ford would never accept cash, never pocketed any of his campaign contributions and refused to hear the scandalous tales he bore of the Speaker's alleged skullduggery. Yet the picture he drew of his good friend was splattered with terms like "plodder," "drab," "naïve," "unabashed country bumpkin" and "a dull and greedy man."

This came as something of a shock to me, since I had never laid eyes on the man. If Winter-Berger had been virtually camping in Ford's office for several years, accompanying him on trips to Michigan and New York, it seemed highly unlikely that I would never have bumped into him.

But the name was familiar; it is the kind of name that is hard to forget. The name "Robert Winter-Berger" began appearing on Ford's appointment list frequently enough to cause some wondering, at least by Miltich and me. Just who was this guy? When one of us went to lunch we'd wisecrack, "I'm going out to grab a Winter-Berger."

Winter-Berger's revelations created a mild stir in Michigan, though they were discounted by knowledgeable Washingtonians. The Grand Rapids *Press* had its Capitol reporter, Bob Lewis, fly to New York to interview Winter-Berger and examine his "evidence." Lewis found only a couple of form letters from Ford and a stack of Ford's old newsletters. Lewis reported that Winter-Berger told him that "Jerry Ford never personally received a cent from me," and the national media lost all interest in the subject.

But now Winter-Berger appeared in a new incarnation, under the sponsorship of none other than Jack Anderson. And he hurled serious new charges at Ford on the eve of the Senate hearings into his fitness for the Vice Presidency.

"A former lobbyist has sworn to the Senate Rules Committee that

57

he 'loaned' vice presidential nominee Gerald Ford $15,000 to cover urgent personal needs," read the Anderson–Whitten column in the Sunday Washington *Post* of October 29. 'The loan,' said lobbyist Robert Winter-Berger, 'was never repaid.'

"In his affidavit, Winter-Berger stated: 'Between 1966 and September of 1969, I personally loaned Gerald Ford in the neighborhood of $15,000 . . . this money was given to Ford in cash to cover an illness and hospitalization of his wife . . . at other times he complained that he was short of money.' "

The rest of the long column was largely a repetition of allegations in the earlier book.

"That——!" Ford exploded with an expletive he rarely resorted to. "He just wants to sell more books!" We had only twenty-four hours to get the answer, affidavit and all.

Winter-Berger's new, last-minute allegation of cash payoffs for Ford's personal use was the most difficult, not only because such transactions are easier to deny than to disprove but also because it was the only shadow cast on his moral integrity.* It was totally out of character, but the nation was still reeling from the shock of Agnew's shattered rectitude.

Fortunately, Winter-Berger was his own undoing. His small corroborating details rang false. The payments had been made in increments of $50 to $250 over about three years. By simple arithmetic, this would have required 300 meetings with $50 bills or 60 visits bearing $250. We searched Ford's appointments and found less than a score.

Betty's illness? We dug out her 1969 hospital bill for $1,427.55, of which Blue Cross–Blue Shield paid $1,399.55.

Without further belaboring Winter-Berger's fairy tales, it is certainly worth noting that in October 1973 the population of the United States was estimated by the Census Bureau to be about 211,000,000. Out of that number only one individual could be found willing to accuse Jerry Ford under oath of moral turpitude. That alone is a rather remarkable achievement.

The unanswered question for me has always been motivation. Why was Winter-Berger so savagely vindictive? A brief whirl in the

---

* After both Senate and House committees found Winter-Berger an incredible witness without an iota of proof, Jack Anderson and I were persuaded to sit down at the same lunch table by Jack Gertz, a mutual friend. Anderson apologized and said his associate had been taken in by Winter-Berger—as to some extent Ford was. Thereafter, I must testify, Anderson was scrupulously correct in his treatment of Vice President and President Ford.

national limelight, another book advance, a primordial wish to gain a great warrior's strength by eating his vital organs? But why did Ford put up with Winter-Berger at all, let alone for three years? What did the guy ever do for him, really?

Well, he admitted he was duped, and who hasn't been deceived by a false friend? As Confucius say, "Fool me once, shame on you; fool me twice, shame on me."

On other occasions Ford demonstrated a disconcerting blind spot in dealing with people. He had difficulty seeing the obvious when ingratiating scoundrels were trying to use him, and he rather resented suggestions that their motives might be less than pure. It is possible that he believed, as Members of Congress have ample reason to conclude, that *everyone* he encountered was using him in one way or another and that he could reciprocate by using them as long as they remained in fact useful. His friends were legion but his real intimates remarkably few.

Essentially, Jerry Ford is a very self-contained and self-reliant man. If he had gnawing doubts in the night or feelings of insecurity that harass most Presidents, he kept them to himself. His self-confidence was enormous but always stopped short of immodesty. He could tell a self-deprecating joke about himself, but one always wondered whether he *really* enjoyed the laughter.

The true story of Ford's 1970 showdown with the late Associate Justice William O. Douglas has never been told despite the torrent of words written about it at the time and thereafter during two Congressional inquiries.

The verdict of the press—and presumably of the public—was that Jerry Ford had been prompted three years earlier by President Nixon and/or his sinister associates to launch his "attack" on the aging New Dealer as a diversion and reprisal for the Senate's refusal to confirm his second and third appointments to the Supreme Court, U.S. Circuit Court of Appeals Judges Clement F. Haynsworth, Jr., of South Carolina and G. Harrold Carswell of Florida.

Even an old Michigan friend such as Jerry terHorst of the Detroit *News* concluded, in his semisympathetic biography (published shortly after he resigned as White House press secretary to protest the Nixon pardon), that "although Ford's anti-Douglas move was undoubtedly motivated by his loyalty to Nixon, it was nevertheless ill-advised and certainly constitutes a dark blot on his Congressional career."

TerHorst missed the mark. Ford was "undoubtedly" manipulated by Nixon's devious political appointees—White House Special Coun-

PALACE POLITICS

sel Clark Mollenhoff, Attorney General John Mitchell and Will Wilson, Assistant Attorney General in charge of the Criminal Division—but that was long after he developed an acute distaste for Justice Douglas.

Ford disapproved of Douglas the way a Grand Rapids housewife would deplore the behavior of certain movie stars. The old man took too many young wives, and he seemed to encourage every new fad in youthful rebellion. Though Ford is an Episcopalian, he had absorbed some of his constituents' Calvinism by osmosis; though as a lawyer he studiously read the major Supreme Court decisions, his difference with Douglas was not so much liberal vs. conservative as swinger vs. square.

What brought this visceral mass of umbrage to a critical stage was the dramatic downfall of one of Douglas' brethren on the highest bench, Abe Fortas. When Earl Warren retired near the end of President Johnson's term, LBJ named his friend Justice Fortas to be the next Chief Justice. The fight in the Senate against Fortas' confirmation was led by Ford's ally, Bob Griffin. The most damaging charge against Associate Justice Fortas was that he had accepted a $20,000 retainer from the Wolfson Family Foundation, a nonprofit organization set up by Louis Wolfson, a financier serving a Federal prison sentence for Security Exchange violations.

The furor continued until the Senate adjourned without elevating Fortas. Following an exhaustive exposé in *Life* magazine in May 1969 on his connections with the Wolfson Family Foundation, Justice Fortas resigned from the Court, still protesting his innocence of any impropriety.

Back in 1966 (October 16) an investigation by Ronald J. Ostrow of the Los Angeles *Times* had disclosed that Justice Douglas had been doing substantially the same thing as Fortas for nearly a decade. The story that Douglas was moonlighting for the Parvin Foundation as its president for $12,000 a year was now revived. It became newsworthy because Douglas' benefactor, Albert Parvin, had been named a co-conspirator (but not a defendant) in the same SEC case that sent Wolfson to prison, and the current attorney for the Parvin Foundation was none other than Mrs. Abe Fortas.* Douglas maintained that Parvin, who set up his foundation in 1960 after selling his interest in the

---

* Mrs. Fortas, who practices law as Carolyn Agger, was retained by the Foundation in November 1966. An expert on tax-exempt organizations, she insisted that its by-laws be changed to remove Parvin from control of its investments, which was done. There never was any suggestion of impropriety on the part of Miss Agger, a highly respected Washington attorney.

Flamingo Hotel in Las Vegas, was inspired to good works after reading one of the Justice's books about developing leadership in Latin America.

Inquiring AP reporters, however, dug a bit deeper than Ostrow and turned up the fact that Parvin's company had agreed to pay $200,-000 to Meyer Lansky, a well-known figure in organized crime, purportedly as a finder's fee in the 1959 sale of the Flamingo, and was making regular installment payments to Lansky during the same period that Justice Douglas was getting his from the Parvin Foundation.

Ford read these revelations with relish. He could not have been oblivious to the favorable publicity his former protégé, Senator Griffin, garnered from his relentless pursuit of Fortas. But he genuinely felt—perhaps from the old Yale Law School tie—that Fortas would be getting a raw deal if Douglas were to go scotfree.

Justice Fortas resigned from the Supreme Court on May 14 and precisely a week later Justice Douglas also resigned—not from the Court but as president of the Parvin Foundation. Just prior to this he dashed off a "Dear Al" letter to Parvin on yellow legal foolscap. Justice Douglas termed the current IRS investigation of the Parvin Foundation's tax-exempt status "a manufactured case" and concluded that "the strategy is to get me off the court, and I do not propose to bend to any such pressure."

Although Justice Douglas suspected that the FBI was out to "get" him, the Foundation's attorney, Carolyn Agger (Mrs. Fortas), believed the press leaks were coming from the IRS. In any event, Douglas' letter to Parvin, when the New York *Times* published it on May 25, 1969, only served to further inflame Douglas' foes in the Congress. His resignation from the Parvin Foundation, though premised on health and a heavy judicial workload, suggested a belated recognition that the association, from which he had derived $101,000 in outside income over the years, was bringing discredit on the Supreme Court.

Representative H. R. Gross (R–Iowa), a former radio newscaster and the conservative gadfly of the House, went further. He alleged in the *Congressional Record* that Douglas might have violated the Federal statute prohibiting judges from practicing law. There began a persistent drumfire of anti-Douglas insertions in the *Congressional Record* by Gross and other conservatives of both parties. Eventually, fifty-nine Republicans and fifty-two Democrats co-sponsored a House resolution calling for a select committee to investigate the conduct of Justice Douglas.

This preface is necessary because it demonstrates conclusively that Jerry Ford did not personally initiate the Congressional vendetta against the elderly Justice and that it was well under way long before President Nixon nominated Judge Haynsworth on August 18, 1969, or had any notion that the Senate would turn him down, as it did on November 21. The idea that Ford was acting as an errand boy for the White House in the Douglas matter was invented much later when, in fact, it was the Nixon Administration that jumped aboard an already rolling bipartisan House bandwagon as a tactic to ensure Senate confirmation of Nixon's second choice, Judge Carswell. And this was frustrated because Ford refused to move against Douglas until the Senate disposed of the Carswell nomination.*

What Ford did do, in the summer of 1969, was to ask me to look into the Douglas–Parvin connection, through whatever channels an old investigative reporter might remember, to see what facts were already on the public record and what new information I could develop from them.

"With all the smoke, there ought to be some fire," he told me. "Be very circumspect about your inquiries. Don't make any big deal of it, but see what you can find out. I can't for the life of me see what is the difference between what Fortas was doing and what Douglas did for a whole lot longer, except that Abe gave the money back when he got caught."

After I had researched most of the news accounts and looked into the House procedures in impeachment cases (the last of which had been in 1936), it became obvious that we could not go much further without more resources of legal and investigative manpower and money. In early October I wrote a memo to Ford saying that although any Member of the House may make impeachment charges as a question of high privilege (meaning that the Speaker must take some action and cannot rule them out of order), the House had, in practice, always referred them to a committee for examination. In modern times this had always been the Judiciary Committee, but precedent existed for creation of a select or special committee.

We were concerned because the Judiciary Committee was heavily

---

* In February, Ford passed along for me to answer a letter from Representative Wilmer Mizell of Vinegar Bend, North Carolina, asking, "Jerry, do you intend to pursue your promise to seek impeachment proceedings against Justice Douglas?" On it he had scrawled: "Bob: write him I believe, *after Carswell,* we might write and give a full-blown speech summarizing Douglas' problems."

weighted with liberal lawyers whose regard for Justice Douglas was akin to reverence. I also noted in my memo that "there is much controversy as to what are impeachable offenses."

I concluded there was little doubt that Douglas' conduct stretched the Fourth Canon of Judicial Ethics of the American Bar Association, which states that "A judge's official conduct should be free from impropriety *and the appearance of impropriety.*"

But I added that "this has no force of law and is extremely broad." I was of the pragmatic opinion that Ford should not get himself hooked up with the ultra-right-wing Congressmen who were crying for Douglas' scalp. Until harder evidence turned up they seemed to me bound to lose, and the Minority Leader loses enough roll calls in the course of nature not to go about looking for more.

About this time nature took another of its courses. My inquiries about Douglas and impeachment, however casual and guarded, had reached the press gallery. Inevitably, people take note of what the Minority Leader's right-hand man is up to. So when Ford held a news conference on November 7, someone asked him whether he was getting ready to impeach Justice Douglas.

"No, I have no such plans," he said, somewhat nonplussed. Then his admirable habit of candor overcame him, and he added, "All I have done is to ask my staff to investigate what the facts are."

"How long has your investigation been going on, and when will we know the results of this staff investigation?"

"Well, we have been looking into it ever since Mr. Fortas resigned and Mr. Douglas decided to quit the Parvin Foundation. I haven't come to any conclusions, and the results of the investigation will be made known at the appropriate time," Ford said.

My heart sank. His big "staff investigation" was only me, and I certainly didn't have any results to speak of. But maybe Ford figured that going public with his probe would start some information coming in. In any event, that was the case.

Our office mail suddenly became an avalanche. Much of it was applause; people prematurely inferred that Ford had grasped the battle standard and saddled up to lead the crusade. Some was vitriolic; how dare he impugn one of America's greatest jurists? There were the usual number of nuts, the kind who use both the black and red ribbons on their typewriters. But there were a few, no more than a dozen or two, who actually appeared to have some firsthand information concerning the Justice's extrajudicial behavior.

PALACE POLITICS

Not everyone wrote letters. There were telephone tips, too, most of them not very credible. One, however, seemed authentic.

Late one night in November, as Ford was drifting off to sleep, the phone rang. It was a long-distance call from a person, unknown to Ford, who even now might remain healthier if his or her identity remains unknown. (For grammar's sake, I shall employ the masculine pronoun.)

The caller said he was not a Parvin employee but he had long-standing business connections with the Los Angeles-based Parvin–Dohrmann Company and its predecessor, which was engaged in the hotel and restaurant supply business. When Parvin bought a controlling interest in the company and became its president, he told Ford, Parvin–Dohrmann began acquiring Las Vegas hotels with gambling casinos, most of which were its customers. The office gossip was that Parvin, the new boss, was a very close buddy of Supreme Court Justice Douglas, gave him lavish presents and allowed him the use of a company credit card for travel, all of which was charged to company expenses.

Ford quickly became wide awake and began closely questioning his nocturnal informant for dates, details and corroborating witnesses. The informant said he didn't mind Ford knowing who he was, if his name were kept confidential. Actually, he admitted, all his information was secondhand hearsay. But he would give the Congressman the names of a half dozen former officials and employees of Parvin's firm who claimed to have firsthand knowledge of the transactions.

Ford took copious notes, promised to respect the caller's request for confidentiality within the limits of the law, and told me about his conversation the next morning. We debated whether or not it would be wise for him, or even for me, to try contacting them. I was fearful, following all the publicity, that the midnight call might be a trap to embarrass him. Still, it was a tempting potential breakthrough.

Once again fortune intervened. Miltich had a request for an interview from two Associated Press reporters, Gaylord Shaw and Jean Heller.

"Maybe the same guy telephoned AP," I said.

Curious, Ford agreed to see Shaw and Heller and asked us to sit in on the session. The AP, Gaylord Shaw explained, had set up a special task force for in-depth investigative reporting. In 1969 this was a new trend in journalism. One of the avenues they were going into was the Douglas connection with the new government of the Dominican

Republic. This had turned up some curious coincidences, but there were still a lot of loose ends.

They proposed a simple trade of information. They'd give us what they had if we'd help them get some answers to perfectly proper inquiries to which a Congressman can demand an answer in twenty-four hours. This is a normal working arrangement in Washington.

The line of inquiry Jean Heller was pursuing was briefly this:

1. Parvin's business connections with legal Las Vegas gambling were a matter of public record, particularly after he was named a defendant in an SEC action against the Parvin–Dohrmann Company on October 16, 1969 (although Parvin had sold his controlling interest in 1968 to Delbert Coleman; and Justice Douglas, apparently on the legal advice of Mrs. Fortas, in March 1969 got rid of all the Parvin–Dohrmann stock in the Parvin Foundation's portfolio).

2. Well-known gambling figures in Las Vegas were interested in obtaining casino concessions in the Dominican Republic, which were up for grabs following the revolt and exile of Trujillo and the election of Juan Bosch as President. At least one of these figures had been associated with Parvin, an attorney named Edward Levinson, who handled the 1960 sale of the Flamingo Hotel from which Meyer Lansky received a $200,000 finder's fee. Levinson was also associated with Bobby Baker, LBJ's former aide, in his vending-machine venture, and Baker and Levinson had flown to Santo Domingo in February 1963 at the time of Bosch's inauguration.

3. Justice Douglas and Albert Parvin were also in the Dominican capital on that occasion, in connection with an educational television project which the Parvin Foundation was financing with the cooperation of President Bosch, who was described by Justice Douglas as an old friend. Bosch had also asked the Justice to advise his government on the drafting of a new Constitution.

Question: Was there any connection between all these people suddenly showing extreme interest in Dominican developments on the one hand and Parvin's tax-exempt foundation headed by a Supreme Court Justice on the other? Since Bosch was toppled from power in September 1963 and the Parvin Foundation's projects in Santo Domingo were thereafter abandoned, there was no ready answer. But the IRS was sufficiently interested to start an investigation as to whether the Parvin Foundation's tax-exempt status should be revoked.

Ford, for a start, decided to let the AP ask some questions for us. He directed me to give Ms. Heller his notes on the six persons who purportedly knew of favors shown Justice Douglas by Parvin above and beyond the Parvin Foundation's presidency. We agreed to see if we could find out anything more about the Dominican connection.

Subsequently, during a meeting on another matter, Ford mentioned what he had heard to Attorney General Mitchell and asked if there was anything to it. Mitchell puffed noncommittally on his pipe, Ford told me afterward, and promised to look into it. Ford didn't think he'd get anything.

Three days after our conference with the AP reporters, the Senate rejected President Nixon's nomination of Judge Haynsworth. And three weeks after that Will Wilson, Assistant Attorney General in charge of the Criminal Division at the Department of Justice, turned up at Ford's Capitol office and handed him a nine-page synopsis of information about the Flamingo Hotel in Las Vegas, Albert Parvin, the Parvin Foundation and the events in the Dominican Republic.

The document was neatly typed in single space on plain bond stationery, without any identifying letterhead or sign of authorship. Nevertheless, Wilson, during his December 12, 1969, visit to Ford's office, represented it to be the response of the Attorney General of the United States to the Congressman's informal inquiry and gave Ford every reason to believe it was fully supported by investigative evidence in the possession of the Department of Justice.

If so, it was highly disturbing. I had a verbatim copy typed up and we locked the original in Ford's office safe. Among other things, the document disclosed:

SEQUENCE OF EVENTS IN DOMINICAN REPUBLIC

1. When Trujillo was in power, Morris Lansburgh operated the Jaragua Hotel in which, by repute, Meyer Lansky controlled the gambling casino. Juan Bosch came into power in the Dominican Republic when Trujillo was deposed and, at least on the surface, the Lansky gambling interests were ousted. Morris Lansburgh emerged as owner of the Flamingo in Las Vegas.

2. In 1956 one Fronkin became the operator of the gambling in something known as the "Coney Island Amusement Park"

in the Dominican Republic, which was on its surface a partnership of a man named Allen, Benjamin Golob and Joseph Mangone. This is believed to be a front for Angelo Bruno, boss of the Philadelphia La Cosa Nostra family. There have been indications from time to time of other Mafia figures who have moved in and out of the gambling establishments in the Dominican Republic, including Joseph Sicareli of New Jersey, Eugene Pozo of Florida, and Santa Trafficante, Jr., of Florida. In the spring of 1963 Louis Levinson was negotiating with the Dominican Republic, as well as Leslie Earl Kruse of Chicago and also Sam Giancanno of Chicago. None of this is directly related to the Parvin matter except to show the interest of American racketeers in the Dominican Republic.

3. December 1962. Bobby Baker and Juan Bosch met in New York City.

4. January 1963. Albert Parvin Foundation decides to abandon all projects in Latin America not related to the Dominican Republic, and it is proposed to send some Directors, including Douglas, as representatives to Juan Bosch's inauguration. It is believed that Bosch visited Douglas in Washington. Douglas called Bosch an old friend and indicated Bosch was anxious for representatives of the Parvin Foundation to come to the Dominican Republic and collaborate with the new government on various projects, including the drafting of a new constitution.

5. Parvin Foundation efforts in the Dominican Republic began in January 1963 and tapered off in August 1963.

6. February 27, 1963. Bosch's inauguration. Douglas, Parvin and Harvey Silbert traveled to the Dominican Republic, at which time Douglas saw Bosch and various of his cabinet members and aides. Harvey Silbert was a member of the Board of the Parvin Foundation and a Los Angeles lawyer who had represented racketeers.

7. At the time of Bosch's inauguration various American gambling figures attended and discussed gambling concessions with Bosch and other Dominican Republic officials, and there seems to have been considerable interest in gambling concessions during the spring and summer of 1963. Some of these included Angelo Bruno, John Simone, Bobby Baker and Ed Levinson.

8. April 16–18, 1963. Bobby Baker and Levinson in the Dominican Republic concerning a tobacco factory and gam-

67

bling concession in the Ambassador Hotel and concerning a concession of vending machines for the Serv-U Corporation, which was then represented by Fortas.

9. June 1963. Baker with Levinson in the Dominican Republic attempting to get gambling concession for Levinson.

10. August 1963. Gambling concession in the Dominican Republic acquired by Cliff Jones (former Lieutenant Governor of Nevada and an associate of Bobby Baker).

11. In the New York *Times* of September 3, 1964, is an article dealing with the J. M. Kaplan Fund, Inc., which is a tax-exempt corporation headquartered in New York City having an interest in the Dominican Republic. For some reason not apparent a very strange figure named Sacha Volman was employed by the Albert Parvin Foundation as its agent in the Dominican Republic.

Nothing much happened over the Christmas recess. Ford and his family went off to ski at their newly acquired Vail, Colorado, condominium. I took advantage of his absence to fly south to my recently acquired condominium in St. Croix, U.S. Virgin Islands.

★

On January 5, 1970, Jean Heller came by to see me and reported a near blank on the six former Parvin–Dohrmann employees. She had checked them all out, but they were uniformly reluctant to talk. One, however, did volunteer the name of a former comptroller of Albert Parvin & Co., Irving J. Marcus of Anaheim, California (subsequently identified by the Celler subcommittee), who presumably would know about any financial transactions of the kind alleged.

Ms. Heller said that when she first telephoned Marcus at his office he couldn't talk and gave her his home number. Later that night at home, November 25, he sounded very cooperative. But he asked that she write him a letter outlining her specific questions. The next day she did but heard nothing. On December 9 she called again.

"It seemed to me somebody had gotten to him in the meantime," she told me. "He just said over and over again that he couldn't help me at all. As if somebody were listening or he thought his phone was bugged."

It was later represented that Mr. Marcus had suffered a heart attack. Nevertheless, he was interrogated in February 1970 by an investigator for the Department of Justice Strike Force on Organized

Crime, to whom he gave a statement that remains confidential. On August 20, 1970, investigators of the Celler subcommittee, having been given Marcus' name by me in accordance with Ford's instructions to turn over to them everything I had, interviewed Marcus in his Beverly Hills attorney's office and found that his initial responses "differed substantially" from those he had given the Justice Department six months earlier. His attorney advised Marcus to refuse to answer further questions unless he was given a copy of the Justice interview, which they refused to do. There the matter rested, unresolved to this day.

On January 19 President Nixon nominated Judge G. Harrold Carswell as his second candidate for the Fortas vacancy on the Supreme Court. Our "staff investigation" continued in a desultory fashion, with plenty more pressing House business. Early in April, Ford summoned me and asked, "Bob, what have we got on the Douglas matter?"

"We have a lot of questions," I replied, "but not many answers. I just haven't had time, as you know, to concentrate on them. And I can only go so far without showing your hand. We have what Wilson gave us. We have what's already been published, in various places. We have the public documents in the IRS and SEC proceedings. We have a lot of rumors and gossip that can't be checked out without an official investigation. That requires a lot more clout than any individual Congressman, even the Minority Leader, can command. We just don't have a case."

"Bill Scott and some others came to see me today," Ford said. His jaw was set tight in a way I had rarely seen. "They gave me an ultimatum. If I wasn't willing to impeach Douglas, then next Tuesday, by God, they would do it themselves in spite of me. And you know, they can."

"If they do, it will be voted down on the spot," I ventured.

"Of course," Ford said. "What I want you to do over the weekend is to put together on paper everything we have about Douglas and let me look it over."

"O.K.," I said. "I'll have something for you on Monday, but I can tell you now we aren't ready to go."

"I don't have any choice, Bob," Ford explained. "What I'm thinking about is not a resolution of impeachment but one like we had in the Adam Clayton Powell case, a resolution calling for a select committee to consider whether or not there are grounds to warrant

Douglas' formal impeachment. This would give us the time we need and get the crazies off my back. All we have to show is a *prima facie* case of judicial improprieties."

I agreed. I went through my files and strung together all the facts and allegations in them, including those from the Assistant Attorney General of the United States which we considered incontrovertible. The result was the lengthy speech Ford gave on the House floor at the end of the April 15, 1970, session.

The Members who customarily drift away around cocktail time remained riveted in their seats. The press galleries were packed. Ford laid down his indictment of Douglas in measured and, at times, eloquent terms.

The Douglas camp was on its toes, however. Representative Andrew Jacobs (D–Indiana), a member of the Judiciary Committee and a champion of Justice Douglas, slipped almost unnoticed to the Clerk's desk during Ford's speech and dropped into the hopper (where new bills and resolutions are introduced) a sheet of paper with a single sentence stating: "Resolved, that William O. Douglas, Associate Justice of the Supreme Court of the United States, be impeached of high crimes and misdemeanors and misbehavior in office."

Jacob's impeachment resolution was referred to Judiciary, and, predictably, it conducted a farcical five-month "investigation," the main purpose of which was to exonerate Douglas and excoriate Ford.

Not a single witness was questioned under oath, not a single subpoena was issued, not a single public hearing was held. Douglas was never interrogated but was permitted to sort through his own files and voluntarily supply documents purporting to be evidence. His attorney, former Judge Simon H. Rifkind of New York, virtually served as coach and counselor of the committee staff.

Ford took his initial setback gracefully and made the error of cooperating with the Celler subcommittee. We turned over all our investigative information to them, with the exception of the identity of the midnight telephone caller and the source of the Justice Department memorandum.

We were confident that when the time came, Attorney General John Mitchell would officially furnish the House investigators with concrete proof of the damaging allegations and Ford would be vindicated. Mitchell did nothing of the kind. He stonewalled. Chairman Celler complained to Ford that the probe was stalled because the Department of Justice refused to respond to his investigators' inquiries.

Frustrated and angry, Ford set up a meeting between Mitchell and Celler. But Mitchell produced nothing of consequence to support Ford's charges and, in fact, went a step further: He made a speech on Law Day forcefully condemning "irresponsible and malicious criticism of the Supreme Court." The Attorney General mentioned no names, but everybody—including Jerry Ford—assumed he meant Jerry Ford.

Though Ford's suspicions were awfully hard to arouse, he began to get the drift. "Bob," he said, "do you suppose John Mitchell made a deal with the Senate? If they'd confirm Blackmun [Nixon's third nominee for the Fortas vacancy] he would call off the pack that's after Douglas in the House?"

"It looks that way," I replied. Blackmun had been easily confirmed on May 12. That was about the time the freeze set in and Mitchell took his oblique shot—which could hardly have been unintentional.

Now Ford had his fighting dander up. "Well, the SOB isn't going to call me off," he thundered. "We'll conduct our own investigation and the hell with him."

We were too far out on the limb to stop even though Mitchell was sawing it off. Ford plugged doggedly ahead. He asked an old lawyer friend from a prestigious Detroit firm, Bethel Kelley, to undertake an exhaustive legal brief on the impeachment of Federal judges and the precedents involving the "good behaviour" clause of the Constitution.

Ford had no more money in his staff payroll to hire any additional investigative help, but Joe Waggoner (D–Louisiana), leader of the Southern conservative bloc, obliged by retaining Benton Becker to assist our private probe.

Becker and I worked well in tandem. We followed the leads implicating Justice Douglas to California, Nevada and Indiana. We turned up a lot of interesting but inconclusive new information. Lacking the investigative clout of either the legislative or executive branches of government, we could not assemble a legal case.

In mid-August, Ford and I drove downtown to Wilson's office to confront him and demand to see the proof. He called in Henry Peterson, his deputy, and they tossed us a few more dry bones of putative charges involving Douglas—but no real evidence.

"They're giving us the run-around," Ford said as we left empty-handed.

As Congress was about to adjourn, the Celler subcommittee issued its final report, 924 pages long. The three Democratic members found no creditable evidence of an impeachable offense. McCulloch, the Republican liberal, courageously abstained. Only Representative Edward Hutchinson (R–Michigan) dissented, concluding that "the evidence is not all in." But by now the House was rushing to go home and campaign, and nobody was listening. Douglas' defenders never forgave Ford.

But we all—the late Justice Douglas included*—learned something from the episode. Douglas cut down his moonlighting and disqualified himself more regularly in borderline cases before the Court. Ford found out that without the necessary votes (counted in advance) a minority Member—even a popular Minority Leader—cannot compel the House to investigate anything seriously. I learned that my boss had a deeply hidden and seldom used character trait, a combination of a gambler's stubborn streak that tells him he can beat the odds with one more throw, and excessive confidence in his own gut hunches. In the future I would have to argue my doubts more emphatically to protect his political rear not only against his foes but also against supposed friends.

The Senate confirmation hearings began on Thursday, November 1. The press tables were crowded, and the TV lights cast their hot glare that politicians prefer to a lover's caress. Betty Ford sat in the front spectators' row, with Roberta beside her, off to the left of center so they could see the star witness' face.

Behind Ford was his phalanx of Cramer, Becker, Buchen and me, and he was flanked by the Secret Service men, whose constant presence we were now getting used to. Chairman Cannon gaveled the cavernous hearing room to order and got right to the point.

"Prior to this year, the office of Vice President has been vacant sixteen times for a total of thirty-seven years since seventeen ninety-eight," he began. "But if history is to instruct us, this committee should

* Though he'd reportedly vowed to stay on the bench as long as Nixon was President, Douglas retired for reasons of health November 12, 1975, giving President Ford his one and only opportunity to appoint a Supreme Court Justice (John Paul Stevens). Never a grudge-bearer, Ford warmly wrote Douglas: "Your distinguished [36] years of service are unequaled in all the history of the Court. . . . Future generations will continue to benefit from your firm devotion to the fundamental rights of individual freedom and privacy under the Constitution."

view its obligations as no less important than the selection of a potential President of the United States."

Noting that "an original and historic power" conferred separately on the Senate and the House by the Twenty-fifth Amendment was being exercised for the first time, without any precedents, the chairman proceeded to make one.

"We must perform our task with the utmost concentration upon his views of the Presidency itself, on the issue of executive privilege, of impoundment of funds, of campaign financing, and on what Congressman Ford would do if he were President and faced decisions . . . in which the Executive Branch confronts an independent Legislature and Judiciary."

Cannon said the FBI's 1,700-page raw report on the nominee was the biggest single investigation ever conducted. It was the first time any nominee for President or Vice President had ever been subject to scrutiny other than by the press, he noted.

The senior Republican, Marlow Cook of Kentucky, said he had been through every page of the FBI file, too,* and drew the first laugh of the session by adding, "I feel that I know as much about Jerry Ford as does Jerry Ford."

Then Ford took the oath and launched into his opening statement. The guts of it was that Ford was uniquely qualified to "be a ready conciliator and calm communicator between the White House and Capitol Hill, between the re-election mandate of the Republican President and the equally emphatic mandate of the Democratic Ninety-third Congress."

Of Nixon he said, "He has always been truthful to me, as have my good friends in the Congress. I have never misled them when they might have wanted to hear something gentler than the truth. Truth is the glue that holds government together," Ford declared, "and not only government but civilization itself."**

* We never did see the raw FBI file. But apparently the worst the 350 G-men could discover about Ford's past was that he was once ejected from a South High School football game for tackling after the whistle blew. And the IRS tax audit decided he'd have to fork over $435.77 for new summer suits he wore to preside over the 1972 Miami Beach GOP convention which he'd claimed as a business expense.
** Phil Buchen insisted this most quotable of Ford's lines should be "Truth is the bond . . ." I argued vigorously for the homely, sticky, vivid word "glue." Ford took no sides, but when he read the sentence he murdered it by saying, "Truth is the glue on the bond that holds government together."

PALACE POLITICS

The opening statement impressed not only the Senators but also the unseen television audience that was getting its first good close-up of Jerry Ford.

Other Senators followed Chairman Cannon's lead, probing to preview Ford's views if he became President. Senator Byrd (D–West Virginia) was the sharpest at this, and he had the Saturday Night Massacre very much on his mind. Byrd pressed hard on executive privilege, throwing back at Ford his own words in a 1963 debate over President Kennedy's aborting the Bay of Pigs invasion and finally demanded, "Can you conceive of any justification, Mr. Ford, for anyone—including the President of the United States—to disobey a court order?"

No person in the country is above the law, Ford answered. If the highest court in the land had spoken, a President ought to obey. This undoubtedly caused some groaning at the White House, but it probably ensured unanimous committee approval. (The Senate confirmed Ford on November 27, 92 to 3.)

The Senate's turn over, there was no time for a breather. The House hearings were only ten days away. The networks had lost interest in the confirmation, and the hearings were recorded only on film for the nightly news shows. Ford was kept on the hot seat for four days and a total of nineteen hours. His patience was equal to Job's.

The Nixon-haters in the ultraliberal wing of the House Committee on the Judiciary were out to lynch the President and, in the meantime, to discredit his choice for Vice President. The Constitution and the grave crisis endangering the country's posture in the world were no deterrents to their consummate demagoguery.

Ford's liberal House colleagues concentrated not on his fitness to be Vice President or even President but on his generally conservative voting record, his alleged insensitivity to civil rights during his House service and his relations as a Congressman with Federal agencies on behalf of constituents. The Justice Douglas matter was their angriest concern. After some sadistic pleasure, they gave Ford a clean bill of health. While we waited for the roll call I whispered, "What's your guess?"

Ford hadn't forgotten how to count votes. It would be 30 to 8 or 29 to 9, he forecast. "Which ones will be against you?" I asked.

"Edwards, Conyers, Waldie, Rangel, Holtzman, Kastenmeyer, Drinan and Jordan," he replied. "Seiberling I'm not sure about. He could go either way."

Sure enough, when the committee voted on Ford on November

29, the vote was 29 to 8. John F. Seiberling, the Ohio rubber heir, abstained. All seventeen Republicans and twelve Democrats recommended that the House confirm.

The Speaker scheduled December 6 for the House debate and vote on confirmation and proposed to have Ford sworn in as soon as the roll call was concluded. The House vote was 387 to 35, with 11 not voting and one vacancy. Ford won 202 Democrats and all 185 Republicans, an amazing 84.7 percent of his colleagues. In the whole Congress, only 38 Democrats of a total of 534 Senators and Representatives opposed his elevation to the Vice Presidency.

Ford wanted a simple ceremony in the House chamber. Speaker Albert enthusiastically agreed, but the Praetorians at the White House wanted to stage another TV spectacular in the East Room. There the President would be completely in charge and in the center of the spotlight. They were also afraid that Nixon might be booed by some of the "crazies" if he entered the House chamber.

Ford, now that his new position was a foregone conclusion, dug in his heels. It was our first test of wills. Ford resolved the impasse by going directly to Nixon. The President understood perfectly; he, too, was counting impeachment votes in the House. His Praetorians had been doing him a disservice.* He came, marched to his place on the second tier of the House rostrum with head high, and there were no discourteous noises.

After Chief Justice Burger administered the oath, Ford addressed the audience in brief but moving remarks. "I am a Ford, not a Lincoln," he began. "My addresses will never be as eloquent as Mr. Lincoln's. But I will do my very best to equal his brevity and plainspeaking." His voice broke as he turned to Betty. "For standing by my side as she always has—" Ford swallowed hard and continued—"there are no words to tell you, my dear wife and mother of our four wonderful children, how much their being here means to me."

Then his adrenaline flowed while the audience in its turn wiped their eyes. He couldn't tell the difference between the Senators and Representatives he saw out there. And beyond them, in homes across the land, he didn't see Democratic faces or Republican faces.

* Prefacing everything with "The President wants . . ." is a heady but dangerous habit easily adopted by Presidential aides and probably has been common practice since Washington's day. Nobody knows whether it is true or not, but chances are that if an underling feels it is necessary to say it, it is a bluff. In the West Wing I instructed my staff never to presume to speak for the President unless he himself so directed.

"At this moment of visible and living unity, I see only Americans.

"I see Americans who love their country, Americans who work and sacrifice for their country and their children. I see Americans who pray without ceasing for peace among all nations and for harmony at home.

"I see new generations of concerned and courageous Americans—but the same kind of Americans—the children and grandchildren of those Americans who met the challenge of December seventh just thirty-two years ago.

"Mr. Speaker, I like what I see."

It all took only twenty-one minutes. Amid a final standing ovation Vice President Ford led the members of the Senate back to their chamber. His fans in Statuary Hall stretched the barricades to grasp at his hand. I followed at a discreet distance, not even sure the doorkeepers would let me on the Senate floor. But Walter Mote and Bill Hildebrand were waiting for me and found me a place in the rear. The Majority Leader, Mike Mansfield, was beginning his introduction of the new presiding officer.

Suddenly my heart sank into my stomach. In the excitement I had forgotten to pick up Ford's speech portfolio from the podium of the House and bring it along. Both speeches were in it. Ford was about to be introduced and he had no text.

I was fifty-six and a half years old and in fair physical condition, and there was only one thing to do. I sprinted at top speed the 150 yards down the middle of the Capitol, across the nearly empty Rotunda, raced through the House doors and down the aisle. My prayers that nobody had picked up the portfolio for a souvenir were answered. Grabbing it, I raced back, my heart pounding, and I really wondered if I'd make it. But I did, just in the nick of time.

"Senators, a funny thing happened to me on the way to becoming Speaker . . ." the Vice President began. That broke the ice.

Afterward there was a big party put on by Ford's Michigan friends at the Capitol Hill Club, a Republican rendezvous nearby. Everybody came—more Democrats than the place had ever seen—and everybody had a ball. Everybody, that is, except President Nixon, who returned alone to the White House. I recalled, amid all the rejoicing, when Nixon became Vice President and was the toast of the club.

"The Second Office of the government is honorable and easy," mused Thomas Jefferson, our second Vice President and third President. "The First is but a splendid misery."

76

4

THE AWKWARD OFFICE

A generation before Art Buchwald, Americans chuckled over the political jokes of Will Rogers, and a generation before that they opened their newspapers at the breakfast table for a few laughs from Finley Peter Dunne.

Dunne wrote about politics as seen by an Irish-American immigrant named Mr. Dooley, explaining the mysteries of democracy to his friend, Hennessy, somewhat more recently off the boat from the old sod. His dialect recalls an age of innocence when all Americans told ethnic stories and the transplanted sons of Erin had not yet acquired Harvard accents.

"It's sthrange about the Vice-Prisidency," said Mr. Dooley. "It isn't a crime exactly. Ye can't be sint to jail f'r it, but it's a kind of disgrace. It's like writin' anonymous letters.

"What are his jooties, says ye? Ivry mornin' it is his business to call at th' White House an' inquire afther th' Prisidint's health. Whin told that th' Prisidint was niver betther he gives three cheers, an' departs with a heavy heart."

The Vice Presidency of Jerry Ford began precisely as prescribed by Mr. Dooley, with a call on President Nixon at the White House. Thereafter, it was about as different from any previous Vice Presidency as it could possibly be.

Only a few of the forty-two Americans who have held the second highest Constitutional office have had much fun in it—only Alben Barkley comes to mind as one who did. Our first Vice President, John Adams, called it the most insignificant office ever devised by the genius of man, and John Nance Garner, who left the powerful Speakership to take it, refined this by allowing "the Vice Presidency ain't worth a pitcher of warm spit."

Be that as it may, it is by all odds the safest and surest way of get-

ting to be President of the United States. "Not a steppingstone to anything except oblivion," Teddy Roosevelt grumbled, but he soon found
out how wrong he was. Including Ford, thirteen Vice Presidents have
gone on to the White House, nine by succession and four by subsequent election.

What made the eight-and-a-half-month Vice Presidency of Jerry
Ford unique was that none of his predecessors—including John Tyler,
Andrew Johnson and Chester A. Arthur, whose terms as No. 2 were
even shorter than Ford's—was perceived right from the start as the
next President. As President Nixon's terminal illness was political
rather than medical, nobody felt constrained to whisper about it. Nobody did.

Under a banner headline FORD SWORN IN AS VICE PRESIDENT the
next morning's Washington *Post* added, "Nixon Ouster Talks Get
New Impetus." My eyes were only half open when I read this, after the
emotional tension and exuberant victory celebration of the previous
day. I was drained, dog-tired and curiously depressed, but there was
no stopping the merry-go-'round.

Ford as usual was up before the birds, and I was there to meet
him in our old House Minority Leader's office at eight. We were all
packing furiously to make room for his successor; we hated to leave
the familiar old nest, the comfortable camaraderie of the House, for
who knew what?

I greeted him with a sour smile. "Well, now you're trading real
power for false prestige."

A delegation of Republican pages arrived, bearing a gift. These
bright-eyed youngsters (who are treated by some Congressmen as if
they were faceless automatons) had pooled their meager resources and
purchased him a new briefcase. (His old expandable one was disrepu-
table and patched with Scotch tape, but I suspect he's still carrying it.)

We set a small historic precedent that day, though it didn't last
long. Speaker Albert, with the consent of the minority heir apparent,
John Rhodes, agreed to let the Vice President keep a small windowless
office next to his old House suite ostensibly to use for conferences with
his former House colleagues. (When Ford became President, this arrangement ran afoul of the separation of powers prescribed by the
Constitution, and Rhodes got the room back.)

While the House Republican Conference was caucusing to choose
a new leader, with Ford absent for the first time since he won a decade
earlier, we walked across the Rotunda to the office of the Secretary of
the Senate, Frank Valeo.

This was an amusing interlude. As a follow-up to Senate Majority Leader Mike Mansfield's only half-joking reminder the night before that a Vice President is to "be seen and not heard" in the Senate chamber, the senior Senate staff Pooh-Bahs sat the new boy down at a table and lectured him on his new job—the forms he had to fill in to draw his $62,500 salary and $10,000 expense allowance, what kind of health insurance would he want, what office space and staff would be available, pension benefits, etc. Ford kept a straight face.

Minutes before 10:00 A.M. Walter Mote led Ford onto the Senate rostrum, where he bowed his head during a prayer by one of Billy Graham's assistants and then banged down the gavel to open the session. Ken Belieu and I, not yet accorded the privilege of being on the Senate floor, peeped through the Senate lobby door and then retired to the Vice President's formal office nearby.

It hadn't changed much since I used to call on Vice Presidents Nixon and Johnson there during my rounds as a Washington correspondent. Gone was the spooky old horsehair lounge upon which Vice President Henry Wilson expired in 1875, but a marble bust of this martyr to Senate oratory was still on a wall bracket above the new sofa. A larger-than-life Texas portrait of John Garner still hung on the opposite wall where LBJ had put it. Over the big desk was a huge crystal chandelier that Jefferson reputedly ordered from Paris to adorn the White House. Its tinkling prisms annoyed Teddy Roosevelt, a former Vice President, and he ordered it sent up to the Capitol "to help keep the Vice President awake."

We had decided to keep Mote, his assistant H. Spofford Canfield (a former Dirksen page) and their small staff who had served Agnew in the Senate, augmenting them with some of Ford's House people who preferred to remain on Capitol Hill.

We were frequently interrupted by legislators wanting to congratulate Ford, among them Senators Bob Dole (R–Kansas), Jack Javits (R–New York) and Representative Garry Brown (R–Michigan), who had masterminded the Michigan "inaugural" party the night before. Senate Minority Leader Scott (R–Pennsylvania) brought in a beaming Representative John Rhodes, who had just been elected to Ford's old leadership post by acclamation. They all had their pictures taken.

When the early editions of the evening *Star* arrived, they echoed the morning *Post*'s interpretation of Ford's confirmation as the start of a new impeachment drive against President Nixon. "Ford Enters Upon Troubled Scene," the *Star* said, with one front-page column headed "Ford" and another, alongside it, "Impeach."

PALACE POLITICS

This was hardly the way to get off to a good start with the White House, it suddenly struck the new Vice President. After all, the President had nominated him, had acquiesced in his desire to be inaugurated in the House chamber and had kept as inconspicuous as a President ever can during Jerry Ford's big moment. Ford got in his limousine and headed for the White House. He owed Nixon one.

The night before, in an atmosphere of celebration and sentimental reminiscence, Ford had met with the President alone. Nixon had earnestly repeated solemn assurances that he was innocent of Watergate complicity. It was not a time for Ford to press his old friend hard, even if that had been his nature. The President confided some of the steps he planned to recoup his daily diminishing credibility.

On December 7, the thirty-second anniversary of Pearl Harbor (which so abruptly altered Nixon's and Ford's lives), the Oval Office meeting between them was more formal. The President, reading from a briefing paper dutifully prepared by the Haig Praetorians, reviewed for the fledgling Vice President some of the responsibilities he would be expected to undertake. More to the point in newsworthiness, Nixon vehemently rejected any thought of resigning under pressure and urged Ford to accentuate the positive accomplishments of his stewardship.

Ford left the Oval Office encounter reassured and ready to help stem the rising tide of impeachment rhetoric. He did not linger to spar with the White House press but returned to the Capitol and immediately held a news conference with longtime reporter friends.

The Vice President had rehearsed his view of his new relationship on the eve of his "inaugural" with Neil McNeil, *Time* magazine's Congressional oracle, saying that "when all the facts are out, he [Nixon] assured me that he will be completely exonerated." Yet he revealed a wariness the candor of which surprised me, telling Neil that "what I have to watch out for is not to become Nixon's apologist—that wouldn't help either of us."

Ford's maiden news conference as Vice President produced stories like this: "Gerald R. Ford began his first full day as the 40th Vice President of the United States with a ringing defense of President Nixon's record and a categorical denial that the President has any plans to resign."

Spencer Rich went on to report in the Washington *Post* that Ford raised the question in his meeting with the President because "I'm going on one of the quiz shows on Sunday and I wanted it straight from the President himself."

The Washington *Star* noted that Ford felt "the American people are far more interested in peace than they are in Watergate" and that Nixon's accomplishments—"a superb job in foreign policy" and "many more pluses than minuses on the domestic front"—would soon swing the pendulum of public confidence back in the President's favor.

On November 8, during the intermission between the Senate and House committees' interrogation of Ford, I accepted an invitation from W. Dewey Clower, a White House advance man on loan to us for Ford's travels, to meet with him and Bruce Kehrli, Haig's staff secretary, to discuss arrangements for the new Vice President. A noon appointment was suggested.

I supposed they were going to take me to lunch at the White House mess, which is a great treat for those who don't have to eat there every day. Moreover, the Navy mess prices are easy on the host. Old friends like Herb Klein, Roger Johnson and Murray Chotiner had taken me there before the Praetorians squeezed them out.

Instead, I was treated to an instructive demonstration of the classic Praetorian put-down, neither my first nor last. First, none of the guards at the White House gates had my name on his list of expected callers. After several phone calls to establish my identity, I was escorted into Kehrli's cramped cubicle in the basement of the West Wing. There I cooled my heels for a full half hour.

Finally Kehrli appeared, a harried young man in shirt sleeves, making a marvelous impression of being terribly busy, so what can I do for you, whatever your name is. He summoned Clower and then chewed at a hamburger which his secretary brought to this desk. She refilled his coffee cup three times without offering a cup to Clower or me. Dewey did most of the talking.

Indeed, he talked far too much. If I had blown my top and stalked out at Kehrli's rude reception I would have missed an amazing revelation. After the earlier meeting Ford and I had with General Haig, Clower related, an *ad hoc* committee had been created composed of General John C. Bennett, Haig's deputy; General Lawson, Nixon's Military Assistant; General Mike Dunn of Agnew's staff; Dave Parker, the chief White House scheduler; and David Gergen, head of the Nixon speech-writing shop. (Ray Price and Pat Buchanan were the President's top writers, but they held more exalted rank.)

The purpose of this group was to assist the new Vice President in "getting aboard" and organizing his enlarged staff. The members were extremely busy, I should understand, but they had asked Kehrli and Clower to brief me on their conclusions.

PALACE POLITICS

"The objective is to relieve Ford of most administrative problems so as to allow him to concentrate on the more pressing problems the President wants him to address," Dewey declared. "Now, we have identified four priority areas.

"First, Congressional relations, including, of course, his duties as presiding officer of the Senate.

"Two, fulfilling major speaking engagements outside of Washington, including those the President has to decline, and important Republican affairs.

"Three, being a focal point for the Nineteen seventy-four off-year campaign.

"Four, being available for foreign travel as directed by the President."

I broke in to ask if any overseas missions were in the works. Not at the moment, they said, evidently dangling the suggestion as a reward if the less glamorous chores were done properly.

"All these activities will require the assistance of speech writing, scheduling and advance personnel," Clower continued, "as well as the services of various experts—Brent Scowcroft [Kissinger's deputy] for national-security affairs, Roy Ash and Fred Malek on management and budget, Kenneth Dam and Herb Stein in economics, Ken Cole for Domestic Council matters and John Love on energy." (Love was about to be sacked.) "We would recommend that Ford call upon these key advisers to the President for whatever briefings he desires," Clower intoned.

Two things were quickly obvious to me, but I bit my tongue as Dewey droned on. These guys figured the Vice President for an empty-headed neophyte who knew little or nothing about what was going on. They also intended to integrate his supporting staff so completely with the White House that it would be impossible for him to assert even the little independence Agnew had managed for five years. I decided this was a time to listen, not to talk.

After more than an hour, Kehrli rose from his swivel chair, ran the back of his hand across his mouth and, a small rivulet of catsup remaining in the corner, said he was already late for an *important* meeting and it was nice to have met me.

"What we want to do," the staff secretary declared grandly as his exit line, "is to make the Vice President as much as possible a part of the White House staff."

As I shook his damp hand, it occurred to me that this was really intended as a compliment. What could be more wonderful than to be part of the exalted White House staff! Kehrli and Clower were telling me the stark, simple truth and saw nothing indelicate in it; they had eaten and slept in the Praetorian discipline so long they had lost the art of dissimulation.

"Simmer down, Bob," the Vice President said when I unburdened my story on him. "They can't help it, so just play along and save important business for Bryce [Harlow] and Bill [Timmons]."

I took his advice and had almost forgotten the episode until I heard almost the identical "briefing" from President Nixon coming out of Ford's mouth a month later. In the meantime, I had managed—mostly in the middle of the night—to find time for thinking about a permanent Vice Presidential staff.

While we had cleared the confirmation hurdles without a mishap, by the grace of God and our tireless volunteers, the moment the race was won we had to escalate rapidly from Ford's Congressional staff of seventeen to at least fifty persons, man four offices instead of one* and learn two brand-new sets of rules—the Senate's and the Executive Office of the President's.

The Vice President's annual salary, then $62,500 a year plus $10,-000 for expenses, was paid by the Senate. The Senate also provided him with office space and a modest $430,200 allowance, mostly for staff. Before the twentieth century, the Vice President was always regarded as part of the legislative branch. After inauguration, Presidents rarely consorted with them.

When Woodrow Wilson left U.S. soil to go to Versailles—the first time an incumbent President ever traveled abroad—he asked Vice President Thomas Marshall (he of the good five-cent cigar) to preside over the Cabinet in his absence. Marshall had strong Constitutional reservations and did so reluctantly.

Warren G. Harding was the first President to invite his Vice President to attend Cabinet meetings regularly, which Calvin Coolidge si-

---

* As Vice President, Ford had two offices in the Senate, one in the Capitol and another in the new Senate Office Building; a hideaway on the House side of the Capitol; and the extensive suite in the Old Executive Office Building alongside the White House. Until a special election in Michigan filled his vacant House seat, there were also interim offices in Grand Rapids and Washington managed by Gordon Van der Till, his home-town assistant.

PALACE POLITICS

lently did. But when Charles Dawes was elected as Coolidge's running mate, he refused. Only since FDR have Vice Presidents been routinely included in every Cabinet.

The sumptuous Vice Presidential suite in the Old Executive Office alongside the White House dates only from President Kennedy's effort to corral the energies and caress the ego of Lyndon B. Johnson. It was then that the Executive budget began to include sums for "support" of the Vice President, already entitled to half a million from the Senate.

During the incumbencies of Humphrey and Agnew, the Vice President's downtown digs in the EOB spread over half the second floor, which formerly housed the entire Department of the Navy. A $657,000 annual allocation of Executive funds, plus a sizable military contribution, was at the Vice President's disposal when we arrived on the scene.

This budget of more than a million dollars, though no larger than many large supermarkets', mostly went (as most Federal money does) for personnel. Unfortunately, it did not permit the Vice President to retain the best people he could find because a ceiling of $36,000 was placed on all but one staff position, which paid $42,500, equivalent then to that of a Member of Congress or a Cabinet Under Secretary. That was a welcome $6,500-a-year raise for me, but nobody gets rich in government unless they steal.

As money makes the mare go, so the tilt of the Vice President's dual allegiance has subtly shifted in recent decades from Capitol Hill to the other end of Pennsylvania Avenue. His duties as a partisan campaigner date far back beyond Mr. Dooley, but his role as year-round political hatchetman really began with Vice Presidents Nixon and Johnson. They also established the tradition of serving as supergrade good-will ambassadors when the jet age made it feasible.*

Nor did we lack for solicited and unsolicited advice as to how Ford should approach his new job. Clower reduced the decisions of the White House control committee to a seven-page memo, proposing that most of our needs be met by borrowing second-raters from the Nixon Praetorians.

Phil Buchen, who had returned to his Grand Rapids law firm

---

* As soon as he gained the rank, as well as the power, of Secretary of State, Henry Kissinger took a dim view of roving Vice Presidents abroad—their minds on U.S. voters and their mouths wide open. Henry permitted Ford and Rockefeller to attend only a few state funerals.

84

after the confirmation, sent several perceptive memos about staff organization to the Vice President. He urged that Ford maintain a continuous input of independent counsel on major public issues apart from what the Administration and Washington lobbyists would inundate him with, and communicate regularly with opinion leaders around the country through a trusted confidential intermediary. Buchen wisely warned that we ran a risk of taking on experienced people "unattuned to your ways and desirous of gaining the power which comes with being on your staff when you cannot be absolutely sure of their reliability and willingness to serve unselfishly the ideas you have for your new office." When Nixon gave the Vice President charge of his Privacy Commission, a cosmetic effort that Ford chose to take seriously, Buchen was brought back to Washington as its executive director and ensconced in an office close to ours in the EOB. But Ford took only as much of his old law partner's counsel as suited him.

Bryce Harlow and Bill Timmons were able to see both sides of our problem. In Eisenhower's White House, Bryce had watched the tension build up with Nixon's staff, and in Nixon's the same thing happening with Agnew's. Ford and I hoped to evolve a golden mean—to be his own man but, at the same time, loyal to his President. We felt that Nixon would fully understand that Ford was much more valuable to him if he were not seen as a Charlie McCarthy being manipulated by the White House and invariably parroting the President's line.

I think President Nixon generally did. But his suspicious streak was stronger than his sophistication, when suspicions were artfully encouraged by his Praetorians. Perhaps we undertook the impossible, but we started out trying to be cooperative and completely aboveboard.

We had literally hundreds of old and new admirers who wanted jobs with the Vice President, from Grand Rapids, Washington and points north, south and west. Ford was always somewhat uncomfortable about personnel problems; he made it plain that was something he wanted me to handle.

I did get one important and revealing guideline from him.

"Just one thing, Bob. I don't want to take on any former Members of Congresss," he warned me. "A lot of them are volunteering and most are good guys, but they wouldn't be able to adjust to the new situation. They'd expect things to be just like before."

I understood perfectly. It would be hard for them to serve as a twelve-hour-a-day subordinate to a former colleague and even harder to take direction from me. On Capitol Hill there's a great gulf between "Members" and "staff," even the most senior professionals, and the only way to cross it is to go out and get elected yourself. With a President, nobody gets too familiar. But with a Vice President we'd take no chances.

When Ford was first nominated in October, what we needed almost immediately was an experienced scheduler and advance man. W. Dewey Clower was thirty-two, had a nice young family, made $34,-000 a year as a Special Assistant to the President of the United States and was fairly typical of the Haldeman breed of advance men who rallied around Nixon's campaigns.

The average American endures or enjoys these political extravaganzas every few years without ever encountering an advance man or knowing there is such a critter. But they are absolutely essential to a successful campaign; no candidate ever won without them nor, it should be added, would Watergate ever have happened without them. Recruited from the ranks of amateur political activists, often from such fields as advertising, sales, public relations or promotion, they take leave from their jobs and go forth with virtually unlimited pocket money to prepare the way of the candidate and make his paths easy.

If their candidate is the President, they flash their White House credentials and generally get instant obedience from the likes of mayors, chiefs of police, local political Pooh-Bahs and the best hotelkeepers. They fend off publicity hounds, eccentrics, minor celebrities and—not always with the same degree of success—the throngs of pretty girls who throw themselves into political campaigns. After all, they have dutifully sewed up a luxurious Presidential suite days in advance and stocked it with all manner of booze and viands.

They hire fleets of cars and carefully go over every mile of the arrival and departure route, timing it with stop watches down to a split-second schedule. When the great man arrives, they hover at his elbow, telling him just where the microphones have been set up and where the most boisterous crowds—and the most television cameras—can be expected. They pack the meeting halls and connive with the cops to blockade protesters and get their friends in for a handshake with the hero.

Advance men even tend to look alike. They wear natty junior-chamber-of-commerce fashions for the young executive; they speak a special walkie-talkie lingo even when relaxing in the bar; and it is perfectly natural that they come to regard themselves even more highly than most bright, aggressive, energetic, resourceful, rootless and ruthless young achievers.

W. Dewey Clower deftly disguised this with a soft Virginia speech and a cherubic countenance. He had graduated an electronic engineer before joining the White House in 1970. He had advanced more than a hundred of President Nixon's domestic and foreign trips. He chaperoned the Chinese ping-pong team on their ice-breaking U.S. tour and seemed to be, as he described himself, a "quasi-diplomat"—just what we needed.

Clower did a good job in the various out-of-town trips Ford took as Vice President-designate. Ford had never had a real advance man before. Once in a while Paul Miltich would accompany him to Grand Rapids, or I would go along to California or to a Governors' conference, but it was mostly for the ride.

Clower faced his first test when the House hearings ended and it was clear Ford would be confirmed. He brought me the Praetorians' plan for Ford's swearing-in, at the White House, of course.

"Mr. Ford wants to take the oath in the House chamber," I said. "The House has been his home for twenty-five years. He really hates to leave it. And whether you believe it or not, it will be better for President Nixon."

"The President thinks," Clower said, "that it should be in the East Room, where Ford's nomination was announced."

"I believe you meant to say 'Mr. Ford' or 'the Vice President'— but never mind. Just take this expression of Mr. Ford's preference back to your people and let me know what they say."

"But the President might be booed up here," Clower said with incautious but genuine alarm.

"Look, these people in Congress are civilized people," I replied calmly. "Some of them have been pretty nasty in the hearings, but they'll all be on their feet applauding when Mr. Ford is sworn in. He's one of their boys. I'll guarantee you there won't be any discourtesy when the President walks down the aisle with Jerry Ford. Tell your people that."

I reinforced my argument with calls to Harlow and Timmons. The Vice President-designate resolved the matter easily with Nixon himself. But Dewey and the Praetorian control committee were bitterly disappointed at losing their first skirmish. They felt they, and Nixon, had lost face.

Ford didn't react at all except to whisper to Dewey, when Clower took his elbow and tried to steer him through the Capitol corridors he'd roamed for a quarter century, "Thanks, but I know my way."

Despite these early displays of eager-beaverism we decided to keep Clower on the Vice President's permanent staff. We also decided to retain General Dunn and his military contingent at the EOB. They had served Agnew well and were holding the fort for whatever Ford had in store for them. Midway in the confirmation ordeal, Dick Cook, who had been Timmons' deputy for the House and a former minority counsel of the Commerce Committee, invited me to lunch at La Bagatelle, and there I found Mike Dunn.

Dick said Dunn was a solid citizen and he hoped we wouldn't start off at cross-purposes. I had been thoroughly teed off at my first encounter with Dunn. Ford had told me to look over the layout in the EOB, and the general, after greeting me with the usual Black Irish pleasantries, turned me over to an enlisted assistant who showed me around the empty rooms (for some of which he had no key) in an acute state of terror. He knew none of the answers to my innocent inquiries and afterward admitted that he was acting under orders from General Haig himself to tell Hartmann no more than was absolutely necessary.

After two martinis Dunn loosened up and allowed that he was disgusted with the White House attitude toward Vice Presidents. "I just don't think it's right," Mike said. He was close to retirement, after a distinguished Army career that won him two stars without benefit of West Point. But he would like to help Ford over the initial rough spots if he could.

My instinct told me to take him at his word. For the time being, we loaded Dunn with the administrative responsibilities he had been carrying during the vacancy in the Vice Presidency, and in addition I put Dewey Clower directly under his thumb. My ability to suffer fools gladly is notoriously low, and I wanted a cushion between me and Dewey, who evidenced a proclivity to take orders from nobody but Ford himself.

The next thing we urgently needed was our own lawyer. Ford's confirmation team was overloaded with good lawyers, but they had their private practices to return to after two months of *pro bono publico*. Nixon's legal eagles, even if they had been champions, were already up to their collective ears trying to keep their uncooperative client out of jail.

We quickly settled on William E. Casselman II, then general counsel of the General Services Administration. An Illinoisian, Bill had a tall and lanky frame that reminded one of young Abe Lincoln.

He'd studied law at George Washington University while working as legislative assistant to Representative Robert McClory (R–Illinois). Harlow and Timmons had recruited Bill for their liaison team during Nixon's first term, which made him an early Ford fan and us good friends.

"The first thing I want you to do," I told Bill the day he agreed to join us, "is to draw up a code of standards of conduct for our staff. I want it to be the strictest in town. You can draw on the White House and Civil Service codes and House and Senate rules, but in no case should our standards be less than the most rigid that now exist."

(Later, Bill's scruples cost me thousands of dollars when I had to sell all but one of my stocks, but I never regretted my first order as chief of Ford's Vice Presidential staff. It was never touched by a whiff of impropriety.)

Of the confirmation volunteers, only Ken Belieu stayed on, with the temporary title of Consultant for Legislative Affairs. Besides Dunn, we retained two superb younger officers, Commander Howard Kerr, USN, and Lieutenant Colonel Americo A. Sardo, USMC, and two retired military men who had served on Agnew's staff as transportation and supply specialists, Ralph Martin and Jim Brown. Both really knew their business.

Jim Brown had learned as an Air Force sergeant how to procure (the military word is "scrounge") anything capable of being found on this planet. If our democratic society allows anyone to be truly indispensable, it is a responsible and resourceful supply officer like Jim Brown.* Moreover, Brown was invariably cheerful, and I never heard him badmouth a single soul. I wish we'd had more like Jim.

By Monday, December 10, after we labored over the weekend moving all our office possessions to the new Senate or EOB offices, I was able to announce a skeleton staff organization that would at least hold us over the holidays. Miltich would continue as press secretary, and Mildred Leonard and Dorothy Hessler were retitled personal assistant and personal secretary to the Vice President. The rest of our House staff was also transferred.

I was asked by Bob Shogan of the Los Angeles *Times* why the Vice President thought he needed a lawyer. Agnew hadn't had one until he got in hot water, and previous Vice Presidents hadn't either, relying on the White House. I didn't want to knock the President or

* Throughout the Ford Presidency, Brown kept the key to the "autopen" machine that legally signs the President's name. He never goofed in more than 4,000,000 signatures.

Agnew, but this gave me the opportunity to reveal our code-of-conduct plans.

"In the climate in which we now live in Washington, things have changed," I said.

The most obvious change was our physical transfer to the Old Executive Office Building. This massive neoclassical pile of rock and cast iron,* sitting adjacent to the White House, has been called "the ugliest heritage of the nineteenth century in America." It was completed in 1888 after seventeen years in construction at a cost of $10,000,000 which the Congress regarded as excessive for ten acres of floor space to house the combined State, War and Navy departments.

Since World War II, during which an inoperable antiaircraft gun was mounted on its roof to comfort employees in the Executive complex, it has been an overflow annex for the White House and sundry Federal agencies. Presidents Truman and Eisenhower held news conferences in the ornate fourth-floor Indian Treaty Room, and President Nixon had a "hideaway" office, actually larger than the Oval Office, on the third floor.

The spacious suite on the second level of the east side, which had become the Vice President's, was usually the Secretary of the Navy's, though General Pershing briefly occupied it and President Hoover used it temporarily after a 1930 fire swept the West Wing. The smaller (but still huge) office connecting with it, which became mine, belonged to young Franklin D. Roosevelt as Assistant Secretary of the Navy.

As Agnew had left it, the Vice President's suite was carpeted and draped with a deep royal blue, and most of the furniture was upholstered in the same cold hue. Roberta told Ford it didn't look like him and enlisted the volunteer help of our decorator neighbors, Rose and George Tiralla, who expertly warmed it up at minimal cost.

The Vice President's office could be entered from two sides. Dorothy, Neta and Gail were within quick buzzer call from the back, a working room between his office and mine. Joann was stationed at the main entrance, along with a uniformed guard, and Mildred had a handsome private office on the other side of Ford's.

For the better part of two decades, Mildred had handled virtually everything for Ford that was important. After Frank Meyer's death

* The structure is entirely granite, with iron interior moldings. Doors are solid mahogany with solid brass fittings. Scrubbing the marble halls and circular staircases originally required eighty cleaning women at $5 a week. Touring it for the first time, President Coolidge asked one question: "Is it insured?" When it was, he supposedly commented: "What a pity!"

Ford made her his Administrative Assistant at top pay. But now, with an enlarged staff and the necessity to distribute the workload, Mildred understandably had difficulty letting go of her responsibilities. She couldn't, alone, keep above the flood.

Even before the hectic two months of confirmation ended, Ford and I began to get telephone and personal inquiries about invitations and other mail he hadn't answered—in fact, hadn't even seen.

This very human tragedy had to be dealt with, not only with kid gloves but without another day's delay, before the Vice President was seriously embarrassed. He agreed to talk with Mildred.

It came off fine. Mildred would sort out the backlog and let others share in the catch-up. In the future only letters from dear old friends would go to Mildred for personal handling. She would extract all invitations and speech requests from the envelopes and turn them over to Dewey Clower, who was taking over scheduling.

"Do you mean I'm not even going to make up our daily appointment schedule any more?" Mildred imploringly asked.

This was the unkindest blow of all. Every day for thousands of days she had typed up this essential reminder. But now it had become a full-time project for a whole office force to wrestle with. It had to be coordinated with a half dozen people besides Ford himself—with the Secret Service, the military aides, Mrs. Ford's secretary, his chief of staff, administrative officer and others if he were traveling.

Mildred bit her lip and dutifully turned the long-neglected invitations, as directed, over to Clower. But thirtyish White House Praetorians, however sweet they may be to their own mamas, do not let little old ladies get in their way. They run over them.

For several weeks we had been getting two Ford schedules every day—Mildred's old familiar format and Clower's elaborate one on the White House model—in fact, on White House stationery. When Ford was confirmed and Clower was invited to join our staff, I told him to knock off the White House letterhead and use the Vice President's. He ignored the order.

I was busy with a dozen more important matters and told General Dunn to handle him. They were both, I knew, fraternity brothers on Haig's *ad hoc* committee to control Ford's settling in, but Mike was a military man. He knew how a chain of command works and where I stood in it. I made it clear that Dewey was to make no final appointments or commitments of any kind without either Dunn's approval or mine. If necessary, we would obtain the Vice President's.

The first fortnight of Ford's new job was frenetic but exciting. Everyone wanted to pay him a courtesy call—General Moshe Dayan; David Rockefeller*; Soviet Ambassador Dobrynin; Sheik Yamani, the Saudi oil minister; Alan Hoover, son of the former President; Dr. Glenn Campbell, director of Stanford's Hoover Institution; and Governor Winthrop Sargent of Massachusetts.

Everyone wanted to interview the new No. 2 man: the *Christian Science Monitor*'s Godfrey Sperling and his elite group of political pundits; John McGoff, president of Michigan's Panax newspaper chain; Saul Pett of the AP; the Washington *Post*'s Roger Wilkins; and photographer George Tames to take a new formal portrait for the files of the New York *Times*.

When Ford showed up for an appearance on a network talk show in a December morning drizzle, a photographer snapped him getting out of the limousine with a Secret Service agent holding an umbrella over his thinning pate. This prompted letters of outrage to the papers. Why couldn't he carry his own umbrella? Security men were not provided by the taxpayers for such menial chores but should have their right hands ready at all times to draw their guns.

Perhaps prompted by all the public attention Ford was getting, President Nixon couldn't seem to see enough of him. The President asked him to join a strategy huddle with the Republican campaign chairmen—George Bush, Senator Bill Brock and Representative Bob Michel—to chart his role in the '74 elections. The next morning he was back for an Oval Office session with Congressional leaders Scott and Rhodes and in the afternoon for an energy meeting, the next day for a session with Governors, the day after for the Domestic Council.**

The Fords' social calendar was crowded, too. They danced expertly at the Symphony Ball, dined at the Georgetown Club at a party honoring House Majority Leader Tip O'Neill (D–Massachusetts),†

---

* David's brother, Nelson, sixty-five, announced on December 11 his intention to resign as Governor of New York after fifteen years in that exacting job. He would devote himself, he said, to his newly formed Commission on Critical Choices for America, which most observers considered a vehicle for Rocky's one last try for the Republican Presidential nomination in 1976. Ford was named a member of the commission, which sort of expired after he chose Rockefeller as Vice President in 1974.
** Ford happily told newsmen the President had assured him they would be in touch every day, either in person or by telephone. Most Presidents promise their Vice Presidents that, but in this case it lasted only about two weeks.
† One of the hosts was Tongsun Park, last of the big-time South Korean spenders. Years later an FBI agent called me to inquire why Roberta and I attended. I told him because I was invited by former Representative Bill

weekended with President Carl Humelsine of Colonial Williamsburg and spent a sentimental evening hosted by Bill and Alice Cramer for the confirmation-team volunteers and their wives.

Before he was confirmed, Ford had accepted an invitation from our mutual friend Jim Reinke, Washington vice-president of Eastern Airlines, to attend an Aviation Club dinner on December 14. He was to say a few words and assist in presenting the coveted Wright Brothers trophy to the 1973 winner, Senator Barry Goldwater.

Roberta and I were to be guests of the Reinkes and looked forward to an evening out together, since we had hardly seen each other since Ford was nominated. Besides, December 14 was the thirty-second anniversary of our first meeting, a blind date for Sunday dinner in Long Beach, California. Our date had to be postponed for a week because Ensign Hartmann, USNR, was suddenly kept on duty due to unforeseen developments in Hawaii on December 7, 1941.

I was to face a somewhat less formidable challenge on December 14, 1973. As I was about to go home, a newsman at the White House called to say he'd heard that the former secretary of two of the most celebrated Watergate characters was joining Ford's staff. He couldn't believe this was true. Was it?

I was flabbergasted and said of course not. Then I thought I'd better not be so positive. A lot of things had been going on during the past week. What was the young lady's name? I'd check and be sure. The name (which isn't important now) rang a bell. Neta checked our personnel files and, sure enough, Dewey Clower had hired her three days before and I had routinely approved her transfer papers along with his.

Clower didn't answer his phone, so I went through the corridors looking for him. I found him in Mike Dunn's office and asked him if it was correct that his secretary had previously been employed by certain White House aides who had become household words. He left without a word, and Dunn quickly assured me he knew nothing about the connection.

Dewey returned and flung a résumé at me, which confirmed all.

"Why didn't you send this to me along with the papers?" I demanded. "I'm sure she's a nice girl and an excellent secretary, but it

---

Minshall (R–Ohio) and because Tip O'Neill had been nice to me in the House and because the Vice President and numerous other solid citizens like Mel Laird were going, and it was a dandy party. I never heard anything more.

isn't fair to the Vice President, it isn't fair to her, and it isn't fair to me to conceal these facts. The press will have a field day with this. Do you understand that this is a serious problem?"

Clower had taken his chair with his back half turned to me, and the general, like the tar baby, said nothing.

"Dewey," I said, "I'm asking you a question. What do you propose we do about it?"

He turned slowly, his little raccoon eyes radiating defiance. Then the young Virginia gentleman elevated his middle finger and replied, "I understand perfectly, and this is what you can do with it."

I realized he might well be acting under orders to provoke me. Dunn was sizing us both up. So I sat there a long time until I stared Clower down and then asked very calmly if he was finished. He nodded.

"Dewey," I said, "you *are* finished. Clean out your desk within a half hour and go back to your job at the White House and thank you for helping out during the transition period. Now it's over.

It was an effort, but I held out my hand. Clower's lips silently formed the phrase "F--- you!" and he was gone. I turned to Mike.

"You had to do what you did," he said. "But don't expect him to be a good sport about it."

The next morning, after a disturbed anniversary night caused by the suppressed anger inside me and some doubt as to whether Ford would back me up or tolerate Dewey's insubordination, I found Mildred in virtual hysterics. Clower had cleaned out his office as ordered and, as a final gesture, carried a full cardboard carton of Ford invitations into Mildred's office and upended them unceremoniously atop her meticulously clean desk, scattering some on the floor. She was sobbing and trying to pick them up.

The Vice President put his arm around Mildred to console her while I picked up the papers.

"I don't ever want to see that Clower's face again," Ford said grimly.*

---

* Clower returned to the bosom of the White House Praetorians, probably warning them they could expect the same fate from Hartmann if he wasn't ruined before Ford became President. He next turned up in a better job on the Domestic Council staff, boldly sending a memo to President Ford proposing that he telephone Chicago's ailing Mayor Daley and telling him what to say. When the President saw this he exploded and told Haig to get rid of Clower. But when Air Force One arrived in Bonn, Germany, in 1975, there

Mildred was due to start a much needed Christmas vacation, but now she insisted she'd have to straighten up the appointment mess. The Vice President and I did what any old Navy veterans would have done: We called for the United States Marines.

Rick Sardo, Ford's Marine aide, sized up the situation instantly, moved onto the devastated battlefield and gently but firmly took charge.

I also hired Frank Pagnotta, on the recommendation of Belieu and Casselman, as a deputy to Dunn for administration. Fifty-nine years old, Frank had retired as a lieutenant colonel after twenty-three years in the Regular Army. Enlisting in World War II, he won a Silver Star for gallantry under enemy fire in France. When he retired in 1965 he was an aide to the Secretary of the Army. In 1973 Frank had a similar administrative job with the Director of Central Intelligence. He knew the EOB like a rabbit knows his warren.

Pagnotta's references read like a bipartisan Who's Who of official Washington, including Richard Nixon, Joe Califano, Representative Olin (Tiger) Teague (D–Texas), Spiro Agnew and even Representative Gerald Ford. I felt that General Dunn couldn't carry both the administrative and national security workload unaided, and he agreed Frank was just what we needed. Inadvertently, Pagnotta promptly plunged me into my second personnel crisis. He had rolled up his sleeves and was helping move some files and furniture into a new office when he called out to Air Force Master Sergeant Ulysses A. Owens: "Put that down over there, boy."

Sergeant Owens stiffened, announced that "colonel or no colonel, nobody calls me 'boy'!" and marched out. His assigned duty was driving Vice Presidential staff cars, but he had pitched in to help the secretaries with the heavy lifting.

The grapevine soon brought the story to me. I knew I had to do something, but I didn't know either Frank or Al Owens very well. I told my troubles to George Willis, who had once been a Pullman Company employee and doubtless had suffered a lot of unthinking

---

was Dewey giving orders to the White House advance team. Ford spotted him and told Donald Rumsfeld to get rid of Clower. Months later, he turned up at the foot of the airport ramp in Jakarta, Indonesia, still advancing Presidential trips. When Dewey appeared again as a White House functionary at the Kansas City convention, Ford simply gave up. A President can only do so much. At last report, Clower was heading an alumni group of Nixon Praetorians in Washington, faithful in his fashion to his first benefactor.

PALACE POLITICS

"boy"s in an earlier era. George knew from years in the Capitol that there was no trace of racism on Ford's staff, nor any tolerance of it. George said he'd have a talk with Owens and try to cool him down. Much self-mortified, Frank didn't deny it. "I just wasn't thinking," he said. "It was just like I'd call the secretaries 'girls'—they don't mind. I'm not prejudiced at all. Owens is a fine lad, and I'm old enough to be his father. Now what can I do to make it right?"

"Well, I think you ought to just come right out and apologize to him before it gets any worse," I said. "But first let me have a talk with him."

Sergeant Owens was now willing to forget the whole deal. "I've been taking a course in the Air Force on race relations," Owens said. "And maybe I wasn't applying what we learned when I fired back so fast. I've been thinking. No, I don't believe Colonel Pagnotta is really prejudiced in his heart. It's just a habit. He didn't really mean anything personal, but I sure was burned up."

So the story had a happy ending, and now we all three laugh about it. Al Owens became more than my favorite driver; he was a loyal friend and confidant. The White House motor pool is manned by Army sergeants, and when we moved to the West Wing there was no way I could get the Air Force a toehold. But on the night of January 19, 1977, when I left my White House office for the last time and turned in my pass, it was Sergeant Owens who waited around to drive me home.

Ford was itching to get to his Vail condominium and out on the ski slopes. I was equally eager to hit the 80-degree water in front of our Virgin Islands condominium, as we had done for six Christmas recesses.

Washington is a town of fits and starts. Things inch along for weeks at a glacial pace. Then a long holiday—Easter, Fourth of July, Labor Day or Christmas—looms, and everything rushes to some kind of impasse or conclusion. Lights burn at night as the high and mighty as well as lowly bureaucrats toil to empty their "In" boxes and finish long-avoided assignments in order to clear their decks for a short spell of rest and recreation.

Believe me, it is needed—not so much because government officials and employees work harder than other people (though many do) but because they take their work and themselves so seriously.

There had been a number of hints from the White House that, on account of the energy crunch and the lengthening lines at the gas stations, President Nixon might go to Florida on a commercial jet (though why it burns any less fuel than Air Force One was not explained) and maybe the Vice President ought to reconsider his traditional family outing in Colorado.

Ford got his stubborn streak up and said, "By thunderation [or some such phrase] I am going to Vail on December twenty-first, and that's it, period!" He started doing extra knee-strengthening exercises so we'd all know he meant it. And he was going in his new perquisite, Air Force Two. And Betty and the kids were going along for what might be the last time all of them would be together.

Commander Kerr volunteered the suggestion that servicemen are always trying to hitch rides across the continent for Christmas leaves, so why not dampen any criticism by filling up the plane with those heading for Colorado and nearby points. The Vice President said that was a great idea.

Everything was rushing smoothly toward his December 21 departure when Haig called and said something very serious had come up. The Premier of Spain, Admiral Luis Carrero Blanco, had been assassinated in Madrid in a plot so bizarre as to surpass all the television spy dramas. Unknown conspirators had disguised themselves as utility servicemen and, tunneling for two months from the basements of unsuspecting residents, had planted an antitank mine under a quiet street the seventy-year-old Carrero used every day to go to Mass. That morning they had blown him and his car 180 feet in the air. It landed on a nearby rooftop.

All Spain was waiting for Franco to die and for Prince Juan Carlos to reclaim the old Bourbon throne. Premier Carrero Blanco had been holding things together, moving gingerly in the direction of liberalization. But the assassins were immediately presumed to be leftists, and the ugly heritage of Spain's Civil War seemed about to explode in new violence. It was important that the United States show sympathy and support for its strategic Mediterranean and Atlantic ally, especially as the rest of NATO still treated Spain as a pariah.

President Nixon would like Vice President Ford to represent him at the funeral, which had been set for Friday afternoon, the next day. If we were airborne by 6:00 P.M., we could just barely make it. It was not a request but a command. I told Haig we'd be ready.

My first reaction was a short Anglo-Saxon word and my second observation to the Vice President was scarcely statesmanlike.

"Well, the little p----s have figured out a way to keep you from going to Vail after all," I said. But Ford was way ahead of me. While I was rushing home to throw a few things into a suitcase, he arranged to have the plane that took us to Madrid fly back after the funeral the same day, stop at Andrews Air Force Base, pick up Betty and the family and fly right on to Colorado. He'd be only a few hours later than planned.

I gave Roberta a kiss and said she'd have to go to the Motion Picture Association party alone that night. "But hang onto our Saturday-morning reservations for St. Croix," I said. "Of course you'll have to pack for me."

"So what else is new?" she called after me.

General Dunn, Paul Miltich, Howard Kerr and I accompanied the Vice President on his first foreign mission. It wasn't much of an entourage. It wasn't much of a plane, either, with only four bunks and limited galley service. Cabinet and Congressional junketers had commandeered all the fancy jets.

It was a grim, gray morning in Madrid, truly funereal, and we could feel the tenseness the moment we stepped from the plane. Our Spanish hosts with unfailing courtesy had a brunch ready for the new American Vice President; he was outranked among foreign mourners only by the King of Morocco. Then Ford was whisked away for a courtesy call on the eighty-one-year-old Generalissimo, who was too ill to attend his old friend's last rites.

We marched a mile or more through the main avenues of the capital, the dignitaries closely following the cortege. The weather had improved, but the crowd was surly. I fell in step with a uniformed U.S. naval officer, the aide to our Ambassador and the biggest man in sight. His ceremonial sword comforted me. Though troops lined the curbs shoulder to shoulder, their discipline seemed to evaporate as soon as the VIPs had passed, and the grim spectators swirled in among us from the rear.

One particularly hard-jawed Spaniard marched abreast of me and continued to fix me with a scowl. When I smiled back, he shouted angrily to his companions, who also scowled. My Navy friend quickly translated: "He says why does the foreigner smile—is something funny?" I wiped it off, as if in boot camp, and scowled my best for the rest of the procession.

The power of a mob is terrifying and claustrophobic. Never before had I seen the unsunny side of the Spanish character, the preoccupation with death that Hemingway caught so brilliantly. We were all glad to get back to the American embassy for—was it late lunch or early supper? The whole twenty-eight-hour journey was kaleidoscopic.

On the way home, racing the setting sun at 33,000 feet, Ford crawled into one of the bunks and was soon dead to the world. Midway across the Atlantic the pilot came back and huddled with me and Dunn. Snow had started to fall in the Washington area, he said. Andrews was closed and so was Dulles. There might be a chance of landing at Baltimore–Friendship, but if not, we'd either have to turn back to the Azores or chance flying on west to an open runway. If we wanted to go back, we'd have to do it now.

My decision? Or wake the boss? The Ford family was supposed to be waiting at Andrews to board the plane for Vail while some of us dropped off. I'd heard the Vice President vow he'd be on skis the next morning. I woke the boss.

Jerry Ford's first command decision as Vice President wasn't very dramatic, but it was very positive. The military men were watching closely to test his decisiveness as the pilot repeated the options.

"Have we enough fuel to go on to a safe landing if Washington is completely closed by the time we get there?" he asked, rubbing his eyes. "There's no safety reason for turning around?"

"Sir, we could go nonstop to Vail if it weren't for picking up Mrs. Ford and the others."

"Very well. Radio ahead to divert them to Friendship and head for there. The sailors who want a ride, too. I may have to ski in my front yard tomorrow but I'm going to ski," the Vice President said and fell back to sleep.

All's well that ends well, the storm shifted, and we landed safe, sound and looking as though we'd slept in our clothes, as we had.

"Why don't you come along and enjoy the snow?" Ford kidded me as I said goodbye. After spending my childhood in Rapid City, South Dakota, and Niagara Falls, New York—and two wartime winters in the Aleutians—I swore I'd never, ever voluntarily be cold again. (How could I know in two years I'd be dying to accompany Ford to Vladivostok?)

"Thanks, but I'm heading south," I called back. "Have a good vacation and I'll see you in January."

5

APOTHEOSIS IN CHICAGO

★★────────────★★

The Roman deity Janus, who gave January his name, has a considerable following among the media pundits and politicians of Washington. It is not merely that he has two faces but that he looks both
forward and back. Looking back invariably fathers the thought that
things cannot help but be better in the future, though of course nothing can be foreseen there.

Lazing in the St. Croix sun in the waning days of the old year, I
reflected on the tremendous surprises that drastically changed my life
in 1973 and felt sure that 1974 would be far more normal and predictable.

We had settled fairly comfortably into the new and unfamiliar
Vice Presidential pattern. While there was a certain amount of traditional conflict with the White House, I was confident it would yield to
the President's urgent need for Ford's help—to shore up Nixon's
front-line defenses on Capitol Hill and in the coming fall elections,
which would render a precise reading on how much overall damage
Republican fortunes had sustained.

The worst of Watergate must surely be over. How could there be
more major bombshells after the Ervin hearings? Special Prosecutor
Leon Jaworski had announced "We're getting the kind of cooperation
I'd hoped we'd get" from the White House.

The clamor for impeachment, though strident, seemed concentrated in Washington and within clearly partisan circles. A strong plu-
rality, 45 percent to 31 percent, told Louis Harris pollsters they'd
respect Nixon more if he resigned and let Ford take over. But there
was no overwhelming public demand for the traumatic exorcism of
House impeachment and Senate trial, nor were the votes there to con-
vict in either house. The current Republican line, therefore, was to demand an early impeachment vote by the House and get the question
disposed of before the '74 campaign. Ford was telling reporters that if

Rodino's committee didn't get a move on and the Democratic leadership dragged its feet beyond April, the whole exercise would be considered rank partisanship.

Agnew's shock wave had passed as suddenly as it had hit. The scandal was personal and failed to rub off. Since it produced Ford as a new face in the Vice Presidency, it actually proved to be a plus for the disspirited party.*

So, like Ford, I contemplated 1974 as a year of on-the-job training, conciliating Congress and campaigning for Republicans around the country. I hoped to help by building a Vice Presidential staff tailored to this and congenial to his personal style. But neither I nor Ford, if I read him rightly, believed as 1974 began that Nixon would do anything but finish out his second term. We both believed the hard core of thirty-four Senate votes against conviction and removal would surely hold. Nixon had weathered more adversity than most politicians, living or dead. Many who had written him off long before were themselves forgotten.

The primary question facing us for the new year was one of recovery from what seemed to have been another Nixon low in 1973. It would be rough, given the complexion of the Congress and the political ineptness of the Praetorians who had survived Haldeman, Ehrlichman, Colson, *et al.,* in the White House. But Laird and Harlow had returned to restore some measure of realism around the President. Nixon had picked Ford, and we had reason to hope that his new Vice President would have a good influence on him. Perhaps the worst was over.

I found Ford voicing the same sort of optimism in a pre-Christmas interview in *U.S. News and World Report,* under the heading "Why I Will Not Run in 1976." He was pretty categorical, to the point of saying that even if he succeeded to the Presidency before 1976 he "would step aside and not run to stay in that office." He explained that he felt he could do a better job as Vice President if he were not perceived as conducting a personal campaign and named Reagan, Rockefeller and Connally as the leading GOP prospects.

I wasn't sure Ford's premise was valid for his unique unelected Vice Presidency. People are drawn to a leader because they think he is

* Already Ford led Ronald Reagan by five percentage points in Republican polls (Harris, 12/10/73) and both Teddy Kennedy (48 percent to 44 percent) and Henry (Scoop) Jackson (43 percent to 41 percent) in Harris' first 1976 trial heat.

101

going somewhere, not because they know he is going nowhere. Never having been through a national campaign, Ford would need to create a constituency of his own independent of Nixon's to enable him to function well even in the No. 2 role.

When he was still a Senator, Jack Kennedy told me he hadn't wanted a political career. When he was younger he thought he'd like to be a writer or a journalist. By contrast, Robert F. Kennedy had the driving ambition and plans that characterize most Presidential aspirants. Certainly Lyndon Johnson, Richard Nixon and Jimmy Carter demonstrated the single-minded purpose it usually takes to gain the White House.

Harry Truman and Dwight D. Eisenhower acquired their Presidential ambitions late in life. Had destiny passed them by, doubtless they would have been not only content but properly proud of attaining the pinnacles of U.S. Senator or Army general. They were Ford's heroes.

Ford never was possessed of the furies that afflict many politicians of lesser renown. Only once, during the time he was Vice President, can I recall him revealing that the prospect of being President might have certain appeal.

We were about to land in Air Force Two, and three of us were sitting around a table with the Vice President. It was the last stop of the day. Nothing was programmed for that evening, so we had been relaxing with glasses in hand. Ford's bourbon and water was sitting on the table, about three-quarters full, as the wheels gently hit the runway. Then, as the pilot braked to decelerate, Ford's glass slid gracefully and silently to the edge of the table and dumped full in his lap. His fly was sopping wet, and within minutes he'd have to stride down the ramp to face the greeters and the television lights.

"Goddamit!" he roared. "We pay half a million dollars for these things! If I am ever President of the United States, every airplane we use is going to have some little round sockets to set your glass in so it can't slide." (He definitely said "if" and not "when." But when he did become President, the Air Force had prudently installed such handy little gadgets on Air Force One and all the back-up jets. On that critical occasion, despite ideal weather, Ford deplaned with great dignity, wearing his raincoat.)

It takes much more to become President than wanting to be, and fate is never far from the process. The times make the man, more often than not, but the man must be ready. That is why I felt the best five words I ever assembled for Ford were "I am my own man." If fate, by whatever route, brought him to the Presidency, that was the essential quality the people would demand. This was the side Jerry Ford had to show to a public that hardly knew him until he became our first instant Vice President. Whatever else Ford might be as Vice President, he could not be merely Nixon by another name. He had to be his own man, right from the start.

But, even as I was pondering these provocative ideas, the Vice President was setting in motion a seemingly routine chain of events that would nearly wipe out that notion.

The White House called Ford at Vail and explained that the President, who had accepted an invitation to address the politically supportive American Farm Bureau Federation at its January 15 convention in Atlantic City, would like to have the Vice President appear in his stead. Sure, said the Vice President. Have your speech writers get me up what the President thinks I should say.

Perfectly natural. It was the President he was accommodating, so why not let the President's people do the work? David Gergen, head of the Nixon speech shop, assigned the speech to Ken Khachigian, an able writer who later went to San Clemente to assist the ex-President with his memoirs.

When Ford was in Congress, Miltich and I had written most of his formal speeches—and he ad-libbed the rest. Since his nomination as Vice President we'd done our best to keep up, but we were both swamped. So the White House had supplied Ford with serviceable scripts on bland subjects such as energy, tourism, civil service and the perennial plight of the American farmer. All we had to do was edit them a little and insert a few authentic Ford lines.

Khachigian's draft for the Farm Bureau convention in Atlantic City was something else. The Vice President handed it to me on Monday morning, the day before he was to deliver it. The first three pages were the usual praise for farmers as the unsung heroes of our economy and upbeat stuff about the American spirit overcoming all obstacles, past and future.

But then the fireworks began. The rest was a barroom brawl with Ford singlehandedly busting the skulls of any and all varmints so vile as to suggest that Richard M. Nixon was not "a wise and good President." The worst villain was the "Democrat 93rd Congress," riding hell-for-leather to an impeachment lynching party. Egging Congress on was "a coalition of groups like the AFL-CIO, the Americans for

103

PALACE POLITICS

Democratic Action and other powerful pressure organizations waging a massive propaganda campaign against the President of the United States." These extreme partisans were "bent on stretching out the ordeal of Watergate for their own purposes, whatever they might be . . . but when you look back on the past years of the Nixon administration and think of his really magnificent achievements, then Watergate is a tragic but grotesque sideshow."

There was more. Surely it was not the speech that had been written for the President. It might have been one left over from Agnew. As soon as I finished reading it, I ran back into the Vice President's office.

"Do you really want to say this?" I asked. Curiously enough, he did. He was spoiling for a fight.

"I told 'em I wanted a real tough speech," Ford said.

"But not this tough. You're supposed to be the 'calm communicator and ready conciliator' with the Congress, remember? Do you really want to castigate the AFL-CIO when Leonard Woodcock just finished giving you a glowing, unsolicited endorsement?"

"Well, maybe it is a little rough on Congress. Work that part over. Make it clear that it's only a few extremists I'm talking about," the Vice President grudgingly agreed. "As for the AFL-CIO, I've been reading a lot of their local union papers. They all use the same canned editorials and cartoons screaming for Nixon's scalp. Obviously, it's organized from the top, but the members think it's the word from their locals," Ford added.

I worked over the White House draft but, I regret to say, didn't censor it enough. I cut out most of the barbed blasts at Congress and reduced the malevolent conspiracy to a "relatively small group of activists" while allowing that "the vast majority of my former colleagues in the House have taken a highly responsible approach to the impeachment question." But I failed to argue with Ford when I should have about the shotgun aim of the speech as a whole and the effect it would have on his emerging image of reasonableness and relative independence. It hadn't yet really been driven home to either of us that every word the Vice President uttered would be broadcast to the nation and endlessly analyzed.

He flew off to Atlantic City, and I stayed behind to attend to what I thought were more important things. Before Air Force Two returned at 3:00 P.M., the news wires were clacking with Ford's slashing counterattack in defense of President Nixon. The air was full of angry comeback from his unsuspecting victims.

I was mad at myself for failing him. I was furious at the White

House for testing how far they could lead him down the Agnew path. But when the Vice President got back he was elated. The hall had resounded with applause. Audiences like a bit of bloodshed.

Ford brushed aside my lamentations, and the next day he tossed away a prepared speech to a Washington group and replayed the hard-charging denunciation of Nixon's tormentors. This could have been the beginning of the end, had he not taken off that evening for "Jerry Ford Day" in Grand Rapids. The folks back home really laid it on the line. They bluntly told him he was nuts to stick his neck out for Nixon like that. If there was any conspiracy of concern about Watergate, they were part of it and proud of it. Watergate was no "grotesque sideshow"; it was the center ring.

Grand Rapids was Ford's Rubicon. Whatever else his critics charge, his grass-roots hearing was acute. He knew how to listen, and he heard what his old friends and supporters were trying to tell him. When he returned to Washington, his old buddies at Burning Tree golf club told him the same. He could go on rallying the rear-guard defenders of President Nixon and share their fate, or he could march boldly across the stream and raise his own standard at the gates of Rome.

"We can't go on getting our speeches from the White House," he told me. "We're going to have to do our own. I know how busy you and Paul have been, but—"

"And we're going to be even busier," I interrupted. "But we'll work it out. Let's start with Paul. He needs an assistant who can handle the media so he can get back to doing speeches part of the time. I've begged him to pick one, but he won't, so let's pick one for him—Bill Roberts."

"Fine," the Vice President said. "I don't think we could do better—if he'll come."

Roberts had already assured me he would. Bill was the kind of guy everybody likes. He'd been a Congressional correspondent for Time-Life Radio-TV, which had an outlet in Grand Rapids. We'd all known him for years. He was capable, courteous and conscientious—and we could use a resident expert on the electronic media. Bill was soon hard at work as deputy press secretary—and writing fine speeches.

"Now, we're still going to need a full-time speech writer, at least one and probably two," I continued. "I've been thinking about . . ."

"Milt Friedman?" Ford took the name out of my mouth. "He'd be fine, but hasn't he just gone to work for Bob Michel?"

Representative Robert H. Michel (R–Illinois) was chairman of the Republican Congressional campaign committee and a close Ford ally. Milt, formerly Washington correspondent for the Jewish Telegraphic Agency and a public-relations aide to B'nai B'rith, had just been hired as a writer by Jack Calkins, executive director of Michel's committee. An intense, idealistic and intellectual bachelor, Friedman had done some freelance speeches for Ford during his House days. When Ford appeared before a Zionist organization, Milt's Middle East expertise and awareness of the code words of the Arab-Israeli conflict were valuable. He could write the simple, punchy sentences Ford liked, and we liked him.

But Congressmen are reluctant to raid one another's staffs. Ford agreed to clear the idea with Michel and I promised to mollify Calkins. Jack reacted explosively but relented for Ford and the larger cause. But first Friedman had to finish a current project.

"I've been feeling guilty about neglecting your speeches myself," I continued. "But you know how it's been. I spend all my time trying to pry some more office space out of the White House and interviewing secretaries. What I need is a really good staff administrator."

"Well, I know where one is." The Vice President smiled. "I have to tell you in advance, though—he'll start right off going after your job."

"I can take care of myself," I boasted. "It's been tried before. If he can do it better than I can, then he should have it. What's his name?"

"Bill Seidman," Ford said. "I think you've met him. He's from Grand Rapids, runs a big accounting firm with offices all over the country. He's younger than we are, very hard charger, sometimes rubs people the wrong way like you do. But he's good, and he'll be loyal. Maybe you and Bill could get along."

He didn't sound entirely convincing, but I was desperate—so I said let's get him down here.

Getting the green light to beef up the staff greatly encouraged me. The reinforcement of Ford's own ranks would itself send a strong signal to the White House that he was not going to be led around by the nose.

But the Praetorians didn't wait. Emboldened by their success in the surprise attack at Atlantic City, they tried to set up the apparently willing Vice President for an even bolder strike. On Monday morning, January 21, the President summoned Ford to the Oval Office. When he returned, he told me the President had assured him that there was evidence on the secret tapes that would completely clear Nixon of Watergate complicity. Nixon volunteered to let Ford see the transcripts that established his innocence. Ford, fortunately, was both sufficiently wary and in a hurry to get to the Capitol. He was already late for a ceremony at which Senator Mark Hatfield was to present him a mint edition of his Inaugural medal—the first ever struck for a Vice President alone. He said he'd think about it.

"Do I really want to read those partial transcripts?" he asked me. "Do you think I should?"

"I don't think you should get involved," I said. "Up to now you're completely clear of Watergate. What you don't know won't hurt you. Once you know anything, there'll be no end of it until you have to know everything. It's their problem. Stay away from it."

"I think so too," Ford mused. We both knew General Haig had made the same pitch to Senate Minority Leader Hugh Scott. Scott scrutinized what later turned out to be a highly sanitized transcript of John Dean's "cancer close to the Presidency" warning in March 1973. Scott had dutifully stated publicly that the tape contained no evidence that Nixon had done anything impeachable.

"I'll just say I'll take the President's and Hugh Scott's word for it and let it go at that," the Vice President concluded.

At a Capitol press conference the next day, Ford did exactly that.

The Praetorians weren't through trying. First, they leaked to the media that the Vice President's controversial Farm Bureau speech in Atlantic City was actually written by President Nixon's writers. Why did they do it? Because the Praetorian mentality is such that they had to flaunt the fact that the Vice President had been broken to obedience, that they were still calling the shots.

Even more incredible, Gergen and his speech writers kept coming up with texts studded with slavish adulation of the President. Their next offering was again by Khachigian, author of the Atlantic City debacle. Gergen adroitly bypassed me and delivered it to Miltich, with copies to Haig and Ziegler. He suggested it be used at a "major forum."

It blasted the Washington *Post* for asking whether Ford were still "his own man" and denounced nameless enemies trying to drive a wedge between Nixon and his new Vice President. Next, Ford was supposed to downgrade his own staff and praise the Praetorians. The draft read as follows:

The staff I brought with me had the well-deserved reputation of being one of the best on Capitol Hill. . . . They have done a

107

first-rate job during the transition. But I have recognized, and they have recognized, that this is an extraordinary change.

We had a small staff, designed to meet the needs of a Congressman, not a Vice President. So we've needed help.

That help has been forthcoming . . . from a President who has been as generous and as courteous as any man I've ever met. I want to say for the record that I've appreciated that help from the White House . . . totally professional, courteous, and very thoughtful.

Let's be clear. Jerry Ford has been his own man for 56* years now, and God willing he'll continue to be his own man for a good many years to come. When Jerry Ford speaks out, he speaks for Jerry Ford—no one else!

Ford was outraged when he saw the draft. He told me to call Bob Michel and see if he wouldn't let Milt Friedman go right away. We totally junked another Gergen draft for Ford's appearance before the Anti-Defamation League of B'nai B'rith in West Palm Beach. Friedman's maiden Ford text focused on peace as the common dream of the three great monotheistic religions born in the Middle East. Milt gave Nixon his due, but he really spread it on about the vision, genius and diplomatic gifts of Henry Kissinger. The Vice President (with similar astuteness) cleared it personally with Kissinger, who readily agreed that Friedman's draft was far superior.

In his next two major speeches in Columbus, Ohio, and Jamestown, Pennsylvania, Ford somehow forgot to mention Nixon by name. He spoke of "this Administration" and about himself. In response to newsmen's questions, he was supportive of the President on the impeachment question but said he wasn't going to "lobby" against it and had definitely decided not to read the proffered Watergate transcripts. We thought that would get the message across.

Among the first outside observers to sense the change in the Ford camp were Rowland Evans and Robert Novak, whose lively Washington column expertly combines exclusive leaks from politicians with their own intuitive speculations. "The most significant indication of how Ford now views his future came in the aftermath of his blooper speech in Atlantic City," they wrote. "It exploded in his face. The private reaction of Ford and his chief of staff, Robert Hartmann, was in-

* Actually, Ford was then sixty.

stantaneous: instead of trying to operate with a small staff as a White House appendage, face the hard truth that Ford is fast becoming the operating political head of the Republican Party, whose nominal chief is not welcome across the country.

"Pressing Ford hard toward a similar conclusion was George Bush, Republican national chairman, who forcefully urged Ford to hire an experienced politican as go-between with the committee, campaign committees and state party organizations," Evans and Novak continued. "That led to the hiring of National Committeewoman Gwen Anderson of Washington State as Ford's fulltime political adviser."

Back in November, George Bush had highly recommended Gwen, saying it would do wonders for party morale to have someone from the National Committee on Ford's staff. The wife of a nuclear scientist and mother of two teenagers, Mrs. Anderson had combined her own business career with Republican politics in Washington State since 1960. I was impressed with her businesslike manner and broad acquaintance among party leaders and also wanted to have at least one woman in a visible and responsible position on the staff. Gwen joined us as a Consultant for Public Affairs, dealing with all manner of nongovernmental organizations—from the Boy Scouts to the GOP.

We also felt it would be a good idea to demilitarize our national security set-up. There were too many generals and former military officers running around the White House in those days, and Ford felt it was a bad precedent, however competent the individuals involved. General Dunn was due to retire, so we began discussing a civilian replacement.

Ford wanted someone who could promote the Nixon defense budget in an increasingly peace-oriented Congress. Ford's earlier experience as ranking minority member of the House defense appropriations subcommittee made him both expert and concerned in this area. Many of the advanced weapons systems he had fought to start were just becoming operational. He also felt that Defense Secretary James Schlesinger, like Robert S. McNamara before him, was prone to irritate and infuriate the staunchest champions of adequate defense spending on Capitol Hill by condescendingly talking down to them.

Schlesinger had inherited from Secretary Richardson an affable and popular Assistant Secretary for Congressional Relations, former Virginia Congressman John O. Marsh, Jr., a conservative Harry Byrd-type Democrat who had retired to practice law after eight years in the House.

"If it weren't for your rule against former Members of Congress, I'd say try and shanghai Jack Marsh," I replied.

"Well, there's an exception to every rule," said Ford, grinning. "Let's get Jack over for a talk."

Marsh was surprised but readily agreed to give up the salutes and perquisites of his high Pentagon position for the inconspicuous daily grind of the Vice Presidential staff. To augment his department, we took on two more younger officer aides, Lieutenant Colonel Robert Blake, USAF, a hot fighter pilot with a cool head, and Army Colonel Jack Walker. We already had Commander Howard Kerr, USN, and Lieutenant Colonel Americo A. Sardo, USMC, so all four services were now represented.

Midway in all this staff shuffling Ken Belieu, who had been our legislative liaison, was hospitalized for surgery, which would sideline him for some time. I put out an SOS for Dick Burress to fill the job temporarily. When Ken decided to accept a private position instead of returning, Dick was able to arrange an open-ended leave of absence from the Hoover Institution and served with loyalty and distinction through Ford's transition to the Presidency.

Bill Seidman had arrived from Michigan and was busily stream-lining our office operations, to my considerable relief. We also got a lot of snide criticism in scurrilous media leaks from the frustrated Praetorians, among them an unending stream of rumors that Ford's staff was torn with jealousies and infighting. I called a meeting of all hands on January 29 to introduce the new members of the staff and to urge everyone to cooperate fully with Seidman in his reorganization inquiries. By and large we were happily on top of our new jobs at the end of the two months' shakedown, and Ford was obviously pleased with his.

He made some lighthearted points about it before the annual dinner of the Washington Press Club. Turning to Speaker Carl Albert, who had been next in line to succeed Nixon until Ford's confirmation, he said, "You and I, Carl, are probably the only two people at this table who would rather be right than President. I don't want to suggest that the thought has ever crossed my mind."

Recalling his 1968 Gridiron Club debate with Hubert Humphrey when Humphrey was Vice President, Ford revived his concluding joke: "At that time I said to Hubert, Mr. Vice President, I want to assure you that I have absolutely no designs on your job. I'm serious. I love the House of Representatives, despite the long, irregular hours. Sometimes, though, when it's late and I'm tired and hungry—on that long drive home to Alexandria—as I go past 1600 Pennsylvania Avenue, I do seem to hear a little voice saying, 'If you lived here, you'd be home now.' "

The Vice President again brought down the house.

But at the White House, they didn't find it any funnier than LBJ had.

Juan Cameron of *Fortune* interviewed Ford at length, as well as some longtime friends, early in 1974. His reflective assessment in the March issue was titled "Suppose There's a President Ford in Your Future?"

One Ford fan willing to be quoted was Mel Laird, ever the kingmaker. "The trouble with Jerry," says the hard-driving Laird, "is that he is not ambitious enough. However, I'm doing what I can to push him toward the Presidency."

"Since he was confirmed, Ford has been forced to think about his own qualifications to be President. In public, he says nothing about that. In private, he has confided that he thinks he could do the job. A lot of other Americans, it appears, have begun to think so, too," Cameron concluded.

Scotty Reston of the New York *Times,* however, complained that the Vice President should be given the sort of on-the-job training that would prepare him for the Presidency. "He is an open, friendly and intelligent man, who is trusted . . . and does his homework," Reston wrote. "But he has little experience in foreign affairs or economic and financial affairs, which are increasingly dominating the relations between nations. And partisan work and legislative work are not the same as managing vast staffs and presiding over the great departments and agencies of the Executive."

True enough, but Ford was already preparing himself in his own systematic way. He flew to his birthplace, Omaha, in freezing February and took refuge in the deep underground headquarters of the Strategic Air Command. He and Mrs. Ford stood in three interminable receiving lines at Blair House to meet every diplomatic representative in Washington.*

* At the first of these, Ford sternly scolded Betty for "always being late" within the earshot of the society scribes. This time she had a good excuse: The doctor had removed a cinder from her eye. Nevertheless, it didn't happen again.

111

PALACE POLITICS

Ford continued his calls on Cabinet officers in their own baili-wicks. The irrepressible Earl Butz greeted him at the door to his impressive office at Agriculture and with deadly seriousness insisted that the Vice President take his high-back Secretarial chair. When the Secretary's assistants and Ford's had arranged themselves around the desk in a semicircle, Butz began: "Mr. Vice President, I understand you came over here to get a better idea of what the Secretary of Agriculture does. So I asked you to sit there and pretend for a moment that you are the Secretary. Now, I'll show you how it goes."

Butz leaped to his feet, leaned clear across the big desk, poked his forefinger at Ford's nose and roared, "Now, you SOB, what are YOU going to do for us farmers?"

There were also the daily briefings by the CIA and frequently by Scowcroft or Kissinger himself on foreign developments; by the OMB and Domestic Council staffs; meetings with a continuous parade of organizations and ethnic groups; Vietnam POWs and Skylab astronauts; interviews with news people; an appeal to the National Governors' Conference to back his new Privacy Committee as a worthy bipartisan endeavor.*

It wasn't all work and no fun. There was a big tango party at Argentine Ambassador Alejandro Orfila's, a smashing Irish stag on St. Patrick's Day in Charleston, South Carolina, and another fun dinner of the Gridiron Club.

At the latter Ford was paired against Senator Henry Jackson (D–Washington), and Bob Orben again helped with his speech. Claiming not to be one, the Vice President roasted all the Presidential candidates,** awarding Jackson "the Calvin Coolidge Award for Conspicuously Concealed Charisma" and observing of California's Governor Ronald Reagan: "He's made California a state where the movies are dirty but the Governor is clean. . . . Governor Reagan does *not*

---

* President Nixon appointed Ford to head this Domestic Council subcommittee, which most Washington cynics dismissed as a diversionary spinoff of Watergate. The Vice President, wary of "being taken over by the staff," insisted on naming as executive director his old friend and law partner, Phil Buchen. They did much fine work on the growing threat of private computer data as well as government intrusions on individual privacy. This could have been a primary plank in Ford's 1976 campaign—but it got lost somewhere by the image-makers.
** Jimmy Carter of Georgia was nowhere mentioned in the skits and speeches.

dye his hair. That's ridiculous. Let's say he's turning prematurely orange."

Thus are great friendships born.

Looking back on it, a Vice President couldn't have had any better cram course. There is no on-the-job training for being President except being President.

The apotheosis of Jerry Ford as a potential President occurred at approximately 9:10 A.M. on Saturday, March 30, 1974, in the Hyatt Regency Hotel at O'Hare Airport in Chicago, where so many candidates have been anointed. The Vice President flew up early that morning to speak at a breakfast of some 1,000 GOP party officials and precinct workers from the eight Midwest states, organized by Ohio's former National Chairman Ray Bliss, the best political pro since James A. Farley.

Senator Charles Percy of the host state, Governor Reagan and Governor Rockefeller were also scheduled as major speakers. None had formally declared themselves as 1976 candidates, but they, along with John Connally, led the speculative lists of those who believed Ford's disclaimers. The breakfast hour was the worst spot on the program but the only time the Vice President could accept. President Nixon was in Key Biscayne, Florida.

Ford startled the sleepy audience to attention by asking the blunt question: "What lessons can Republicans learn from Watergate?"

By the time Ford finished his short, hard-hitting speech, he was soaring on waves of applause and cheers. At last, somebody high in the Republican Party had faced the ugly fact of Watergate and admitted it was a disaster.

"Ford Attack on CREEP Delights GOP Audience," read one headline. "Ford Denounces Nixon's '72 Aides," "Ford Blames 'Elite Guard' for GOP Ills" were others. The Associated Press carried the entire text to its clients and began its long dispatch thus: "Vice President Gerald R. Ford said Saturday the political lesson of Watergate was 'never again must Americans allow an arrogant, elite guard of political adolescents' to dictate the terms of a national election campaign."

By focusing his attack on CREEP, Ford touched a sensitive nerve among party workers, who were generally ignored and pushed around in 1972 by arrogant little Praetorians on leave from the White House. He won immediate hosannas from every Republican who had run that year, most of whom were left to their own devices while CREEP concentrated, as its name implied, on the re-election of the President. CREEP also skimmed off most of the campaign money while other GOP candidates went begging.

Furthermore—the point was not lost on anyone—it was an oblique but devastating criticism of Nixon's responsibility in reducing Republican morale to near zero. Ford did not yet believe the President guilty of any impeachable offense, but he did believe that Nixon's handling of Watergate was stupid and politically devastating to the party. And at last he said so aloud.

What had galvanized him to action was a special election in his old Fifth District of Michigan on February 18. The seat had been held by Republicans ever since 1912, and Ford's chosen successor lost it to a Democrat. A post-mortem survey showed 73 percent of Ford's own folks considered Watergate the chief issue of the special election, and, accordingly, 60 percent voted for the Democrat even though they considered his Republican opponent better qualified.

The effect of his Chicago CREEP attack was electric. The Vice President was instantly hailed as the *de facto* head of the Republican Party. The other hopefuls present—Percy, Reagan and Rockefeller—were barely mentioned in news reports, but all hastened to endorse Ford's formula for future victories.

Stunned, the "arrogant, elite guard of political adolescents" back in Washington declined all comment except the obvious one: the Vice President's remarks were neither written by nor cleared by the White House. Indeed they were not.

About two weeks before the Chicago speech, Ford asked me, "Do you remember that memo you wrote me some time ago about CREEP?"

I didn't, but he did. It was, in fact, ten months ago—long before anybody imagined Ford being Vice President. It was written shortly after the resignations of Haldeman, Ehrlichman, Kleindienst and Dean and two days before the Ervin Committee opened its televised Watergate hearings.

"There's some good thoughts there about amateurs versus the professionals in politics," he went on. "Since I'm going to be talking to the old pros, let's kick CREEP around a little and they'll love it."

I dug out my old memo, which was written in Navy lingo:

114

The Republican Party is in a Damage Control situation. We know that we have taken multiple hits. We do not know how serious the damage is, or whether the integrity of the ship can be maintained.

Communications are disrupted and the crew is starting to abandon ship. The primary duty of all hands is now to keep the ship afloat. While praying for the captain's safety, senior officers cannot deny that damage has occurred or pretend that somebody else will repair it in time.

Damage Control procedure must be undertaken immediately to:

1. Restore discipline and stop—or at least slow—the tendency to panic into a "every man for himself" response.

2. Minimize damage to regular Republican organizations (National, Congressional, Senatorial and state and local committees) *by sealing off the flooded* CREEP *compartment* and emphasizing its isolation from, and antagonism for, the traditional party apparatus in 1972.

3. Mount an effective counterattack and get off the defensive.

I had gone on to argue that to protect the Presidency, the Republican Party must maintain a degree of independence from the Presidency and articulate political positions which "will be able to weather and survive *even heavier damage* in the future."

I supposed Ford had read the memo and forgotten it. Not at all. He had waited almost a year for the right time, and the right place, to use it for maximum effect.

Buoyed by his success, Ford flew off to Clearwater, Florida, where he repeated his CREEP speech before nine hundred stomping and shouting Republicans. He added a little praise for the President's peacemaking efforts and some equally mild criticism of the "opposition" Congress. Then he threw in, almost as an afterthought, a gratuitous, extemporaneous and rather strange observation: "President Nixon," he said, "is in great health, mentally and physically."

At that point there had been no public suggestion that anything might be *mentally* wrong with the President. But Ford was worried and let it slip. At his most recent private meetings with Nixon, the President hadn't seemed himself. He rambled, didn't appear to be listening and talked endlessly about trivialities. Kissinger also stoked Ford with similar fears, hoping it would not adversely affect foreign policy.

None of the traveling newsmen picked up this hint—none except John Osborne of the *New Republic.* His weekly articles, "White House

Watch," afforded him the luxury of reflection, besides which he is one of the best political reporters in the business. On the late flight back to Washington, Osborne casually asked Ford if they could sit and talk for a minute.

They talked nearly an hour before Air Force Two landed in the small hours of the morning. The Vice President was exhilarated by the applause ringing in his ears, and he really let down his hair. Later, he said he thought the conversation was "off the record"—meaning personal and private. That is not what Osborne thought, nor the way he habitually worked. And when Osborne's summary appeared in print, Ford didn't deny saying it or meaning what he said.

Osborne revealed the Vice President's current thinking as follows: Ford concluded that it was foolish to go on pretending there was no possibility that he might become President by succession and become the Republican nominee in 1976. If he were President, he would keep Henry Kissinger and had so assured the Secretary of State. Kissinger had initiated the exchange and had agreed to stay.

He had high regard for and would keep Rog Morton at Interior and Peter Brennan at Labor. He would like to get George Schultz back as Secretary of the Treasury (which Schultz had just turned over to Bill Simon) or in another high post. He didn't know some of the others intimately but was impressed with Jim Lynn at HUD. He would get rid of James Schlesinger as Secretary of Defense because he didn't understand Congress or know how to deal with it.

As far as Presidential staff was concerned, he'd fire Ron Ziegler (who had publicly rebuked him once too often) and would take Bob Hartmann, Bill Seidman, Phil Buchen and Bob Orben to the White House with him. He'd like to—but doubted if he could—persuade Counsellors Mel Laird and Bryce Harlow to return. He thought General Haig "a great manager" and would ask him to stay. But Osborne wondered "just how Bob Hartmann, William Seidman and General Haig would fit into one White House" and prophetically surmised Haig would return to his Army career.

Next Osborne discoursed on the amount of time Nixon had been spending lately in small talk with Haig, Ziegler and with Ford himself.

"The hours he's had to spend with the President, mostly listening to Mr. Nixon talk about this and that, have on a few occasions driven the Vice President close to distraction," he wrote. "This impression of Ford's impression of Richard Nixon indicates that the President has undergone a change of personality in the past year or so."

When Osborne's clean beat appeared, the Washington press zeroed in on Ford's alleged intention to fire Ziegler and Schlesinger. But the White House Praetorians focused on his disparaging attitude toward the President.

Their old comrade, William Safire, launched a savage counterattack. Safire had recently quit as a Nixon speech writer to become the New York *Times*'s idea of an objective Republican columnist. He misread or twisted Osborne's careful words to conclude that "the new Haldeman at the White House would either be L. William Seidman or Philip Buchen, both cronies from Grand Rapids" and dismissed Ford's confidences as "hardly in good taste . . . while the body of the sitting President is still warm."

I believe that President Nixon understood perfectly that Ford had to put some space between them—as Nixon had done with President Eisenhower in 1960—as a matter of political realism. But the President *was* concerned, even as the impeachment circle closed in on him, about the fruition of his peacemaking plans in the Mideast, with China and the U.S.S.R.

This was reflected in such calculated blurts as Pat Buchanan's during a Public Broadcasting interview with Bill Moyers, LBJ's former press secretary turned pundit, whose footsteps Buchanan would soon follow. UPI reported it thus: "Presidential Assistant Patrick J. Buchanan said Monday one reason President Nixon's impeachment would be 'genuinely harmful' is that Vice President Gerald R. Ford lacks Nixon's foreign policy skills."

Buchanan said Ford would make a conscientious effort to continue Nixon's foreign policies, "but I do not think he has the knowledge or range or capacity that the President currently has to conduct American foreign policy."

Ford sent Pat's subsequent memo of apology to me with a curt "No comment" scrawled on it, eloquent comment enough. He was even more upset by a *Newsweek* report that the President, during a visit by Governor Rockefeller, had leaned back in his Oval Office chair and said sarcastically: "Can you imagine Jerry Ford sitting in this chair?"

The Vice President queried Nixon about this crack, and the President, naturally, denied saying it. But his Praetorian guard adopted it as an article of faith.

While relations between the White House and Vice Presidential staffs grew increasingly embittered, Bill Seidman was finishing up his reorganization proposals. One of his most useful ideas was to create and train an independent network of Vice Presidential advance persons. Seidman, Warren Rustand, and Ford's two regular advancers, Robin Martin and Jim Brock, organized a two-day school in Washington for twenty-one volunteers. They were trained to be the antithesis of the Haldeman-trained alumni, unpushy, unpretentious, polite and penurious.

We even shocked the chauvinists by having advance*women,* such as Mary Fisher of Detroit and Sally Roberts of Denver, who were terrific. Most of Ford's volunteer crew, alas, were eventually squeezed out by the Praetorian professionals at the White House.

At the end of April the spotlight swung away from the Vice President and back to the White House. On the twentieth, a calm and confident President appeared on national television, stacks of bound transcripts behind him, and announced that tomorrow he would release all 1,254 pages of his taped conversations. More than national security had been edited. Expletives had been deleted in vast profusion. Characterizations of individuals, presumably offensive, had been deleted. Americans, however they talk among themselves, don't like their Presidents to talk that way. Doubtless they imagined even fouler words to fill the blank spaces than those Nixon actually used. Despite the permissiveness of the period, Americans were shocked.

And Jerry Ford was shocked. Not because of his strict Christian upbringing (he'd heard Nixon's private language for a quarter of a century). What bothered him was the tone of the President's discussions with his principal subordinates—Haldeman, Ehrlichman, Colson, Dean and others. They were so cheap, so vulgar, so devoid of dignity or respect for the highest office in the land. It was like a gang of dirty little boys plotting to fix a rival gang.

I found the Vice President's reaction puzzling. Like most of us he was disappointed, but Richard Nixon still seemed to be his hero, more sinned against than sinning. Ford was more concerned by the Praetorians' protocol lapses than by the shabby picture of the President that emerged from the transcripts.

"They *never* address him as 'Mr. President,' " he mused. "I *always* do."

When he asked what I thought of it, I said the White House release was a blunder. Pandora's box had been opened and sooner or later everything would fly out. Nobody—not the prosecutors, not the press, not the public—would ever be content with this partial and sanitized script.

118

For the first time I began to wonder why the President was willing to accept such indecent exposure unless it was a desperate gamble to divert attention from something even worse.

Ford managed to avoid comment for a while by claiming he hadn't read the bulky document. But on May 1 he flew to Charlotte, North Carolina, for a fund-raising dinner and was cornered by the press. The first query was:

Q: In your opinion, should the House Judiciary Committee be satisfied with the transcripts released by the President or should the committee have full access to the subpoenaed tapes?

FORD: I think the committee ought to be satisfied with the evidence the President turned over. . . .

Q: Mr. Vice President, have you read any of the transcripts yet?

FORD: I read some on the plane coming down—probably 100 or 200 pages. I hope to read some going back. But I've read a number of the summaries, so I'm reasonably familiar if you'd like to ask any questions.

Q: Do you still think President Nixon is innocent?

FORD: There is no question in my mind that the documentation which has now been made available to the American people . . . proves the President is innocent and exonerates him of any involvement in either the planning of Watergate or any cover-up.

How could Ford have made such a statement? The transcript was not evidence. It may not have proved the President guilty, but by no stretch of law or the English language could it possibly exonerate or prove anyone innocent. And why would the Vice President make *any* statement without even a question in his mind? If he'd forgotten that he was a lawyer, he could at least remember he was a politician.

Ford soon began answering questions about the transcripts by saying that they "do not exactly confer sainthood on anyone concerned." But the issue was getting too sharp to straddle.

Privately, the Vice President took two steps that suggested to me that he was now less than certain of Nixon's innocence and eventual exoneration. He asked Dick Burress, an expert on House procedures, to give him a memo on the exact steps of the impeachment process. And when his legal counsel, Bill Casselman, and I conferred with him about revising his form letter replying to inquiries about impeachment, he struck out a sentence that read "I look forward to the exoneration of the President with respect to all the allegations against him."

But far more significantly, regarding his plans for 1976, he

119

hedged. Previously, he had assured his correspondents that "I do not intend to again be a candidate for any elective office."

Now, he changed "do not intend" to "do not have any present plans to be a candidate."

In part, Ford was disillusioned by Nixon's repeated refusals to take his advice and turn over the contested tapes, if they would clear him. He also was becoming increasingly alarmed that, guilty or not, the protracted conflict between the President and the Congress, the President and the courts was upsetting the Constitutional equilibrium of government and further eroding public confidence in our institutions themselves.

In the short four months since his Atlantic City attack on the impeachment lobby, Jerry Ford had changed his primary purpose. No longer was it to save the President who appointed him but to save the Presidency he might inherit. No longer was it to prevent a Constitutional confrontation (which was already here) but to get the crisis over with as soon as possible.

He never said this to us in so many words. But it became clear in an address he and Milt Friedman worked on for May 9 at Eastern Illinois University, in which he warned of "a crisis in confidence."

Ford called upon "all public officials" to speak frankly and publicly. He said legal processes already begun would settle the guilt or innocence of those involved. "This cleansing process," he declared, "would bring about needed recognition that the law applies to holders of high office as well as to the citizen who elects the office-holder."

Repeating his belief that "truth is the glue that holds government together," the Vice President conceded that truth can be "brutal" and cited the tape transcripts as a painful example. But he warned: "The time has come for persons in political life to avoid the pragmatic dodge which seeks to obscure the truth."

The applauding students knew exactly what he meant. So did the reporters. And so did the White House.

President Nixon called Ford into the Oval Office the next morning and solicitously wondered if he ought not to slow down. He was concerned about the Vice President's health—making so many trips, so many speeches; perhaps he was working too hard and should take it easy for a while. Get a good rest. Not a whisper of criticism of what Ford had said.

Ford ignored Nixon's not so subtle hint. He told the President he was leaving again that afternoon for Buffalo, New York, Texas, Loui-

120

siana and Florida and would be back in Washington for two days before taking off for a week in Hawaii and a stop in Tacoma, Washington.

After that they pretty much went their own ways.* The President flew to the Middle East, then to Moscow. Events were moving inexorably toward impeachment by the House on the one hand and indictment by the Special Prosecutor on the other.

Neither, of course, was satisfied with Alexander Haig's and Fred Buzhardt's doctored transcripts. The President, after personally reviewing some of the subpoenaed tapes, dug in his heels and declared nothing more would be handed over. The Supreme Court would have to resolve the impasse.

Ford made one more try one May 23, when he returned from Hawaii, to persuade the President to change his stonewall strategy. After that he resumed his travels, covering 115,000 miles ostensibly campaigning but actually seeking every possible excuse to stay out of Washington, D.C.

It would be nice to say that Ford's subsequent public utterances stuck consistently to his high-level "crisis in confidence" theme that the truth must prevail. The fact is that he waffled, zigzagged, backslid and contradicted himself.

"After seven months, Ford still walks the tightrope," lamented *Congressional Quarterly.*

Norman Miller in the *Wall Street Journal* wailed: "Someone ought to do Jerry Ford a favor and take his airplane away from him."

But Air Force Two was rarely on the ground. The Vice President stumped for conservative John Rhodes in Arizona one day and for liberal Jack Javits in New York the next. "Ford's Flying Circus" was his last refuge from the time bomb set to explode in Washington.

There was even less time than he thought.

* When the mother of Dr. Martin Luther King died in Atlanta, Georgia, Ford told me he'd like to lead the Administration's delegation to her funeral. Stan Scott, a King family friend and Nixon's Republican bridge to the black community, recommended this to General Haig. Instead, the Praetorians contrived that the Vice President must fly to Loring, Maine, to welcome Nixon home from Moscow at almost the same hour. Mrs. Ford went to the Ebenezer Baptist Church, at her own insistence, and was the most prominent Republican mourner present.

6

THE LONGEST WEEK

★★————————————★★

WEDNESDAY, JULY 31, 1974

We had flown all night from San Diego in "The Flying Submarine"—
a windowless converted tanker that the White House sometimes
fobbed off on the Vice President for long trips instead of the plush 707s
used by Cabinet members. A few hours after our return, Ford was up
at dawn for a breakfast with his Chowder & Marching buddies on
Capitol Hill. Then he dashed back to the EOB for the retirement ceremony of General John C. Meyer, USAF.

By noon Ford was back aboard Air Force Two, headed for a
long-promised golf game with his former sparring partner in the
House, Majority Leader (now Speaker) Tip O'Neill (D–Massachusetts). At the airport in Worcester, Massachusetts, a Democratic town,
a summer weekend crowd of some 500 excited parents and kids—described by the egalitarian New York *Times* as "working class"—
waited to press around the arriving Washington golfer-politicians and
reach for the Vice President's hand.

"It surprised the hell out of me," O'Neill commented. The House
Democratic leader was certain Jerry Ford was fully aware that he
might soon become President. But, he noted sympathetically, the
American public might deem Ford guilty of disloyalty if the Vice President were an outspoken critic of the embattled Chief Executive who
nominated him. "Before we got to the first green," Tip said, "Jerry was
telling me how much he was looking forward to retirement—and all
the golf he wanted to play."

Exactly a week earlier, Ford had expanded on the same note to
Godfrey Sperling in a long interview. When the Washington Bureau
Chief of the *Christian Science Monitor* bluntly asked Ford how he
could resist Republicans' pressure to be their Presidential nominee in
1976, he conceded it would be hard. But he recalled his commitment to
Betty and their children and insisted: "I have no intention of being a
candidate in 1976."

122

Why was Gerald R. Ford deceiving himself, or deceiving the press and public, by this transparent fantasy? When the floodgates opened on the final act of Watergate, how could he still play in minor golf tournaments between laps of a 115,000-mile political stump schedule because he had made "promises" months before?

The truth is he had decided to separate himself from the gathering *Götterdämmerung* physically instead of morally, geographically rather than intellectually. It was a kind of cop-out, but given the circumstances and Ford's desperate internal dilemma it appeared the best of a bundle of bad options.

The Vice President was in an impossible political position. He never fully articulated it, but I knew him well enough to read the sighs and groans and sad headshakes of genuine disbelief with which he received each new revelation of another Nixon setback. I felt for him, but even more I feared he would destroy his future ability to unite and lead the country if he waited too long to take a forthright posture of his own. And I was not alone.

Without any conspiratorial communication among us, I knew that Betty, Phil Buchen and most if not all of Ford's real friends both inside and outside of government were sharing the same anguish. I also knew that our agony was nothing compared to his and that in the end this man was going to do what he alone decided to do. In fact, if pressure from friends became too intense, he might impulsively do exactly what they were urgently warning him not to do—just to prove he could not be bent.

So I did not strenuously resist his instinctive reaction to his steadily growing peril. He doggedly went on doing the very things he had been doing for years—fighting for the Defense budget; racing around the country for Republican causes, large or small; and obliging old friends, not a few of them Democrats.

I had come to learn that one universal instinct of durable legislators—to postpone making an irrevocable decision until the last minute of the last roll call—has considerable practical merit. It is an echo of the old Navy adage: "When in trouble, when in doubt/Run in circles, scream and shout."

The last day of July, then, I put in a fairly easy day at my desk, thankful the boss was busy on a distant golf course. Calls from two job seekers and a man in Michigan with a secret solution to cure inflation I put off until tomorrow, or never. I was getting skittish of press calls and referred most of them to Miltich. I did return one from Bonnie Angelo of *Time*.

Bonnie was a longtime friend who had always been honest with me. She asked about a rumor that the Ford staff was secretly planning for his succession to the Presidency. I told her no; if anything like that was going on I would surely know about it. Bonnie's call upset me. If nobody was doing any preparation, why *weren't* we? We all knew the moment was coming, yet subconsciously we played for more time.

About 5:00 P.M. I took off; the Vice President wasn't due back until late that night. Roberta greeted me cheerily as I let myself in the door.

"Honey, General Haig wants you to call right away."

My first thought was an eerie premonition that the moment had arrived. Haig rarely called me at home.

The general came right on, expressing mock surprise that he had failed to find me at my desk at 5:39 P.M. I explained what he already knew, that Ford was playing golf in Massachusetts and wouldn't be back until late that night. Well, said the general, it wasn't important enough to bother Ford at home, but could he have a few minutes with the Vice President in the morning? Despite his casual tone, it obviously was not something Al wanted to talk about on the phone. I pulled the Ford schedule for Thursday, August 1, from my coat pocket and said sure, we'd work him in sometime before 11:15.

"Fine," Haig said, thanked me and hung up.

Again I had a strong premonition that something big was brewing. Maybe the tension was getting to me. After dinner, though, I was still vaguely upset, and I thought the Vice President should be alerted to Haig's appointment. I called the Ford home in Alexandria and left word for the Vice President to call me when he got home.

About 11:00 P.M. Ford called. He was just about to have a swim and hit the sack, he said, not sounding particularly weary.

"Al Haig wants to see you in the morning," I said. "I put him down for right after our staff meeting. He didn't say what it's about, but I want to talk to you before he does."

"Sure," he said cheerily. "Thanks for taking care of it. I'll see you at eight." We hung up. I took a swim and hit the sack myself. I had a lot of wild dreams, but they were tame compared to the week ahead.

THURSDAY, AUGUST 1, 1974

As soon as I reached the office, I plowed as usual through the Washington *Post* and New York *Times*. They, and the other morning papers I found on my desk, were full of an obvious "trial balloon" story floated by Pat Buchanan, President Nixon's longtime speech writer and conservative confidant. The gist of it was that Nixon and his advisers were now seriously considering a sharp shift in strategy. They believed the House was lost. If President Nixon himself requested a quick *pro forma* vote in the House, he would avoid a bitter debate that might further weaken his public support and damage his last-ditch stand in a Senate trial. It was the first official admission by the White House that impeachment was inevitable. At least it *seemed* official.

Buchanan, more than Ziegler, had some credibility left. In his youth an editorial writer for the St. Louis *Globe-Democrat*, he was among the longest in Nixon's service of the senior Praetorians. Passionate loyalist to the bitter end, Buchanan did not wholly share the blanket loathing of all "press people" that marked the Haldeman cult of true believers. For their part, the White House watchers could not conceive of Buchanan planting such a momentous story without the President's express approval.

Buchanan himself was not keen about shortcutting the procedure to the Senate, but he did believe the President was considering it. Unfortunately he didn't know this firsthand but from Haig via Timmons, who considered it the only hope remaining. It was common talk on the Hill, and Hugh Scott and John Rhodes had discussed it between themselves. If the President could be persuaded to ask for a quick House vote, it certainly would take off the hook a lot of Republicans seeking re-election in another three months.

I wondered whether, after all, this was what Haig wanted to talk about. The Vice President hadn't ventured any opinion of it to me, although he was a seasoned vote-counter. For weeks I had been urging him to issue a formal statement firmly cutting off all public comments on the impeachment issue, but he kept saying the time was not right. He still saw himself, I realized, as an honest broker between the President and the Congress whose good offices might be needed.

As Ford strode into his cavernous office at 8:00 A.M. and plunked his bulging briefcase on the table beside his desk, I was waiting to pounce through the back door. I knew he'd already devoured several papers, but I mentioned Buchanan's breakfast with Godfrey Sperling's group. Yes, he'd read it. Then I reminded the Vice President about Haig's appointment, which didn't show on the printed schedule.

"I don't know what's on Haig's mind," I said, "but I think this time you ought to have somebody with you—me or Marsh or both of us. I just think you might want to have a witness to who said what."

125

PALACE POLITICS

"O.K., you sit in," he agreed.

It was time for him to chair the regular meeting of the "Action Group," which consisted of Marsh, Seidman, Burress, Mote and me and sometimes other senior aides.

He walked a few paces through a connecting hall to the Vice President's conference room. They rose, and he went through the usual protest. Ford took his place at the head of the table, and I sat in my usual seat to his right.

Discussion that morning centered on two upcoming trips, one a foray into the deep South, ending in New Orleans, on which Ford would leave day after tomorrow and return August 5. Then with fewer than three days back in Washington, he would head back to California for a big fund-raising telethon being put on by the Republican National Committee. There were twelve other appearances. Perpetual motion had become our way of life. I was looking forward to sneaking off for a few hours with my father, who was eighty-five and living alone in Beverly Hills.

General Haig was a little late. It wasn't like him but a forgivable flaw for anyone who works beside a buzzer connected to the President's desk.*

When Haig arrived, the Vice President waved him to a seat on the sofa. Haig obviously hadn't been getting much sleep for a long time, and the strain was evident. When it became obvious that I was not going to leave, Haig began guardedly. There had been a new development. He had just been told about it himself, and it was bad.

One of the tapes that would have to be turned over to Judge Sirica—he hadn't listened to it himself but had been briefed by Nixon's lawyer, James St. Clair—apparently contained conversations very damaging to the President's whole defense. Since the Vice President had been outspoken in maintaining the President's innocence of any impeachable offense, Haig felt he should forewarn him that a bad surprise was coming.

How bad? the Vice President asked. And when would it break?

---

* The President's desk phone enables him to summon, or speak directly to, five stations—his secretary-receptionist, the Navy steward who served coffee, etc., from a tiny galley off the Oval Office, and three others. Throughout the Ford Presidency, "RTH" was on one of these buttons, the initials of Kissinger-Scowcroft on one and Haig-Rumsfeld-Cheney on another. As the ultimate in status symbolism, this phone arrangement was duplicated even in the President's private toilet.

126

Haig reiterated he had not heard the tape himself. But the lawyers were very concerned. Sirica had to be given the tape under the Supreme Court's order, and after that it would be only a matter of time before it would reach the House Judiciary Committee and the press. If what he had been told was correct, Haig said, the new evidence would reduce to virtually zero whatever chance there was of defeating impeachment in the House.

And the Senate?

It would be very, very rough going. It wouldn't just be a storm that would blow over like the deleted expletives on the earlier tapes. It was certainly going to be very damaging.

Haig was being obviously unspecific; it was equally obvious that he wished I would go away.*

There was a more immediate problem, Haig continued. The new evidence directly contradicted what St. Clair had told the court and the Judiciary Committee. His professional reputation was at stake, and St. Clair had no time to lose to convince Sirica and the Congress that he had misled them in good faith. But how could he do this without compromising his client, the President?

The Vice President quickly saw that more than St. Clair's credibility was at stake. Instinctively, he thought as a Congressman would. He had, in fact, helped to arrange meetings between Dean Burch, a Nixon Counsellor, St. Clair and some of his former House colleagues. He was keenly aware of how far some Republican members had stuck their necks out in defense of Nixon during the impeachment debate. They were on record, their own political careers were at stake in November, and how many could survive another setback?

"How is the President holding up?" the Vice President asked Haig. He didn't, I remember noticing uneasily, directly ask what was the President's reaction to the tape discovery or even whether Haig's fears had been disclosed to Nixon. Was the general, I wondered, ever so subtly testing the Vice President's loyalty—or was he preparing to jump ship and sign on with the next President-to-be?

President Nixon's mood was constantly changing, Haig said. One minute he was all for fighting it out, right down to the last Senate vote. Then he would appear strangely indifferent, concentrating on other

* A version of this meeting is related by Woodward and Bernstein in *The Final Days*. There were only three of us present. The Vice President and I could not have told the story to them, since it is hardly flattering to either of us. Woodward and Bernstein are extremely generous to the general.

127

business as if the impeachment matter were all a problem for his lawyers. Nixon's staff and his family were pulling him this way and that, the general related. Some of the time Haig had to try to carry out his wishes without being certain what his wishes really were. But the President had enormous reserves of stamina and prided himself on being at his best under pressure.

The Vice President told Haig that, as the President well knew, he would always be available if the President wanted to talk to him. In their recent meetings, he assured Haig, the President had appeared confident and in good spirits. He said that maybe he could think of some way to solve St. Clair's dilemma with the House Members, but not just offhand. He asked Haig to keep him informed of developments, especially since he would be doing a lot of traveling. Now, he said, he had to go up to Capitol Hill for some Congressional appointments.

Haig left. Jack Marsh and I rode up to the Senate office with the Vice President in his limousine. I was waiting for a cue from Ford, as I fully expected him to fill Jack in on Haig's revelations. He valued Jack's judgment and also knew how important it was to Jack's good relations on the Hill for Marsh not to be taken by surprise. But Ford said nothing.

The big Lincoln turned into the carriage-wide arch under the steps on the Senate wing, and we scrambled out and after the Vice President. He made his way through friendly tourists to his office off the Senate lobby.

Spoff Canfield had hardly closed the door behind us when a call from the White House came through. Marsh and I sat mute during a one-sided conversation in which the Vice President's part was a series of "uh-huhs." At the conclusion of the call Ford told us it was General Haig. He wanted to see him again that afternoon and strictly alone.

I started to protest. "Never mind. I'll fill you in," the Vice President said firmly.

Marsh and I exchanged helpless glances and went on about our business. Jack was as worried as I was that the Vice President might get too deeply into the White House quagmire. We had talked about it privately and without formalizing it had reached a tacit understanding that one or the other of us would try to be with him wherever he traveled and whenever he met with anyone who might carry away an unguarded comment. Most of the time Ford went along, but not always. A veteran politician's proclivity for one-on-one conversations is not easily shed.

128

I had long since learned that there is a certain point beyond which you don't press Gerald R. Ford about what is best for him. The storm warning was a visible tightening of the facial muscles, often accompanied by elaborate pipe-lighting or some physical action as he inwardly reined in his temper, over which he had developed such control that many people thought he had none. When that signal flashed, you just relaxed and let him go ahead and do it *his* way.

When Haig arrived at the EOB for his 3:30 appointment, I asked Joann to let me know the minute the general left. Exactly what was said at the fateful *tête-à-tête* may never be known. We had no hidden tapes or microphones. The only authoritative account was given by President Ford in his personal testimony before the Hungate subcommittee two and a half months later. Haig has never been publicly quoted by name, to the best of my knowledge.

The trouble future historians will have is that the committee reached no collective conclusion. Incredibly, it never summoned Haig to the witness stand. Its inquiry left the question "Was there a deal?" essentially unanswered—a time bomb that ticked silently away throughout the 1976 election campaign and continues to divide the defenders and detractors of the Ford Presidency.

One curiously forgotten fact is that there certainly was no secret about the meeting at the time. When newsmen picked up rumors that Haig had been closeted with the Vice President, Paul Miltich was authorized to say the general had briefed the Vice President on developments in the impeachment process and had given him the latest White House assessment of Nixon's defense strategy.

Among the broad spectrum of the post-pardon commentators on this crucial Ford–Haig discussion there is a curious consistency to a strange assumption: that Gerald Ford, the certified honest man, must have had ulterior motives but that Alexander Haig, Nixon's closest collaborator, acted only from purest patriotism.

Among the questions the committee never asked: Why was Haig so insistent on seeing him alone?

Who planted the seed of a "deal" in the first place—and why?

Was Jerry Ford deliberately drawn into a compromising situation which, hanging over his head, crippled his Presidency even before it began, clouded his subsequent pardon decision and helped ensure a Democratic comeback in 1976? To how many others did Haig "confide" his version of the meeting after it occurred? I cannot answer these questions, but I wonder why nobody has ever asked them aloud.

PALACE POLITICS

I was not present, thanks to Haig, and can only relate what happened during the next twenty-four hours.

Haig stayed for what seemed an eternity. The record later showed it was about forty-five minutes. Finally the direct line on my desk rang and Ford told me to come on in. He was leaning back in his chair, staring up at the iron ceiling molding. His face was grim. He looked as if a two-hundred-pound blocker had just hit him in the stomach.

"Bob," he began, "what I am going to tell you must not go any farther than this room."

(He rarely bothered with this prelude. He knew I could, and would, keep his secrets well.)

Haig had now read a transcript of the June 23 tape, and it turned out to be even worse than he thought. It was devastating to President Nixon's defense, proving that he knew about the cover-up almost from the start. He had misled the American people, his own family, his own lawyers, his own Vice President. When the tape was turned over to Judge Sirica, Nixon would be finished—in the House, in the Senate, in the history books. It was all over.

I asked, "What happens next?"

The obvious answer was that Gerald R. Ford was going to be President sooner rather than later. But he didn't say that. He was still thinking in terms of Nixon's next move, not his own.

Haig wasn't sure what the President would do, but he reviewed the rapidly dwindling number of options left. One, Nixon could declare himself incapacitated under the Twenty-fifth Amendment and turn things over to the Vice President as Acting President until the disability ended with his acquittal or removal by conviction in the Senate. Though nothing like this was contemplated by the framers of the Twenty-fifth Amendment, the Constitutional language was certainly broad enough to cover it. I had researched the history and intent of that amendment exhaustively in preparation for the Vice Presidential confirmation hearings and immediately spotted the defect in that option.

"I hope you nipped that one in the bud," I said. "Nothing in the Twenty-fifth Amendment would prevent the President from taking back his office any day of the week he felt like it. All he'd have to do is declare that his disability, whatever it was, no longer existed—and to prevent him from recovering all his Presidential powers you, the Vice President, would have to take the lead in deposing him."

The Vice President indicated that the Twenty-fifth Amendment route wasn't a really serious alternative. And then, he said, Haig had talked about the possibility of Nixon pardoning himself before resigning, which the lawyers thought he had the power to do, or of resigning and then being pardoned.

"Jesus!" I said aloud. To myself: So that's the pitch Haig wouldn't make with me present! Aloud again: "What did you tell him?"

"I didn't tell him anything. I told him I needed time to think about it."

"You what?" I fairly shouted.

It was almost the worst answer Haig could have taken back to the White House. Far from telling nothing, Ford had told Haig that he was at least willing to entertain the idea—probably all Haig and Nixon wanted to know.

Well, he wanted to talk with Betty and a few close friends. The trouble was, who could you talk to about something so sensitive? What did I think?

"I think you should have taken Haig by the scruff of the neck and the seat of the pants and thrown him the hell out of your office," I stormed. "And then you should have called an immediate press conference and told the world why."

It was as if he hadn't heard a word of my outburst. I could see that he had not yet grasped the monstrous impropriety of Haig's even mentioning the word "pardon" in his presence. Especially alone, at Haig's insistence. Clearly, Ford was still in a state of shock.

So was I. I knew whatever damage had been done was irreversible, but maybe I was unduly suspicious. I, too, wanted time to think and to check my judgment with others. We were playing with political dynamite.

I said I would give careful thought about whom it might be safe to take into his confidence. The fewer the better, I thought. I was fairly certain Betty's intuition would sense the danger and turn him off Haig more effectively than I had. But, as a fallback reinforcement, I also suggested Jack Marsh.

Marsh had a much higher opinion of Haig than I did, but Jack's loyalty to the Vice President was primary. Ford muttered his agreement but looked at his watch and said not right now; he was already late for his next appointment.

He was to meet Betty for an inspection tour of the Admiral's House, the Victorian mansion atop the Naval Observatory hill which for generations had been the prized perquisite of successive Chiefs of

131

PALACE POLITICS

Naval Operations and which was in the process of being converted to the official residence of the Vice President.

I went back to my own office, telling Joann and Gail I didn't want to be disturbed except in the gravest emergency. The calls had piled up on my desk, but I decided it was no time to answer them. I was under a vow of secrecy.

I desperately needed to talk to somebody. If the Vice President were even contemplating a prior pledge to pardon Nixon, he would have to be dissuaded—as quickly as possible. I knew from experience that changing Gerald Ford's mind was not easy. I doubted that I could do it single-handedly; I needed help. I jotted down a short list of his closest political friends, then crossed off those who might not be able to keep such a matter strictly to themselves. I was left with Betty, Marsh, Bryce Harlow and one or two more.

I asked Jack Marsh to drop over to my office when it was convenient. He came right over. We shared a lot of problems; such parleys were not unusual.

"Jack," I began, "you know that Al Haig was in there alone with him half the afternoon."

He nodded. As he remembers, I looked like death warmed over.

"I can't tell you what went on or even hint at it, but I am scared witless he might make a terrible mistake. I made him promise me he would tell you, himself, what he just told me—before he does anything. That's all I can say, except he'll be coming back here, so don't go away."

Marsh laughed. Neither of us left very often before 8:00 or 9:00 P.M.

We went on talking about other things, and before long I heard my phone buzz. Gail said, "The Vice President just got back."

"Wait here," I told Jack. I rushed into Ford's office through the back door. He was in the bathroom, the only private john on that floor of the EOB. "It's me," I called through the door.

"I'm going to take a shower," he said. "Something important?"

"You wanted to talk to Jack Marsh, and I want to talk to you."

"I haven't got much time," he said in a tone I'd heard before. It meant this wasn't a very good time to engage him in argument. But I had to strike, even if the iron wasn't very malleable.

"We won't take long," I said.

"O.K.," he said, "I'll call you."

I rejoined Jack and he agreed to stand by. When the Vice President summoned me, he was adjusting his black tie. "Boss," I began, "you just can't get involved with this thing in any way. Whatever the President decides, whatever Haig and his lawyers tell him, the Vice President must not have any part of it. And you ought not even be thinking about pardons. Nobody has any power to pardon anybody except the President, and you're not President yet."

"Al says it could happen within a week," he said almost sadly. "Maybe this weekend—maybe not for some time, but I should be ready."

Migod! I said to myself. He still doesn't see the danger. He snapped his briefcase shut and was about to start for the door.

"I know you're rushed, but I've been waiting all day to say this: You are going to be President. But you won't be able to run the country if you have anything at all to do with the way Nixon leaves office. You can't advocate resignation any more than you can advocate impeachment. Somebody else has to push him over the cliff, or he has to jump himself.

"You didn't ask to be Vice President; you can't let anybody ever say you lifted one finger to make yourself President, or the job won't be worth having. I think this is terribly important."

I waited for his reaction.

"Well, I'm going to sleep on it. I want to talk to Betty. And I told Al to send St. Clair over first thing in the morning," he said impatiently. "I'll see you at nine." He started for the door. Then, turning with his old smile, he added with some feeling, "Thanks, Bob. I'll talk to Jack then, too."

He was gone. I called Jack, told the girls to go home and closed up shop.

"Something is bothering you," Roberta said almost as soon as I'd kissed her hello. "Bad day?"

"No worse than usual," I lied.

FRIDAY, AUGUST 2, 1974

James St. Clair, President Nixon's lawyer, arrived at the Executive Office Building about the same time I did and was closeted with Ford shortly after 8:00 A.M. There was nothing particularly unusual about his visiting the Vice President; he and Dean Burch had been briefing Ford about impeachment developments for some time. I assumed that St. Clair was explaining more precisely what was on the damning tape and its legal consequences. But the Vice President's subsequent account of the meeting, a single paragraph in his Hungate subcommittee statement, reveals a couple of interesting questions that were on Ford's mind that morning.

"Shortly after eight o'clock," he recalled, "James St. Clair came to my office. Although he did not spell out in detail the new evidence, there was no question in my mind that he considered these revelations to be so damaging that impeachment in the House was a certainty and conviction in the Senate a high probability. When I asked Mr. St. Clair if he knew of any other new and damaging evidence besides that on the June 23, 1972, tape, he said 'No.' When I pointed out to him the various options mentioned to me by General Haig, he told me *he* had not been the source of any opinion about Presidential pardon power." (Emphasis mine.) Instantly sensitive to the impropriety of such a discussion, St. Clair quickly took himself professionally out of being party to it.

Then who *was* the source of Haig's "understanding from a White House lawyer that a President did have authority to grant a pardon even before any criminal action had been taken against an individual?" Was it Fred Buzhardt, the other White House lawyer then privy to the self-incriminating taped evidence against Richard Nixon? It would seem so.

Yet there was another individual in the White House who was a lawyer—Richard Nixon himself. A damn smart lawyer, too. In his extremis, facing the Constitutional waiver of double jeopardy for Federal officials impeached and convicted, watching his closest friends and factotums facing long felony sentences, can anyone imagine that Richard Nixon had not thoroughly familiarized himself with the pardoning power of the Presidency?

Why did Haig, in the process of imparting the most dire secret of the Nixon White House to the Vice President, fail to identify his legal source by name? Why did St. Clair, if he knew, fail to identify the "White House lawyer" beyond saying he was not the one? Did both these men, sharing with the President knowledge that was to bring him to resignation, rush over to brief the Vice President on their own, without the approval of their Commander-in-Chief and client? It is unthinkable.

As soon as St. Clair left, Marsh and I went into Ford's office together. It was about 9:00 A.M. Much of the previous day's tension had gone. The Vice President motioned for us to sit down and calmly began to recite, for Jack, what Haig had revealed in his two visits. Marsh listened without comment. Ford went on to something that was news to me as well.

Betty and I talked it over last night, he began. We felt we were ready. This just has to stop; it's tearing the country to pieces. I decided to go ahead and get it over with, so I called Al Haig and told him they should do whatever they decided to do; it was all right with me.

I couldn't believe my ears. Ford had promised me he'd talk to Marsh before he did anything. But now he'd telephoned Haig* in the middle of the night, and God knows what they'd said to make matters worse. Jack was as stunned as I—hearing the whole story for the first time. We both tried to elicit exactly what words passed between Ford and Haig, but it was never clear. He just wanted to get it all over with.

Finally Jack, in his gentle Virginia way, asked flatly what had been said about pardons in his midnight talk with Haig. Well, nothing that Ford could recall. But then mightn't Haig conclude, on the basis of their earlier talk, that a future pardon was still a viable option as an inducement to get President Nixon to resign? Of course not, Ford snapped, Haig knew better than that. There was no commitment, just conversation—and in strict confidence.

We both lit into him like Dutch uncles. It didn't matter how confidential it was; it was a matter of public confidence. There must be no appearance of any improper conduct on his part. The Presidency was in panic. The rats were swarming all over the ship. Haig had talked with him on the subject of pardons. He had talked with St. Clair about pardons. They would talk to others. Certainly they would tell the President. The White House was a leaky sieve. That midnight phone call to Haig went through the switchboard and was logged. How would he ever explain it?

---

* In his autobiography, *A Time to Heal*, Ford maintains that after talking with Betty, "as we prepared to go upstairs, I received a phone call from Haig. 'Nothing has changed,' he said, 'the situation is as fluid as ever.' Well, I replied, I've talked with Betty, and we're prepared, but we can't get involved in the White House decision-making process. 'I understand,' he [Haig] said. 'I'll be in touch with you tomorrow.' It was almost one-thirty and time to go to bed." Memories are fallible, but I know what most upset me was the fact that Ford had called Haig. Why would Haig telephone the Vice President at 1:30 A.M. just to say nothing had changed? And why, if Ford informed Haig that night that "we can't get involved," did he have to go through it all over again the next day for Harlow, Marsh and me? I will have to stand by my own vivid recollections.

135

PALACE POLITICS

The Vice President was a little shaken by our vehemence. What did we want him to do?

I looked at Jack, and he looked at me. He was asking us how to unmake an omelet. I cannot recall who spoke first, but the gist of it was this: You have got to talk to the President, hopefully before anyone else does, and tell him that you can't have any part in whatever he decides; you cannot contribute any advice or recommendations to Haig or others on his staff, and you do not intend to make any more public statements on the matter.

He would think it over, the Vice President said, and see us later.

Back in my office, Jack said, "Bob, we're losing this argument. I tried my best but . . ."

"We *can't* lose it. We've got to turn him around. This thing is a time bomb ticking away, and he must defuse it—right now. Why did he have to make that phone call? He promised me he'd talk to you first."

Jack shrugged. "Nobody likes their staff ganging up on them. Maybe we need reinforcements. Who else will he listen to? You know his friends a lot better than I do."

I showed him my list. "I think our best bet is Bryce. But we're sworn to silence. I'll have to ask the Vice President first. Maybe we could all have lunch."

At my next chance, I sought permission to bring Bryce over and get his opinion. Sure, the Vice President said, he'd be happy to see him. I immediately phoned Harlow, who already had a luncheon engagement.

"Can you come over right after lunch, then?" I asked. "It's important."

Bryce agreed. When he arrived, Jack and I poured out our concern. It was midafternoon before the Vice President called for us.

After greeting Bryce and thanking him for coming over, he said that Bob and Jack felt he had some kind of a problem and then rehearsed his version of the past thirty-two hours. "What do you think, Bryce?" the Vice President asked.

"Well, Mr. Vice President," Bryce began, "the thing is that I cannot for a moment believe that all this was Al Haig's own idea or that the matters he discussed originated with 'the White House staff.' It is inconceivable that he was not carrying out a mission for the President, with precise instructions, and that it is the President who wants to hear your recommendations and test your reaction to the pardon question.

136

"But the President knows that he must be able to swear under oath that he never discussed this with you and that you must be able to swear that you never discussed it with him. Therefore, he sends Haig, and therefore I would not advise you to try to clarify the matter with the President himself. That would only make matters worse, if that's possible.

"Bob and Jack are absolutely right, however, that there is grave danger here of compromising your future independence, because there is bound to be suspicion and bitterness when you take the place of the man who nominated you. You are going to be President for nearly three and hopefully seven years. Whether Nixon resigns or is convicted, the probability is that the question of a pardon will come before you sometime before you leave office.

"There must not be any cause for anyone to cry 'deal' if you have to make that decision, or any mystery about your position now that you know what Haig and St. Clair have told you. But the most urgent thing, Mr. Vice President, is to tell Al Haig, straight out and unequivocally, that whatever discussions you and he had yesterday and last night were purely hypothetical and conversational, that you will in no manner, affirmatively or negatively, advise him or the President as to his future course, and nothing you may have said is to be represented to the President, or to anyone else, to the contrary."

Harlow's soliloquy ran much longer than the above, and he warmed to his subject as he went. The Vice President sat back with his hands clasped in front of his lips, impassively, as he did when concentrating.

All right, he announced, reaching for the phone, I'll call Haig right now.

The general was with the President. He would call back.

The three of us made no move to leave. This time Gerald Ford was going to have his own witnesses. When Haig returned the Vice President's call, none of us moved to eavesdrop on the extensions, nor did he signal us to do so. We heard him tell Haig that he wanted to be doubly certain there was no misunderstanding; that he had no intention of recommending whether President Nixon should or should not resign and that nothing he and Haig had talked about should be given any consideration whatsoever, by Haig or by the President, as indicating any intent or inclination on the part of the Vice President to involve himself in the President's ultimate decision.

He hung up and told us, "Al agrees."

PALACE POLITICS

We had decided not to stir up St. Clair by further explanations; after all, he had been summoned and they had merely conversed about a range of legal technicalities. The Vice President began loading his briefcase again; he and Betty were going out to dinner with David Kennerly, the Time-Life photographer who had been covering some of our travels.* Bryce, Jack and I returned to my office.

"Whew, that was close!" we said, almost in harmony.

"Joann," I called, "as soon as the Vice President leaves, swipe some of his ice cubes."

We toasted a good day's work. We thought that was the end of it.

SATURDAY, AUGUST 3, 1974

Never before in American Constitutional history had a Vice President held it in his power to elevate himself to the Presidency by speaking one declarative sentence: "The President is guilty." Indeed, this Vice President could accomplish almost the same result simply by remaining silent when asked, "Is the President guilty?" But Ford still could not bring himself to do or say anything that might contribute to the President's fall. Quite simply, Richard Nixon had been his friend for twenty-five years. And Jerry Ford was no Judas.

Ford was scheduled to leave Washington on Saturday morning on a swing through Mississippi and Louisiana. It was primarily designed to boost the re-election campaigns of three Southern Republican freshmen in the House, Thad Cochran, Trent Lott and Dave Treen. All three had been staunch defenders of President Nixon. Press conferences had been scheduled at almost every stop, and the Vice President was certain to be asked, once again, his views on Nixon's guilt or innocence.

In the light of our new knowledge of how close Nixon's day of reckoning had come, it was decided that I would accompany the Vice President and Marsh would stay behind and keep an eye on the White House and Camp David, where it was rumored Nixon was going to hole up with his speech writers. We would just have to wait and see what happened.

During the first leg of the flight I showed the Vice President the

---

* Ford got a kick out of Kennerly's brashness and braggadocio. Perhaps Dave replayed for him the carefree bachelor Jerry Ford once was or the Peck's bad boy he could never be.

draft Marsh and I had worked on, the gist of which was that he had nothing to add on the question of impeachment. If there were any significant change in his opinions or the basis for them, he would let the newsmen know.

"But there *has* been a change," he observed. "I can't say that now."

"I know," I said. "But you're going to get asked at the first opportunity they have. So what *are* you going to say?"

"I can't let Trent Lott and the others down," he said. "I'll try not to talk about anything but the President's efforts for peace—you can't fault him there. Maybe they won't ask. Nixon is very popular down here."

I said we couldn't be that lucky. Well, he'd have to play it by ear; maybe he might have to just go on saying what he'd been saying for a few more days. It couldn't do anyone much harm. But it did. I wish I had seen that as clearly then as I do now.

Shortly after we touched down at the Golden Triangle Regional Airport at Starkville, Mississippi, our advance man, Elliot Serrafin, located me. "There's an urgent long-distance call for the Vice President," Serrafin stage-whispered over the noise of the crowd, "from Senator Griffin in Michigan." He guided me to a nearby hangar where there was a small office and a telephone.

Bob Griffin was one of a dozen people in Washington from whom the Vice President or I would take a phone call no matter how busy we might be. Like Ford, he had been a Nixon defender as the impeachment storm darkened the Republican horizon. When Bob Griffin tried to reach Jerry Ford on a Saturday morning in Mississippi, I knew he had something to say.

I got through to him right away, using my home credit card rather than the White House switchboard. I told Bob the boss was on the platform speaking.

"Tell Jerry that I have just sent a personal letter to the President suggesting that he should resign," Griffin told me. "I won't make it public until Nixon's had a chance to read it, but I may release the gist of it before you all get back here Monday. I thought Jerry ought to know. . . ."

I said I would have the Vice President call him on a secure phone as soon as possible, but I doubted if we could do it before the next stop. The Senator said he was moving around in Michigan himself and gave me some telephone numbers. Usually he was not so guarded, but I could tell he knew something he didn't want to say. (Later we learned that Haig had called Griffin on Friday afternoon, before he left for Michigan, to warn him of the upcoming *coup de grâce*.)

On the way to our next stop, Jackson, I quickly told Ford about Griffin's call.

"Griffin's letter comes pretty close to being an ultimatum," I said, "and all the time we've been reading that the end would come when Barry Goldwater decided to pull the rug."

The Vice President smiled. Bob wasn't what you'd call a hip-shooter, he observed, but when he moved he meant business.

"We are going to have to decide fast what you're going to say next," I said.

He thought for a moment, then said, "If Bob is telling the President—and the public—what he intends to do if it comes to trial by the Senate, why can't I do the same? What I intend to do is *nothing*. The Constitution expressly says that the Vice President has nothing to do with an impeachment trial of a President; he is deprived of his presiding role and the Chief Justice takes over. Why don't you see if you can work something out along those lines—but first, let's talk to Bob."

In Jackson, where Ford would be campaigning for Representative Thad Cochran, the Congressman greeted us at the airport and rode with the Vice President into town. Jackson was strong Nixon territory, and it might well be the end of Cochran's short Congressional career to abandon the President, but he was troubled by the evidence—though he had no notion how much more was soon to come.

The Vice President didn't disclose anything but patted Cochran's shoulder in encouragement and said with a Delphic smile, "Don't worry too much over it; you may not ever have to cast that vote."

Political crowds in the South are always noisily friendly in their welcome, even to Republicans. Hospitality is part of their tradition. But for a humid noon day in Mississippi, the people of Jackson were exceptionally eager to see a Michigan Vice President, to reach out and shake his hand and murmur a few words like "We're praying for you, Jerry!" When we reached the Hilton suite Cochran excused himself. Ford's Army aide, Colonel Walker, got Senator Griffin on the phone, and the Vice President motioned for me to stay and listen.

As usual, I got only one end of the conversation, but Griffin began reading his letter to President Nixon, which was being typed about that moment. Ford was noncommittal, saying only that Bob had to do what he thought was right.

Ford did ask how soon the Senator expected to make his letter public, and Griffin replied that he would wait until it had time to reach the President. On Monday, he would pass out copies to his colleagues at a meeting of the Senate Rules Committee considering trial procedure. Griffin implored Ford not to get any farther out on the limb in defending the President.

I was not sure when Griffin told Ford of his call from Haig, but Ford—at least in this conversation—did not disclose to Griffin what Haig had told him.*

It was time to go to the VIP reception and luncheon, but I stayed behind in the suite, grabbed a sandwich and a cup of coffee, put in a call to Marsh and told him he'd be getting a copy of Griffin's letter. I asked Jack to let me know immediately if the Griffin story leaked out and said that I was about to unhitch my portable typewriter and try another statement. I outlined the new tack we proposed. Marsh liked it and wished me luck.

For just such emergencies, I always carried a World Almanac in my briefcase when we traveled. It is the second most useful book in the world, and thanks to the Gideons, you can usually find the other one. (Since LBJ's delay in Dallas, a Bible is always aboard Air Force One and Two as well.)

This was surely a Constitutional crisis, so we would start with the Constitution. I ran over the sections about impeachment.

I went on to review the single precedent of a Presidential impeachment, in the seething wake of the Civil War, which "failed by a single vote of a courageous Senator at the cost of his own political future." (Here my memory relied on John F. Kennedy's *Profiles in Courage.*) Then to the real issue.

"I have thereby concluded that, because as a party of interest the Vice President should have nothing to do with a Presidential impeachment, because the Constitution specifically removes him from the presiding officer's chair during the Senate trial and turns it over to

---

* In *The Final Days* Woodward and Bernstein, obviously drawing on both Haig and Griffin as sources, assert that when the Senator's letter reached President Nixon (by some route other than Haig) he summoned the general in a furious rage and denounced cowardly and weakhearted legislators who deserted him in extremis. Woodward and Bernstein state flatly that "Haig did not mention his call to Griffin the day before . . . [but] to complete his cover, Haig told Buzhardt that *it was probably Ford who had tipped his old friend Griffin.*" (Emphasis mine.)

the Chief Justice, I should now take myself completely out of the whole impeachment debate and keep my own counsel."

I thought the ending was a little weak. There should be a more ringing conclusion, but the luncheon was breaking up and the advance man, Roger Whyte, was hurrying me along to the motorcade. This would have to do.

Air Force Two's next stop was Hattiesburg, Mississippi—a thirty-five-minute hop. This was Representative Trent Lott's district. Lott was on the Judiciary Committee and was one of the President's last-ditch defenders.

As soon as the Vice President was buckled into his seat, I thrust my draft statement at him. He read it carefully. Handing it back to me, he said, "You're on the right track, but this is way too long and there's too much history. And I don't want to sound like I'm shutting myself up from *ever* saying anything. The time might come when I have something important to say."

Most politicians like having it both ways if they can, and he was right. He shouldn't take any *absolute* vow of silence.

"You know they're going to ask you at the press conference," I said. "They are already asking me why you have hardly mentioned Nixon all day."

The Vice President frowned as he relit his pipe. Then he said, with some finality: "I'll handle it, Bob. Maybe they'll get tired of trying. Anyway, an important statement like this should be issued in Washington when we get back. And we have to think of Trent Lott. See if you can shorten it up and give it more punch."

The crowd awaiting in Hattiesburg was the biggest and most enthusiastic yet. Next there was the press conference in the Pine Belt Airport terminal.

As we moved through the throng, one sign struck my eye: "Ford Support the President for Us." The Vice President must have seen it too.

"Does the Vice President now think Nixon will be impeached?" was almost the first question.

Ford conceded that "the situation has eroded to the point that it is possible. I suspect the odds are such that unless there is some change, he will be."

Did the Vice President still consider Nixon not guilty? Would he support the move by Representative Paul Findley (R–Illinois) and others to have the House vote to censure the President rather than take the extreme step of seeking to remove him from office?

142

"If I had my druthers, I'd rather have the House vote the facts as I see them and vote for acquittal," Ford replied. I shuddered. He hadn't changed his line a bit, only his estimate of the odds.

The next questioner went for the clincher.

"Mr. Vice President, we have noticed that you have scarcely mentioned President Nixon in three speeches all across Mississippi today, whereas in the past you have vigorously defended his innocence. We have also heard reports that various Republican leaders and some of your own staff have been urging you to soft-pedal your support of the President. Is this a deliberate change of tactics on your part?"

"In the limited time I have in these engagements," the Vice President answered, "I believe it is vitally important to speak on affirmative matters, as I have done today. However, I don't want anybody to get the wrong impression. My views today are just as strong as they were two days ago. I still believe the President is innocent of any impeachable offense."

I groaned silently. His views *must* be different.

He went on to make matters worse by signaling what we had been confidentially planning: The time might come, he said, when he would have to refuse further impeachment comment, but that time hadn't come yet. Well, what was done was done. On to New Orleans, a city one usually approaches with a glow of anticipated pleasure. Saturday night on Bourbon Street; Sunday brunch at Brennan's. But first there was another damned press conference.

Fortunately, the Vice President got through the New Orleans encounter with the press no worse than he left Hattiesburg. Our traveling Washington reporters were already past their Sunday-morning deadlines.

SUNDAY, AUGUST 4, 1974

I was up half the night reworking the luckless "I'm shutting up" statement. At eleven I dragged myself out of bed to have breakfast at Brennan's with Louisiana State Chairman Jim Boyce. Later I had a visit with Lindy Boggs while Ford was playing golf.

That Sunday afternoon was like being on the moon. We had no idea what was going on at Camp David; our EOB office was tightly closed; the Vice President watched television and I worried over his statement in my room next door.

Treen had arranged a small dinner that night at the Pontchartrain by the lake. The food was superb and there was no political hoopla; it was a thoughtful gesture that we appreciated.

MONDAY, AUGUST 5, 1974

One major nonpolitical event remained on the Southern agenda, a morning address by the Vice President to the national convention of the Disabled American Veterans at the New Orleans Marriott.

The DAV delegates gave Ford a rousing ovation. As it subsided, National Commander John Soave, a Michigander, grabbed the microphone for a monumental Freudian slip.

"Thank you, Mr. President!"

The veterans roared and Ford looked puzzled. Soave quickly recovered with a quip that he didn't have any inside information. Meanwhile, Jack Marsh was reading to me over the telephone a statement that Senator Griffin had confidentially advised him he would issue to the Washington press at about 11:00 A.M. It was both tougher and more tender toward Nixon than his Saturday letter.

"We have arrived at a point where both the national interest and his own interest will be best served by resigning," Bob began. "It's not just his enemies who feel that way. Many of his best friends—and I regard myself as one of those—believe now that this would be the most appropriate course.

"Needless to say, this would be an awesome, most difficult decision for him to reach. But I believe he will see it that way too," Griffin concluded.

This was the first flat-out call for the President's resignation from a top member of the Republican leadership in Congress.

John Rhodes, the House Minority Leader, had scheduled a press conference to announce whether or not he would lead the anti-impeachment debate on the House floor. (He had reportedly decided to do so.*) Haig urged him to delay his announcement without saying why. But Representative Charles Wiggins, Nixon's ablest advocate on Judiciary, had loyally confided the spreading secret to his leader. So Rhodes stayed home.

Marsh went on to warn that what we had been calling "erosion" on Capitol Hill was now turning into a tidal wave. He emphasized once more that if the Vice President was going to get out a statement

* Rhodes still refuses to reveal his decision.

divorcing himself from the Nixon defense, he had better hurry or be the last in line.

"I've tried, Jack," I told him. "But, you know maybe he *wants* to be next to the last to leave the sinking ship. He's an old Navy man, and that's the Executive Officer's role."

Shortly after takeoff there was a call on the radio-telephone. It was our Washington office, wanting us to be alerted that President Nixon would be issuing an important statement at about 3:00 P.M. We were due to land at 2:50.

We supposed that the announcement would be that the President was turning some more tapes over to Judge Sirica, as we already knew.

But the 3:00 P.M. timing was enough to trigger the Vice President into action. He realized that he had procrastinated too long. Once the tapes reached Sirica it would only be a matter of time before they leaked either via Jaworski's staff or the Judiciary Committee. He made a few word changes and handed my latest draft back.

"O.K.—let's put this out as soon as we get back to the office," he said. "No press conference, just hand it out as a statement from the Vice President."

There was a call from Haig waiting when we reached the EOB. The general told the Vice President that things were moving swiftly and he might be called upon to take over within seventy-two hours. But the President, and most of his family, were still resisting the resignation option, Ford was given to understand.

The promised White House announcement had been delayed for an hour or so. Obviously it was something more complex than we expected. It was my turn to hesitate. How could the Vice President issue his statement without knowing what the President was going to say?

The Vice President agreed. I called Haig and asked that he have a copy of the President's statement hand-delivered to me as soon as possible. He readily agreed—but did not hint that anything else was about to transpire. An hour passed. Nothing from the White House. Only the UPI news ticker told us of repeated postponements by Ziegler. Finally Ford announced he was going home, leaving me and Miltich to release his statement.

Finally, a two-page, single-spaced mimeographed "Statement of the President" arrived by messenger. But before I could even scan it, the UPI ticker across the room began to clang for a "Bulletin."

I watched the words as the machine spelled them out.

PALACE POLITICS

UP-128
PRESIDENT NIXON TODAY ACKNOWLEDGED THAT SHORTLY
AFTER THE WATERGATE BREAKIN HE ACTED TO SLOW THE FBI
INVESTIGATION KNOWING IT WOULD PROTECT HIS RE-ELEC-
TION COMMITTEE AND THAT HE WITHHELD THIS FROM THE
JUDICIARY COMMITTEE AND THE SUPREME COURT. . . .

Then the ticker began to quote directly from the transcribed June 23 tape of Nixon's instructions to Haldeman.

"The sons of bitches!" I shouted to the empty room. "They've re-leased the transcripts!"

Haig had not sent a copy of the transcripts to the office of the Vice President of the United States. To send Nixon's explanation of the fatal tape without the text of the tape itself, after the press had both, was unforgivable. It was deliberate sabotage.

I phoned the Vice President and read the Presidential statement rapidly.

"We're trying to get a copy of the transcript now—but we may have to get one from the press room," I said with rising anger. "Shall I send it out to the house?"

"No," he said wearily. "I'll read it in the morning. I guess we know the gist of it."

"Shall we go ahead and put out your statement?"

"Look it over so it doesn't sound silly. You may have to add a couple of sentences referring to the President's announcement. I'll leave it to you. It's too bad . . ."

He didn't finish the sentence, but I knew what he meant. He had missed the chance to disengage himself in advance.

Jack Marsh and Paul Miltich were there, consuming the clattering UPI copy in total shock. "We've got to get our hands on that tran-script," I said. "Jack, why don't you call Haig and see if he'll give you one."

"I'll do better by going over there myself," Jack said.

Marsh took off and I suddenly realized what Ford wanted me to do. He still didn't *want* to know precisely, firsthand, what the evidence against the President was.

I flung a sheet of paper into my typewriter and wrote a new be-ginning for the statement: "I have not listened to the tapes nor have I read the transcripts of the President's conversation with Mr. Halde-man. Without knowing what was said and the context of it my com-ment would serve no useful purpose and I shall have none."

146

Paul read over my shoulder. "We'll have to move fast or the White House story will completely bury us," I said. "Have someone hand-deliver it to AP, UP and the National Press Club. Phone it to the networks; we still might make the late-news shows."

Marsh was back shortly bearing two copies of the transcript.

"I just walked into Haig's outer office and helped myself," he said and grinned.

I showed Jack the updated Ford statement. "This is good," he said. "But I think he ought to say it directly to the President. You know Nixon has called a Cabinet meeting at ten."

"Why don't you work up some notes for him to take along?" I said. I was beat.

"When do you think it'll happen?" Marsh voiced our common concern.

"Probably this weekend," I said. "Everything always happens on weekends. I don't see how we can afford to be in California."

"Well, let's lock it up for tonight," Jack said. "I'll see what I can do for the meeting tomorrow."

TUESDAY, AUGUST 6, 1974

The statement of disengagement that Vice President Ford had finally issued was more than it seemed, more than a mere moratorium on further impeachment comment. He was, at last, truly in a position to be his own man. Roughly, he was in the same status as a President-elect.

We still didn't know the final course Nixon would choose, nor did anybody for sure.* Haig's gingerly machinations to bring about a quick resignation seemed to be having the opposite effect on the President's psyche. Even in extremis, Richard Nixon was too smart, too practiced a manipulator of men, not to be aware he was being manipulated.

I was pleased by the play Jules Witcover gave us in the Washington *Post* under a bold headline clear across the top of page 14: "FORD SAYS HE INTENDS TO BOW OUT OF IMPEACHMENT DEBATE."

George Meany, a wise old Washington weathervane, told the AFL-CIO Executive Council that he was less than enraptured by the Vice President's legislative record and political philosophy but felt the American people and the union movement would support Ford if he

---

* In his memoirs, Nixon claims he decided to resign on August 1. But he admits he wavered afterward.

took over. "A conservative with integrity is far better than what we have today in the White House," Meany was quoted as declaring.

The President decided to postpone his Cabinet meeting from ten to eleven. Jack Marsh had produced a succinct six-point outline of what he felt the Vice President should say at the meeting, and I thought it was right on target. Apparently Ford did too, for he folded it lengthwise and stuffed it in his inside coat pocket. I always accompanied him to Cabinet meetings.

But on this momentous morning—as it turned out, the last gathering of the Nixon Cabinet—my name was not on the White House list at all. I pointed this out to the Vice President and asked what I should do about it.

He grinned. "Nothing. Just follow me in and sit down."

So he, too, had noted how much things had changed.

As we entered from the West Executive basement a few minutes before eleven, the guard for once didn't demand my White House pass.

Nixon showed no sign of strain. While the news cameras clicked he bantered a few remarks across the table which seemed unusually relaxed. He made a point of recognizing me as "Bob." I felt a great surge of pity for this man and a shiver of fear about the Presidency itself. Was it such a prize? He was certain everyone had read the papers. He was sworn to uphold the law, and he was going to let the law take its course. He would take his lumps, but he would not be party to a precedent that would change the Constitution and permit future Presidents to be driven from office under intense personal pressure. He did not feel that he had committed an impeachable offense and he would not resign. He thanked his Cabinet members for their support. Now, they must all work a bit extra to run the government well, whether they agreed with his decision or not.

The President looked straight across the table at his Vice President. His tone softened.

"You don't have to do anything that would be embarrassing to your personal interest—I don't ask that," he said. "You don't have to talk about Watergate. Talk about all the good things that this Administration has done. . . . I intend to fight this battle right to the end."

While Nixon continued his monologue, I glanced at my copy of the notes Marsh had prepared for the Vice President. They read:

First, everyone here recognizes the difficult position I am in. I am a party in interest.

148

Second, no one regrets more than I do this whole tragic episode. I have deep personal sympathy for you, Mr. President, and your fine family.

Third, I wish to emphasize that *had I known and had it been disclosed to me what has been disclosed in reference to the Watergate affair in the last twenty-four hours, I would not have made a number of the statements that I have made, either as Minority Leader or as Vice President of the United States.* [*Emphasis mine.*]

Fourth, I do not expect to make any recommendation to any of the others at this meeting.

Fifth, whether the full disclosures will meet the Constitutional definition of an impeachable offense is a matter that can only be finally resolved by the United States Senate in a proceeding as provided for in the Constitution.

Finally, let me assure you that I expect to continue to support fully the Administration's foreign policy and fight against inflation.

It was a superb job on Marsh's part, covering all the bases. But when the President finished and asked if Ford had anything to say, he never even reached for his notes.

As choked with emotion as anyone, the Vice President got off to a faltering start. He explained at some length his decision to issue yesterday's statement and repeated much of it, when all anybody wanted to know was why he had waited so long.

Then he remembered Marsh's six points and paraphrased them quite effectively, except for one thing: He omitted the third and most important one. This went much farther than my statement of the previous day; it was a repudiation of everything Ford had ever said about the President's innocence. It was also a direct reproach to Nixon himself; "had I known or had it been disclosed to me" was an artful and telling phrase, meaning nothing less than that the President had deceived his loyal lieutenant.

Why did he omit this? I can only guess, but I believe he was simply incapable of inflicting that additional blow. He could not look across the Cabinet table at Richard Nixon and call him a heel. If he had just committed that small cruelty, he might still be President today.

The news of his statement would surely have leaked to the public; the Praetorian Guard would have seen to it. It was Ford's own Declaration of Independence—but he failed to sign.

149

PALACE POLITICS

When the meeting broke up, we made for the back door. Ford was late for the Senate luncheon; I thought he should avoid the waiting White House press. Treasury Secretary Simon did most of the talking for the Cabinet; he conveyed the consensus that Nixon was determined to fight on.

The Vice President was determined to hew to his regular routine and act as if this were another ordinary day. He met with a visiting delegation from the Japanese Diet; officers of the National Association of Homebuilders; Betty Beale, the Washington *Star*'s social doyenne who as instinctively gravitates to Presidential power as a bee to honey; and Vermont Royster, veteran editor of the *Wall Street Journal.*

Both journalists asked friendly but expertly searching questions. Their interviews showed Ford in the best of form, giving nothing away but projecting a sense of calm confidence in his ability to handle the world's toughest job, as well as being a normal, natural nice guy.

George Bush, then the able and adroit Republican National Chairman, dropped by on an unscheduled visit to brief the Vice President about the fund-raising telethon in which Ford was to be the concluding speaker from the Century Plaza in Los Angeles. There would be a lot of celebrities, including Governor Ronald Reagan and John Wayne.

Ford warned his old House colleague that he might not be able to be away from Washington this weekend. They should arrange to have a pinch-hitter ready.

In the late afternoon Ford returned to Capitol Hill, keeping a promise to meet with Senator Pete Domenici (R–New Mexico).

I stayed behind to try to catch up on my routine. There was a list of phone calls two pages long. One was from Mel Laird, who wanted to tell me (which meant he wanted me to tell Ford) that he had been getting calls from the press (which meant that he had planted ideas with the press) about the prospect of his being tapped by Jerry as the next Vice President. He had blown this down, Mel said. He couldn't afford it and, besides, his candidate was Nelson Rockefeller. Ford and he were both upper Midwesterners, and they thought alike. The party needed to rebuild itself in the Northeast and broaden its appeal to ethnics and labor—Rocky's natural constituency.

I wondered why he didn't make this pitch himself. Shyness was never Mel's failing. I said I was sure the boss hadn't yet given this matter much thought.

"He's got to move fast," Mel said. "There mustn't be a lot of agonizing. It will show decisiveness; that's what people want."

The rest of my telephone log read like a roster of the Washington press corps. Miltich reported that everybody wanted to know whether the trip to California was still on. I told him to say yes but to hedge it a little. The boss was going to decide tomorrow; to cancel it now would send up too big a signal.

Dick Burress brought in the final draft of the Vice President's speech for the Hoover Institution at Stanford on Saturday. It was a very good and scholarly speech—one of the best Ford never gave.

The Vice President returned from the Hill, and I took a few minutes to bring him up to date.

"Bob," he said quietly, "I think you'd better start thinking about what I should say after my swearing-in. I don't want anything fancy, but think about it."

"How much time do we have?"

"Two or three days—maybe less. It will probably all be over in seventy-two hours."

"He *is* going to resign, then?"

"Al Haig still isn't one hundred percent sure. The President blows hot and cold. Maybe we'll know more tomorrow."

"Why don't you ask the President yourself?"

"Not unless he wants to tell me." He packed up his battered briefcase and headed home.

I waited in my office until it was time to meet Roberta at the Motion Picture Association for dinner and a showing of Julie Andrews, my secret passion, and Omar Sharif in *The Tamarind Seed.* Jack Valenti's parties are always relaxing, and that I needed.

I went back to perusing the papers, this time to the editorial pages. There, in the *Star,* I found another kind of seed—an evil one. Milton Viorst, obviously writing before Ford's statement, found his continued defense of Nixon not only "bizarre" but downright sinister.

"He seems to be preparing groundwork for a grant of clemency," Viorst surmised, "that would smell terribly of a deal."

What crap! I thought. I turned to Joe Kraft, the latter-day Walter Lippmann, in the *Post.* Joe was usually very perceptive and had excellent sources. Today he wrote: "One of the Vice President's aides has already begun to say out loud: He's going to be President. It's inevitable, and he knows it."

Peering into his political crystal ball, the columnist saw the Republicans returning in 1976 to their Midwestern base while the Democrats were turning back to their native ground, the South.

"The next Democratic President will be the man who can bring

151

the South back into the fold," Joe concluded, "and it just might be a Southerner."

What *utter* crap! I said this time. I snapped my briefcase shut and headed for the party.

I never thought I would sleep through a Julie Andrews movie, but that night I did.

7

OUR NIGHTMARE IS OVER

★★————————★★

Three o'clock in the morning of Wednesday, August 7, 1974, my sub-conscious was already spinning when the alarm sounded. While the coffeepot boiled I focused on the confidential charge entrusted to me by the next President of the United States. It might well be the most important job I would ever have to do. It must bridge—but also di-vide—the past and the future. It was not so much an Inaugural as an invocation. It would be brief, but every word must ring true.

First of all, Ford must take command. He must not merely *act* like a President but *be* President. He must link himself to the unbroken line that began with George Washington.

On a scratch pad I wrote the words "take charge."

Next, he must establish once and for all the legitimacy of his suc-cession. He would be every bit as much President as any of his thirty-seven predecessors, but he would also be different. Nobody outside of the Fifth District of Michigan or the U.S. Congress had ever cast a vote for him. He must acknowledge this and turn it into an asset. He must establish direct empathy with the people.

I jotted down the word "legitimacy."

Third, he would have to set the course on which he would steer the Ship of State, and the polestar which would guide him must be truth. I added: "Truth is the glue."

He would have to pay his respects to the Congress and reaffirm the basics of American foreign policy for anxious ears abroad. I could hear Henry Kissinger at the last Cabinet meeting saying, "I hope no-body decides this is the time to take a run at us."

Somehow, he had to show human compassion for his fallen pred-ecessor. Finally, very simply, he must ask God's help. All Presidents have needed it. So would Jerry Ford.

Now I began to type: "My friends and fellow Americans . . ." Too much like FDR? Never mind. How can you say it better? Besides, in the back of my head I had been nurturing the idea of reviving something like the fireside chat, where Ford was at his best.

"Not an Inaugural speech, not a fireside chat . . . just a little straight talk among friends . . . the first of many.

"I am acutely aware that you have not elected me as your President by your ballots. So I ask you to confirm me as your President with your prayers. . . .

"If you have not chosen me by secret ballot, neither have I gained office by any secret promises. . . . I am indebted to no man and only one woman—my dear wife. . . ."

Then, the operative sentence of the whole speech: "My fellow Americans, our long national nightmare is over."

In the early-morning silence, I could almost hear the collective sigh of millions. I don't know where this phrase came from, but it didn't struggle to be born. It just flowed naturally.

"As we bind up the internal wounds of Watergate, let us restore the Golden Rule to our political process, and let brotherly love purge our hearts of suspicion and hate.

"I asked you to pray for me. . . . I ask again your prayers for Richard Nixon and for his family. May our former President, who brought peace to millions, find it for himself."

I could feel a lump in my throat. I wondered if Ford would be able to say this without breaking up. End it quickly now, on a note of confidence and strength, speak directly to every listening American.

"With all the strength and good sense I have gained from life . . . I now solemnly reaffirm the promise I made to you last December 6—to uphold the Constitution, to do what is right as God gives me to see the right, and to do the very best I can for America.

"God helping me, I will not let you down."

The morning traffic was rolling down Massachusetts Avenue now. I swam a couple of laps, dressed and headed for the office. Roberta was still sleeping.

The Vice President buzzed for me. I showed him the draft of the speech. "I've been sweating over a hot typewriter since three this morning. I haven't even reread it myself. See if you like the approach."

He was a speed reader, and he skimmed through it fast.

"Sounds fine. I'll go over it more carefully tonight." That meant he wanted Betty to pass on it, perhaps the kids. I had long ago trained myself not to mind, though perhaps I did. He folded it and stuck it in his pocket.

154

"The President is going on television, probably tomorrow evening," he began. "It appears now that he will resign. But he's still President, and he could change his mind. If he resigns, it will probably be Friday, effective at noon. That's when I'll be sworn in."

"Where?" It all seemed very matter-of-fact now.

"They're talking about the Oval Office."

I said that he couldn't begin to get half his really good friends and family in there, reminding him of the turn-out at the Capitol when he took the oath as Vice President.

"But they want just a small ceremony," Ford protested.

"Boss," I said, "now is as good a time as any to say this: The hell with what *they* want. It's what do *you* want. *You* are going to be the President."

Marsh smiled but said nothing. The Vice President must have taken my outburst to heart, because the ceremony was rescheduled for the East Room.

I began to spurt rapid-fire questions. What about the Chief Justice? Burger was in Europe, he said, but Phil Buchen's group was handling that.

Buchen's group?

Then he told me, for the first time, of the secret transition planning group that Buchen had pulled together, consisting mostly of bright but unknown young Nixon operators. For months they had been working more or less from scratch on the mechanics of a sudden Presidential succession. Now, Ford said, the transition effort would have to risk coming out in the open. He'd asked some of our old friends to help out—Bryce, Bob Griffin and John Byrnes, Bill Whyte and Bill Scranton.

I noted that Mel Laird was not on the list. This morning, Mel's gambit of tossing Rockefeller's hat into the Vice Presidential ring was all over town. Yes, the Vice President had seen the stories. "Melvin's having fun." He smiled.

I was doing a slow burn about his having kept me in the dark. I had sworn to numerous reporters that nobody on Ford's staff was doing any takeover planning. So had he, I reminded him.

"Phil only told me what he was doing last night," he said sheepishly. "We were perfectly truthful, both of us. Buchen isn't part of my staff."

He asked what I would think of Jerry terHorst as White House press secretary. Miltich couldn't handle that murderous assignment.

155

PALACE POLITICS

Fantastically loyal though Paul was, he was simply no match for the piranhas of the White House press room.

Jerry would be great, I said. TerHorst and I had covered the 1960 campaign, worked well together, and he was highly regarded by his peers.

TerHorst had known Ford from Grand Rapids days and was finishing a book about him. Did he want me to sound Jerry out? What should I tell Paul?

He'd handle it personally, Ford said. The Vice President looked sad. He didn't like to fire anybody or hurt anybody. Just as he was about to assume the most powerful position on earth, he caught a glimpse of what it would cost to keep it.

There remained a million things to be done. For the last time, he went up the House wing of the Capitol for a 75-cent haircut from his favorite barber, Morrison Hansborough. There were short interviews with three longtime friends in the press corps, Maggie Hunter of the New York *Times,* Alan Otten of the *Wall Street Journal* and Paul Martin of *U.S. News & World Report.* Bill Timmons and Ken Cole came over for their regular legislative briefing. It was a farce; nothing was on their minds except the end of their world.

Secretary of the Navy Bill Middendorf and Admiral Holloway, Chief of Naval Operations, came by to get in a few licks for the Navy's budget. Bill knew how hard Ford had come down on his side when the Nixon White House wanted to bring in an outsider for the Navy's top job. He had thoughtfully framed a wartime photo of Ford's old ship, the USS *Monterey.* Ford regaled us with his story of how he was nearly washed overboard in 1944 during a typhoon.

We made some contingency plans for the trip to California. Ford would record a message for a housing-project dedication in the Watts section of Los Angeles. Burress would ask Senator Mark Hatfield to be a standby substitute for the Hoover address at Stanford. The GOP telethon from Hollywood could make do with Ronald Reagan and John Wayne.

The Vice President's "Action Group" assembled at 5:45 for what would be its final session. He thanked everyone and warned all of us to be doubly circumspect for the next few days.

Walter Mote reported from the Senate that Barry Goldwater, flanked by Hugh Scott and John Rhodes, was at that very hour telling President Nixon what everybody knew: The jig was up. He didn't think there were a dozen votes left in the Senate for the President.

156

Griffin had suggested a Congressional resolution of immunity if Nixon resigned. There wasn't much left of the Vice President's future agenda to talk about.

My log of phone calls again filled two pages. The only one I returned was from Leon Parma in California. Before dragging myself home—it had been fifteen hours since 3:00 A.M.—I called Leon back and guardedly suggested he'd better get himself to Washington or he might miss something historic. Parma caught the next plane.

THURSDAY, AUGUST 8, 1974

I can remember with great clarity where I was and what I was doing the day King Edward VIII renounced his throne for love; the day the Japanese attacked Pearl Harbor; the day FDR died; the day Hiroshima evaporated; the day John F. Kennedy was assassinated in Dallas.

But the day Richard M. Nixon announced he would resign the office of President is something of a blur in my memory. There are crystal-clear episodes swirling in a maelstrom of minutiae.

What to the last-ditch Nixon loyalists was a blessed release was to the dedicated Ford people an unwanted conscription. There was no elation, no private celebrations along our third-floor cubicles in the EOB. The President's men and women were drowning their sorrows, their faces glazed. In the Vice President's area there was only feverish work.

Reporters, photographers and television crews camped on the curbing and the neighbors' lawns as Ford left his Alexandria home. Skipping his usual banter, he gravely jumped into his limousine for the short drive across the Potomac. When my battered Volkswagen pulled up at the White House gate, silent crowds were already pressing against the iron fence, hoping to see history happen. I had seen this while covering political crises and palace coups in Europe and the Middle East, but never in Washington.

We were still officially scheduled to leave for California at noon. Air Force Two and the press were waiting. After a hurried huddle, Miltich was sent to tell the newsmen that the Vice President's departure had been delayed.

There were so many urgent things to be done; somehow we did most of them. The Vice President himself was calm and decisive, the coolest head in the crowd.

157

PALACE POLITICS

One official duty, a sad one, remained on his calendar. Weeks earlier, the President had asked the Vice President to stand in for a presentation of Congressional Medals of Honor to the next of kin of seven Vietnam servicemen. There were no dry eyes in historic Blair House as Ford recalled the unbroken chain of courage and sacrifice stretching from Concord Bridge to the swamps of Southeast Asia.

While Ford was still over at Blair House, General Haig was on the phone to say the President would like to see the Vice President at eleven, if it was convenient. The politeness of protocol. Of course it would be convenient. It is always convenient to come when a President calls—even a doomed one. I relayed the word to Marsh. No explanation was needed. It was 10:40 A.M.

At 10:58, the White House intercom rang again. It was Ron Ziegler. In a choked-up voice, he read me the brief announcement he was going to make in the press room as soon as the President and Vice President had met. I never cared much for Ziegler, but I murmured something like "I'm sorry, Ron."

Exactly at eleven, the UPI ticker quoted a White House aide, who asked not to be identified, saying flatly that Nixon would resign. Two minutes later, continuing the flash, UPI identified only Al Haig by name as being "among" the top advisers who had been urging the President's resignation all along.

I went out to meet Ford as he led his party on foot back across Pennsylvania Avenue. He was grave, nodding as I filled him in quickly on the wire bulletin and my calls. Like a new quarterback trotting onto the field near the end of a third-quarter rout, he braced his shoulders and disappeared into the White House, two agents right behind him. I went back to work.

The two old comrades of the political wars faced each other over an empty desk in the Oval Office and talked alone for an hour, maybe a little more.

When Ford returned he ran through the timetable. The President would go on all the networks at nine that night. He would say he had decided to submit his resignation in the best interests of the country. It would take effect at noon the next day, Friday. In the morning Nixon would say goodbye to his staff and then board a helicopter on the White House lawn. The Vice President and Betty would see the President and Pat out and would say their goodbyes last.

At noon the President in Air Force One would be about over Kansas, bound for San Clemente. Then the finger on the button would change. Ford would be sworn in by the Chief Justice in the East Room.

Even as we talked, the news was rolling over the wires. Ziegler had made his last press briefing.

I inquired how the President was taking it.

"Better than I am," the Vice President answered soberly. Nixon had seemed calm and peaceful, as if he were almost glad to have it over. He was businesslike, as sharp as ever about details, anxious to have everything go right tomorrow. "He said he was sure I'd do well," Ford told me.

They had talked some about the world situation. It was very much on Nixon's mind. Ford assured him he'd try to persuade Kissinger to carry on. Nixon must have known, but didn't say, that Henry could not have been dislodged with a crowbar.

When Ford learned that Julie and David would be staying on in Washington, he told the President they could have all the time to pack they wanted. He and Betty wouldn't have to move into the White House right away. Nixon was grateful, even touched.

He would be meeting with Henry at three, the Vice President said. Miltich could annnounce it, but he didn't want a lot of reporters hanging around afterward. Our California trip was scrubbed.

"Have you had a chance to go over the speech?" I asked.

Pulling the rough draft from his pocket, he said he wouldn't change a word—except for one thing that troubled him. His finger pointed to the sentence "Our long national nightmare is over."

"Isn't that a little hard on Dick?" he asked.

"No, no, no!" I cried in genuine anguish. "Don't you see, that's your whole speech! That's what you have to proclaim to the whole country—to the whole world. That's what everybody *needs* to hear, *wants* to hear, has *got* to hear you say. It's like FDR saying all we have to fear is fear itself. Maybe it isn't yet quite true, but saying it will make it come true. *You* have to turn the country around.

"Junk all the rest of the speech if you want to," I implored, "but not that. That is going to be the headline in every paper, the lead in every story. This hasn't been a nightmare just for Nixon and his family," I argued. "It's been a nightmare for everybody—for you, for me, for Nixon's enemies as well as his friends. Don't you think it's been a nightmare for Carl Albert, for Pete Rodino? Most Americans voted for Nixon less than two years ago. Hasn't it been a nightmare for them, listening to their neighbors? This has been a *national* nightmare, and it's got to be stopped. You're the only one who can."

He thought for a moment, then smiled. "O.K., I guess you're right. I hadn't thought about it that way. And thank you—you did a wonderful job. I don't know how you did it."

"Neither do I." I grinned back. "Maybe I had some help from up there."*

He didn't argue. Our emotions were running in tandem. Then he turned abruptly back to business.

First thing next week, probably Monday or Tuesday, he wanted to go before a joint meeting of Congress. There wasn't much time; I'd better get started on it. I said I'd have Milt Friedman begin putting some ideas together that we could work on over the weekend.

The wires were humming with speculative stories about the Ford Administration, the transition plans, prospective new Cabinet and staff prospects. Some were pretty far out; some were obviously inspired and some substantially accurate. Virtually all of the Washington writers and commentators were having a field day over future Vice Presidential prospects, with Rockefeller as the frontrunner.

There was also an avalanche of speculation about granting immunity from criminal prosecution to President Nixon if he resigned. There seemed to be hardly anybody against it if it would speed the President's exit. Ed Brooke of Massachusetts, no big Nixon fan, took the Senate floor to propose a joint resolution commending immunity. "The spectacle of a President going to jail really distresses me," he said. Chairman Rodino was quoted as saying that if the purpose of impeachment (i.e., removal from office) had been served, he had no desire to see further prosecution.

Linda Mathews in the Los Angeles *Times,* however, went further. "To avoid prosecution," she stated, "Mr. Nixon will have to either strike a deal with Jaworski or reach an understanding that Ford will pardon him after the Vice President ascends to the Presidency."

Bill Casselman came in, visibly upset. One of Bill's friends on the Nixon staff had slipped him a copy of a White House memo about to be circulated, setting forth rules to guide the staff in the disposal of their files and official papers. The document read as if a Democratic Administration was about to take over, not ours. Worse, it appeared

---

* It is difficult to express, but I still am haunted by the feeling that some unseen hand was guiding mine that morning. Is there such a thing as inspiration? Can a ghost have a ghost? I don't know.

largely to leave up to each individual's own conscience what documents should be left behind for the use of the Ford staff and which might be destroyed or taken with them.

"People have been hauling suitcases and boxes out of here all this week," Bill said. "If we don't have any records, how can we carry on the government?"

"How do we stop them?" I asked. "They're still running the show."

Bill wasn't sure, but he needed help. There were laws about this. Buchen and his legal people were preoccupied with transition business. He and Barry Roth couldn't do it alone.

"Why don't we call Ben Becker? Tell him to drop everything and get over here," I suggested. Becker got things done and was totally devoted to Ford.

Becker came right over. "Snoop around and find out what's going on," I told him. "Throw your weight around as much as you can get away with. The White House police and the permanent White House functionaries will cooperate. They know who their next boss is going to be. Don't let anyone take anything out of the compound or burn or shred anything that we may need," I concluded.

Ron Ziegler called again—about as many times in one day as he had in five and one half years. He had heard about Jerry terHorst; he would be going to San Clemente with the President, so if he could be of any assistance, it would have to be today. Otherwise his deputy, Jerry Warren, would be available. I passed the word to TerHorst, again feeling an unexpected surge of admiration for Ziegler's steadfastness.

Suddenly I was getting calls from Nixon's Cabinet. Bill Simon at Treasury, who had been quoted in the morning papers as predicting a psychological boost for the sagging economy if Nixon would resign, earnestly said he hoped the new President's first statement would include some reassurance to the business community. I thought it would have that effect, I said, but it wasn't only Wall Street that needed confidence restored; it was also Main Street. The President would try to touch the nation's soul rather than its pocketbook. Simon appeared to understand.

While Nixon was meeting with the Congressional leadership (including Speaker Carl Albert, who had come to the 80th Congress with him) for a poignant leave-taking, Ford gathered his Vice Presidential staff together. It was hard to believe it was the last time. Some had been his devoted slaves for decades in the House of Representatives, some I had recruited during his confirmation hearing and eight-month tenure in the nation's second office and a few were holdovers from Agnew. They were all uneasy about their future, waiting for an encouraging word.

He thanked us for our tireless support and loyalty. He asked our patience in the days ahead. He made no promises. I didn't think it came off very well. He never did find it easy to deal with subordinates—with peers, yes, but not subordinates. It was a bad omen.

He went home, and I went home, to watch Nixon's swan song in privacy. We watched the President, with whom our lives had been intertwined, making the best case he could for himself in departing. It wasn't magnificent, as Dan Rather said, but it was a dignified way to go.

It didn't matter much what Nixon said, anyway. Tomorrow President Gerald R. Ford would wipe the slate clean, and we would make a new beginning.

Did I dream, or lie half awake remembering?

There was Senator Nixon, in a Los Angeles television studio, Pat gallant and gaunt beside him, invoking the fate of their daughters' little dog Checkers, fighting for his political life.

There was I, standing at rigid attention beside the Nixons at Maiquetia Airport in Venezuela, sharing the spittle that was raining down on us as a military band droned through two national anthems. And later, after the murderous mob attack in Caracas, running to reassure Pat that he was unhurt.

There was Goodwill Ambassador Nixon, in the all-electric kitchen of a model American home at the Moscow Fair, bending forward, poking his finger in the burly chest of Nikita Khrushchev, lecturing him on the rewards of capitalism.

There was I, summoned to his suite in the Waldorf-Astoria on the eve of his third debate with Kennedy, being fed some encouraging private polls, being used, being expected to carry the failing candidate's false confidence back to the press room.

There was Embittered Loser Nixon, snarling to the bone-weary newsmen who had followed him all over California that they wouldn't have Richard Nixon to kick around any more. And there was Gracious Loser Nixon, going to Kennedy's Palm Beach retreat in 1960 to assure him he wouldn't contest Illinois and Texas.

There was I, sitting on the podium behind Permanent Chairman Gerald Ford, exactly six years ago at the convention in Miami, listening to Richard Nixon say, "America is in trouble today, not because her people have failed but because her leaders have failed."

There was President Nixon, slipping as unobtrusively as a President ever can into the crowded church, comforting Ginger, widow of my best friend, Congressman Glen Lipscomb of California, cut down by cancer at fifty-one. But there was also President Nixon saying of loyal, long-suffering Herb Klein: "He doesn't have his head screwed on—he's not really one of us, is he?"

And there was I, gulping down scalding *caffè latte,* skimming the morning *Post,* brought starkly awake by Ollie Atkins' poignant picture of Julie Nixon, collapsed in grief on her father's shoulder.

It was the morning of August 9, 1974—gray and humid. It was time to go. *My* long nightmare was over—or about to begin.

8

EUPHORIA
WITH ENGLISH MUFFINS

★★————————————★★

No American President, possibly excepting General Washington, ever entered upon his official duties with a greater reservoir of public good will or with higher hopes for his success than Gerald Rudolph Ford.

He came to the White House without the bruising battle of a national election or the even more savage resentments of a primary struggle. He assumed the nation's highest office, officially certified in advance as worthy of that honor by all but eight Members of the Senate and thirty-one in the House.

He had a loving, handsome family that could not have been better cast by a modeling agency. He was a child of the Great Depression who had worked his way through college and law school. He had played America's favorite game and played it well. He had seen combat in our last popular war but was no professional hero, just one of millions who did their jobs and welcomed their discharge. He had served his Michigan constituents faithfully and well, but his steady rise in politics had made him neither snooty nor rich. He drove the beat-up family station wagon on weekends, made his own breakfast in a modest home and carried his own bags on and off airplanes.

He was an Eagle Scout, an Episcopalian, a 33rd-degree Mason, an Elk, a Rotarian, member of three major veterans organizations. His peers on the minority side of the House five times elected him their leader, and his political party twice chose him to chair its national convention.

"Good old Jerry" was what they called him. When the news of the Nixon "enemies list" that John Dean compiled came over the news ticker during the Watergate hearings, I remember him saying, "Anybody who can't keep his enemies in his head has got too many enemies." No President ever started off with more friends and fewer enemies, and, fully sensing this, Gerald Rudolph Ford rose to the occasion.

Brisk and businesslike, wearing a formal dark-blue suit with a white shirt and conservative blue-and-white striped tie with a thin line of red, the Vice President arrived at his office on the dot of 8:00 A.M., as if it were just another day.

The informal group of proven Ford loyalists, dubbed the "transition team" but lacking any official status or Federal funds, such as the law makes available in normal Presidential successions, had done Herculean labor in a limited time.

Phil Buchen and five Washington old-timers, plus thirty-five-year-old Clay (Tom) Whitehead, a Nixon appointee distrusted by the media but trusted by Buchen, had drawn up the original transition agenda. The group resolved at the outset that they would do their job of making recommendations rapidly and go out of business as quickly as possible. Still, they agreed, there would have to be a continuing cadre of close Presidential confidants to monitor the changeover from a Nixon to a Ford Administration. "You must walk a delicate line between compassion and consideration for the former President's staff and the rapid assertion of your personal control over the Executive Branch," they recommended to Ford.

To help accomplish this imperative, they proposed that they be superseded by a more formal transition group of four, in which Bill Scranton would be the only holdover, with the key role of picking new people to staff the Ford Administration. The others proposed by the team were Jack Marsh for liaison with Congress; Ford's old friend Rogers Morton, Secretary of the Interior, for liaison with the Cabinet; and Frank Carlucci as liaison for the Nixon White House staff. The choice of Carlucci was (and is) a puzzler to me, since Ford had not had close contact with him. Carlucci may have been a puzzler to the Vice President, too; in any case, Ford crossed out Carlucci and wrote in "Rumsfeld." (Later, the President made Carlucci Ambassador to Portugal as a consolation prize. Next he became President Carter's deputy director of the CIA.)

Prefacing their fifty-page loose-leaf presentation of priority objectives, the Buchen team tersely set forth three guiding principles:

1. Restoration of confidence and trust of the American people in their political leadership, institutions and processes. This is the major priniciple and others relate to it.
2. Assumption of control which is firm and efficient.
3. National feeling of unification and reconciliation enabled by the character and style of the new President.

Nobody could quarrel with those lofty goals. When the Ford Administration was finished, the first and last had been admirably accomplished. Where President Ford failed—where in a sense we all failed—was in No. 2. Jerry Ford simply was not a control man. Others were, and they surrounded him. Unhappily, despite the transition group's high collective quota of sophistication, they proceeded from a totally false assumption: "The old White House staff will submit their resignations," they confidently predicted. "But they should be asked to stay on for a time to help with the transition. It will be clear that most of the political types will be expected to leave within a reasonable time."

By "reasonable time" the team was thinking in terms of two to six weeks. The President was expected to receive White House and Cabinet resignations during his first week in office and accept them as soon as Ford replacements could be named.

Ron Ziegler had already been disposed of, and Henry Kissinger had already been embraced, whether the transition team liked it or not. Of the remainder of the Nixon Cabinet, a key role clearly was foreseen for Rogers Morton, but most of the others could go. It was assumed that all of the Cabinet, honorably and traditionally, would be anxious and ready to resign at the pleasure of the new President—and that he would unmistakably expect them to.

As for the White House staff—excepting the career clerical and housekeeping people who see Presidents come and go—the advisers saw clearly the necessity of a thoroughgoing housecleaning as soon as the transition period was over.

"The one exception we recommend is Al Haig," they wrote. "Al has done yeoman service for his country. You should meet with him personally as soon as possible and prevail upon him to help you and your transition team, thus completing the holding-together he has done for so long."

However, it was the team's firm consensus that Haig's unfettered and absolute authority had to be cut back immediately. He could no longer go on being Acting President of the United States, once Ford took over. "He should not be expected, asked, *or be given the option* [emphasis mine] to become *your* chief of staff. We share your view that there should be no chief of staff," the advisers agreed, "especially at the outset. However, there should be someone who could rapidly and efficiently organize the new staff, but who will not be perceived or *be eager* to be chief of staff."

Other false assumptions the transition team made were that Haig would require Presidential persuasion to stay on, that the general would slip gratefully and gracefully back into a subordinate slot, or that any successor—however perceived—would actually not *be eager* to be chief of staff.

I sometimes wonder what might have happened if President Ford had rejected his transition advisers' desire to fade quickly into the background and instead installed most of them immediately as the nucleus of his new Administration, along with the dedicated veterans of his Vice Presidential staff. Scranton to State, Marsh to Defense, Byrnes to Treasury, Griffin to Justice, Whyte to Commerce, Laird to HEW, Seidman to Labor, Morton at Interior, Buchen to the first Supreme Court vacancy, Harlow to whatever he wanted—it's fun to speculate, but things didn't work out that way.

At the same time Vice President Ford was reviewing his team's prescription for a drastic overhaul, General Haig's indefatigable Praetorians in the White House were drafting their own briefing paper. They knew how to humor Presidents, even innocents from Grand Rapids. Considering the expert twist of their one-page memo, one might ask whether a copy of the Buchen team's toilings had not been slipped to them—very little escaped Haig's espionage net.

The Nixon staff memo, handed to Ford when he had been President less than an hour, deserves to be reproduced in full:

MEMORANDUM FOR THE PRESIDENT

Meeting with the White House Staff
Roosevelt Room
1:00 P.M. Friday, August 9, 1974

The main purposes of this meeting are to:
(1) Reassure the staff of your respect,
your need for their help, and your
regard for President Nixon.
(2) Inform the staff of the role the Transition Team will play for the next few
weeks and their relation to it.

We suggest that this be a fairly short meeting,
covering the following general points:

1. The stress on the staff in these last
few days and indeed the last year.

167

2. How important it is that they stayed in
Mr. Nixon's service.
3. The special and heroic role of Al Haig.
4. Your personal need for the staff to
remain intact and in place for a time to
help you and the Transition Team.
5. The Team members will be in touch with
them and General Haig will be actively
involved in the Transition Team's efforts.

Do Nots

At this time, do not commit yourself to dealing directly with
anyone but Al Haig.

Do

Ask each staff member* to be alert to problems and to make
suggestions to Al Haig or to Transition Team members.

This memo is unsigned; its origin can only be surmised from its content. For the official record and the files, Haig initialed another briefing paper for the President, eliminating reference to Haig's "special and heroic role." But it was the anonymous first memo the President carried in his coat pocket to the meeting on Friday, August 9, the day of his succession to the Presidency.

Henry Kissinger came around bright and early that day, as he was to do religiously for the next two years. (It was to the Secretary of State that Nixon would submit his one-sentence resignation in writing that morning.) Kissinger had briefed the Vice President on foreign developments irregularly but fairly frequently in view of his demanding travel schedule over the past eight months. This morning Kissinger's concern was for a nonstop series of short meetings with foreign ambassadors which had been set up from 2:25 to 7:00 P.M., broken only by a ten-minute session with the transition advisers.

As soon as Henry left, the Vice President buzzed. We went over the final text of his Inaugural speech. Then there was the matter of the Bible. Was there a certain verse he'd like it opened to?

He swung around to the credenza behind his desk and pulled out a Bible, recently given to the Vice President by his son Mike, a divinity

---

* Invited by Haig to this meeting were: Len Garment, Ken Cole, Bill Baroody, Dick Moore, Jerry Warren, Dean Burch, Bill Timmons, James St. Clair, Pat Buchanan, Herb Stein, Roy Ash, Kenneth Rush, Fred Buzhardt, Ray Price, Ken Clawson, Bill Eberle and Brent Scowcroft.

student. He handed it to me, saying, "Proverbs three, five and six."

I thumbed for the reference, a bit surprised at how readily he remembered it. Before I found the place he was reciting: "Trust in the Lord with all thine heart; and lean not unto thine own understanding. In all thy ways, acknowledge Him, and He shall direct thy paths."

"My mother taught me that a long time ago," he added. "I've said it to myself often as a sort of prayer."

Betty arrived, pretty in a pale-blue outfit. It was time for them to walk over and see the Nixons off.

"Would it be all right if I came along?" I asked. "I'd like to tell them goodbye."

"I think you should," the Vice President said.

We walked silently across West Executive Avenue to the diplomatic reception room of the White House. From there a single door opens onto the blacktop driveway, curving around an immaculate lawn that sweeps down to fountain and fence, with the Washington Monument beyond.

The Presidential helicopter was parked, boarding steps down, and a red carpet had been rolled across the grass to it.

President Nixon, surrounded by his family, was upstairs finishing an emotional leave-taking from his tearful staff. We were almost alone in the room, except for the Secret Service agents. Nobody talked. Muffled applause from the East Room seeped through the ceiling. Before it subsided, the President, holding Pat's arm, wheeled from the corridor into the room, closely followed by Tricia and Julie, Eddie Cox and David Eisenhower and a few aides. All except the President were choking back tears, and his eyes were red. The scene could have been the funeral of someone very dear.

Betty, the Vice President and I were lined up along the right of the First Family's intended path. Mrs. Ford took the President's hand and quickly turned to embrace Pat. The Vice President and the President clasped hands and elbows for long seconds. I have no recollection of what Ford said, if words were needed, but I seem to recall Nixon, managing a smile, saying, "Good luck, Mr. President."

The President-to-be turned to Mrs. Nixon and kissed her tenderly on the cheek, while the President turned to me.

"Bob," he said, "take good care of him; I know you will." His handshake was firm. His hoarse voice was warm and friendly. What was the right thing to say?

"Thank you, Mr. President, for all the good things you have done for our country . . . and God bless you," I said.

169

PALACE POLITICS

Betty and the Vice President by now were whispering consolations to the rest of the family, their backs to us. There I stood, gripping the hand of the President of the United States, not able to find any more words. But he, who hated small talk, made some to rescue me.

"You won't have a lot of spare time," Nixon said, "but when you get back to California, come and see me. We've got a great place there—you know, you've seen it, of course."

He dropped my hand and consulted his wrist watch. Frowning slightly, he tapped Pat's elbow. The aides moved in, and the outside doors swung open.

"Time to go," the President reminded his wife, almost happily, I thought. I took Pat's hand, and we exchanged a wordless goodbye with our eyes.

They swept out the door, followed by the Fords, down the red carpet and into the chopper. The crewmen stood at stiff salute. Nixon flashed the "V" for victory signal of a thousand campaign send-offs—I don't recall noting the irony of it. The rotors accelerated. The shrubbery and trees of the White House lawn shook and swayed as in a summer storm. We turned our faces from the blast. Then we turned back for a final wave, and it was over.

The Vice President took Betty's arm and guided her at a brisk pace back to the EOB. The White House was not his—not quite yet. Both their jaws were set, lips tight. They stared straight ahead, holding onto each other and their turbulent emotions.

When we retraced our steps through the West Wing, most of the framed Nixon photographs were gone. Atkins' crew was replacing them with shots of Ford and his family.

I broke out of formation at the basement door and took the tiny elevator up to Bill Timmons' office. I needed something to dissolve the lump in my throat. Timmons must have telepathic powers; he was breaking out a bottle of Chivas Regal from the stationery closet as I entered. Bill didn't wait for ice but poured hearty slugs into two water glasses.

"To the President," I said, meaning Nixon.

"To the President," he replied, meaning Ford.

The East Room, with its stately chandeliers and larger-than-life portraits of George and Martha Washington chaperoning all proceedings, is the largest in the White House. But it can hold, with space set aside for the press and camera equipment, only about three hundred sitting down.

We were green as grass, but the Haig staff was a well-oiled machine. This we learned quickly as the guests began filing into the East Room for the historic moment.

The handsome, faultlessly uniformed military aides—male and female officers of all the services—escorted each couple to their assigned places. It was incredible; the stars of the Nixon galaxy filled all the choicest seats. The Ford sons and daughter were allowed in the front row, but the Ford brothers and their wives were placed with their backs squarely to the TV cameras. Most of Ford's friends and faithful aides were lost in the rear ranks.

It wasn't a minor oversight at all, I would soon learn, but an integral element of the Haldeman–Haig control mechanism to condition everyone, not excluding Presidents, into a resigned recognition of their power. The Praetorian Guard never sleeps.

(John Osborne, one of the canniest of White House reporters, recalled in the *New Republic* an incident where an aide put a phone call from Mike Mansfield through to President Nixon without informing Haig. The normally unflappable general had a conniption fit, according to Osborne. Chewing out everybody within earshot, Haig reportedly thundered, "I run this White House and don't you forget it! Don't *ever* let that happen again! *I* run this White House.")

Ford directed Haig not to have the Marine Band play "Hail to the Chief" when he entered. It was not an ordinary Inaugural, and triumphal flourishes would be most inappropriate. Only some soft familiar background music to damp down the crowd noise.

As the hands of our watches closed to noon, all eyes were on the doorway in back of us. The Chief Justice, robed in black, strode down the center aisle and took his place on the right of the lectern. The Presidential Seal was already in place. Nothing in the room had changed since Nixon's lachrymose farewell a few hours earlier—nothing except the atmosphere.

The invisible loudspeaker voice intoned: "The Vice President of the United States, and Mrs. Ford." We rose to our feet, applauding. Looking serious, but the grim tautness in their faces now gone, they marched slowly down the aisle, nodding to the familiar friends who lined it. Ford helped Betty up onto the platform and she took her place between her husband and the Chief Justice. Ford's favorite Vice Presidential aide, Marine Lieutenant Colonel Rick Sardo, handed Mrs. Ford the Bible, open to the proper page.

The Chief Justice broke the total silence. "Mr. Vice President"—it was the last time he would hear himself addressed that way, I thought—"are you prepared to take the oath of office of the President of the United States?"

In a firm voice Ford replied, "I am, sir."

Concluding the oath with the customary "So help me God," the thirty-eighth President of the United States shook Burger's outstretched hand as the Chief Justice became the first to say, "Congratulations, Mr. President." Ford managed a small smile and turned to plant an authentic smack on the cheek of the new First Lady.

More applause.

As Betty and the Chief Justice took their platform seats, the President turned to the lectern, gripped it with both hands and began to speak.

His voice was strong, but one could sense the churning emotions held under stern control. When he came to "our long national nightmare is over," it came out in near perfect pitch, like the pronouncement of an Old Testament prophet. He paused to let it sink in. His delivery was natural and nearly flawless.

But nearing the end, as he recalled asking prayers for himself, the dam began to break.

"I again ask your prayers—" he paused, got a grip on himself and continued—"for Richard Nixon and for his family." Painfully, huskily, the words trailed out: "May our former President, who brought peace to millions, find it for himself."

The whole ceremony took only fifteen minutes. The Marine Band struck up "America the Beautiful" as the President and First Lady, now beaming naturally, left the room. The guests stopped clapping only long enough to unashamedly dab their eyes with their handkerchiefs. This time, though, they were tears of joy and hope.

The President went directly to the Red Room. There the bipartisan leadership of the Congress—sentimental old buddies one moment, bare-knuckle brawlers the next—assembled themselves stiffly on the damask-covered antiques. Speaker Carl Albert, once again number one in succession to the Presidency, was otherwise immensely pleased. He and Senator Mike Mansfield led off the congratulations and assurances of cooperation, and at the time they really meant it. The new President thanked them and tried to be the same old Jerry. But something had changed and could never be quite the same again. From now on it was perfectly O.K., even flattering, for him to call the Speaker "Carl" and the Senator "Mike." But for them, he was now "Mr. President."

I was glad to be there, for I had my own sentimental attachment to Capitol Hill. After seven congenial years, I valued my relationships of respect and trust with people on both sides of the aisle. Friendship is a coin of great worth in the legislative world.

I wanted to sense the mood of this group, so essential to getting the President off to a good start, in taking the right tone in his address to Congress on Monday.

When the meeting broke up, the hour of the Joint Session agreed upon, the President joined the First Lady in the hallway to receive his other guests. Then all the Ford family walked over to the West Wing to inspect his new office and pose for an official photograph.

The Oval Office had been stripped clean of all its previous occupant's paraphernalia; the desk was bare and the shelves empty. It was cold and impersonal, the bold primary colors forbidding and somehow a little savage. But the natural warmth of the happy Ford family pervaded the place, and out of the corner of her eye Betty was already planning changes in the decor.

Showing his family out of the Oval Office, Ford left his speech portfolio planted squarely in the middle of the big desk, instinctively establishing possession. Taking his cue, I promptly planted my own briefcase on the desk in the small adjacent office, recently vacated by Rose Mary Woods. It was heavy with the acrid smell of paper recently burned in the fireplace. But it was, for the moment, the only empty room in the whole West Wing of the White House. TerHorst had already occupied Ziegler's, and Haig's troops clung fiercely to all the rest. I phoned Neta and told her to have her typewriter moved and take up sentry duty outside the door.

The President's next task, according to the tight agenda set up by his transition team, was to meet with the White House staff in the Roosevelt Room, formerly John F. Kennedy's "Fish Room." This windowless conference room in the center of the West Wing is smaller and less formal than the Cabinet Room. All the former President's men were crowded there, in the stiff pecking order that delighted them, the bigger shots around the table, the lesser fry along the walls. Haig was at one end of the table; one empty chair awaited the President at the other. For Ford people there was standing room only.

The President entered, everybody rose, he asked them to please be seated and sat down himself. Standing over his left shoulder, I could see he had no notes, but he was a quick memorizer.

To my horror, however, his rendering of what the transition team urged that he must stress from the outset was way off-key. He was not

173

asserting who was boss but pleading with everybody not to leave him, begging for their help. Al Haig had "unselfishly" agreed to stay on, and Ford's transition people would work *with* Al to bring about an orderly changeover. Glancing around the room, I saw Phil Buchen, Jack Marsh and Bill Scranton, similarly aghast. The general, in full command, responded on behalf of everyone that "in our hour of common cause" the staff would give the new President the same dedication and loyalty they had given President Nixon. Some loyalty, I thought. They rose and applauded, the President beamed, and as in silent drill Haig's Praetorian Guard swept Ford out the door. The room emptied quickly, leaving the Ford interlopers standing there.

The next symbolic stop in the transition team's program was a visit to the press room. But when Ford disappeared into the Oval Office, Haig all but physically gave rookie Press Secretary Jerry terHorst a straight-arm.

"There's no time for that," Haig snapped.

TerHorst sought me out, fuming. I advised him to confront the President personally; it had probably just slipped Ford's mind in the onrush of the day's responsibilities.

The incident made up my mind what I had to do—and fast. I hadn't wanted to bother the President with trivial things on his first day, but if we were still going to play hardball, I had to have a bat. As soon as he was alone, I tapped on the door and went in. I was wondering how to begin, but he beat me to it.

"Do you think I did all right? I mean in there," he said, nodding toward the Roosevelt Room.

Very gingerly I explained that—well, some of his transition people were a little unhappy that he hadn't been more forceful about the changes he intended to make in due course. He seemed surprised, a little defensive.

"Why, I just said it in my own words. Here's what they gave me."

He pulled Haig's page of pointers from his pocket and handed it to me. It wasn't the right time to dissect the deception; he had too much on his mind. So I said, "I think your old friends ought to have some official status around here if we're going to be of any help to you. You know I don't give a damn about titles and all that, but that's the only way these guys know how to play. Right now, I'm nothing to them but somebody getting in the way, and so are Jack and Phil and all the rest. We aren't the President's staff at all—*they* are."

He hadn't given it much thought, but what would I like to be?

174

Maybe he wasn't yet wised up to White House briefing memos, but he sure knew why I came.

"I haven't had much time to think about it either," I said. We both grinned good-naturedly. "But we haven't got much time. I had kind of hoped to be your first Presidential appointment, like Bryce was Nixon's. I guess TerHorst already has that honor, but I'd like mine to be today, anyway. I don't care what you call the job, as long as it's not 'chief of staff.' I've had that."

"Well, what about Counsellor?" the President said. "You could be my first appointment to the Cabinet."

I hadn't expected that. But what was good enough for Arthur Burns and Bryce Harlow was good enough for me. (President Nixon in 1969 had created the appointive position of Counsellor to the President, with Cabinet rank, for Dr. Arthur Burns. Subsequently, he named others as Counsellors.)

"Thank you, Mr. President, I'll try to deserve it," I said. "But I think Jack Marsh should be one, too."

He said he would talk to Jack. As for the others on the Vice Presidential staff, I could tell them to be patient and everything would work out.

His desk, a few hours ago uncluttered, was now piled high with fat file jackets. He fished into one of them and showed me three draft memos Haig's Praetorians had brought for him to sign.

One was addressed to the Vice Presidential staff, one to the White House staff and one to heads of (Cabinet) departments and agencies of the Nixon Administration. They praised President Nixon effusively, containing this statement: "President Nixon fought long and with all his might to serve the American people well, ending his Presidency with a selfless and courageous act. You can still serve him and the Nation by helping me to carry on the essential functions of the Presidency."

It was too late now to revise this dubious and, in my view, demeaning language. But still being chief of the Vice Presidential staff, I strongly let my views be known on that memo. We then recast it to say only: "I hope you will render all possible cooperation to those who will be here to facilitate the transition, as well as to those of Mr. Nixon's staff for whom this time is even more difficult than it is for us."

Doggedly, TerHorst had managed to bypass the Praetorian Guard and took the President in to meet the press. They were delighted by his selection of TerHorst, one of their own, and even more by his flattering camaraderie. It would be a while before they would portray him as an uncoordinated oaf.

Next on the agenda was an economic meeting in the Cabinet Room. Dr. Arthur Burns, an Eisenhower adviser and the architect of Nixon's 1968 domestic-policy pledges, had been eased out of the inner circle to make way for John Ehrlichman and kicked upstairs as chairman of the Federal Reserve Board. When he exercised the independence contemplated by law for that powerful office, Dr. Burns was further excommunicated from the Nixon White House. This was his first return, an important augury to financial circles at home and abroad.

Also on hand was the Secretary of Treasury, Bill Simon, the slick-haired boy of Wall Street, with a classical conservative mind set on economics and a latent political ambition that far surpassed his political assets. Alan Greenspan, a New York guru who mesmerized corporate presidents as readily as he did Presidents of the United States, was there as well. Greenspan had been nominated by Nixon but was not yet confirmed by the Senate to be chairman of the Council of Economic Advisers. Ford, whose orthodox economics were an open record, had already decided to keep both Simon and Greenspan on. Their antirepression conviction boiled down to "let 'em eat cake."

After the economic huddle President Ford fell into Kissinger's outstretched arms for a series of ambassadorial meetings, largely for photographic purposes, laid on in ten-minute intervals rather like a hotbed motel.

I returned to my EOB office for the first time since noon. Guiltily, I realized I had told Roberta to wait for me there until I could break free to take her to lunch. There was a small note on my desk in her handwriting. "Darling, Rob and I have gone home. I love you. Roberta."

Bless her. She always understood. I didn't know how often this would be repeated over the next two and one half years, nor did she. I telephoned and told her of my appointment as Counsellor, and she was glad for me.

The transition team that assembled in the Cabinet Room shortly before 5:30 had been augmented by Leon Parma and by Don Rumsfeld, whose plane from Brussels had arrived too late for him to make the noon ceremony. The rest—Harlow, Whyte, Byrnes, Buchen, Morton, Scranton, Griffin, Hartmann, Marsh, TerHorst and Whitehead—were in various stages of physical and emotional exhaustion.

Al Haig, who looked even worse, was greeted with sincere expressions of sympathy and somewhat pointed suggestions that what he needed was to go away some place and sleep for two weeks.

The President, after twelve grueling hours, was in better shape than any of us. He briskly started off the meeting as if it was the only thing he had to do all day, calling on Buchen to review the initial reorganization moves he had approved.

Phil, I'm sure, had expected the President to lay out the plan, giving it the full weight of his authority. But he began gamely. The unofficial team was dissolving itself and going out of business.

Buchen praised the volunteer labors of Clay Whitehead, whom he called "the real brains" of the enterprise, and asked if anyone had questions.

The President had the first one. "Scranton will work with Al, I suppose," he inquired.

Buchen, whose judicial features rarely betray his true feelings, almost swallowed his pipe.

Rog Morton, a battle-scarred veteran of this kind of jousting in the Presidential presence, came to his rescue with a pointed question. What would be the mission of this new "transition group"?

"Not to make the decisions," the President cautioned sternly, "but to work with the President and see if some input from the outside can't be helpful."

This wasn't quite the group's charter that Rog was after, so he tried again to get his own role defined. How would the Cabinet go about reporting to the President? Was he supposed to have some responsibility for relations between Cabinet departments? In the past that had been the role of the Cabinet Secretary and the Domestic Council.

"Right," said Haig, who didn't want any tinkering with the system by this bunch. But the President responded to Rog as Secretary of the Interior, not to Rog as a member of his newborn transition team of four.

"I'll have an open door to the Cabinet," he declared, "but when you come, talk about something. If you waste my time, it's going to be a long cold winter before you come back."

This was getting nowhere. Better change the subject before the whole carefully planned program went out the window into the Rose Garden. I scribbled a note suggesting the President describe his personal work habits and preferences for the daily routine. This might give the Nixon staff some marching orders instead of perpetuating the status quo.

"I usually start work at eight," the President began. (Nixon was a late-riser.) "We'll stick to the regular routine at the outset—first my intelligence briefing, then I meet with Bob Hartmann [there was the nod I needed], the legislative liaison people and the press secretary."

Starting about 10:00 A.M., he continued, he was ready to have morning appointments with others.

"I listen better than I read," the President noted. "I like to take papers home to read at night, and I prefer brief papers. This is my general philosophy of decision-making: I like to see the alternatives."

Now it was Haig's turn to try to change the subject back onto his track. This was a fascinating tug-of-war, with most of the people around the table on my side but almost everybody else in the building on his.*

Tomorrow morning, Saturday, he would be briefing the President on the White House structure, Haig said. Perhaps some of the rest of us would like such a briefing. If so he would set one up.

He was only interested in organizational restructuring, not philosophical, the President pointed out. He had the same general political philosophy, in liberal vs. conservative terms, as President Nixon, and that would continue.

Bob Griffin asked what the President intended to do about getting a Vice President. The President said he had given that some thought—the process, not any particular people. He thought it should be done quickly, within a week or ten days.

"I expect to spend Sunday listening to a number of people whose views I respect," he told the Senator (who would, of course, be one of them).

The President stood up; he was already late for his next ambassadorial appointment. It was our first, but by no means last, lesson in

---

* Someone at that meeting subsequently gave a detailed account of this encounter to Richard Reeves of *New York* magazine, the scathing Ford hater who had already shown his colors under a cartoon depicting the Vice President as Bozo the Clown. I was listening and watching faces too intensely to write much down, but my scrawls on White House notepad sheets differ drastically from Reeves's secondhand version in his 1975 volume *"A Ford, Not a Lincoln.* According to Reeves, the President was still Bozo, Haig "a commanding presence," and Marsh was thoroughly put down in front of everyone. One would think Jack or I would remember that if it ever happened, but neither of us do. It didn't.

how Henry was somehow always able to pre-empt Ford's time in the face of the most pressing domestic and political considerations.

It was late, but I waited for Ford to pack his briefcase and head home. The names on the Presidential push-buttons hadn't been changed, so he poked his head in my door and motioned me into the Oval Office. He was obviously in no hurry to leave and said to sit down and talk awhile.

First, he wanted me personally to handle the high-priority business of his picking a new Vice President. No one else should be involved, except Neta, of course. She could move into the little study between the Oval Office and mine, where nobody would drop in, and keep all the paperwork locked up when she wasn't there.

He would use much the same process as Nixon had—I knew how they worked it. John Rhodes and Hugh Scott would be asked to collect the choices of all their Republican Members, in sealed envelopes, deliver them to us, and I was to tabulate them. George Bush would do the same with members of the Republican National Committee. He would like the Cabinet and senior staff to submit their recommendations in writing, too.

Starting Sunday afternoon, he wanted to schedule half-hour sessions with the people he *really* wanted to talk to. I jotted down the names as he reeled them off: Mel Laird, Les Arends, Hugh Scott, Bob Griffin, George Bush, Bryce Harlow, Al Haig, Bob Hartmann, Jack Marsh, John Rhodes, Barber Conable, Elford Cederberg, Barry Goldwater, the Speaker . . . (No, it might be awkward for Carl to come down. He would do it by telephone.)

How about Reagan and Rockefeller? I asked. No, not now. He would be calling some others on the phone, but this was enough to get me started.

He had some more thoughts about the address to the Joint Session on the Hill. How to start off—no fancy oratory. Why not just say something like this: "My friends, we've got a lot of work to do. Let's get on with it."

That sounded fine, and I told him how the speech was coming. Milt was pounding away, and we would try to have something for him by Sunday. I wasn't sure how.

"I'll ask the Cabinet for some suggestions tomorrow," he volunteered. "Henry and Brent are working up something on foreign policy."

Mentioning the Cabinet meeting gave me an idea.

179

PALACE POLITICS

"Wouldn't it be a good idea to change the pictures in the Cabinet Room for your first meeting? It will serve notice that some changes are being made, that this is now the Ford Administration. The photographers will be sure to notice."

The President seemed puzzled. But having been a White House reporter myself, I was quite conscious of this clue to a new President's character.

"Every President puts up the portraits of his favorite predecessors," I continued. "Come on, let's take a look."

He unwound his long legs and followed me the few steps into the empty Cabinet chamber with its long oval table. We fumbled for the light switch.

President Eisenhower, painted by his White House assistant, Tom Stevens, smiled down at us from above the fireplace, where Nixon had hung Ike in the place of honor.

"Kennedy had Jefferson up there," I recalled, "and LBJ replaced him with FDR. I think Ike had Lincoln, the one that's now in the State Dining Room, and I can't remember Truman's favorite. Most of them kept Lincoln around somewhere, but for some reason Nixon had Abe taken down and put up his heroes, Teddy Roosevelt and Woodrow Wilson."

The President inspected the portraits to his left and right, noncommittally.

"I think we should leave Ike where he is," he said.

"I've never thought you especially admired Wilson or TR," I said. "Who would you like to have instead?"

"What is your recommendation?"

"Well, I think we ought to bring old Abe back," I began, and he nodded. "And the other one might be a Democrat. How about Andy Jackson?"

"No, Harry Truman," the President said decisively.

I showed my surprise. "You're sure?"

"Absolutely," he said.

It was an inspired choice as well as a genuine tribute. Harry Truman had been drafted as a substitute for a Vice President who had fallen from grace. Nobody knew much about him outside his home state, and nobody expected much of him.

Fate called Harry Truman to assume the Presidency suddenly, in the midst of grave national trial. Not only did he measure up, but he confounded his critics and almost single-handedly won a full term in his own right. He was no orator, no intellectual, a plain man, a family

180

man, a fighter, a patriot. Nobody liked him except the people and the historians.

In selecting him, I could sense that Gerald Ford was foretelling his own hopes. I was totally confident they would come true. What I felt like saying was corny, but I had to say it.

"Mr. President—" it still sounded a little strange—"you are going to be a great President."

"Thanks, Bob." He smiled. "I don't know about that. But I want to be a *good* President."

★

On Saturday the new President was up before six, put the water on to boil for tea, sliced a melon and popped two halves of an English muffin into the toaster. Wearing baby-blue pajamas, he opened the front door of his Alexandria house to retrieve the Washington *Post*. It wasn't there yet, but a gaggle of news people already were. Seeming a bit surprised, he modestly ducked inside.

Fourteen-year-old Shelley Deming, the neighborhood delivery girl, showed up shortly thereafter and a Secret Service agent hurried the paper to the President, who was churning up the pool with his customary forty laps. Photographs* have preserved for posterity this historic ritual, showing a very minimal paunch for a sixty-one-year-old man.

At about the same hour, across the Potomac in Maryland, my more ample fifty-seven-year-old midriff was navigating considerably fewer laps.

I was equally impatient to get the morning papers to find out how the President's first words had been received.

"Ford Becomes 38th President; Promises Openness and Candor," declared the Washington *Post* on my doorstep. His 849-word Inaugural text was printed in full on the front page. I had exaggerated only a little in telling the President-to-be that "Our long national nightmare is over" would be in every headline. It was a bit long for that, but virtually every account of the historic day, news or commentary, focused on that key phrase. The media carried the message to the country.

ABC called the speech one of "simple eloquence" and Senate

* David Kennerly is a superb photographer. When the new President asked Kennerly if he'd like to be his official photographer, Dave hesitated for about a 1/1000th of a second shutter speed before making the supreme sacrifice. Kennerly was on hand in his new role, and his old clothes, to immortalize the Presidential ablutions.

PALACE POLITICS

Majority Leader Mansfield found it "authentic Jerry Ford . . . superb . . . he hit the right notes." The liberal New York *Post* found Ford's simple and candid words flawless for the occasion, on every point striking "precisely the right tone." The New York *Daily News* termed them "simple and straight, without oratorical flourishes" and characteristic of the man. The Los Angeles *Times* proclaimed a "Smooth Transfer—Mood of Stability as Ford Moves In," and the Chicago *Tribune* welcomed Ford's "well-chosen, dignified and simple words."

Actually it is from the wires of the two major news services, AP and UPI, that most Americans get their impressions of important events. The Associated Press's Frank Cormier couldn't have pleased me more than with his simple opening paragraph: "Declaring that 'our long national nightmare is over,' Gerald R. Ford took the oath today as 38th President of the United States and promised an administration of openness and candor."

Helen Thomas' round-up for United Press International got off to a somewhat snide start, I thought.

"Gerald Rudolph Ford, Jr. [he had not used the "junior" since his adoptive father died in 1961], a Michigan lawyer who was never elected to national office, took the oath today as the 38th President of the United States and promised Americans that, 'God helping me, I will not let you down,' " But the rest was straight enough, stressing the emotional atmosphere of the simple ceremony.

The chorus of praise from the professional politicians was all but unanimous, Democrats vying to outdo Republicans. Former Secretary of State Dean Rusk pledged his support to the new President. National Urban League president Vernon Jordan called for "reconciliation and renewal." Nat Goldfinger, the AFL-CIO economist, said Ford was "a man of real integrity" whose unknown policies, while probably not those of organized labor, would at least permit "starting clean."

By cable and wireless, phone and mail, congratulations and expressions of good will poured into the White House—from Pope Paul in Rome, from a kindergarten in Kentucky, from queens and commissars, Presidents and patriarchs, classmates and shipmates and teammates, former friends and future foes and thousands upon thousands of Americans answering the President's call to prayer.

The small staff of the White House correspondence section was swamped. Roland Elliott set out a call for volunteers, who responded nobly. But how could they recognize and cull out the really close Ford relatives and friends who might be mortally offended to get back a formal acknowledgment? The President had an easy answer. Anyone who couldn't understand such a slip under the circumstances wasn't much of a friend. Nevertheless, those addressed "Dear Jerry" or having internal earmarks of personal association were sent to Mildred Leonard or to me for identification.

One I took in to him pleased him immensely. It was from Morrison Hansborough, a tall, black, elegantly sideburned gentleman who had recently retired from the House barbershop in the Capitol. He had cut Ford's hair every two weeks since way back when it was thick on top, while they talked about current events and the Washington Redskins.

"It is true that we don't agree on some things, but I have always appreciated your tolerance and understanding. I think you will agree that disagreeing is as beautiful as a slice of apple pie," Hansborough began.

He was aware that the President was flooded with advice, but he would offer some more anyhow.

"Keep your intestinal fortitude in good shape . . . you only have one set."

"Don't worry about making enemies; just don't make too many friends."

"Don't concentrate on 1976 to the extent that you forget 1974 and 1975."

"Don't forget your sense of humor, it's good for the heart."

"Don't forget the fine arts, particularly jazzy music which is good for the soul."

Hansborough signed it with "Peace, Love, Happiness."

The President was to have no lack of advisers, and I wish all their counsels had been as sound and as sincere.

Saturday's schedule called for a continuation of the new President's visible and confident assumption of all his duties. Following the transition team's thorough timetable, he would meet next with the old Cabinet and National Security Council.

Neither of these bodies had a Constitutional origin. The Cabinet has been a continuous tradition since Washington, always including the heads of major Executive departments but also any other officials a President wishes to include, such as the Vice President, Ambassador to the United Nations, Director of the Office of Management and Budget and his own senior advisers. The Cabinet as such has no legal authority. As President Lincoln announced after polling his Cabinet on the advisability of issuing his Emancipation Proclamation, "Gentlemen, the vote is eight noes and one aye. The ayes have it."

The faces around the twenty-seven-foot Cabinet table at 10:00 A.M. Saturday morning were very much the same as the previous Tuesday. So were those benignly surveying the scene from the walls—Eisenhower, Wilson, Theodore Roosevelt. (Haig and his little Praetorians had encountered insurmountable difficulties in locating a portrait of Harry Truman.) I took a seat just behind the President's and slightly to his left, where I could hear any whispered instructions. Don Rumsfeld had planted himself in a similar spot slightly to the right, more in the news photographers' line of fire. He was an old hand.

President Ford was unstuffy and gracious as ever, but there was no tentative tone in his voice. A few hours' sleep had done wonders. He was telling them now, not imploring.

Among them only Interior Secretary Rogers Morton could be called a close personal associate. They were all Nixon's second choices; not one of his original 1969 Cabinet had survived. By and large they were probably less political and more able; for many months, they had kept the huge Federal establishment running with little direction or help from the beleaguered White House. As Vice President and as Minority Leader, Ford had worked with all of them in the interest of continuity and stability.

Now, he said, stability and continuity were even more essential. For the present, he would like each of them to stay on the job. It would not be necessary to submit the customary *pro forma* letter of resignation. (Ford had been appalled when Nixon, after his 1972 landslide, had Haldeman collect such letters from everyone high in his Administration, undated, for use at the President's pleasure.)

The President explained briefly about the transition group and said he would make no major decisions on personnel changes until he received their recommendations. Over the next few weeks he would talk privately with every Cabinet officer, and his door would always be open to them. Everyone smiled.

Of course, the President added as the smiles faded, at some point he might want to make some changes. Or they might want to return to private life. But when that time came, they would talk it over face to face.

Asserting the primacy of the Secretary of State, Kissinger responded on behalf of all that "we want to express unflagging support and total loyalty to you." Everyone nodded, including James Schle-

184

singer, whom everyone knew Ford had fingered months ago for early retirement.

I studied the faces of the others; Jim Lynn, Earl Butz, Bill Simon, William Saxbe, Peter Brennan, Roy Ash, George Bush, Dean Burch, Caspar Weinberger, Rogers Morton, Fred Dent, Claude Brinegar, John Scali, Kenneth Rush. How many would the President really retain? Kissinger certainly; Morton, but maybe in another role; probably Earl Butz, who went back to the Eisenhower era and was a legend in the corn belt. And George Bush, if George didn't wind up Vice President.*

The President thanked Henry and, eying his old empty chair, invited the Cabinet to submit their confidential Vice Presidential recommendations in writing by next Wednesday. He would also like their suggestions for his first address to the Congress. He started around the table clockwise.

The meeting of the National Security Council, set to follow the Cabinet session, was the first clash of wills between Henry Kissinger and Ford's transition advisers. The NSC was set up after World War II with the intention of synchronizing the President's responsibilities in national defense and international affairs. The President, the Vice President, the Secretary of State and the Secretary of Defense are the only statutory members. The Secretary of the Treasury, the Chairman of the Joint Chiefs of Staff and of the Joint Intelligence Board normally attend, plus anyone else the President wants there.

At this point Kissinger was still serving as Assistant to the President for National Security Affairs, which meant that he was White House director of the NSC staff as well as Secretary of State. Many thoughtful people, some with no personal animus toward Henry, felt this dual role negated the main purpose of the NSC, which was to give the President his own source of input on foreign affairs, independent of the traditional State or Defense Department channels. But Henry coveted both hats and his convenient corner office in the West Wing.**

---

* As a prophet I get about B-minus. When Ford left office, two and one-half years later, only Kissinger and Simon still sat in the same places. Lynn and Dent had played descending musical chairs. So had Morton until he exhausted his failing health fighting little Praetorians.
** When Bryce Harlow occupied the office between Kissinger's and Haldeman's that was later mine, it had the only private toilet in the West Wing other than the President's. Once when Bryce was briefly away from Washington Henry managed to have the door from the facility into Harlow's suite

PALACE POLITICS

When the President's advisers sought his early assertion of command over the nation's top security body as part of the transition symbolism, it did not set well with Henry. To give Kissinger the benefit of sincere misgivings, he argued that the NSC meeting on Ford's second day might be misread abroad (and even at home) as a crisis signal, something like the Cuban missile thing. There were indeed plenty of potential flash points in Cyprus, Korea and the Middle East.

At first, Ford acceded to Henry's arguments, and the NSC meeting was postponed. Marsh, Scranton, Rumsfeld and I saw this as a symbolic danger of its own. Why was Henry alone infallible? The President reversed himself and put the meeting back on his calendar.

Henry lingered only long enough to show minimal respect. As soon as the photographers finished snapping the scene and the President opened the meeting, he excused himself to go back to the State Department; his walkout was a perfectly fail-safe nose-thumbing.

Back in the Oval Office, after the NSC session, Ford announced to Marsh and me that he was hungry and thought he'd go over to the EOB and finish up his cottage cheese that was in the refrigerator. Jack looked a bit shocked.

"Mr. President, there's a pantry with a steward on duty just outside this door here, and downstairs we've got a full Navy mess, you know, and they'll bring whatever you want right here to your desk, and if they don't have cottage cheese they can run out and get it for you...."

The President grinned. Obviously he was experiencing a touch of "You Can't Go Home Again" and wanted to take one last look around his Vice Presidental haunts.

"No, never mind. There's some things I want to get out of my desk. I won't be long."

He headed for the door. The Secret Service agents scrambled in hot pursuit. I followed, not for cottage cheese but to see how Milt was coming on the speech.

As he was finishing his lunch, the President called me in. He said his swearing-in was going to be rerun on TV, would I like to watch it with him? He was a habitual self-critic of his own performances, learning from each mistake. But this time he was more than satisfied. It was a good speech, he said to me. What about the next one?

---

walled up and plastered and the entry moved adjacent to Kissinger's suite. Returning, Harlow made the wry observation that he was "the only *man* in Washington ever to lose his *head* to Henry Kissinger."

I showed him what Milt had done. A good start, but it needed more work. He suggested some changes. Could he have a copy to take home tonight?

Patient and appreciative as he was, I always had a sneaking suspicion that Ford believed his speeches were spun by the light of the moon, perhaps by some distant cousin of the Tooth Fairy after I put a sheaf of blank paper under my pillow.

He felt, I think, that writing was *my* trade, not his. He had little appreciation of literature as an art form; neither poetry nor music interested him much.*

When I returned to my West Wing office, Rumsfeld stuck his head in the door. He still didn't have a roosting place in the White House proper; all the old hands were hanging onto theirs for dear life. Did I have a minute? Sure.

"What is the first thing we need to do to get a grip on this place?" he asked.

"Two things, right away," I said. "First, somebody has to manage the President's time more frugally and systematically. The schedulers are running him ragged. Mind you, it's more than half his fault. He keeps on adding commitments, never subtracts any. He makes these promises in person. Nobody knows until it's done. He thinks he's an iron man, and he can't say no to an old buddy. Somebody else has got to be his abominable no-man. I'm tired of it, and I've lost almost every round.

"The second thing is personnel. Haig and the Nixon personnel office are going right on grinding out Presidential nominations and appointments. They may be fine people, but they're not Ford people. He's got to surround himself with his own team as fast as he can. Nobody's going to vacate until they're told to, and the President has just told them never to mind."

Rummy nodded. Recruiting was supposed to be Bill Scranton's business, but he'd see what he could do. He congratulated me on the President's Inaugural speech and on my new job. We could work together and help each other help the President, he said and hustled off.

Next, Bill Casselman and Ben Becker came by to report they had

* Ford had a good sense of rhythm, but it was muscular, as in dancing or in sports. He could not recite in cadence, nor carry the tune of "The Star-Spangled Banner." He never hummed. I am not a medical expert, but I think he is tone-deaf. But, by rigorous discipline and concentration, he could make a good speech when he wanted to.

found the Burn Room of the White House so jammed with bags of paper to be destroyed that the overflow was piling up in unguarded corridors. Becker had ordered the burning stopped until further notice and the paper-shredder used only for material bearing a national security classification.

"There's a question," Casselman cautioned, "as to whether we really *want* to have possession of all the stuff that's in those burn bags." Bill had a point. Besides, it would take a small army of people a year to go through all of it. If we really wanted to put Watergate behind us, why fool with the natural disposition of old trash?

"Not a lot is going to pile up over the weekend," I said. "We'll decide Monday, after you talk to Phil about it."

A few of the essential tools a senior White House aide must have to maintain his ability to serve the President came my way that first full day in the West Wing, two of them more or less by accident.

As part of its sophisticated security system, the Secret Service maintains a network of electronic gadgets that display at all times the whereabouts of the President, the First Lady and their immediate family, the Vice President and the Secretary of State. One of these was installed in Rose Mary Woods's old office, where I had established a lonely beachhead. It was a fascinating discovery; no wonder they always knew what Vice President Ford was doing.

I could tell by glancing at the gadget whether the President was in the Oval Office, the Cabinet Room, the barbershop, the doctor's office or walking his dog Liberty.

An asterisk (*) would appear on the gadget and an almost inaudible "beep" would sound whenever the President was in transit from one location to another. The time of his departure would be recorded, whether from "Family Quarters" or "Peking, China." His destination did not show up until the President had safely arrived; then the time would change and his new whereabouts would be displayed.

Only a few key offices had these privileged sources of immediate information: Haig's, Kissinger's, the chief of the Presidential protective detail, the Military Assistant and the keeper of the Oval Office door. They were invaluable in getting through to the President in a hurry when he was not at his desk and in spotting surprise switches in his schedule.

Another immensely important piece of machinery was the autopen. Hundreds, sometimes thousands of pieces of paper issue daily from the White House bearing a fully legal pen-and-ink signature of the President. Obviously, he doesn't sign them all by hand.

Whoever controls this facsimile signing machine is an a position to protect the President from such acute embarrassments as calling a lifelong friend "Mister," sending an obvious form letter to a United States Senator or signing an inaccurate or improper statement.

The autopen machines in the bowels of the White House were locked up and the matrices duplicating the hand of "Richard Nixon" became inoperative on the night of August 8. Nixon himself signed his resignation in a steady hand.

Vice Presidents, along with many other government officials, have their own autopens. I had given Frank Pagnotta and Jim Brown strict orders to guard against any abuse of the Ford signature, which was still in our old EOB suite. All of Ford's routine mail had to be taken there for signature. The little Praetorians of the Haldeman–Haig secretariat were frantic.

I was still innocent and was inclined to give up responsibility for the autopen. But already the Praetorians began to overplay their hand. The President wanted to swear me in at two that afternoon. He asked Haig to make the arrangements and to date my commission August 9—the day he became President and made the appointment. The President said he would stand as my witness, and I should get Roberta and anyone else I wanted in for a little ceremony. I called home and my son Rob's apartment; there was no way to get my daughter Bobbie and her family up from Kentucky in the time we had. I asked Neta to invite all the Vice Presidential people and transition-team members and Benton Becker.

Just before my swearing-in, Pagnotta appeared in a high state of agitation, carrying my commission. It had been duly inscribed by the calligrapher and countersigned by the Secretary of State, but the space for the Presidential signature was blank. "They sent this over to be signed *on the autopen,*" Frank snorted. "They only do that for junior ribbon clerks. The President *always* signs for his Cabinet and senior aides. Now you *know* this wasn't any accident."

No, it wasn't. I picked up the parchment and marched through the private door into the Oval Office. Buchen and Becker were there, conferring about some legal question. I apologized for interrupting and told the President merely that this had to be signed before I could be duly sworn.

Sure, he said, fishing for a pen. He didn't have one in his pocket, and neither did I. I picked up one from his desk set, a gift from Mike Mansfield. That's just for sentiment, he said; it hasn't worked for years.

Becker came to the rescue with a black-and-gold Parker from his pocket. The President signed. Benton refused to take it back. "Give it to Bob, Mr. President," he said. "He can have it framed."

I protested. "But it's too good a pen, a Parker."

"Naw," said Becker. "Look closer. Made in Japan."

It was. I took the pen, the commission, said thanks and got out of there. Pagnotta, much relieved, promised to have them both framed.

"We'll keep control of the signing machine," I called to Pagnotta, "until the President himself tells me otherwise." (He never did.)

The impromptu ceremony in the Oval Office at which I became part of the official family of the President of the United States was a moving and soul-searching experience. My job would be essentially the same as it had been for more than eight years—to help Gerald R. Ford in any way I could. Yet the goal would no longer be simply Ford's success or the party's success. Such considerations would not vanish, but they would always be secondary to the best interests of the United States of America, its Constitution and laws.

Roberta brought the Bible she had given me when I sailed from San Francisco in World War II, its brown leather cover worn and cracking, some of the onionskin pages torn. It was opened to the Old Testament passage she had inscribed on the flyleaf thirty-one years before: "Entreat me not to leave thee, or to return from following after thee, for whithersoever thou goest, I will go. . . ." The President was standing to one side. Behind us were the battle colors of the five services, heavy with campaign ribbons, silently proclaiming the powers of life and death implicit in the Presidency. Roberta, standing between the President and me, held the Bible. Rob stood at my left shoulder and, behind him, faithful Neta.

When it was over, I simultaneoulsy kissed Roberta, hugged Rob with my left arm and reached my right hand out to meet the President's. It was quite a feat, and his solemn mien changed to a hearty laugh. He made a gracious little speech for the benefit of my friends, calling me "an invaluable assistant" past, present and future. Everybody crowded around to congratulate me.

Betty Ford called me from home. This happened rarely; I was never quite sure how she really felt about me. For my part, I liked her, sympathized with her loneliness and respected her political instincts. They were often (but not always) more acute than her husband's.

She was intensely jealous of her celebrated mate (at least until she came into her own as "First Mama"), not in any sexual way, for she needn't be. I accompanied Ford on enough overnight trips to know he wasn't afflicted with what Congressional cloakroom wags termed "the Curse of the Kennedys." His eye wandered sometimes, but nothing more. He was as devoted to his wife as he was career-oriented.

But Betty was jealous of his time. She had to have someone to blame for his incessant absences, late homecomings and cold suppers. She didn't want to blame him, so she took it out on the top male on his staff. Her contacts with the staff were minimal; they were part of his other world. Not very subtly, they endured her prolonged telephone ramblings and conveyed the message that they worked for her husband, not for her. I suppose I was unconsciously guilty of this; long ago my eyes had been opened about bosses' wives. I think she resented me, for a time, more than I knew, even more than she confided to a society newswoman who splashed it all over a national magazine.

I say "for a time" because before his death in 1972 Betty's resentment was directed at Frank Meyer, Ford's longtime Congressional aide. Afterward her animus was transferred from me to Rumsfeld, much to my relief.

I don't know what she thought of Cheney, for by the time of his apogee she was whirling happily in her own orbit. I suppose she blames him—or thanks him—for Ford's losing the White House.

But Betty's call on Saturday was simple and touching. Would I, if the occasion arose, conspire with her to get Jerry to go to church on his first Sunday as President of the United States? Of course I would.

When we were going over his plans for private talks about prospective Vice Presidents, I saw my chance. "It's really none of my business, but I think you ought to take Betty to church in the morning," I said. "I think she would like that, and you need all the help you can get."

He allowed that she had been urging him to go, and he would really like to, but he hadn't been very good about attendance lately. Wouldn't it look hypocritical if he suddenly became a regular churchgoer just because he was President? Maybe he should wait a week, anyhow. I said I didn't think anyone would be that cynical. People liked to have their Presidents go to church.

When the President's Sunday schedule came off the Xerox machines, that's how it was. I phoned Betty to tip her off to be properly surprised. I felt I had done my good turn for the day.

On Sunday, when they returned from church, I joined them in their Alexandria home for the Ford family's traditional diet-busting Sunday brunch, waffles with strawberries and sour cream. I brought

191

along my first revision of Milt Friedman's draft for the President's maiden speech to Congress on Monday. Millions of Americans would be watching at prime evening time, and it was important to set the right tone. Many had missed Ford's swearing-in, and the new President would have to show the nation that he was fully in charge.

Two of Milt's original lines are memorable. Taking the laugh line I had written for his first speech as Vice President, "I am a Ford, not a Lincoln," Friedman deftly updated it into a more progressive thrust: "While I am still a Ford, I am not a Model T."

He also coined the phrase "unity in diversity" to describe Ford's concept of America and its system of government. The President liked it; it would turn up often throughout his term of office.

Curiously, Milt's copy of the first draft that went to the President credits me with the triple alliteration "conciliation, compromise, cooperation" (a fourth, "communication," was a late-starter). This was the quote the news media seized on as the keynote of the speech. My copy of the first draft indicates it was Milt's idea. Anyhow, it worked.

With the final details settled, nothing remained but for the final text to be put into large type and for the President to spend some time alone familiarizing himself with it.

Near the back of the First Lady's gallery places had been found for Roberta and Nancy Kissinger. In the front row, on the telegenic side of Mrs. Ford, sat General Alexander Haig, as he always had beside Mrs. Nixon. Other choice seats were taken by other senior Nixon holdovers, all male, who made up the seating chart as if nothing had changed. The President himself asked that David and Julie Eisenhower and Louella Dirksen, widow of the Senator, be invited. Three of the Ford children filled up the rest of the front row.

Now that we were Cabinet-rank Counsellors, Jack Marsh and I would march in with the Cabinet. As we were being lined up in the Speaker's office, Marsh and I discovered that we had been listed by the White House advance men to bring up the rear of the procession, behind not only the Cabinet heads but also Nixon's old Counsellors, Dean Burch and Kenneth Rush and OMB Director Roy Ash.

That was the proper protocol, we were imperiously admonished by one of the Praetorians. Not tonight, Jack muttered between set teeth. This was his turf, where he'd served as a Member for eight years. And I had been the Minority Leader's aide on that same floor for seven. We agreed that when the signal to move was given, we'd lock arms and simply shove our way in at the head of the Counsellors.

"Lucky Anne Armstrong isn't here," I whispered. "We couldn't very well elbow a lady."

The President entered to a demonstration of genuine affection. It was authentic Jerry Ford, who, after finally squelching the applause that accompanied him to the rostrum, brought them to their feet again by saying, "I don't want a honeymoon with you. I want a good marriage."

I overheard a delighted Democratic Senator sitting behind me whisper, "Can you imagine Nixon saying something like that?"

He turned serious for a while and then caught them with a genuine Ford wisecrack: "My office door has always been open, and that is how it is going to be at the White House. Yes, Congressmen will be welcomed—if you don't overdo it. Now I ask you to join with me in getting this country revved up and moving. The State of the Union is excellent. But the state of our economy is not so good. The American wage-earner and the American housewife are a lot better economists than most economists care to admit. They know that a government big enough to give you everything you want is a government big enough to take from you everything you have."

(This favorite Ford line, later erroneously attributed to both Reagan and Nixon, was borrowed from Harold McLean, a business executive Ford heard speak to the Economic Club in Chicago in 1945. He inserted it in almost every speech. The White House press and little Praetorians snickered and groaned, but it never failed to get a big hand.)

The Congressional audience dozed slightly during the familiar recital of Kissinger's round-the-world tour. Soviet Ambassador Anatoly Dobrynin applauded along with the Democrats when Ford invoked the shade of John F. Kennedy: "I say to you in words that cannot be improved upon: Let us never negotiate out of fear, but let us never fear to negotiate. If we want to restore confidence in ourselves as working politicians, the first thing we all have to do is to learn to say 'No.' "

As the President moved without a misstep toward his conclusion, I held my breath. We had encountered some difficulty ending on exactly the right upbeat note. I remembered the President's private exchange with me on his first evening in office and proposed that he say, "I don't want to be a *great* President. I want to be a *good* President."

Ford struck out the first sentence without hesitation. He was right: no harm in wanting to be both. But where I had written "I want your help" he made it "I *need* your help."

193

PALACE POLITICS

And so he looked straight at the red eye of the center camera and it came out simply and with great conviction: "Fellow Americans, one final word. I want to be a good President. I need your help. We all need God's sure guidance. With it, nothing can stop the United States of America."

9

REACHING OUT; DIGGING IN

Sunday in the West Wing of the White House differs from other days only superficially. It is the only day when callers are not expected, and male staff members sometimes show up without jackets and ties. Most of the clerical and secretarial people are absent. The mess is closed, and vending machines are the only source of victuals. There is ample parking on West Executive Avenue, and the President's senior aides come in a few hours later and go home a little earlier than usual.

Otherwise, it is the day when you try to get the work done that was left undone Friday and didn't get finished on Saturday. It is also a day for the tireless Praetorians to plot their future stratagems, hopefully unobserved.

If this was all a mystery to the new President's longtime aides on their first weekend in the White House, we were soon to learn. No sooner had I showed up in my office than Benton Becker brought in some astonishing news.

Working late Saturday night, Becker had discovered rows of military trucks lined up outside the West Basement entrance, waiting to load up material that was to be airlifted from Andrews Air Force Base to San Clemente. From the number of vehicles it was obviously a lot of stuff. Some file cabinets were already being loaded.

Benton didn't know what they contained of Nixon's valuable records, but he notified the Executive Protective Service and, on his own dubious authority, ordered the transfer halted. Becker needed to know what President *Ford* wanted.

The EPS went along, but the Air Force people had their orders. From whom? Haig? General Lawson, Nixon's military assistant? Ex-Master Sergeant Bill Gulley, the real czar? Marine Colonel Jack Brennan, in California with the ex-President? Well, nobody could be quite sure where the order originated.

In any case, the Secret Service wouldn't let the trucks take anything away and made the unhappy airmen unload what they had already loaded. The Air Force lost the night engagement and returned empty to Andrews.

I assured Benton he had done the right thing and said I would take full responsibility for it. The office of President, not Richard Nixon alone, was under court order to safeguard evidence. We next conferred with Phil Buchen, who agreed that Ford shouldn't be bothered with the distressing incident until he had given his big Monday-night speech. We all vowed to say nothing to anyone until we found out more about the operation and who ordered it.

But whoever was frustrated by our intervention must have talked. At his noon press briefing, TerHorst (who was totally in the dark about this) was asked twenty-one questions about the custody of the Nixon tapes, their legal status, and possible contacts between San Clemente and the White House staff.

First, Pete Lisagor innocently asked, "Jerry, can you tell us whether there is anything new on the status of President Nixon's tapes and papers and documents? I think you said the other day they were being studied by the legal people."

TerHorst fell back on his earlier assumption, but Lisagor and Marty Schramm caught him in a whipsaw reminiscent of the old Ziegler-baiting days, except it was more amiable.

Which legal people? Well, Buzhardt was still around, and Justice had lots of attorneys. Specifically who at Justice? Couldn't say. Is St. Clair involved? Don't know, but he's still on the payroll. Then the key question.

"To follow that a moment, are the papers and documents, so far as you know, still intact?"

TerHorst said yes, they were. They were in custody of the Secret Service "and no disposition nor movement of them has occurred."

Thanks to Becker, Jerry was right. Not that it wasn't close.

The sparring went on.

"Jerry, was former President Nixon blocked from taking the tapes out of storage here?"

TerHorst said, again accurately, that he was not aware of that. But the inquisition continued. Had Nixon asserted that the tapes were his personal property?

The press secretary wasn't aware of that.

"Has the President [Ford] been in contact with the former President since Friday?"

196

There it was—the question that was to haunt Gerald Ford and all of his press spokesmen for almost three years.

TerHorst candidly said he hadn't asked the President that, but he was not aware of any contact.

The Attorney General had been spotted in the West Wing that morning. Did he see the President? No, TerHorst said, he believed Saxbe met with General Haig. Ah-ha! What about?

"Specifically, can you rule out the possibility that General Haig might have met with the Attorney General at the request of Mr. Nixon?"

Jerry gamely said he wouldn't rule it out but would have to ask. Yet this was a curious question indeed. So was the next one: "Jerry, does President Nixon still have any mechanism of contacting staff members back here and asking them to do one favor or another for him, or to look up this or check that or whatever it might be, and if so, could you tell us how that works?"

TerHorst's answer suggests both wariness and inner panic.

"There obviously—without accepting, Marty, the suggestions in your specific question—is continuing liaison between the former President and the present one, and the essential mechanism [for] that is of course Ron Zeigler and Steve Bull and Jerry Warren and anyone else to whom former President Nixon would care to talk."

What TerHorst was admitting was the obvious, stark fact that there was hardly anyone in the Ford White House that Nixon or his aides-in-exile could not call, day or night, to ask a favor.

What Buchen and Becker and I knew was that obviously they had already done so.

They would continue to do so as late as February 1976, when former President Nixon's "private" return trip to the People's Republic of China coincided with the critical New Hampshire primary and didn't help Ford a bit. There were recurrent reports, which I could never verify, that the military couriers who shuttled between Washington and San Clemente in government aircraft carried selected vintages from the White House wine cellar as well as classified papers.

The ghost of Richard Nixon would not go west. His Praetorians dug in to defend their past, their positions, their prerogatives and their power. To them the inexperienced new President was primarily a hostage, and his circle of inexperienced new aides were natural enemies to be quickly disarmed.

Mary McGrory, the Washington *Star*'s syndicated columnist, is said to have the charitable heart of a Poor Clare personally. Politically, she is a hybrid of Madam LaFarge and Westbrook Pegler. In her trade, she has no present equal in rectitude, ferocity or skill in the weaponry of words. Her victims are predominantly conservatives; her finely crafted sentences evoke the guilty pleasure of a live sacrifice. Summing up the Ford Inaugural, Mary wrote: "The hope that Ford, a limited man, will grow in the White House is limited. He is a devout partisan." Nonetheless, she concluded, "Ford's character and temperament are ideally suited to the times. After two secretive and surprise-mad Presidents, his plodding style will be restful. For the present it is enough that he replaced a man who destroyed himself by taping his private conversations. Gerald Ford would never do that."

Reading this, and remembering the wild ovation this President received from Congress when he pledged there would be no bugging or taping by a Ford Administration, I could hardly have been more flabbergasted when a very discreet and dependable associate of long standing, who knew his way around the White House by virtue of a sensitive but nonpolitical job, asked if he could have a few words with me in strictest confidence. I got up and closed the office door.

"I'm not supposed to have anything to do with this," he began almost in a whisper. "But I don't think it's fair to the President and you people who are new here. There are a lot of things you don't know."

I nodded agreement.

"Well," my informant continued, "the President ought to know that his Oval Office is still bugged, and you should know that any of these telephones may be bugged, if certain parties just ask the Secret Service to do it."

Of course the President ought to know. But how could we prove it?

"Not 'we,' " he quickly corrected. "I don't know anything about such things. You'll have to check it out somehow for yourself."

I thanked him and promised to tell no one where the tip came from. I put in a call for Becker. Benton would look into it. Pretty soon he was back.

"Would you believe," he began, "that there are two microphones inside the President's desk and two more imbedded in the walls behind the brass fixtures at the other end of the Oval Office?"

I said it couldn't be true. It *was* true, Benton said; he had seen for himself. Then where did the wires lead? Who was listening?

"Nobody, at least not so far as I know. The wires lead to a closet where they have been snipped off, but anybody could hook up a recorder to them. Even I could, and my electronic aptitude is zero. Anyhow, if anybody gets wind of those microphones, who's going to believe the wires lead nowhere?"

He was right. This was too big for us to act on our own. The President had to be told, without another moment's delay. We went in together.

Becker told his story. The President's jaw tightened. I knew the sign. He slammed what he was reading on the desk, hard enough to rattle the sturdiest microphones.

"Dammit! They told me definitely there weren't any—that they'd all been removed long ago. Back when Butterfield first told the Ervin committee that there were tapes. Bob, you remember I asked Al Haig specifically."

The President dismissed us and summoned Haig. What was said only they know, but the Secret Service dug the microphones out that very night and handed them in a plastic bag to Becker. Becker personally delivered them to Stuart Knight, Director of the Secret Service, as possible future evidence. The Oval Office walls were replastered and repainted by morning.*

Perhaps, just maybe, Haig didn't know they were still there. But he was a meticulous detail man. If he didn't know he shouldn't have answered until he made sure. It was the President of the United States who asked and relied on his answer. Those hidden mikes left the President of the United States misinformed and exposed for ten days to the potential of calamitous embarrassment.

The official transition group—Marsh, Morton, Rumsfeld and Scranton—had been hard at work since August 9 to complete its report for the President by the same ten-day deadline he had set for selecting a Vice President.

By one of those feats of legerdemain at which practiced politicians excel, Rummy—who had originally been designated secretary and co-ordinator of the group—emerged in an evolution of press accounts as its chairman or "head."

The agile Ambassador joined me and Haig around the President's desk every morning right after Kissinger excused his new pupil. Don was working hand in glove with me, I thought. At the same time, Rumsfeld was working hand in glove with Haig, preparing to take

---

* Ford issued strict orders against phone-tapping. So far as I know there was none. I even left my dictating machine at home.

PALACE POLITICS

over the veteran Praetorian Guard Haig had inherited from Haldeman, with a few Rumsfeld substitutions. The control system that Haldeman, Ehrlichman, Fred Malek, Jerry Jones and others so effectively
forged in the first Nixon term was intact, except for those who had engaged the attention of the Special Watergate Prosecutor. They were
more than eager to vindicate the system (which was all they ever knew
about government and politics) and to exercise its ironclad control of
the White House staff and the upper Executive establishment.

The common denominator of Praetorians, whether in Caesar's
palace or the White House, is their consummate need for a tough commander. They are basically bullies, playing with vicarious power, protected by the plea that they are carrying out orders.

Bob Haldeman claims credit for having chosen Al Haig as his
successor. In a double backhand, he claims that anyone tough enough
to endure being egomaniac Kissinger's deputy would be able to cope
with Nixon's schizophrenic genius.

Haig was an entirely different personality from Haldeman. He
was usually soft-spoken and polite, seasoned in both battlefield and
bureaucratic combat, infinitely more of a diplomat and politician.
Haldeman, on the other hand, was less driven by personal ambition;
he was totally sublimated to what he perceived to be the interests of
Richard Nixon. Whatever Haig's motives, he preserved and perfected
Haldeman's system.

Rumsfeld had an enormous advantage over Haig and the other
Praetorians. They had been meticulous students of Nixon and Haldeman, but Rummy was also a student of Gerald R. Ford. The rest held
the new President in almost open contempt. They considered him and
his cronies as sorely in need of their sophisticated knowledge of Presidential behavior. Rumsfeld knew better. He knew that he would have
to carry out 90 percent of what Ford wanted in order to get 10 percent
of what he wanted. And he was too smart to take on other longtime
Ford favorites in a frontal showdown.

Thus, to the nervous Nixon holdovers, Rummy was a former
White House colleague, the prodigal returned. On the transition team,
and confiding to Congressional pals, Rumsfeld was the most impatient
of all in prescribing a sweeping, symbolic purge of everyone associated
with Nixon's final spasms.

Without dissent on the part of Rumsfeld, the group recommended
that Haig's eventual successor be stripped of the imperious "chief of
staff" title and the accumulated layers of personal authority Haldeman
and Haig exercised over other White House aides. The Haig operation

had become a bottleneck, they concluded. In the future, this Presidential assistant should "coordinate but not control" the activities of Ford's senior advisers. He would be a traffic cop but not a Berlin Wall at the Oval Office door. There was no suggestion that he even be *primus inter pares.* *

The transition group envisioned that six West Wing assistants, responsible for foreign, domestic and economic affairs, budget, personnel and legal counsel, would have direct and immediate access to the President at all times. They made no recommendations for filling these slots, although Ford had designated Henry Kissinger to fill the first of them. Marsh and I would be generalists and trouble-shooters with wide freedom of action. The press secretary's unique situation was already settled.

Not knowing for certain who the Vice President might be, they were vague about his Executive responsibilities. Certainly he should be a principal Presidential adviser, but he should not be given *operating* responsibility over either domestic or economic policy. This would unbalance the desired parity among senior aides.

Under Nixon, a Babel of official Administration comments about the ailing economy had contributed to its instability. The transition group proposed that the Secretary of the Treasury be publicly and explicitly designated by the President as his sole authorized spokesman on economic policy. (A splendid idea, if one ignores the garrulous nature of economists.)

In the Cabinet Room, together with the original Buchen transition team and those of us who had been joined in his informal "Kitchen Cabinet," the President listened through nearly two hours of recommendations. He interjected sharp questions but betrayed neither approval nor disapproval of the major thrusts.

Finally, he tamped out his pipe in the aluminum Presidential ashtray with a loud clatter, clamped his original copy of the report under his arm, said the group should continue to gather approximately monthly to assess progress and give him candid counsel and took off for a Senate party.

Rumsfeld was slated to fly back to Brussels that night** because of the Cyprus crisis. The group had intended to go out of business after

---

* "First among equals" was the way Rummy liked to be characterized.
** Rumsfeld a week earlier told Clifton Daniel, the New York *Times* bureau chief, that "any suggestion I'll be joining the White House staff is absolutely inaccurate. There has been no such discussion and I have no such intention."

submitting its report, and a liquidation party was laid on. Instead of a celebration, it was a wake.

Nothing had been decided, nothing accepted, nothing rejected. The President would study the recommendations, neatly typed and cleansed of sweaty revisions and the stale-tobacco smell of endless argument.

But of course that is the way the system works. A President makes decisions alone, rarely in full view of a roomful of interested witnesses. Often events make Presidential decision unnecessary; things have a way of working themselves out.

In the end, some of these well-conceived changes *were* made, but it was Donald Rumsfeld who made them. Bill Simon was named the President's chief economic spokesman. The senior White House staff was restructured along the recommended lines, the office of chief of staff was abolished, the Vice President was tendered a major advisory role while his operational clout was carefully circumscribed.

A few key Nixon officials eventually faded into the sunset, to be replaced by other Nixon retreads and Rumsfeld recruits. But beneath all this shuffling of musical chairs on the upper levels of the West Wing, the Praetorian Guard remained.

The Nixon-to-Ford transition was superbly planned. It was not a failure. It just never happened.

None of the senior Nixon aides would budge from his or her West Wing bunker. I shared Rose Mary Woods's former suite with Buchen and his confidential secretary, Eva Dougherty. Dorothy Downton, the President's personal secretary, was crowded into the center room with Neta and Gail.

Jack Marsh took up temporary residence in the inside room across the hall by simply ordering Haig's batman, Major George Joulwain, to get out. Otherwise, the Ford people remained literally shut out of the White House. Somehow, the new broom had been misplaced.

Haig was obviously suffering insecurity pains. He cried on the sympathetic shoulder of UPI's Helen Thomas about his momentous role in recent history despite which "some of Ford's top assistants would like to see him depart." And the transition group had even recommended eliminating his job.

Viewed from his bunker, Haig was acting in the honorable tradition of the combat commander. He was looking out for his troops, and for the foot soldiers and second lieutenants, this was fine. There was no reason why he should not go about it in an open and aboveboard way.

Looking back, I now believe that Haig was less guilty of insubordination than of the habit-forming and heady intoxication of power. At the time I was furious at his refusal to recognize that Gerald Ford, not Alexander Haig, was now President of the United States.

Soon the news columns were full of animated accounts of a bloody, bare-knuckle power struggle between Haig and Hartmann. All of Ford's Kitchen Cabinet wanted Haig out and egged me on eagerly. But they did nothing about it themselves except whisper to the press, write oblique memos and bitch. The President, I knew, hated these techniques. Haig would have to hang himself.

Bill Scranton tangled with Haig early on. The transition group agreed on the day Ford took office that Scranton and Haig would meet with the new President, first thing the next morning, on the way the White House staff system presently worked. Scranton understood this would be at 9:30. I was in the Oval Office when Haig arrived about 8:30 bearing a fat black briefing book. He stood waiting for me to go away. The President took in the situation and said affably that this was something Bob should probably know about, too. General Haig uncomfortably proceeded with the briefing.

Nothing was said or seen of Scranton. For an hour or so Haig displayed elaborate organizational charts and paper-flow diagrams. Nothing was very clear except that nobody could possibly understand the system except Haig.

Ford said he'd like to have the book, which broke down the White House staff and listed the current occupant of each position, tenure, title and pay. He wanted to take it home to study. I said I'd like a copy, too.

Incredibly, the general in mufti told the President of the United States he couldn't have it. It was Haig's only working copy!

I expected an explosion, but Ford blandly told Haig to have a couple more copies made. I don't know whether the President ever got his. I never did.

Scranton had turned up at 9:30 to find the Oval Office door barred by Terry O'Donnell. Always polite, Terry told Scranton the President was conferring with Haig and Hartmann. The general had ordered that nobody disturb them.

Fuming, the former Governor of Pennsylvania and Yale classmate of Ford's sat there waiting for Haig's exit. Haig briskly informed Scranton that the briefing was over. He had handled it—since Scranton apparently was unable to get up on time. The President now wished to be left alone to prepare for his first Cabinet meeting.

The fight had gone out of Scranton. I don't think he ever told the President of the incident, but either he or Haig told at least one reporter. Discouraged, Bill soon went back to his Pennsylvania home, and the shuffling of Ford and Nixon staffs was left to Rumsfeld.

That same day, Haig ran quickly through a list of pending Nixon appointments to high-level political jobs requiring confirmation by the Senate. Twenty-four of them had already been sent to the Hill. The White House staffing process had been completed on fourteen others, but they had not moved beyond Haig's final approval. Should he proceed?

The President, his thoughts elsewhere, casually told Haig sure, go ahead. Later, apparently reconsidering, he told me what had transpired.

I said, not knowing who they were, perhaps he'd better take a longer look at them. He told me to retrieve the lists from Haig and, after a three-day stall, I saw they contained a number of Nixon's old Praetorians whose elevation to well-paid sinecures could have acutely embarrassed Ford.* The general was no fool, however. His covering memo baldly claimed that it was Haig's idea, not mine, to allow Ford to reconsider.

Reconsider he did, approving seventeen of the twenty-four nominations already before the Senate and demanding to see the files on those who had been as good as appointed by Haig.

What neither the new President nor I knew on his second day in office was that Haig, not Nixon, had been making most of these key Presidential nominations for months. Put more precisely, nobody except Haig and Nixon will ever know.

The Haldeman–Haig system called for "decision memos" to be submitted to the President. At the bottom would be a space for the President to initial "Approve," "Disapprove" or add his choice of candidates or options.

* Typical of these was Daniel T. Kingsley, one of Fred Malek's lieutenants among the Nixon Praetorians, who was nominated for a $36,000-a-year sinecure on the Federal Power Commission. Ford balked at this, and Kingsley was switched to the less visible post of Associate Administrator of the Small Business Administration. Most of the others eventually found places in the Ford Administration. That they were perfectly capable public servants does not mitigate the fast shuffle Haig tried to pull on the new President.

These papers were then carefully filed away as permanent proof that the decision actually was the President's and even, on occasion, to show him that he personally made it. But in the archives of the last Nixon years historians will find a point where the familiar circumscribed "R" for Richard is more and more frequently replaced by a bold "H" for Haig.

It was Haig alone who carried in to Nixon's desk the daily grist of governmental actions which Constitutionally only the President can direct. When Haig emerged, the stacks of decision memos would bear his initials, and only he knew what Nixon had said. Probably it was something like "You handle it" or "Take care of it; I don't give a [expletive deleted]." Haig did what he had to.

So maybe it was merely combat fatigue and force of habit. But Haig neglected to tell President Ford, at the very outset, that he—the President—was supposed to put *his own* initials on those papers.

The papers purporting to record a Presidential decision continued to come out initialed "H" instead of the southpaw "GRF" I knew so well. Haig's Praetorian Guard accepted them as commands. I did not.

One of my assistants asked me casually one morning, "Why do you suppose the President is sending Pat Buchanan to South Africa?"

"First I've heard of it. Who said so?"

"His nomination came over this morning to be signed by machine, along with a lot of others."

"Well, to the losers belong the spoils," I snorted. I had nothing much against Buchanan. Pat had married one of Nixon's sweetest secretaries, and while we were hardly palsy I admired his last-ditch loyalty.

The next time I was alone with the President I asked in an offhand way why he hadn't told me he was going to make Buchanan an ambassador, along with Shirley Temple.*

"What?" he demanded. "Pat Buchanan? Ambassador to where?"

I related what little I knew. He had no recollection of ever approving such a thing. Yes, there had been some discussion of Pat's wanting to leave, but . . .

That ended my part in it.

The battle-smart political general, master manipulator of Presidents, pupil of Henry Kissinger in chicanery and charm, walked right into the trap Ford had set and I had baited.

* My friendship with Shirley goes back to her first career, when her oldest brother, Jack, and I were roommates at Stanford.

205

PALACE POLITICS

Exuding efficiency, Haig flipped papers prepared for signature onto Ford's desk and off again with practiced dexterity. All went well until he came to the Buchanan nomination.

Alas, I did not witness this moment. All I know is that nothing more was ever heard of the appointment and no decision memos ever again issued from the Oval Office without the initials "GRF" validating them.

The President was, or pretended to be, very upset with me when a somewhat garbled version of the Buchanan episode was prominently displayed several days later in an Evans–Novak column entitled "General Haig Must Go." I immediately and unashamedly confessed to him that I had lunch with Bob Novak at Sans Souci only hours after his confrontation with Haig took place. Novak already knew about it, probably from Pat. I had confirmed only as much as I knew. After all, I reminded the President, "You yourself ordered us to be open and candid."

Novak related another story that I hadn't heard—that Staff Secretary Jerry Jones at Haig's direction was outfitting two plush EOB suites, 348 and 353, as Washington retreats for Nixon's San Clemente aides Ron Ziegler and Steve Bull. Somebody else sunk that idea.

Haig hung on, of course, until the unconditional pardon for his former boss was a *fait accompli*. His contemporaries in the Army whom Nixon had jumped over in elevating Haig to Vice Chief of Staff didn't want him back at the Pentagon. Besides, that would have required Haig to submit to Senatorial interrogation.

So the NATO command was determined upon, despite some public grumbling by the Dutch government that the Atlantic alliance was not a repository for Watergate refugees. It also involved the rather brutal eviction of a fine officer, General Andrew Goodpaster, who had been Ike's senior White House aide.

Rumsfeld, impatiently waiting to use Haig's corner office, arranged all that. Ron Nessen announced Rumsfeld's appointment and Haig's "promotion" and return to uniform at Nessen's first press briefing on September 24.

The President gave Haig a farewell dinner in the Residence. Some of the press noted that Hartmann appeared to be the winner. I was not. Rumsfeld was.

In the first weeks of his Presidency, Ford was faced with a fistful of urgent tasks—setting a new tone at the White House, repairing the blown-up bridges to the Congress, disposing of the contaminated

Nixon tapes and papers, asserting America's continued commitments to peace and the security of the Free World and simply settling in to the unfamiliar routines of a new home and a new job.

He was confronted by a crumbling economy, an ominous turn of events in Cyprus, a veritable Niagara of well-intentioned advice and for him the not insignificant calamity of losing his swimming pool.*

Despite all this, the President appeared unflustered and unhurried, moving from one immediate panic point to the next. And he found time for the thoughtful personal gestures that more than compensated me and other Ford loyalists for all our frustration and fourteen-hour days.

Jack Marsh was to be sworn in as the second Ford Counsellor on Thursday, August 15, in a brief ceremony much like mine. But by now the Praetorians were back to battery, "staffing it out" so that all the informality and spontaneity was lost. Their argument was that it would be more "Presidential."

Scarcely consulting Marsh, the ubiquitous Haig aides constructed an elaborate memorandum proposing who should be invited as guests, who should be permitted in the official photograph and even where each of us should stand.

Ford did not then, or ever, precisely define Marsh's duties or mine. Although certain areas of primary responsibility were to evolve from our respective talents, we remained on call for any special missions the President wanted to entrust to us. He made it clear to both of us that there was no subject, no individual and no agency of government that we should regard as "none of our business." Any intelligence or observation that came our way, which in our judgment the President ought to know about, he was always ready and willing to receive.

This is not to say that others were deliberately trying to keep things from him—though often that did seem probable—or that he always accepted our interpretations or recommendations. Sometimes he did not, but he never failed to appreciate them, because he knew our intentions were to advance his interests, not our own.

President Ford was not the kind of person who could be a recluse, voluntary or involuntary. He saw too many people and read too many

* My good neighbor, Bill Markert, Washington executive of the National Swimming Pool Institute, and Jack Stiles, Ford's lifelong Grand Rapids pal, spearheaded a program to build a new White House outdoor pool through public contributions.

PALACE POLITICS

publications to be isolated or out of touch with reality. But there is a grave defect, and a growing danger, in the institution of the Presidency itself. No matter how extroverted his disposition, no matter how curious his mind, a President invariably finds himself hearing mostly what people believe he wants to hear. The longer he lasts in such a sterile environment, the easier it becomes to accept—first with annoyance, then with resignation, finally with gratitude.

The Roman Caesars traditionally had a slave riding in the imperial chariot whose duty, during a triumph, was to keep whispering in the imperial ear, "Remember, Caesar, you are only mortal!"

Every American President, even one who toasts his own English muffins or totes his own suitcases, needs one or more close associates who can and will remind him when he is full of baloney.

First ladies with the spunk of a Bess Truman or a Lady Bird Johnson or a Betty Ford perform this useful function in the bedchamber. Some Presidential mothers, fathers, brothers and close cronies also come to mind. Still, Americans are wary of royal families and Kitchen Cabinets.

The official position of Counsellor was one of Nixon's better ideas. It is, however, an uncomfortable role, because it constitutes an intolerable threat to the schemes and security of lesser Presidential subordinates—the little Praetorians.

Jack Marsh and I never relinquished the difficult and demanding charge President Ford laid upon us, although we went about it differently. Nor did we ever become rivals, although it would seem to be a built-in hazard of our situation. Jack is a lover; I am a fighter. His gentle Virginia requests made subordinates purr; my gruff California commands made them scratch back.

As a Member of the House he had been my senior, as chief of the Vice Presidential staff I had been his senior, as Counsellors to the President we were equals. But we always respected, and indeed sought, each other's opinions. Neither of us ever tried to make Brownie points with the President at the expense of the other. And when we agreed, as we did frequently, the President relied upon it—probably because we dared to disagree with him more often than most, but obeyed and defended his decisions, once made, as if they were our own.

After the ceremony, Bill Roberts dragged Jack out to the press room, where he finessed a fusillade of questions about the current progress of the transition group.

The fact was that we were slowly sorting out the most urgent tasks of the transition, though not the long-range ones.

208

Phil Buchen was formally named legal counsel to the President with Cabinet status. Buchen's appointment would shortly be announced, along with James St. Clair's immediate return to private practice and Fred Buzhardt's imminent resignation.

Bill Seidman, a self-starter who understandably was not content to sit around supervising the bewildered Vice Presidential staff, had pitched into crash-planning for the President's promised economic summit without waiting for a formal title. Later, he became Assistant to the President for Economic Affairs and director of Ford's Economic Policy Board.

Jerry terHorst was firmly installed at Ron Ziegler's semicircular desk, aided by Paul Miltich and Bill Roberts from the Vice Presidential staff and Ziegler's deputy, Jerry Warren. TerHorst was looking for his own deputy,* though Warren was immensely helpful in the interim.

Bill Timmons, an Assistant to the President, would stay on as long as he liked, with all his gang. Marsh had been given a general mandate over Congressional relations. He would also have some responsibilities in the area of national security and intelligence, which sent some shudders through Kissinger's shop. But Marsh's immediate concern was a closely held secret which only a half dozen of us knew: President Ford wanted to offer conditional amnesty to Vietnam deserters and draft dodgers.

I am not certain where this idea originated. It is clear that the President was influenced by his older sons, Mike and Jack. Neither had been called for military service, but they reflected the prevailing disenchantment of their generation with the Vietnam conflict.

Jack Ford, a senior at Utah State, had some difficulty adjusting himself to being the President's son but never was averse to being thought of as having influence politically. Jack was quoted in the press afterward as having had a long talk with his father on the plight of Vietnam deserters and draft dodgers.

Mike, the Fords' firstborn, married and living in Massachusetts, generally avoided the limelight. But his independent and religiously oriented mind would naturally empathize with contemporaries who refused to bear arms for reasons of moral conviction. I know the President highly valued Mike's utter candor.

The President, like most men who experienced World War II, had little natural pity for those who shirked their duty to let others die for

* He chose Jack Hushen, like himself a former Michigan newsman and the chief information officer at Justice.

them. Ford had been a hawk on Vietnam until convinced that the Johnson Administration had no intention of winning decisively. Then he supported (at some political hazard to himself) the rear-guard Kissinger–Laird strategy that would permit a face-saving "peace with honor."

But it was not lost on Ford that the drawn-out war was destroying the country's traditional unity in the face of foreign challenge, that it had created bitter divisions in our political system deeper than any since Reconstruction. Particularly, it had alienated and turned to mindless apathy or lawless protest a vast segment of American youth.

Of course, ever since the cease-fire, some militant draft dodgers and deserters in foreign exile, mostly in Sweden and Canada, had been demanding unconditional pardon. Ford had frequently spoken out emphatically against this, but now he was calling upon a sorely troubled nation to put the past behind it and move forward in unity.

Vietnam and Watergate were inextricable, divisive and deadly poisonous. To start with a clean slate, to let bygones be bygones, to write a new chapter required that the ugly recriminations of both be buried.

Marsh had been working, at the President's direction, to devise a formula that would allow the deserving to escape the worst consequences of their desertion or draft evasion but would not be a blanket exoneration and confession, which the extremists demanded, that the government had erred.

The problem was complicated by the fact that while they might be lumped together in the public mind, we were dealing with two quite distinct categories of offenders whose crimes fell under two completely different legal jurisdictions.

While public sentiment has always regarded desertion as a far more heinous crime than draft dodging, and military justice of necessity must be more severe than civilian, those who have known battle have much more understanding and compassion for the typical combat deserter than for the typical civilian shirker. Running away from certain death is somehow more comprehensible than running away from your draft board.

Still, it is impossible to generalize. Every case was unique, and the peculiar glory of the American ethic is that every individual existence has a worth of its own, which the state is bound to recognize. President Ford was acutely conscious of this imperative and determined to find a way to cope with it.

The law, as it stood, was just and equal. It would be a fatal precedent to tamper with it, to signal future generations that defiance of the universal obligation to defend one's country would eventually be forgiven. Or that any individual has the right to decide for himself whether his country's call is worthy or not. Nations do not long endure that way.

There were two good nonpolitical forums on the President's upcoming speaking schedule from which he could unveil his amnesty program. One was the annual national convention of the Veterans of Foreign Wars in Chicago on August 19, another the summer commencement of Ohio State University at Columbus on August 30.

Milt and I were concentrating on the choice when the President came up with his own solution.

"Bob," the President said, "I have decided that the place to make my announcement about a conditional amnesty—no, it's really not amnesty; let's call it 'earned re-entry'—is right there in front of three thousand tough Veterans of Foreign Wars, most of whom are against the whole idea."

"You could do it at Ohio State," I said. "And the students would probably go crazy."

No, the President said, you and I know these organized veterans of World War II. They're really good guys. Our generation was the worst idealists of all; we thought we were saving civilization, and who knows, maybe we did. It would be hypocritical to pick an audience you know would applaud wildly; it's much better to go to the VFW and lay it on the line.

It was a daring opener for his first out-of-town address as President, to go into a lion's den of professional patriots and plead the case for draft dodgers and deserters. I was elated.

"There's just one thing," I cautioned. "If you are going to use the VFW as your sounding board, it has to be a total surprise. If the audience has any advance inkling of what's coming, it won't fly."

The President replied, rather more kindly than I deserved for stating the obvious, that he had been thinking about that. Only the two of us, he said, would know that he was going to launch this "earned re-entry" vehicle at the VFW convention in Chicago.

We would go over it on the plane to Chicago and insert it into the prepared text at the last moment. The Defense and Justice departments, both of which were generally hostile to the idea, could just go ahead thinking they were preparing option papers for Marsh to present to the President at some indefinite future. And Al Haig, as a Vietnam commander and outspoken hardliner against any form of amnesty, need not have any knowledge of our secret.

I went to work with a will. In the course of my research, I read a long background analysis of previous Presidential amnesties, starting with Washington's pardon of the indignant farmers who made the Whiskey Rebellion. I was struck by the coincidence that the most comparable acts of clemency, and the best remembered, were undertaken by two of Ford's favorite predecessors, Lincoln and Truman. It seemed all the more imperative, then, that the portraits in the Cabinet Room should be changed simultaneously with the amnesty announcement.

The President had directed that portraits of Lincoln and Truman be hung in the Cabinet Room before his first Cabinet meeting. He accepted the plausible alibi that a satisfactory likeness of Truman could not be located in time for that session. But he still wanted it done and definitely done before his surprise amnesty announcement.

He kept asking me about it, and I kept asking Haig, and nothing happened. Sunday night I stuck my head into the Cabinet Room to see if the portraits had been changed. They had not.

I returned to my office and dictated this memo to Neta, to be hand-delivered in a sealed envelope marked "Private":

PRIVATE

MEMORANDUM TO GENERAL HAIG   August 18, 1974
FROM ROBERT T. HARTMANN /s/ RTH

This is a reminder that it is important to have the portraits of Presidents Lincoln and Truman hung in the Cabinet Room while we are away on the Chicago trip tomorrow.
President Lincoln should be by the window, and President Truman should be by the door.
Since time is of the essence, we can forget about showing samples to the President.

That Sunday the Fords spent their last night in their Crown View Drive home. After church they had open house during the afternoon for their neighbors, a sentimental leave-taking which the President climaxed by the playful but prophetic promise: "We'll probably be back to see you all in two and a half years."

Betty decided to get away from the moving for a few hours and accompany the President to Chicago, her birthplace. Our vertical take-off from the White House lawn by helicopter, and the luxury of Air Force One waiting at Andrews Air Force Base, was an exciting new experience that would soon become routine. But it was marred by tragic news.

Word was flashed to the President that our Ambassador in embattled Cyprus, Rodger Davies, had been fatally shot during a riot at the American Embassy in Nicosia. This was Ford's first appreciation, I believe, that when you are President the people who are working for you are liable to get killed. It is different when you are a Congressman or Vice President. He was deeply saddened.

There was an outsize delegation of Presidential guests on this first Ford foray into the heartland of America: Senators Vance Hartke, Strom Thurmond and Clifford Hansen; Congressmen Les Arends, Dan Daniel, William J. B. Dorn, Olin Teague and John P. Hammerschmidt; the bipartisan elders of the Armed Services and Veterans Affairs Committees. Bill Timmons and I were entertaining them in the VIP cabin when a steward whispered in my ear, "The President would like to see you."

The President and First Lady had finished breakfast and he was anxious to go over the surprise amnesty announcement. TerHorst already had distributed a VFW speech text to the ninety-three media people accompanying us. We had worked out the gist of his bombshell, and I had the only copy of it—three and a half triple-spaced pages—in my coat pocket.

Ford unscrewed his heavy felt-tipped pen and wrote this insert: "I will then decide how best to deal with the different kinds of cases. There *are* differences. Decisions of my Administration will make any future penalties fit the seriousness of the individual's mistake."

Still less than crystal-clear, the President's amnesty bid established that he was inclined to view Vietnam offenders as Americans who had made mistakes, not as criminals. This would not be enough to satisfy the professional agitators, but it was a far cry from Nixon's "Never!" stance.

The flight to O'Hare was only an hour and forty minutes. Al Haig came into the Presidential cabin with a folder full of papers and dispatches. Ford handed him the amnesty announcement with the casual comment that he had decided to insert it into his VFW speech.

The general read rapidly, turning white. When he got his anger and astonishment under control, he declared with some passion that he considered it a grave mistake. "They'll boo you," Haig warned the President.

Ford seemed unperturbed. He didn't think so, but if they did, so be it. It was imperative, though, he added pointedly, that no warning of what was coming reach the audience.

Mayor Richard Daley's reign is now history, but in those days one could read the political temper of the Windy City by the turnout he arranged for visiting dignitaries. It was hot and humid as the motorcade made its way along the Loop, but the Fords' reception was even warmer. Daley had really gone all out.

Confetti poured from office windows, sidewalk crowds waved and whistled and reached for the President's hand whenever the procession slowed. Standing in the bubbletop, Ford grinned broadly and waved back. Fireboats spouted purple and blue-green water high above the Chicago River, and aerial salutes burst noisily amid the skyscrapers.

As we neared the Conrad Hilton, we sighted the first protesters, a small band of Greek-Americans bearing placards and shouting slogans aimed at U.S. policy in the Cyprus crisis. But even they were all smiles as they waved such signs as "Partition Kissinger, Not Cyprus."

"Hail to the Chief" was revived for this martial occasion, and the VFW comrades rose to their feet with a roar as the distinguished member of Old Kent Post 830, Grand Rapids marched into the International Ballroom.

The predominately World War II-vintage veterans were on their feet again when he announced that Dick Roudebush, the 1957 National Commander of the VFW and a longtime Ford colleague in the House, would be nominated as the next Veterans Administrator. They whooped when he pledged to humanize the agency and, in a subtle swipe at Watergate, declared: "I don't like red tape. As a matter of fact, I don't like *any* kind of tapes."

(I watched the faces of the Nixon Praetorians in the Presidential party. They were not smiling.)

But the biggest standing ovation of all came when the President, departing from his advance text, recalled that as Minority Leader and as Vice President, he had "stated my strong conviction that unconditional blanket amnesty for anyone who illegally evaded or fled military service is wrong. It *is* wrong."

"Hold your hat," I whispered to Marsh. "Here we go!"

When the applause subsided, Ford gripped the lectern with both hands and plowed gamely on.

"Yet, in my first words as President of all the people, I acknowledged a Power higher than the people who commands not only righ-
teousness, but love; not only justice, but mercy."

Then he described the Vietnam-era deserters and draft dodgers as
another class of casualties, "still absent without leave from the real
America." You could have heard a pin drop.

"I want them to come home, if they want to work their way back,"
the President told the stunned and silent auditorium. Betty's was the
only face on the platform that wore a smile. But there were no boos, no
hisses, not a scintilla of disrespect. These were men who had fought for
freedom.

They listened intently as the President described his last duty as
Vice President, presenting posthumous Medals of Honor to the next-
of-kin of fourteen Vietnam heroes. His voice quivering a little, Ford
recalled, "As I studied their records of supreme sacrifice, I kept thinking how young they were. The few citizens of our country who, in my
judgment, committed the supreme folly of shirking their duty at the
expense of others were also very young. . . . All wars are the glory and
the agony of the young."

He called upon the veterans for help and understanding in giving
these young Americans "a second chance."

"As I reject amnesty, so I reject revenge," the President concluded.

At the end of this twenty-seven-minute address the VFW gave
him another standing ovation. Unconverted, but not unmoved, these
guys admired guts. Haig scowled.

Another priority, in Ford's early days of the Presidency, was his
effort to reach out to the black community. He was acutely aware, and
somewhat perplexed, that of the sixteen black Members of the Congress only one in the Senate (Ed Brooke, R–Massachusetts) and one in
the House (Andy Young, D–Georgia) had voted to confirm him as
Vice President. He couldn't quite understand what the others had
against him.

Ford frequently recalled his first brush with racism, in 1934, a
year when Mrs. Roosevelt's lunching with Mary M. Bethune at the
White House was considered a shocking breach of racial convention
by some and a heroic deed by others.

Willis F. Ward, a track star who could outrun all pursuers, was
Ford's University of Michigan teammate. Black athletes were still
fairly rare in Northern universities and segregated out in the South.

PALACE POLITICS

When the Wolverines traveled, not all the players wanted to share a hotel room with Ward, but Jerry Ford didn't give it a second thought. They became good friends, and when Georgia Tech refused to play Michigan with Ward on the field, Ford—a senior and star center—almost walked out in protest.

Almost—but he didn't. He wrestled with his conscience and finally decided he had an equal duty to the others on the team. They won that one for Willis—9 to 2—and Ford was voted the most valuable player. (If he *had* refused to play unless Ward did, would he have beaten another Georgian in 1976?)

He is, actually, color-blind and (if there is such a word) creed-oblivious. He chose Bill Coleman for his Secretary of Transportation not because he wanted a token black face at the Cabinet table but because he had been impressed with Bill as a young lawyer on the Warren Commission staff. And Coleman richly returned Ford's confidence as one of his finest Cabinet choices.

Long before the date acquired any significance in Ford's life, August 9, 1974, was the ninth anniversary of the rioting and arson that devastated the black ghetto of Watts in Los Angeles. As Vice President, Ford had accepted the invitation of L.A. County Supervisor Kenneth Hahn and the private developers to help dedicate a 200-family housing project erected on the ashes of the 1965 fire. Again, Ford probably wanted to show his support of privately financed housing for lower-income families as opposed to massive government projects, rather than merely making a bid for black favor. In this appreciation of economic self-interest rather than racial emotion as the ultimate key to the black vote, he was simply ahead of his time.

No matter how pressed he was on August 9, Ford found time to record his Watts speech for telephone transmission to the housing dedication ceremony. It was proudly claimed by the grateful sponsor that this was, in fact, his first public utterance as President, and the largely black audience roared its appreciation whether Ford could hear it or not.

Other omens were good in the fall of 1974. Representative Shirley Chisholm (D–New York) called upon all Americans—black and white—to "give him a chance." Her colleague Charlie Rangel of the House Judiciary Committee, which confirmed Ford and impeached Nixon, joined Mrs. Chisholm in a conciliatory telegram to the new President.

Even as Vice President, Ford had worked closely with Stan Scott, the able White House special assistant for liaison with minorities, to improve his rapport.* So when Scott brought the Rangel–Chisholm telegram to me, I rushed him right in to see the President.

The President raised his eyebrows in pleasant surprise. As Stan was explaining that the Black Caucus, of which Rangel was then chairman, had been boycotting Nixon's recent appearances before the Congress, Ford reached for the telephone.

"I want to speak to Congressman Charlie Rangel," he said. There was a slight delay; Rangel's secretary thought it was a practical joke. But shortly Rangel was on the line. It had doubtless been many a cold winter since he had heard a cheerful voice saying, "One moment, sir, the President is calling."

"Charlie, how are you?" Ford boomed. "It was certainly nice of you and Shirley to send me that telegram."

The genial banter went on, like long-lost brothers, with Ford saying he'd like nothing better than to have the Black Caucus down to the White House and that Stan Scott would set up a mutually convenient time.

In less than an hour Scott was back.

"Rangel and all the rest will be there. Didn't I tell you? He's tickled pink!"

We both laughed.

"What is more," Stan continued, "Charlie wonders if it would be all right with the President if he told the press about the call."

"Of course," I said. "He will anyhow. And if he doesn't, you do."

The meeting was a very relaxed and good-humored reunion. The President mostly listened and made no specific promises other than that his door would remain open to them. Even this much made the skeptical Democrats beam.

Representative Barbara Jordan of Texas termed it "a good meeting," and Michigan's Charlie Diggs found it "very productive." Rangel was cautiously optimistic and generous in his personal praise of the President. The Washington *Post* was editorially ecstatic.

While the new President was reaching out to young Americans, black Americans, dissident Americans, disillusioned Americans, the old Praetorians went on digging in.

---

* Such outstanding leaders as Vernon Jordan, Hobart Taylor, the Reverend Leon Sullivan and former Assistant Secretary of Labor Art Fletcher had been receptive and helpful.

PALACE POLITICS

In the final year of the Ford Administration it was often charged that the President was devoid of imagination, barren of ideas, had no vision of where he wanted to lead the nation, offered no original initiatives on how to get there. Coming from political rivals, such criticism would be standard campaign rhetoric. The tragedy is that it was spread surreptitiously, and thus confirmed, by the very Praetorians who doggedly sabotaged every innovative idea President Ford and his real friends put forward. Most of the Ford initiatives were therefore stillborn; the rest died from lingering neglect.

This is a continuing story, and the most charitable explanation of how it happened is that the Nixon holdovers could not change their set attitudes. They could not work up any enthusiasm for programs that departed dramatically from those they had helped to evolve. They wanted no part of ideas that reached out to elements of the electorate they instinctively despised and feared—alienated young Americans, academics, the AFL-CIO, Afro-Americans, to name only a few.

As soon as they realized they were not earmarked for early retirement but could remain in control of the system by which Presidential wishes are supposedly carried out, the Praetorians skillfully deflected every Ford proposal designed to break sharply with the Nixon past and to put his own tolerant stamp on a bright new beginning.

One of Ford's better ideas, one that was wholly his own, illustrates this point perfectly. He was scheduled to address the summer commencement at Ohio State University, Michigan's traditional football rival, on August 30. At one of our morning sessions he told me what he had in mind.

"Kids in college today keep complaining their education is irrelevant," the President said. "Of course they love that word and use it for everything they don't like. But when you really try to get to the bottom of their gripes they mean that what they're required to master on the campus has little or nothing to do with getting a job afterwards, or getting ahead in life."

"We talked the same way in the Thirties," I replied. "The economy is nowhere near as bad as it was then, but finding the right job isn't easy."

"There's something more fundamentally wrong," Ford continued, pondering aloud. "The Federal Government now spends billions furthering higher education, but it's throwing good money after bad if we're just perpetuating an irrelevant system. The young people I talk to claim that the professors go on preparing them to be professionals and junior executives and teachers and homemakers with a thin coat of culture and that the real world doesn't need all that many such types."

"I've heard the same. So they wind up in the Black Panthers or in the Red Brigades or in a Blue Funk," I wisecracked.

"All the big corporations send their recruiters around to the campuses to woo the smartest students and their best executives to counsel them," the President went on. "Now, why don't we get big labor into this? They spend millions studying where the jobs are going to be in the next decade or two. Why can't there be more collaboration between the world of work and the academic world?"

He admitted he didn't have the answers, but they were good questions. We made them the theme of his Ohio State speech. We checked all the pertinent bills before the House Labor and Education Committee (this dual jurisdiction may have sparked Ford's idea) and picked the brains of specialists at HEW and Labor. The President specifically charged Secretaries Caspar Weinberger and Peter Brennan to sit down and work out a concrete program.

The commencement speech in Columbus was a great success, and the President's idea was hailed editorially as an exciting new approach to an old dilemma. But the Praetorian "coordinators" in the White House conspired with the career bureaucrats to smother the infant in its crib—it wasn't one of theirs. By the time Ford replaced the Secretaries of Labor and HEW with two career academics the foundling had vanished without a trace.

The Praetorian pattern was a thing of beauty. What they could not prevent they could delay. What they could no longer delay they could cause to fail. What they could not make fail they could alter. What they had altered was no longer the President's idea and should be discarded. After a while initiators of new ideas simply gave up.

Jack Marsh, for instance, started off determined that he and other Ford loyalists should not accept the Praetorian discipline of running all their communications to the President through Haig, Jerry Jones, *et al.* He took a memo to Ford adapting for the White House the system we'd worked out in the Vice Presidency, though half of Washington had the unlisted telephone number in the Fords' bedroom. President Nixon, he'd been given to understand, permitted only calls from his immediate family, General Lawson (his military assistant) and Steve Bull (his civilian aide) to be put through to him outside of office hours. Knowing the new President, Marsh felt that Ford would want a somewhat wider circle of friends able to talk to him at any time. He suggested, for starters, Speaker Albert, Buchen, Haig, Hartmann, Lawson, Marsh, Rumsfeld and a few personal friends as well as the First Family. Any other urgent calls, if the White House switchboard operators were in doubt, would be referred to Marsh or me to determine whether Ford should be disturbed.

The President promptly approved Marsh's proposed procedure. But the Praetorians simply ignored it. All calls were routed through Haig or Rumsfeld/Cheney or the military aides either promoted from the old Nixon crew or hand-picked to replace the devoted trio Ford brought with him from the Vice Presidency. Defying the President's specific order, no calls ever were referred for screening to Marsh or me. Nobody ever dared to keep us from getting through to Ford directly, but Nixon's Praetorian Guard retained control.

All his life Ford had been used to a totally loyal, even worshipful, staff that made mistakes but was never deliberately disobedient, never presumed to put their political judgments above his. This had been Ford's good fortune throughout his tenure in the House and as Vice President. Perhaps naïvely, he expected the same as President.

Probably no White House staff in history has been an unmixed comfort and blessing. Talent and tenacity are usually alloyed with ambition and the often unintentional arrogance of proximity to power. But Ford's gravest flaw was that he was never able—perhaps he never fully tried—to draw around his Presidency a phalanx of aides and advisers whose selfish interests were either identical to or sublimated to his own. Nor would he permit anyone else to create one.

There was never, for all thirty months he was President, a truly Ford Cabinet or Ford staff. There was an incompatible, uncontrolled, contentious collection of Praetorians, many bitterly resentful of the few old Ford loyalists who hung on until the end. The surviving Praetorian Guard, shifting its allegiance from Haldeman to new masters but never really to the "accidental" President, stubbornly shielded Jerry Ford from his better self.

With the coming aboard of Nelson Rockefeller, the surviving Nixon Praetorians really closed ranks. Here was a giant roadblock to their common purpose.

As over the years Rockefeller had been the principal Republican challenger of Nixon's domestic policies and political strategy, he would as Ford's Vice President threaten the very basis of Praetorian power, Oval Office control. He would neither be awed nor owe them anything. He would be far harder to manage than Agnew or Ford.

Unlike the Buchens and the Hartmanns and the Marshes and the Seidmans and the Nessens, Rockefeller could neither be encircled nor enlisted by the Praetorian Guard. Nor would his skill at palace politics be easily countered.

But there are ways to cut down Goliath if a David appears.

10

WHO ELSE BUT NELSE?

★★ ——————————————— ★★

On the night of August 28, 1974, shortly after he was nominated to be the forty-first Vice President of the United States and the second chosen under provisions of the Twenty-fifth Amendment, Nelson Aldrich Rockefeller slept in the Lincoln bedroom of the White House. Neither Happy nor he saw the famed Lincoln ghost. It was nonetheless a memorable occasion. Although he had served in high appointive and consultative posts in every Administration since Franklin D. Roosevelt's, Nelson had never before been an overnight guest in the home of his dreams.

Reams have been written about Rocky's unabashed but unfulfilled yearning for the Presidency. Was his passion for public service a form of atonement for the legendary frugality of his grandfather? Was his career a dramatic vindication of the theory that there are some things money can't buy? Or was he simply a citizen of extraordinary gifts who had both the time and the inclination to better his country if he could?

I do not know whether Nelson Rockefeller would have been a great President or not; fate has more to do with that verdict than most of us suppose. I do know something of how great a Vice President he was.

Speculation as to whom the next Vice Presidential nominee would be got started even before Ford stepped up to the Presidency. Melvin Laird kicked off early with a big plug for Rockefeller on August 6.

After he returned to private life, I was reminiscing about this period with Rockefeller and rather by accident got his version of the Laird gambit. Rocky apparently misunderstood a question about early rumors being floated and thought I was accusing him of putting Mel up to it. He denied it with surprising vehemence.

"I never heard about it. I didn't know about it. I was up in Maine and I closed off all the phones. Just as I was getting in the car in Tarrytown to go to Maine, he [Laird] called and said he thought I ought to be the one and he had recommended it to the President."

Rocky's inflection indicated that he knew what Mel's game was and that he wasn't above returning the compliment.

"Well, you know, we have all been in politics a long time. And I said, 'Mel, you are the man who ought to be the one. You have been in the White House. You know all this stuff. You've been in government. You are in touch. You have no problem in Congress.' And he said, 'No, I've got to make some money. My year is nineteen-eighty.' "

Leaving a prayer meeting with John Rhodes and Minnesota Representative Al Quie in his old Minority Leader's office, Ford was startled two days before he became President by crowds on the Capitol steps shouting, "Don't pick Rockefeller! Don't pick Rockefeller!"

At about the same time, Senator Jim McClure of Idaho was huddling with hard-line conservative colleagues to head Rocky off at the pass. The next day he delivered to the Vice President's Senate office and, almost simultaneously, to the United Press International a two-page letter listing thirteen men and one woman who would be acceptable to him and at least six other right-wing Senators.

McClure's list was headed by Barry Goldwater, Ronald Reagan and Senator Jim Buckley, in that order. Rockefeller was nowhere mentioned by name, but McClure said his list was prompted by "the concern that many of us have."

Jim McClure baited his hook skillfully. He knew the press would give short shrift to an anonymous bunch of conservatives supporting Goldwater and opposing Rockefeller. So he added, "One rather intriguing thought that has occurred to me . . . is to consult with the gentlelady from Oregon, Mrs. [Edith] Green. If she can see fit to change her party registration, her selection would throw consternation into the ranks of the opposition and would find much favor with myself and many of my friends." (Mrs. Green, a delightful and savvy lady, did not change her Democratic registration but campaigned valiantly at Ford's side in '76—and he sure carried Oregon.)

Two more campaigns surfaced immediately, one on behalf of George Bush and one, less visible, on behalf of Donald Rumsfeld. Dick Herman, the energetic National Committeeman from Nebraska, flew into town to set up shop openly for Bush. This may have been embarrassing to George, but he did not directly repudiate it.

George Bush had a lot of advantages. He was the popular Chairman of the National Committee. He had been a well-liked Member of the House for many years. He had been an ex-officio member of Nixon's Cabinet, and while he had failed in his bid for the Senate from his adopted state, Texas, his father had been a pillar of that body from Connecticut. Furthermore, he was a Ford loyalist and had kept his skirts completely clean of Watergate.

Traditionally, nobody ever runs for Vice President. You run for President, no matter how slim the odds. If the breaks don't come your way you settle, for the sake of the country and the party, and accept the second spot.

As the week went on without any firm clues, the press began printing unsubstantiated smears against the supposed frontrunners. The first smear to surface was a strange one. A Philadelphia lawyer named Hamilton Long, well identified with right-wing causes, telephoned the White House saying he had urgent and important information to convey to the President about one of those under consideration for the Vice Presidency. He eventually got through to Phil Buchen as the new legal counsel to the President. He would not be specific on the telephone but persuaded Phil to invite him to come in and talk privately.

Long's story was that Howard Hunt had not, as widely believed, destroyed all of his Watergate files. He had secreted seven boxes. Someone had made copies of key documents and locked them in a bank safety-deposit box. In that cache, Long said, was evidence that Nelson Rockefeller personally financed a clandestine dirty-tricks operation by Nixon to disrupt the 1972 Democratic National Convention that nominated George McGovern in Miami Beach. Long did not know any of this firsthand, he admitted. But he volunteered the bank location and box number.

Buchen realized he had a hot potato and we all huddled with the President about it. The consensus was to relay Long's report immediately to Leon Jaworski and ask the Special Prosecutor to report back promptly. The President clearly considered such smear tactics deplorable and gave them little credence.

TerHorst, meanwhile, was being quizzed on a similar charge in Jack Anderson's column. He said that the President was aware of the charge and had directed it be investigated fully. He also said the President probably would meet his self-imposed decision deadline of ten days, probably next Tuesday or Wednesday.

Typical of the press reaction was CBS' Bob Pierpoint, who speculated that, considering how long it took Jaworski to investigate anything, Rocky had been effectively ruled out of the running.

This was unfortunate, but we were all babes in the White House. We had done the right thing and truthfully told what we had done, but it was unfair to Rockefeller to give Presidential credence to Long's hearsay. And, of course, the press castigated us for that the next day, by which time a counterrocket had been launched.

Actually, the smear aimed at George Bush must have been planted even earlier, with *Newsweek* magazine. (*Newsweek* appears on the newsstands on Monday but, to intrigue buyers, often issues a news release for Saturday-evening newscasts and Sunday-morning papers.) *Newsweek* claimed unnamed "White House sources" told them that "there was potential embarrassment in reports that the Nixon White House had funneled about $100,000 from a secret fund called the 'Townhouse Operation' into Bush's losing Senate campaign against Lloyd Bentsen in Texas in 1970. There were indications that $40,000 of the money may not have been properly reported as required by election law."

It was carefully worded but enough to set the rest of the Washington reporters off on the cry that Bush had slipped badly and to send Buchen off for clarification a second time. Eventually both charges were totally disproved; the Special Prosecutor found the bank box empty. Rockefeller disclosed that he had indeed made a trifling contribution ($250,000) to the Nixon war chest in 1972 but with strict stipulations that it be spent entirely in New York State under his supervision. Rockefellers don't get rich by subsidizing the disruption of Democratic conventions which Democrats usually can be counted upon to do for free.

Bush's people easily established that the Senatorial campaign sums received from Washington were part of a well-publicized program to help all Republican candidates and had been fully reported to both state and Federal authorities.

There were no smears directed at Rumsfeld. He took no visible interest in the Vice Presidential process, being preoccupied with transition team planning. When the Cyprus flare-up threatened to force Greece out of NATO he received the President's permission to rush back to Brussels, so he was not personally on the scene when the eleventh-hour smears surfaced.

The only overt activity by Rumsfeld supporters was the clearly coordinated planting with Washington reporters of the fact that Rumsfeld was one of those under consideration.

The President had set a deadline of Wednesday, August 14, for written recommendations from his Cabinet and staff, all the Republi-

PALACE POLITICS

can Members of the House and Senate, Republican Governors and members of the Republican National Committee.

The total number of first-, second- and third-choice ballots received by the deadline was 910, not counting, of course, several score who chose to whisper their choices in the Presidential ear and not commit them to writing.

Neta tabulated all the returns in the little office sandwiched between the Oval Office and mine, which the President used for a hideaway. I didn't even look at them myself and saw the final tabulations only an hour before handing them to the President.

Counting merely the number of times their names appeared, the top ten contenders in the poll were George Bush (255), Nelson Rockefeller (181), Barry Goldwater (83), Ronald Reagan (52), Elliot Richardson (40), Melvin Laird (38), Howard Baker (32), Bill Brock (24), Anne Armstrong (20) and Governor Dan Evans (20). Don Rumsfeld tied with Senator Mark Hatfield for fifteenth place with eight mentions each.

When only first choices were counted, the story was somewhat different but not decisively. Bush had 125, Rockefeller 100, Goldwater 32, and Reagan dropped to 16. Baker followed with 14, Laird 12, Richardson 9, Brock 7, and Evans and Scranton had 6 apiece. Rumsfeld had 1.*

If popularity in the party was to be the guide, Bush and Rocky were far ahead of the pack. Predictably, Bush prevailed as the first choice of the more numerous categories, his National Committee and his former colleagues in the House, and Rockefeller was the heavy favorite among Governors, with eight votes to two each for Bush and Evans, plus scattered singles. Rocky topped the Senate list as well, with ten ballots to Goldwater's five and four each for Baker and Bush. Surprisingly, Rockefeller was also the first choice of half the old Nixon Cabinet who submitted written recommendations.

There were several surprise entries. Dr. Billy Graham got one mention, as did Bryce Harlow, former Interior Secretary Wally Hickel of Alaska and Dr. Franklin Murphy, former Chancellor of UCLA and then president of the Times-Mirror Company in Los Angeles.

The hour for women and blacks obviously had not struck in the Republican Party. Anne Armstrong got five first choices, Ed Brooke

---

* It was not his own. But two distinguished United States Senators, who shall be nameless, modestly listed themselves as their only candidate.

one, and that was it. (Betty Ford, however, was lobbying persistently for consideration of a woman Vice President.)

There were a couple of other indices of public sentiment, highly unscientific but dearly beloved by elective officials—mail and phone calls. The day before the President announced his decision, the White House mailroom had tallied 11,782 letters and telegrams from the public on the subject. In such samplings the "aginners" always have the upper hand; Americans have more fun writing tirades against somebody than tributes for anybody.

Three thousand two hundred and two citizens warned the President against the wicked Rockefeller, and 383 were equally upset at the prospect of Chuck Percy. Goldwater outdistanced his closest competitor, Bush, by 2,280 to 887, and Reagan, Rockefeller and Richardson followed with 690, 544 and 544 pen pals respectively.

One of the most intriguing aspects of this Vice Presidential sweepstakes was the abundance of "authoritative" news accounts that had utterly no factual basis. Only the President, Bryce Harlow, Neta and I had any knowledge of the inner process, and the President was extremely careful about exposing the tilt of his own thinking.

Thus all the press and television speculation had to be inspired either by hopeful aspirants, White House Praetorians pretending to know when they didn't, or else they were masterful works of fiction.

Almost everybody, of course, had Bush and Rockefeller at the top of their lists. But they all shot wildly in every direction to hedge their bets.

Christopher Lydon of the New York *Times* came up with a final long-shot list of Baker, Evans, Richardson, Rumsfeld and Laird. The United Press International reported on Sunday, August 18, that the President had narrowed his choices to two, one of whom was believed to be Rockefeller. The AP was intrigued by "indications" that the choice would be neither Rocky nor Bush.

NBC's Ron Nessen, who had been a close Ford-watcher during his Vice Presidency, indicated that the organized campaigns for Rockefeller and Bush were annoying to the President. With dubious prescience, Nessen also claimed that Reagan, Goldwater, Laird and Richardson were coming up fast.

The first evidence Ford gave of the narrowing process came on Friday, August 16, when he summoned FBI Director Clarence Kelley to the Oval Office and asked him to do a quick check on three

PALACE POLITICS

names—Rockefeller, Bush and Rumsfeld—in the utmost confidence and with no significance attached to the order.

Rummy did not show much strength in the statistics—eight mentions out of 910 and only one as first choice. But there is only one preference that matters, and Rumsfeld was definitely on the President's mind.

On Wednesday, the deadline set by the President for recommendations from his Cabinet, Ford chided me that my own choices were missing.

"Since I'm so involved with this thing, I thought it would be better not to say," I said. "Besides, before I could say who I think would be best for you, I would have to know the answer to another question: Are you going to run in Nineteen seventy-six? It makes quite a big difference."

He chuckled. "You know what I promised Betty."

"Yes, and what you promised the Senate, too."

"I didn't promise them I wouldn't run," the President corrected me. "I said I had no such intention at the time—and I didn't. But I really did promise Betty."

I waited for him to volunteer more, but he turned to some other topic. Maybe he really hadn't crossed that bridge after five days as President.

Thinking it over, I scribbled my own recommendations on an old Vice Presidential memo pad, with one copy. I sealed both in envelopes and told Neta to lock one in my safe.

I personally handed the other to the President. Dated August 14 at 2:00 P.M., it read:

> A—If you want to run in '76:
> Rockefeller
> Rumsfeld
> Bush
>
> B—If you want an electable successor in '76:
> Bush
> Laird
> Richardson

When the President picked Rocky, I assumed from that moment he was a candidate.

Sunday afternoon, August 18, the President went to Burning Tree to play golf with Les Arends, Mel Laird and George Mahon (D–

Texas), chairman of the Appropriations Committee. Ambushed by newsmen at the gate, the President announced that he would make his decision by Tuesday.

Early Monday morning, before we left for the VFW convention in Chicago, the President took a slip of yellow foolscap and wrote in his familiar southpaw:

Bush
Rumsfeld
Richardson
Rockefeller
Raeygon [sic]

"While we're gone, have Phil [Buchen] check these names out with Jaworski," he said as he handed me the note. "I want the answer when we get back, because tonight I'm going to make my final decision."

I noted he had added Richardson and Reagan to the trio the FBI had already cleared. Was he really serious about them? Well, there are a lot of leaks from the Special Prosecutor's office, he replied. Have Phil give them all five names.

I noticed too that there were no Senators or Congressmen on the list and wondered aloud about it. He said he had considered some and was fully aware that Goldwater, Baker and Brock had considerable support. John Rhodes would probably have had, too, if he hadn't publicly disclaimed interest. But he had ruled out all the incumbent Republican legislators for a variety of reasons, one of which was that he'd need all their votes.

Afterward, though, it wouldn't hurt if Goldwater and the others thought they had made the finals, I suggested.

The President agreed I had a point there. "Well, let's say that I narrowed it down to six. We won't ever tell who the sixth one was, and they'll all be happy."

Later, when I had to brief the press about the process by which the President picked Rockefeller, I writhed over that little subterfuge, but I got away with it.

Phil Buchen was still operating out of the EOB. I met him in the middle of West Executive Avenue and, in a cloak-and-dagger maneuver, showed him the five names, which I had copied onto another slip in my own hand, correcting the mangled spelling of Reagan's name. I checked the three that really mattered with a pencil. He told me to keep the slip; he would carry the names to Jaworski in his head. We trusted each other, but the President's worrying about leaks was contagious.

On the flight back from Chicago, the President dropped into the press section of Air Force One for a little social chitchat in his shirt sleeves.

"I'm a sphinx," he said, trying to look like one.

The traveling press quickly noted that the Nixon name "Spirit of '76" had been quietly removed from the Presidential aircraft for Ford's first trip out of Washington. TerHorst confirmed that in the future it would be simply "Air Force One."

Jack Marsh and I had both recommended it be done immediately, because if the President used the plane in political campaigning, it could be legitimately criticized as making partisan use of the Bicentennial theme. Whereas Nixon could not have been a candidate in '76, Ford could.

Unbeknown to us, Ford had already given strong indications that he was determined to run in a private telephone chat with Nelson Rockefeller the previous Saturday. The President, as Rockefeller remembered it, said he had not reached any decision but that he was looking for a partner with a background and experience in domestic affairs. Would domestic affairs include campaigning as a candidate in 1976? The President was cagey, Rockefeller recalled, but gave the definite impression that he had every intention of running himself. That was what Rocky wanted to hear. The Ford Administration was not going to be just a short-run, caretaker extension of Nixon's second term. It would be worth a fling.

In perspective, what was said in that Saturday telephone call about the 1976 campaign is less intriguing than what may have been said about responsibilities Ford wanted Rocky to undertake as his Vice President in 1974 and 1975. In December of 1977 I talked for hours with Governor Rockefeller in his modest Rockefeller Plaza office and questioned him closely about this.

"Since you have said since the 1950s you weren't interested in being Vice President, and turned Nixon and Humphrey down, what caused you to accept President Ford's offer?" I began.

"It was entirely a question of there being a Constitutional crisis and a crisis of confidence on the part of the American people," he replied. "I felt there was a duty incumbent on any American who could do anything that would help contribute to a restoration of confidence in the democratic process and in the integrity of government. I felt

230

President Ford was taking over the job on that basis. He understood the Congressional–legislative side of the issues and I understood the Executive–administrative side. And, therefore, I might be able to contribute something.

"He wanted me to give him support in the domestic field and wanted me to head it up as Henry [Kissinger] would in the foreign field. And he wanted me to help him on recruitment, which, he said, could be very helpful, as I was known for having attracted good people," Rockefeller concluded.

"Did these conversations come *after* you were Vice President?" I asked him.

"No," he said. "This was on the phone, the first time."

"Before it was actually announced?"

Rocky nodded affirmatively. "Although General Haig called me first, a couple of times," he explained, "President Ford then called me and said he was thinking it over and wanted to ask me some questions—whether I knew of anything that would be embarrassing or might work against his asking me, and I said I didn't think so."

"Was this a day or two before?"

"Yes.... Then he said I'd hear from him. Next, I think it was Haig called and asked me to come to Washington because they'd made a decision. By that time I was up in Maine. Happy and I talked. I said to her if this is something the President wants I will do it, although I recognize it may be just what I've always thought it was. I've known all the Vice Presidents since Henry Wallace. They were all frustrated, and some were pretty bitter. So I was totally prepared to go down (to Washington) and just be there," Rockefeller continued. I persisted:

"The President didn't make any firm commitments, in advance of the announcement, as to the specific things he wanted you to do?"

"He may have mentioned heading the Domestic Council. I don't remember because I was a little bit from Missouri about this—they'd have to show me. But he did mention this question of helping him on recruitment. He said, 'We want—I want you to be a partner in this thing,'" the former Vice President recalled, somewhat sadly, I thought.

"Did you feel at the time," I asked, "that the President envisioned a rather complete housecleaning in terms of personnel?"

"No, we didn't talk about that at all."

On Monday evening, at the end of a twelve-hour day, the President had invited all the agents of his Vice Presidential Secret Service detail, with their wives, to a reception in the Residence.* As it broke up, the President told me he was going upstairs to make his final decision. He would meet first thing in the morning with the Democratic and Republican leaders of the Congress, then the Cabinet, to give them a few minutes' advance notice of his choice. Then he would announce it and introduce the new Vice President over live television to the nation. Would I tell TerHorst to get everything ready?

I was scribbling notes on the back of an envelope.

"Aren't you going to ask me who it is?" he demanded.

No, I said, reminding him that my written guesses were sealed in the envelope I'd given him five days ago. And why should I, I kidded, when I'd known for days? But how was the lucky guy going to know he should be there?

"He'll be there," the President said mysteriously.

I knew Rockefeller was the only candidate under serious consideration who was not in Washington panting beside his phone. Had he, after all, picked Bush or Rummy? Well, I would have no trouble sleeping and would find out in the morning.

But mention of the Cabinet Room meeting reminded me of the Truman and Lincoln portraits. I said good night to the President and, on my way back to my office, stuck my head in and turned up the lights in the darkened chamber. Sure enough, Haig had finally found Harry Truman, and he and Lincoln hung in their places of honor as Ford had commanded a full ten days earlier.

But all the drama of the Presidential change had drained away, as the Praetorians intended. The Rockefeller nomination dominated the next day's news, and it took the press corps several days even to notice Abe and Harry.

The President had privately instructed Haig to call Rockefeller at Seal Harbor, Maine, and arrange for him to be at the White House early the next morning. Haig was not to tell the Governor he was Ford's choice, not in so many words. But with Happy included in the invitation and elaborate instructions for Rockefeller's car to slip in by a side entrance to avoid the media, Rockefeller had no difficulty guessing.

Somehow the secret held overnight. At our early encounters the next morning, the President told me and TerHorst, and the press secre-

---

* Shortly after he became President, Ford changed the traditional nomenclature from "the Executive Mansion" to "the Residence."

tary went about setting up the Oval Office for live network and press-pool coverage of the announcement. At 8:30, we both followed Ford into the Cabinet Room, where the Democratic and Republican leaders of Congress were munching on Danish pastries and coffee.

They rose and applauded. Bipartisan consultations at the White House had been few and far between in the final days of the Nixon era. Ford was making good on his pledge of "communication, conciliation, compromise and cooperation."

The Democrats, moreover, were pleased by the new President's embrace of an economic summit and his public acknowledgment of Mike Mansfield's authorship of the idea.

The President let them stew awhile, however, on his Vice Presidential secret. He said he was anxious to keep the upcoming fiscal 1975 budget under $300 billion and called upon Roy Ash, Nixon's budget director, who assured them of his desire to work with the new Congressional budget committee during its trial run.

Henry Kissinger was allowed to chew up some more time by briefing the Congressional group on the tense Cyprus situation.

The President thanked them for moving quickly on his week-old request for a wage and price monitoring agency, but he made it very emphatic that he did not, and would not, want either standby or mandatory authority to impose Federal controls.

Finally, as it approached ten o'clock, the hour the networks expected to carry the Vice Presidential nomination, he told them—who else but Nelse? It had been a hard decision, but Rockefeller was his choice on the basis of being most qualified to take over the Presidency if the need should arise. He would sign and send the formal nomination to the Hill that afternoon. There were nods of approval around the table.

The President asked the leaders to remain for a few minutes in the Cabinet Room while he met with Rockefeller and the Oval Office was readied for the announcement. Then he would like them all to be present for the ceremony.

This seemingly casual afterthought was carefully planned. We were in effect locking the leaders of the House and Senate up so they could not rush out and spill the beans to their favorite reporters.

The President next ducked into the Roosevelt Room, where the Cabinet and senior staff were assembled. They also applauded his brief announcement, including some who would later undercut Rockefeller with unprecedented ferocity.

233

PALACE POLITICS

I then followed him through my office into his small hideaway adjacent to the Oval Office. Rockefeller and Betty Ford were seated on the couch chatting, and the President grasped Nelson's hand and said somewhat anticlimactically that he was the one.

Rockefeller replied that he was honored by the President's confidence and hoped to be worthy of it, apologized for Happy's inability to accompany him on such short notice. Dave Kennerly squeezed into the tiny room to record the moment for posterity, and Ford told Terry O'Donnell to get former President Nixon on the telephone.

Betty and I silently exchanged looks of surprise and wonderment. Was this call really necessary?

The conversation was brief. Ford addressed his predecessor as "Mr. President," inquired as to his health and Pat's, and said after much consultation and deliberation that he had chosen Rockefeller. Nixon, as the President later recalled, called it "a good choice" and thanked Ford for his thoughtfulness in notifying him.

"Here, I'll put Nelson on," Ford said to Nixon, quickly passing the phone to his startled Vice Presidential nominee. With that he grabbed my arm and darted into my adjoining office, where he asked me to get George Bush on the line.

The President explained, a little sadly, that George was a very close contender in his mind and that he didn't want him to get the word first from anybody else. Bush took the bad news like a man. (Rumsfeld, of course, had been at the earlier White House meetings; he congratulated Rockefeller warmly and betrayed no visible disappointment.)

Four minutes late for the 10:00 A.M. telecast, President and Mrs. Ford led the way into the Oval Office, followed by Rockefeller.

"After a great deal of soul-searching," the President began, speaking extemporaneously, "I have made a decision. . . . It was a tough call for a tough job . . . but I have made the choice and that choice is Nelson Rockefeller of New York State . . . a good partner for me and I think a good partner for our country and the world."

Rockefeller responded with a warm tribute to Ford.

"You, Mr. President, through your dedication and your openness, have already reawakened faith and hope, and under your leadership we as a people and we as a nation have the will, the determination and the capability to overcome the hard realities of our times. I am optimistic about the long-term future. Thank you, sir."

After backslaps and handshakes all around, the President and

TerHorst led the Vice President-designate over to the press briefing room, where Ford, after saying, "He will make a great teammate," left Rockefeller to his moment of glory alone.

The newsmen immediately zeroed in on whether Rocky would disclose his personal finances as fully as Ford had, and he rather testily told them it would be impolite to answer such questions before they were put to him by the appropriate Senate and House chairmen.

In general the press was friendly and the news reports almost ecstatic.

"Choice Wins Praise in Both Parties," said the New York *Times*.

"Ford's Choice Is Hailed by Leaders on the Hill," the Washington *Post* proclaimed next morning. Dave Broder wrote that "the Republican Party settled on what seems likely to be a Ford–Rockefeller ticket for 1976, and opened what many of its leaders saw as an opportunity to overcome its status as a permanent minority in American politics."

R. W. Apple, Jr., in the New York *Times,* discoursed on Ford's "reversal of national political tides of potentially historic proportions." He quoted an admiring, if staggered, Democrat as conceding the new President "hasn't made a wrong move yet."

That afternoon I had a forty-five-minute session with the White House press. Ron Nessen of NBC adroitly sought to read into the Rockefeller selection some clue as to the President's own political plans. "Some people at the White House had sort of spread the word," Nessen began, "that he [Ford] was looking for a man who would be young enough to serve as Vice President for six years and then be in a position to run himself in 1980. Rockefeller would be seventy-two—"

I saw where the question was leading and cut it off.

"I think the President's decision answers that question, Ron," I said. "He was not looking for the survival of the Republican Party but of the Republic—if anything happens to him."

Did the President envision a substantive role for his Vice President?

"Go back and read Ford's words on how he envisioned the role of Vice President," I countered; "they probably haven't changed very much in eight months."

Did the President think Rockefeller should make the same complete financial disclosure that Ford had during his own confirmation?

"The President," I said with finality, "has already indicated what he thinks should be done by what he did."

235

PALACE POLITICS

I shall return to the Ford–Rockefeller story later. But there are a couple of questions I have been asked a hundred times since, and this a good place to deal with them.

First, why did President Ford pick Nelson Rockefeller? Second, why did Governor Rockefeller accept? Were there any prior commitments or understandings between them?

After five years I have found no reason not to accept the President's stated objective, which was to choose the most competent person in the country to govern as President of the United States, should the need arise.

Incumbent Presidents also toy with the intriguing idea of grooming a successor. Under the Constitution, Ford was eligible for a maximum of only six and a half years. Obviously, ambitious young Republicans like Bush and Rumsfeld, Baker and Brock hoped to be anointed and get one leg up on the 1980 nomination. But Jerry Ford was no stranger to the discomfort of impatient younger politicians panting to inherit his job. And he had been in his new job for only ten days. How much easier to let Nelson Rockefeller, at sixty-six his senior by five years, occupy the number-two spot at least long enough to keep the eager beavers off his back while he mastered the political powers and perils of the Presidency.

However uncomplicated a President may seem, and however genuine his primary motive, there are bound to be corollary considerations which at least subconsciously affect his decisions.

There is the theory that, foremost among prominent Republicans in August 1974, Nelson Rockefeller was completely "clean" of association with the discredited and disgraced Nixon Presidency. Of the other leading prospects for the Vice Presidential nod, all had enthusiastically carried Nixon's banner for long periods. Reagan was his chief cheerleader in Nixon's native California; Richardson had fallen from grace only after gladly filling a wide assortment of high Nixon appointments; Bush and Rumsfeld both had forsaken safe House careers at the President's bidding; so had many others who were not serious contenders except in the newspapers. The Republican Party, except for its failing Rockefeller wing, was largely composed of former Nixon defenders.

Nelson Rockefeller, on the other hand, had been the recipient of Nixon campaigners' dirty tricks for years, when Watergate was nothing more than the drainage end of Washington's Rock Creek into Foggy Bottom.

Considering Ford's determination to restore public confidence, put Watergate behind us and bind up the bitter divisions it had inflicted on our political system, what could be more logical, and more dramatic, than linking himself with Nelson Rockefeller at the outset of his Administration?

How better could he prove that he was indeed his own man, not illiberal, open to new ideas, unprejudiced toward the Eastern Establishment, sincerely reaching beyond his own conservative Midwest constituency to recruit the best available talent for the country's renaissance?

I am convinced, however, that there was another consideration in the choice of Rockefeller, subsidiary but substantial. The President had, of course, read all the columns suggesting that he would never nominate Rockefeller because the New Yorker would upstage him in fame, fortune and charisma. This was silly stuff, because the only Vice Presidents in history who ever came close to outshining the President were Thomas Jefferson and Teddy Roosevelt, and Rockefeller, at sixty-six, had no reason even to try. Nevertheless, it must have been tempting to Ford to prove that he had no hang-ups about choosing one of the richest and most renowned men in the world as his Constitutional subordinate. And doubly so because Richard Nixon, who was always mesmerized by great wealth, had tried and failed to enlist Rocky. So while Ford was perfectly at ease with wealth and social status, it no doubt gave him some satisfaction to ally himself politically with the Rockefellers and demonstrate he was definitely the boss. He may never have admitted this to himself, because there was an eminently compatible cover motive.

The fabulous Rockefeller resources go far beyond mere money. They include a wealth of talent, skill and scholarship—a world brainpower bank unprecedented in our history. The Rockefeller organization, although never able to win the Presidency, would be a formidable auxiliary to a Ford Administration sorely in need of new intellectual input and ideas. As a member of Nelson's newly established "Commission on Critical Choices," Ford gained a firsthand glimpse of these personnel and policy-generating resources.

For his part, Rockefeller was certain this was a major factor in Ford's choice. In one of our long conversations after the Ford Administration faded into history, Rockefeller contended that he was dubious from the start that he would ever fare much better than any recent Vice Presidents in sharing real responsibility with a President. But the hope, however hedged, was clearly the reason he came.

PALACE POLITICS

"After you were sworn in as Vice President did you find the job to be just about what you had expected, or different?" I asked.

Rockefeller squinted his eyes shut and thought hard for a moment. He clearly didn't want to appear critical of Ford in anything he said.

"Well, let me put it this way. I feel that the President very sincerely meant what he said when he asked me to come down for the reasons he said. And I admired his dedication to the country and to the whole concept of restoring faith in government and doing a good job for the country and his courage in picking me as his Vice President."

Why did that call for courage?

"I say courage for this reason. I was on Dan Rather's TV show with Happy, and this was after Nixon had nominated Ford. And he asked Happy, 'When President Nixon was faced with a loss of a Vice President when Agnew resigned, did you expect Nixon might ask your husband to become Vice President?'

"She said, 'Of course not.' She answered so fast it took him aback, and he said, 'How can you be so positive about that?'

" 'Well,' she said, 'it's very simple. Weakness never turns to strength.' "

Rockefeller was obviously pleased with his wife's perspicacity.

"Now, I am a reasonably strong personality and have been in this business for a long time. So I think it took a great deal of strength and confidence and showed that President Ford had a great deal of both to pick somebody who was a political figure, who had been a national candidate and had a great deal of experience. To me that was evidence that he wanted to do a job, that he meant what he said about Henry helping him in the international field and me helping him in the domestic, and that was fine."

The disintegration of the Ford–Rockefeller partnership, like an off-again, on-again marriage, is a fascinating story. I was often the middleman, but I could not save it. As usual, there were faults on both sides and other parties deeply involved.

However unhappy the ending, the beginning of the Ford–Rockefeller romance was one of almost total triumph for the new President.

Hugh Sidey of *Time,* who has made President-watching his particular thing, accurately reflected the euphoria at the end of Ford's first fortnight in office when he wrote: "For ten years this nation has suffered from cardiac insufficiency. Now the heart is beginning to pump again under Jerry Ford. One can feel the renewed strength running through the Federal government. . . . The transformation is doing so well not from mystique but from candor, not from majesty but from humility, not from complexity but from plainness," Hugh concluded. "Ford's first days look like genius because they are so ordinary, so like the rest of America."

Tom Braden in the Washington *Post* grudgingly pondered the same phenomenon and detected the hand of public relations in it. "Somebody—Robert Hartmann or J. F. terHorst or Melvin Laird or Mr. Ford himself—must have taken time during those final hours between Nixon's disgrace and his departure to make up a list of things to do which would turn a nation from rancor to affection and give the new President the goodwill which might stand instead of a mandate," Braden wrote. "Whoever did it did it well."

He too hailed Ford's choice of a Vice Presidential nominee, his VFW olive branch to war resisters, his invitation to the Black Caucus and other signs of change. "It's been a first-rate performance, and it has rallied the nation and restored the nation's self-respect. . . . It has also proved that the art of public relations is a useful art, that it need not disguise or conceal but may be used wisely by well-meaning and honest men in order to make it clear that they are well-meaning and honest," Braden added. "But there is a limit to what public relations can accomplish, and it is not too soon to say that Gerald Ford seems now to have reached it," he concluded.

Ironically, in the face of all the praise for Ford's choice of teammates and advisers, the first Presidential decision he took absolutely alone, in which his closest political and public-relations counselors had no prior part and little subsequent influence, was the pardon of Richard Nixon.

The pardon was the *real* Jerry Ford.

11

SNAKE RIVER:
THE NIXON PARDON

★★——————————★★

Sunday, September 8, 1974, was the day Evel Knievel, the professional daredevil, rocketed his red-white-and-blue Sky-Cycle above the 1,600-foot Snake River Canyon in Idaho. Something went wrong with the launching. As thousands gasped in happy horror, Sky-Cycle shot upward and then nose-dived into the riverbank far below. Evel was extricated with only minor scratches.

The same Sunday, Gerald R. Ford took an even greater gamble.

After receiving early Communion that day at St. John's across the square, the President returned to the Oval Office, which had been his for exactly thirty days. He sat down at his desk, leaned forward and looked squarely into the red eye of a single video camera, around which a score of puzzled news reporters had just been herded. For nine minutes, earnestly and sometimes eloquently, he explained what he was about to do. Then, taking his pen in hand, he signed with a firm stroke a "full, free and absolute pardon" of Richard Nixon.

In California, shrouded in early-morning fog, Nixon accepted President Ford's "compassionate" pardon without directly acknowledging either gratitude or guilt. He had been wrong in not "acting more decisively" and "more forthrightly" in dealing with Watergate, but he always did what he thought best at the time. He deeply regretted his "mistakes and misjudgments" and hoped that the pardon would help lift the burden of Watergate from our country.

The President left the White House for a long-scheduled golf game at Burning Tree with some old cronies.

Jerald F. terHorst, also in his thirtieth day at the White House, finished up the myriad details of announcing the pardon to the media, readdressed a farewell letter to the President, broke the news of his resignation to his top aides and went home.

It is dangerous, it is foolhardy, it offers a dubious prospect of success, but it is not *absolutely impossible* to ride a rocket bike across the

240

Snake River Canyon. When success would amply reward the high risk, men are sometimes drawn to such gambles.

Life is full of Snake Rivers, you might say.

But sometimes things go wrong at the launching.

Gerald Ford's tenure of office was two years, five months and twelve days. Only four Presidencies have been shorter, and history associates little of moment with the terms of Harding, Garfield, Zachary Taylor and William Henry Harrison. Camelot lasted five months longer than the Ford Administration. John F. Kennedy is remembered for his religion, his remarkable family, his youth and the perplexities of his death. Gerald Ford may be remembered for never having been elected, for healing our land, for falling down steps and for pardoning Richard Nixon.

So much rubbish already has been piled up around the pardon that it is indeed distasteful to paw through it, sift it for missing links and concealed clues and reorder it for proper disposal. But we all, Ford's companions as well as his critics, have completely missed the key point about the pardon decision and why he made it and disclosed it in the way he did.

We have become obsessed with the specter of a "deal"—(1) there must have been a deal, or (2) there was no deal, period. Further, that the place to look for proof or disproof of any deal must be in the long prior relationship between Richard Nixon and Jerry Ford, between whom such a deal (1) was or (2) was not consummated.

This either-or approach characterizes every question that has been raised about the pardon, by the media or by the Hungate Committee, in magazines or books, slanderous or serious. Take your choice. Either the pardon was exactly what Jerry Ford said it was, or it was the most outrageous piece of skullduggery in U.S. history.

Obviously, this won't do. What Jerry Ford said it was on several different occasions does not all add up. There is a perplexing, stubborn persistence in sweeping denials that defy the norms of human behavior and the laws of probability. On the other hand, no hard evidence impeaches President Ford in any essential element of the pardon decision. To fit the skullduggery theory into the long and open record of Ford's career requires a full suspension of reason and logic.

Why is the pardon still a mystery, then? Where are the missing pieces? Is there a simple explanation?

241

PALACE POLITICS

To begin with, we need not look for the genesis of the pardon in the quarter century of political friendship and alliance between Ford and Nixon. Both men had taken the other's measure and admired the strengths and deplored the deficiencies each discerned. It could be assumed, when Nixon nominated Ford for the Vice Presidency, that he would generally support and defend the embattled President of his party. This was in fact the assumption of the Democratic Congress which led to his overwhelming confirmation.

What is now largely forgotten is that, prior to the pardon, it was also universally assumed—and quite generally approved—that if the former President ever really faced the prospect of imprisonment, his successor would intervene to prevent further public humiliation of Nixon and his family. This impression was certainly reinforced by Ford's own comments at his first Presidential press conference on August 28, but it was seen as an unlikely contingency a long way down the road.

Public thinking on the question of leniency for evicted Presidents had no historic precedents to guide it, although the climate of opinion undoubtedly was influenced by the fate of Spiro Agnew, until then the highest Federal officeholder ever forced out by allegations of criminal wrongdoing. Once Agnew resigned the Vice Presidency there was little clamor for additional punishment and little criticism of the plea-bargaining "deal" by which he faded into private status.

The central mystery of the Nixon pardon was not—and is not— whether President Ford exercised a proper Constitutional power but rather why he did it *when* he did it and, particularly, why he seemed to say only eleven days earlier that he had no such *imminent* intention.

I will begin this re-examination of the pardon decision by saying that I was in part to blame for it. I took responsibility for stopping the caravan of military trucks from carting off all of Nixon's files to be flown to San Clemente the night after Jerry Ford became President. I issued the orders, on my own, to stop the shredding machine and the paper burning and not to let anyone carry anything bigger than a briefcase or purse out of the White House gates that weekend. At the time, I considered these holding actions to freeze things over until a proper decision could be made. But looking back, what I did for the first time—and I think the last—was to make a *Presidential* decision which I had no right or authority to make. Had we looked the other way, much of the Nixon problem might have gone out the gate and never come back. The courts and the other Watergate defendants might have tried to get those records back, but they would have had to get them back from Nixon and others, not from the Ford White House. We certainly would have been criticized for letting them go, but the onus would have been on those who moved them out in the dark of the night.

As it was, my temporary decision was tantamount to a permanent one. When we reported the details to Buchen and to the President, both agreed we had done the right thing by stopping the unauthorized removal. But we were now clearly stuck with a mountain of Nixon records and, worse, nobody in the Ford Administration had the foggiest notion what they contained.

For all the fuss and fury about the Nixon tapes, most Americans simply have no notion of the sheer volume of records that even a normally prudent Presidency can amass. Without having been caught taping anything, the official files and papers of recent Chief Executives fill huge storerooms. From the time of George Washington, tradition and custom had unanimously held that the papers and records of a President were his personal property and he carted them away from the White House when he left, or donated them to libraries.

The big difference with the Nixon records was that they were believed to contain evidence that might be relevant to ongoing criminal proceedings. Some were the subject of outstanding court orders and subpoenas directed to the President of the United States, holding him responsible for their safekeeping and delivery to the court as directed. And the President of the United States was now Gerald R. Ford. How was he to respond to these and future court orders?

This was the burning question that President Ford was faced with during his first week in office. He still had no legal adviser of his own. We all assumed that his friend, Phil Buchen, would soon be named Counsel to the President. But Buchen's hands were more than full with transition matters.

Like the others Ford had urged to stay on the day he became President, Fred Buzhardt still was in charge of the White House legal staff. Buzhardt had come from the Pentagon to the White House about the same time as Haig replaced Haldeman. Although St. Clair had been the front man in Nixon's Watergate defense, it was Buzhardt who bore the daily burden. He worked himself into a heart attack trying to organize Nixon's defense and returned to it as soon as he could get out of bed.

Nevertheless, Buzhardt knew the ethical limits of a lawyer's loyalty to his client. He was determined not to become party to any criminal obstruction of justice, and he was one of the first to propose that Nixon consider resigning. It was Buzhardt who, under Nixon's instructions, listened to the June 23, 1972, tape after the unanimous Supreme Court ruling against the President on July 24, 1974. He immediately realized it was the lethal "smoking gun." Thereafter, he helped Haig orchestrate Nixon's resignation.

Almost from the first day TerHorst faced his former colleagues in the White House press room, he was peppered with increasingly insistent questions about custody of the Nixon tapes and papers. At first he tried the routine dodge that this question was "under study" by the legal experts and that he was not competent to answer legal questions. But as the questioners became more adamant, the new press secretary had no one to turn to for guidance except Buzhardt.

Unfortunately, TerHorst did not discuss his problem directly but sent a subordinate who had dealt with legal matters on the old Ziegler press staff. The answer came back that in the opinion of the White House office of legal counsel, based not on statute but on unbroken tradition since the early days of the Republic, papers and records of a former President were considered his personal property. TerHorst got the impression that this represented a consensus of the Buzhardt legal office, St. Clair, the Justice Department and the Special Prosecutor.

On August 14, TerHorst told the press that St. Clair was returning to his practice in Boston and that Buzhardt was remaining as legal counsel.

This exchange followed:

Question: "When are we going to get the word on what the status of these tapes are? . . . It seems like it has been dragging on for a few days now."

TerHorst: "I can't give you very much on that. . . . As I mentioned, the tapes are in the protective custody of the Secret Service, but they have been ruled to be the personal property of former President Nixon."

By whom, he was asked. By the legal counsel. Which one, St. Clair?

TerHorst: "I am not sure which particular attorney but the judgment was a collective one. . . ."

Question: "Did the President have any part in this decision?"

TerHorst: "No, he did not. This was made independently of President Ford."

Question: "Does he concur in it?"

TerHorst: "Yes, he does."

Question: "Do you know how it can be determined that these tapes are not relevant to an ongoing investigation?"

TerHorst: "I presume that was a judgment made by the respective legal counsels, both those who served President Nixon and those who serve in the Special Prosecutor's office, but that is a legal area and . . . I am not really competent to answer that question."

Question: "Are you saying there was agreement among the different staffs, the Special Prosecutor, the Justice Department and the White House legal staff?"

TerHorst: "I am assuming there would be, because I am sure neither one would just take unilateral action."

But that, of course, is exactly what *had* happened. The reporters raced off with their big news, and Jaworski's office immediately let it be known that the Special Prosecutor had merely been "informed" of Buzhardt's ruling, never "consulted," and by no means concurred in it. They could hardly say it was not a correct statement of past practice, because it was, but they obviously wanted no part of letting the Nixon tapes and records get away, even if new legislation would be required to retain them.

The resulting front-page stories were a disaster. Uniformly, they suggested the Ford Administration was trying to pull a fast one in the interests of former President Nixon. The fact that we had prevented the midnight airlift of the Nixon files to San Clemente was still unknown even to TerHorst; only the President, Buchen, Casselman, Becker and I—plus those of the Nixon holdovers whose orders had been frustrated—were aware of this redeeming action and somehow it had not leaked.

(Equally interesting, in view of Haig's repeated complaints that the "Ford people"—primarily me—were leaking all sorts of adverse information about him during this period, is the fact that Haig had successfully removed all of his own files from the White House even earlier. When this was discovered, Haig agreed to bring them back. This we never disclosed.)

At our regular session in the Oval Office the next morning, August 15, a livid Jerry terHorst faced a grim Jerry Ford. As was his custom, the President had read the full transcript of his press secretary's briefing the previous day. Ford was angry—but not with TerHorst. The press secretary started to explain how he had been had by Buzhardt's office, but it was evident where the problem was. President Ford simply could not be getting his legal counsel on such touchy questions from one of former President Nixon's lawyers, no matter how honorable Buzhardt was. He decided that Phil Buchen would be named Counsel to the President immediately, and however belatedly, Phil would consult with everybody concerned, the Special Prosecutor, Justice and counsel for former President Nixon.

Meanwhile, TerHorst would take his cues only from Buchen or the President, and there would be no press-room elaboration until Buchen could reach some resolution of the dilemma.

Knowing that Phil was up to his ears already, the President suggested he could have Bill Casselman, Ford's counsel as Vice President, and call upon Benton Becker to backstop him. Though younger, both were veterans of the Washington legal jungle.

Ford stressed that he wanted the views of independent authorities and not simply government lawyers who already had a stake in the unprecedented situation.

Ford was at his best in this early crisis, decisively directing what we should do to minimize it.

Looking back, I see something we all overlooked at the time. The crucial concern was not that Nixon wanted his records back, not that Jaworski and Nixon's even more implacable press pursuers wanted to prevent Nixon from getting them. The key factor was that *Ford wanted to get rid of them.* He had no desire to be the daily arbiter of this no-win contest. Nixon's files were a millstone hung around his fledgling Presidency; he desperately wanted to cut himself free.

TerHorst went out to face the reporters just before 1:00 P.M. and announced that Buchen had been named Counsel to the President and that Buzhardt "has not yet resigned, but will resign."* He confessed to having been "in error" about the Special Prosecutor's participation in the Buzhardt ruling.

(Actually, Buzhardt hung on for some months. John Osborne wrote in the *New Republic* on October 12, 1974: "The chief and in some instances the only source of information that Buchen needs in dealing with the Watergate aftermath is Fred Buzhardt's memory of what went on.")

The next day the pack was back in full cry.

---

* Haig was furious over what he called "firing a sick man at a press conference." He and TerHorst nearly came to blows about it. Neither the President nor Buchen objected, however.

TerHorst was able to explain that Buchen had sat down with Buzhardt and with representatives of the Special Prosecutor's office and they had agreed that the controversial records would remain in White House custody pending "an orderly and more studied effort to resolve questions of when and under what conditions possession and sole control of the property would be transferred."

One week later, newspapers reported that former President Nixon, forewarned that he could no longer count on absolute cooperation from his old White House staff, had retained his own Washington attorney, Herbert J. Miller.

Miller was an interesting choice. Although a Republican, an unsuccessful GOP candidate for Lieutenant Governor of Maryland in 1970, he first won Washington attention as Bobby Kennedy's choice to head the criminal division of the Justice Department. Later returning to private practice, he defended former Attorney General Richard Kleindienst against Watergate charges and won him a suspended sentence on a reduced charge. So if Nixon were looking for a skilled plea-bargainer, the consensus was he couldn't have done better than "Jack" Miller.

Buchen didn't know Miller, but Becker did. Buchen was thus able to deal with the ex-President's lawyer (and eventually with Nixon himself) through Becker, who had no official White House status. It was a sound arrangement to protect Ford.

The immediate legal and practical problem, remember, was what to do with the Nixon records. More precisely, how the Ford Presidency could get rid of primary responsibility for resisting or permitting access to them without surrendering or abandoning the duty of safeguarding them.

Nobody except Nixon himself, or Nixon and Haldeman, in many instances, knew what was on the tapes. To an undetermined extent, the written logs and records of the Nixon Administration held clues as to what *might* be on certain day's tapes at certain hours. But the Ford staff had no personnel to find out and furthermore and fundamentally would really *rather not know*.

To say that the tapes should never have been made is well enough. But they *were* made. To say that they should have been destroyed promptly when their existence became known is well enough. But they were *not* destroyed. And there they were, figuratively piled on top of President Ford's desk, taking precedence over every pressing business before the nation.

The President was spending hours every day pondering this dilemma. His press secretary was spending hours trying to satisfy the clamor of the news media about it. The first serious challenge to the credibility of the new "open" Presidency had already arisen over it. Nixon's tapes and records were a time bomb left behind, ticking ominously.

I was not privy to all the legal deliberations in this period, but the upshot was a brilliant improvisation. Simply stated, it adopted the custodial principle of a bank safe-deposit box. There would be two keys, and both would be required to open—but only one to lock up the box. Nixon, or his duly designated agent, would hold one key; Ford, or his agent, the other.

Since Ford didn't really want a key, his agent for ordinary purposes would be the Administrator of the General Services Administration, who by law is responsible for the Federal Archives and Records Service.

Miller and Becker hammered out a draft letter of agreement in which the tapes were treated differently from other records.

The rest of the Nixon records were to be moved to California and, until a permanent Nixon library could be established, would be kept in custody of GSA. For a three-year period access would be limited to Nixon or his agents, but no originals could be removed. After three years Nixon could dispose of them any way he pleased, but presumably the bulk would be deeded to the government for the Nixon archive, the way prior Presidential papers had been handled.

For the tapes, however, two consecutive five-year periods were contemplated. During the first five years they could neither be destroyed nor the originals removed from GSA custody, and only Nixon or persons authorized by him in writing could listen to them. On September 1, 1979, legal title to the tapes would pass to the United States, but Nixon could then direct the GSA administrator to destroy some or all of them. Upon Nixon's death, or at the end of ten years, on September 1, 1984, all the original tapes automatically would be destroyed.

Buchen later explained that within the first five years the statute of limitations would have run out on Watergate-related crimes. Nobody ever satisfactorily explained what the second five-year period was for, unless Nixon had additional literary plans.

In case any tapes were subpoenaed or ordered released by a court, both Nixon and the government were to be notified and either could assert an objection, defense or privilege to prevent their release. Thus

248

Nixon *alone* could fight an attempt by the Special Prosecutor, or another Watergate defendant, to produce a tape in evidence; but Ford *also* could claim future national security would be jeopardized by certain disclosures.

It seemed to me a good compromise. Nixon came off very well, to be sure, but in the absence of any statutory law on the subject, he got less than any other ex-President had.

The question of a pardon for Nixon was not, during these early negotiations, linked with the problem of disposing of the records. Indeed, it was generally assumed that Nixon's eagerness to get possession of his tapes and papers was (1) to prepare his defense against possible prosecution or his testimony if called in other trials and (2) to speed publication of his memoirs so that he could pay for a legal defense. Moreover, if access to his records were long denied him he might well have good grounds for dismissal of any charges that might be brought.

Pardon talk, however, continued to fascinate the press. As an inducement for Nixon to resign voluntarily, the tacit promise of clemency had found considerable favor even among his foes.

Public opinion was ambivalent. Most people didn't want a former President cruelly hounded, but neither did they want him to get off scotfree. They sensed something unfair about subordinates serving prison terms while the boss drew full pension. But it was all unjelled, and only time could contrive a consensus.

It never crossed my mind that President Ford was giving a pardon serious thought until Sunday, August 25, when Nelson Rockefeller was on one of the Sunday quiz shows. He was asked and agreed with Senator Scott that Nixon had, in effect, been punished enough and should not be drawn and quartered as well. Being of a suspicious nature, I wondered why these liberal Republicans were floating the immunity idea.

It would have been smarter for Rocky's own cause to waffle. Was he perhaps testing the waters for President Ford? No, after our close call with Haig on August 2, I couldn't believe the President was even contemplating anything like a pardon so soon. Rockefeller was probably just saying what he felt: Nixon was down and out and it wasn't much fun kicking him.

But on Monday, inevitably, TerHorst was asked if President Ford agreed with Rocky and with Scott, and the press secretary ducked and said Rockefeller had not been told by the President what to say or not to say.

PALACE POLITICS

The pardon dilemma did not surface again until August 26, two days before Ford was to hold his first formal news conference. That night, when I got around to my telephone messages, I saw that Clark Mollenhoff had called me twice. I was still avoiding press calls, but Clark might be trying to tell me something I should know.

Mollenhoff began by saying he had heard the President—he still called him "Jerry," which rather annoyed me—was going to hold a press conference. He was sure that someone would ask him about pardoning Nixon.

Clark, who has a law degree, said the *prima facie* case against Nixon was overwhelming. He had talked about this with "Jerry" as Vice President, but he hadn't seemed very impressed. Now, his first formal news conference was a perfect opportunity for him to put speculation to rest and say in no uncertain terms that he would let justice take its course. If he didn't, Mollenhoff said, his good start on the Presidency would be sorely crippled.

In my innocence, I asked what was the urgency. Nobody had suggested that Ford planned to pardon Nixon, so why should he deny it? Clark said that was how much I knew. After Ford's surprise proposal for conditional amnesty to Vietnam evaders, which everyone knew was a Haldeman ploy to prepare for Watergate pardons, Nixon's was sure to follow.

I said the Vietnam amnesty had nothing to do with Nixon or his former aides, most of whom were against it. But I would try to convey Clark's views to the President.

In anticipation of the Wednesday-afternoon press conference, we set aside all Tuesday afternoon and several hours on Wednesday for preparation. Ford was not exactly an amateur at handling tough questions, but we realized the extra importance of his first time up to bat as President.

TerHorst and I were there, along with Paul Miltich, Jack Marsh, Milt Friedman, Paul Theis, Bill Seidman and, I think, Alan Greenspan. I don't recall Buchen being present, and I believe Haig was in and out. We sat around the President's desk, acting the role of reporters, and peppered him with every dirty question we could think of. The White House press corps never approached us in venom. Ford greatly enjoyed it and flattened most of his sparring partners with ease.

When my turn came I asked: Would the President put a stop to all the talk about his pardoning Nixon or his Watergate confederates?

Without hesitating, Ford declined the opportunity. He had heard no such talk, he said, nor had he authorized any. It was an inappropriate subject for him to comment upon while many of these matters were still pending in the courts.

"Does that mean," someone else asked, "that you disagree with your Vice President-designate, Governor Rockefeller, and your Senate leader, Hugh Scott, both of whom have stated publicly that President Nixon has suffered enough?"

Not at all, Ford said. He believed that both Rockefeller and Scott had a very good feeling for the sentiment of the American people and he would be inclined to agree. But they did not have the legal responsibility of the President and were therefore free to express themselves as they pleased.

Very good, we all felt. He was in effect putting further legal questions out of bounds. He should just stick to that line.

TerHorst asked another question about Nixon: The former President reportedly had been calling friends in the Congress complaining that Jaworski was still persecuting him—"picking the carcass" was the phrase he used. Had President Ford gotten any such calls from San Clemente, or had he talked to Nixon about possible immunity?

Ford said flatly that he had not talked to President Nixon since he left the White House except, as had been announced, to tell Nixon of his choice of Rockefeller.

After the others had left, I told the President about Mollenhoff's call. If he recognized Clark, he could expect a question about ruling out any pardons.

He shook his head sadly.

"Clark is very bitter," he said. "It's too bad."

When the real news conference began, however, it was not Mollenhoff but Helen Thomas of UPI who was recognized for the first question.

"Mr. President," she began, ". . . do you agree with the [American] Bar Association that the laws apply equally to all men, or do you agree with Governor Rockefeller that former President Nixon should have immunity from prosecution? . . ."

(In logic, it would of course be possible to agree with both or with neither. But logic was neither Helen's nor Ford's long suit. He smiled and let Helen tie up the loose ends of her elongated question.)

". . . and specifically, would you use your pardon authority, if necessary?"

Just as rehearsed, Ford recalled that in this same room on the day

251

he became President, he had expressed hope that Nixon, who brought peace to millions, would find it for himself.

"Now the expression made by Governor Rockefeller, I think, coincides with the general view and the point of view of the American people. I subscribe to that point of view, but let me add . . ."

My stomach turned into a knot. Whenever I heard Ford use that phrase, I knew we were headed for trouble. He was going to toss away the carefully plotted chart and sail into unknown waters.

". . . but let me add in the last ten days or two weeks I have asked for prayers for guidance on this very important point."

This was news to me. I had spent a good many hours with him over that period, and not once had he evidenced such a deep concern. Of course I did not attend his prayers, but he shared a lot of his worries with me. Still, it was not like Ford to talk publicly about prayer in any frivolous context.

"In this situation, I am the final authority," the President continued. "There have been no charges made, there has been no action by any jury, and until any legal process has been undertaken, I think it is unwise and untimely for me to make any commitment."

Following up on Helen's opener, another reporter asked the President if he meant to say that a pardon for Nixon was still "an option that you will consider"—depending on what the courts might do. Of course, he would make the final decision, but he would make no commitment "until it gets to me," Ford replied.

They persisted. Then he was not ruling out the pardon option? No, he was not ruling it out. It was a proper option for any President. Then how could Jaworski pursue cases against Nixon's aides if there were a possibility Nixon would escape trial? In effect, Ford said that the Special Prosecutor should do his duty as he saw it.

"What do you plan to do as President to see that we have no further Watergates?" was the next tangent. This was not one we had foreseen, because the answer was so obvious: Ford was not Nixon.

But the President's answer—in retrospect—was as curious as it was completely extemporaneous. It reflected clearly the congenital Congressman's fear that he may be done in by his "staff" and seemed to say this was Nixon's undoing.

"There will be no tightly controlled operation of the White House staff. I have a policy of seeking advice from a number of top members of my staff. There will be no one person, nor any limited number of individuals, who make decisions. I will make the decisions. . . ."

Question: "Do you plan to have a code of ethics for the Executive Branch?"

The President: "The code of ethics that will be followed will be the example that I set."

Near the end of the traditional half hour, the press came back to the Nixon problem.

Question: "Mr. President, you have emphasized here your option of granting a pardon to the former President . . ."

The President: "I intend to."

Question (continuing): "You intend to have that option. If an indictment is brought, would you grant a pardon before any trial took place?"

This blunt question had not been anticipated.

The President: "I said at the outset that until the matter reaches me, I am not going to make any comment during the process of whatever charges are made."

(This answer is a textbook classic of incoherence and inarticulateness. It would surely seem, at least, to mean that nothing would be cooking for quite a while, so it would be useless to keep asking. If his answer was exquisitely artful, one must suppose that Ford had already determined his course. If it was simply clumsy, for which plenty of precedent exists, he was still groping his way toward a firm decision, fighting for a little more time.)

A clutch of his closest aides followed the President back to the Oval Office and smothered him in ecstatic praise. We all felt the news conference had gone supremely well.

That evening the President and First Lady had invited the Rockefellers, the Cabinet, senior staff and their spouses for an informal dinner and dancing. It was supposed to promote camaraderie between the Nixon and Ford people, though we were grossly outnumbered. Everybody except Rocky, Buchen, Marsh, Seidman, TerHorst and me was a Nixon retread. But it was a fun party, anyhow.

The ladies joined in praising his press conference. The President loved it.

"I was a little nervous at first, but after the first five minutes it was just like any football game," Ford told the admiring circle around him. "I had a little practice at that sort of thing—fifty-five press conferences in the last eight months."

The next morning's press reports were in general fair and objective, and most reporters made a point of the relaxed atmosphere and new civility of the encounter, contrasting it with the increasingly savage shootouts of the Johnson–Nixon years.

Almost universally, they read into Ford's replies a definite intention to treat former President Nixon with compassion and to reserve the option of intervening, if need be, to spare him the ultimate humiliation of a prison cell. And there was virtually no criticism, but considerable applause, for what they believed to be his position.

The Washington *Post*'s headline read: "PRESIDENT HINTS HE WOULD WEIGH PARDONING NIXON" but qualified this in Carroll Kirkpatrick's lead story by saying, "if charges are brought against him in the courts."

The New York *Times'* unique triple headline summarized its account thus: "FORD SAYS HE VIEWS NIXON AS PUNISHED ENOUGH NOW; PARDON OPTION KEPT OPEN.—DECISION PUT OFF—PRESIDENT CITES DUTY OF JAWORSKI TO ACT AS HE SEES FIT."

Clifton Daniel, President Truman's son-in-law and then chief of the New York *Times* bureau in Washington, wrote a very perceptive column of analysis—quite the best of any I saw. For one thing he made the correct distinction between Ford's earlier pronouncement and his latest one, something nobody else ever got around to.

" 'I do not think the public would stand for it,' Mr. Ford told the Senate Rules Committee at hearings on his confirmation to be Vice President," Daniel recalled. "But that was in response to a question on whether, if a President resigned, his successor would have the power to *prevent* a criminal investigation or prosecution of the former President. The question that was asked him today was whether he would use his pardoning authority."

Daniel saw the gist of the President's comments as a signal to Jaworski to get cracking. And so did the Washington *Evening Star,* which predicted that Nixon's new lawyer, Herbert J. Miller, would seek to work out some kind of three-way deal involving the Special Prosecutor and the White House.

The *Star*'s reporters, Barry Kalb and Fred Barnes, struck a new note in their next day's account which takes on special significance in light of later developments. They wrote: "Ford aides acknowledged that the President is well aware of his authority to act at any time to pardon Nixon. Even before Nixon left the White House, sources said, the Justice Department's office of legal counsel studied the extent of the President's clemency power. It was determined that clemency can be given at any point. . . . *Ford was told* of the Justice Department's findings, according to White House sources, *and chose to pass up his first opportunity to grant Nixon clemency* in favor of allowing Jaworski to act." (Emphasis mine.)

The *Star's* startling allegation was echoed by the *New Republic's* John Osborne in a probing piece published a month later. Osborne asserted that "a fact that Mr. Ford . . . has not confided to his closest and most senior associates is that he briefly but seriously considered announcing his intention to grant the pardon at his first press conference on August 28."

Was this true? In retrospect, I suppose he probably did. Ford is a lousy liar. When Helen Thomas asked her first question every impulse in him surely wanted to say, "Of course I'll use my pardon authority if necessary."

But he plunged ahead with the prepared answer we'd worried over, and when he got halfway through his conscience was pricking because he knew damn well it wouldn't do. He relieved the pressure by adding a clue that nobody then caught: If he was going to do nothing, *what was all the praying about?*

Who were the "Ford aides" who acknowledged that he was "well aware of his authority to act any time to pardon Nixon?"

Ford subsequently testified before the Hungate subcommittee that no member of his staff, or of Nixon's, or anyone acting on behalf of the former President, and specifically not Haig, urged him to grant the pardon prior to his decision to do so. I cannot contradict my respected boss, but "never" and "nobody" statements are always suspect. Probably his denial hangs upon the floating character of the term "decision" and upon what, in his mind, would constitute an "attempt to influence."

Almost everyone around the President, day and night, owed their jobs to Richard Nixon, and most of them felt both affection and sympathy for him. It is simply too much to believe that for four weeks not one Nixon holdover ever lifted a finger to get Ford to pardon him.

It has subsequently been reported that Haig in fact did, and Leonard Garment and Ray Price earnestly tried to win Ford over. Garment and Price both wrote memos on the day of the first press conference, according to a Washington *Post* story that didn't surface until December 18, 1975. The rehash of the Nixon pardon, by Bob Woodward and Carl Bernstein, attributed to "a reliable source" the allegation that Ford had given Haig "private assurances" on August 28, 1974, that a pardon for Nixon would be forthcoming.

PALACE POLITICS

Woodward and Bernstein admitted they could not establish that Ford ever saw the Garment and Price memos, of which copies obviously had been supplied them. Garment's was a humanitarian plea, fearing that Nixon might crack up or even attempt suicide. Price, they said, had drafted a pardon statement that he hoped the President would use at the outset of his first press conference. I can say that announcing a pardon on August 28 was neither suggested, discussed nor even hinted at during any of the many hours I spent with the President in that period. But the *Post* called General Haig at NATO headquarters and said the general obligingly confirmed there was a pardon discussion about that date.

All of this is less illuminating than the fact that, almost sixteen months after the event, with an election being held, someone familiar with the transition and the pardon was using White House documents to revive the dormant controversy and do Ford grievous harm.

A virtually identical story came out of San Clemente, about a week after the pardon, by Everette R. Holles of the New York *Times.* It was attributed to "a long-time friend and associate of Mr. Nixon in touch with affairs inside the Nixon estate" who said that Haig told President Ford on August 29 that unless he moved quickly to announce a full pardon for Nixon—without waiting for legal action as implied at his news conference the previous day—the former President might suffer "a personal and national tragedy."

The source of this stuck to his guns after it was denied by everybody concerned—Ford, Haig and Jaworski, with whom Haig reportedly had conferred.

Going back over this elaborate game of "Who Struck John," one is primarily puzzled why everybody—and particularly Haig—was at such pains to deny any and all involvement. So what if they all implored Ford to pardon their former boss? Could anything be more normal and natural? The only circumstances under which it would be improper to attempt to influence a President to grant clemency to someone would be to give him false information, to use illegal persuasions such as blackmail or bribery and, finally, to seek the pardon of an accomplice or fellow conspirator *in order to prevent one's own prosecution.*

Of course, one of the effects of the Nixon pardon was to prevent that. Except for those already enmeshed in the criminal-justice system, no further prosecutions were undertaken against Nixon's subordinates.

256

On September 17 in the Washington *Post,* Joe Kraft demanded that Haig be hauled up to the Hill for confirmation as NATO commander. "Circumstantial evidence connects General Haig with a mountain of dirty work," Joe began (a sentence Joe McCarthy couldn't have improved). "But the President—and this is the principal lesson of the pardon—*is not in a good position to deal with the Nixonite Old Guard.*" (Emphasis mine.)

"As White House chief of staff, in 1973 and 1974 [Haig] presided over the Watergate cover-up," Kraft thundered, "[but] the details are obscure and full of question marks. What exactly was Haig's role in the Saturday night massacre of . . . Archibald Cox? Didn't Haig think something was fishy when Lt. Gen. Robert Pursley, a distinguished officer serving as military aide to Secretary of Defense Melvin Laird, was subjected to wiretapping? What was Haig's role in the 'Pentagon spy ring' and the White House 'plumbers'? How about the 18½ minutes missing from the most critical White House tape?

"The Ford White House staff cannot possibly explore such questions. If nothing else, as the pardon blunder indicates, Mr. Ford and his staff are too decent to deal effectively with the Nixon gang," Joe concluded.

In reconstructing the circumstances and events surrounding the Nixon pardon it would be nice to relate that I was the first and only associate to whom President Ford confided this most momentous of his initial moves. It would be even more flattering to my reputation as a Presidential Counsellor to say that I fought tooth and nail to dissuade him from so disastrous a course. Alas, that is not what happened.

What happened, to the best of my recollection, was that early on the morning of Friday, August 30, 1974, the President summoned his three senior advisers—Buchen, Marsh and me—to the Oval Office. General Haig was there with him. We were due to take off for Columbus, Ohio, very shortly. When we had arranged three of the side chairs in a semicircle around his huge walnut desk, Ford said that what he was about to say must be kept in the utmost confidence because he had not made up his mind with absolute finality.

(Nobody made any notes, so I shall put in paraphrase the spirit of the discussion, if not the letter.)

The President said he had been doing a lot of thinking since his first press conference two days earlier. Upon reading the transcript of the questions and his answers, he was concerned that so many questions were about Watergate, former President Nixon and the possibil-

257

ity of his prosecution or pardon.* He was not sure his answers had been clear.

As a lawyer, he felt a little chagrined that he had not been sufficiently certain what the law actually was concerning the pardoning powers of the President. It was his own fault, he said. He should have studied up on this before the press conference, but that was water over the dam.

Turning to Buchen, Ford said he wanted this legal point researched as thoroughly and as rapidly as possible, consulting independent authorities. But he cautioned Phil on the Byzantine ways of Washington. Any outside inquiries would have to be made very gingerly. Phil said he could handle it.

The President leaned back in his big chair and elaborately filled and lit his pipe.

Matter-of-factly, Ford said he was very much inclined to grant Nixon immunity from further prosecution as soon as he was sure he had the legal authority to do so.

There was a deafening silence.

There is an antique clock on the Oval Office wall, just to the right of the principal entry door. I don't know its history, but it must have overheard many state secrets. Its pendulum ticks loudly. At this moment it shattered the silence like a burst of machine-gun fire.

I had been watching the faces of my colleagues almost as closely as the President's. Face-watching is a very inexact science. Jack Marsh, the most amiable of men, wears a slightly puzzled frown when listening intently. Haig, to whom shocking revelations had become old stuff, cleared his throat and wondered if, considering the course the conversation was taking, his presence might be inappropriate. He asked to excuse himself.

The President waved him back down in his chair. Calmly he ticked off his reasons. It was not merely a matter of avoiding the degrading spectacle of a former President of the United States being dragged into the prisoner's dock in a criminal court. It would be a long time before it came to that, if ever. He doubted that, under current Supreme Court rulings about pretrial publicity, an unbiased jury could be empaneled anywhere in the United States for such a proceeding.

But with each legal maneuver by the defense or the prosecution, with every ruling, every appeal, every delaying motion, the whole rot-

* Nine out of twenty-eight questions.

ten mess of Watergate would be revived; all the old divisive passions would be rekindled. It could go on and on, for years and years, and in the end Nixon would either escape any penalty or, if convicted, public opinion would cry "enough!" and compel whoever was then President to pardon him.

"If eventually, why not now?" he asked. If a Presidential pardon would be the inevitable end result of a long-drawn-out process of "justice taking its course," why not get it over with and get on with the urgent business of the nation?

We sat mute. Haig wiggled nervously in his chair, Buchen's scowl deepened, Marsh's frown was accentuated by a sickly pallor, and God knows how I appeared. The President's logic was unassailable, yet I felt as if I was watching someone commit hara-kiri.

The President pressed on. His conscience told him a pardon was right, and his mind was about 99 percent made up. It was a decision he alone could make, and he would make it alone. He wanted no leaks and no test of public reaction. But if we wished, he would appreciate hearing our views.

I had been with him through many tough decisions. I could smell whether he really wanted an argument or not. It was written all over him that he didn't want to be talked out of this one, that he had already decided to pardon Nixon, and the only open questions were *when* and *how*.

It was Phil Buchen, who had known him longest and was far and away the most cautious of his Counsellors, who spoke first.

"I can't argue with what you feel is right," Phil began, "but is this the right time?"

"Will there *ever* be a right time?" the President shot back.

Before anyone could reply, the President's telephone buzzed. He picked it up, and I darted into my adjoining office to dig up the transcript of the news conference. Haig also took off and never returned. It was obvious that Al wanted to be able to call upon the three of us as witnesses that he had not raised his voice as a pardon advocate. His fine sense of honor left me cold; he had been alone with the new President no less than two or three hours a day ever since he took office.

By the time Ford hung up, I had skimmed the key media questions and answers. He turned to me and said, "Bob, what do you think?"

"I think, Mr. President," I replied with a wry grin, "that the fit is really going to hit the shan."

It was the President's turn to grin—for the first time that morning.

Mine was an in-house joke. Susan's frequently incontinent kitten had been named "Shan."

I waved the papers in my hand. "Here are your own words," I read aloud. '. . . until any legal process has been undertaken, I think it is unwise and untimely for me to make any commitment.' And then they asked if you meant that pardon was an option you would consider 'depending on what the courts will do.' And you answered that 'until it gets to me, I make no commitment. . . . I am not going to make any comment during the process of whatever charges are made.' "

Ford's jaw tightened, and he knew I was going to lay it on hard.

"You didn't read the part about my not ruling it out. I refused to make any commitment one way or the other. I said that too, every time, and I was very firm about it," the President said somewhat testily.

"Well, O.K. Maybe that's what you meant, but that isn't what I heard or what most people heard. What everybody believes is that you may pardon Nixon some day but *not* right away. And not until there have been some further legal steps in the case. And if you do, the professional Nixon-haters in the press and in the Congress will go right up the wall. You are going to have a firestorm of angry protest that will make the Saturday Night Massacre seem mild."*

"Sure, there will be criticism," Ford readily agreed. "But it will flare up and die down. If I wait six months, or a year, there will still be a 'firestorm' from the Nixon-haters, as you call them. They wouldn't like it if I waited until he was on his deathbed. But most Americans will understand."

I was tempted to say that most Americans will understand only what they see on television and read in the papers, and the media would be furious because they would believe Ford had deceived them. The last thing we needed was a new credibility gap. But I had hit him pretty hard, so all I said was "I agree with Phil: This isn't the right time. It takes time for public sentiment to shift. Sooner or later they'll get a bellyful of those people who keep on hounding a former President and howling for more blood. Why can't you wait until some sympathy sets in? It's already begun. *Newsweek* says fifty-five percent of the people think further prosecution should be dropped."

---

* In retrospect I was too mild in my estimate, not of the protest's *intensity* but of its *durability*. Of course I could not anticipate TerHorst's dramatic defection, which set the tone for the press.

The President said he wasn't going to depend on public-opinion polls to tell him what was right.

Jack Marsh agreed with my forecast of adverse reaction, especially on Capitol Hill. There would be a lot of hot rhetoric for the record. But secretly, Jack surmised, down deep in their hearts, the legislators would be glad to have the President take them off the hook. Most elected politicians, he observed, are not really keen about criminal prosecutions of other politicians after they have fallen from grace. To them, even more than to most Americans, being forced out of the White House would appear the ultimate political punishment for an essentially political offense.

None of us, to my recollection, raised the question of what a pardon would do to Ford's own election prospects in 1976. We could not have been so naïve as to assume the Democrats would not attempt to capitalize on it. Probably we skipped the subject because Ford's own earnest insistence on doing what was best for the country was contagious. In those days we were all intensely aware that for the first time in history the *institution* of the Presidency was in jeopardy. We believed Jerry Ford was the man to restore confidence in and respect for the office. If he could, we were certain he would be nominated and elected to a full term; if not, the job wouldn't be worth having.

Outwardly, nobody was wildly enthusiastic, but neither did anyone violently object—the way TerHorst did later. Maybe that was why he was not invited; Ford knew him better than any of us. It was pretty clear the odds of changing his mind were close to zero. The President paid us the compliment of his confidence not because he needed our *opinions* but because he needed our *help* to execute his decision and to build a solid front among his senior aides before riding out the expected storm. The meeting broke up with all of us in a state of semishock.

Over the long Labor Day weekend, Buchen and Becker sought to unscramble the problem of the Nixon records. Buchen had asked the Special Prosecutor to provide him with a list of the areas of possible prosecution of former President Nixon and with his estimate of the time it might require to bring Nixon to trial if such a course were followed.

Jaworski put his deputy, Henry Ruth, to work on this and obliged Buchen with a memo outlining ten possible violations of law and his own conclusion—that Nixon could not be brought to trial for a year or more. That Wednesday, Buchen and Becker met with Miller. The

261

President authorized them to pass word to Nixon through his attorney that he, Ford, was of a mind to grant him a pardon, although the final decision had not been made. This was done by telephone, and it seems clear now that its purpose was to prod Nixon into accepting the compromise custody agreement limiting his absolute access to his tapes and records.

Nixon was no novice at negotiating the best possible terms for himself, and instead of grabbing at the proffered pardon, he instructed Miller to fly to San Clemente to iron out some technical points in the agreement. Buchen, with Ford's concurrence, told Becker to go with him and close the case as quickly as possible. They flew to California on Thursday, September 5, arriving fairly late.

That Thursday the President assembled the same group—Buchen, Haig, Marsh and me—in the Oval Office and announced that he had definitely decided to pardon Nixon. I recall little surprise and no argument. If I had my life with Jerry Ford to live over again I would have thrown myself across the track in front of the onrushing locomotive, however futile it might have been. But I did not, nor did the others.

"I want to make the announcement right away. How about tomorrow morning?" he declared.

Phil interjected that drawing up the necessary legal documents, proclamations, etc., would take some time. Besides, he cautioned, you don't want to do anything until Becker gets back here with Nixon's signature on that agreemment.

"When's Benton getting back?" the President asked.

"Not before tomorrow night or Saturday, assuming Nixon signs," Buchen said.

"Well, I have decided and I want to make my decision known without any more horsing around," Ford said very emphatically. I hadn't heard that expression since my high-school days, but his meaning was clear. "I will not wait one day later than Sunday."

Nobody at the time noticed the coincidence of dates: Sunday, September 8, would precisely mark the completion of the first month of his Presidency. Nor did any of us raise, as we should have, the question of why the President's press secretary, Jerry terHorst, was not included in this important planning. We just supposed the President would tell him in his own way. But it was a serious omission.

The following day, on a flight from Philadelphia after his maiden Bicentennial speech, the President called Haig, TerHorst, Marsh and me to the forward cabin and began going over the logistics of the pardon announcement on Sunday. To my knowledge, this was the first the press secretary had been told of it. Curiously, he neither evidenced surprise nor voiced objection. Later TerHorst would bitterly complain about not having been taken into the President's confidence earlier and being deliberately misled by Buchen. I will not arbitrate this sad business except to say that I know how much it hurts to be kept totally in the dark by a President to whom you have dedicated all your waking hours. On the other hand, TerHorst was informed only a few hours later than the Vice President of the United States, a good thirty-six hours before the event, and there was no spontaneous outburst of moral indignation from him at that point.

While we were headed homeward, Becker was flying back from San Clemente, the custody agreement signed by Richard Nixon in his pocket. He also brought a draft statement, which the former President had worked out with Ron Ziegler, accepting the pardon.

A somewhat red-eyed crew gathered around the President's desk on Saturday to listen to Becker's account of his encounter with Nixon.

Nixon seemed mentally as sharp as ever, Benton said, but otherwise the change in his appearance was startling. His stoop was more pronounced and his movements painful. He spent most of his time seated with his phlebitis-swollen leg elevated. Becker noted that Nixon's color was poor and that his collar seemed several sizes too large, as if he had lost a lot of weight.

Becker had done most of his business through Miller and Ziegler, but at the end of his visit Nixon invited him into the house for a chat. He tried to be a cordial host, and when the time came for Becker to leave he almost automatically began fiddling around his desk drawer for a souvenir. Finally he came up with cufflinks and a tie clip bearing the Presidential seal and his signature.

"I used to have an aide who'd stand by and hand me these," Nixon recalled. "I used to have all kinds of things, ashtrays, you know, paperweights and all that. Lots of them. I'm sorry, but this is the best I have now."

We were all moved by his pitiful word picture and glad to turn to the legal specifics of the agreement. All that remained, it seemed, was for Arthur Sampson, the GSA administrator, to add his signature.

Then there was Nixon's proposed statement accepting the pardon. Legally, an acceptance was essential, and at least theoretically, it would have been possible for Nixon to let Ford get clear out on the limb of offering a pardon and then dramatically refuse it. The idea that Nixon should be required to acknowledge his guilt or, as Buchen put it, include in his acceptance a "statement of contrition" was apparently Phil's idea and it was more theological than legal. Nixon, the lawyer, knew it was necessary only for him to say "I accept," and he went only a little bit further.

For a pardon to be "free" as well as "full" it must be unconditional, and thus Buchen, as well as the President, was compelled to insist, afterward, that no strings were attached, such as the custody agreement. But it is patently obvious there was such a connection and that, having got the vexing tapes and records out of the way (as he thought), President Ford was not inclined to jeopardize the agreement by forcing Nixon to eat more crow.

None of us, excepting Haig, was very happy with Nixon's acceptance draft. But it was really not ours to write. Becker and Haig went off to telephone Ziegler a few minor "suggestions" and to arrange with TerHorst for simultaneous release of Nixon's statement in San Clemente and the White House press room, as soon as Ford signed the pardon document.

The President leaned back in his big leather chair and clasped his hands behind his head. Staring at the ceiling, he began to recite tentatively the reasons he would give for his pardon decision. From time to time, Marsh or Buchen or I would suggest a different phrasing or point out a legal or factual imprecision. But for the most part Ford spelled out his statement in his own words. He clearly had given it plenty of thought.

Before saying good night I hesitated at the doorway. "Can I ask you just one question?" I said.

'Sure," the President said, grinning. "So long as you don't try to talk me out of it."

"No, that's not it. I think I understand your reasoning. But one thing still bothers me, and you haven't answered it. What's the rush? Why must it be tomorrow? Why not Christmas Eve, or a year from now, when things quiet down?"

His answer wasn't at all what I expected. But he was perfectly serious about it.

"Well, someone—one of the news people—might ask me about it again."

"But all you'd have to do is say you haven't decided," I protested.

"But I *have* decided," the President declared firmly, and that was the end of my last delaying action.

On Sunday morning TerHorst wanted to know where the text of the President's remarks was so he could duplicate it for the press. I gave him a copy but warned it still hadn't had a final O.K. from the President, so it shouldn't be passed out until we got one.

TerHorst's eyes were red from lack of sleep, but none of us had much. What I didn't know—and I would never have guessed from his calm pipe-sucking demeanor—was that he had spent the rest of the night composing a letter of resignation as press secretary, which he termed "the most difficult decision I ever have had to make." The key paragraph read:

> So it is with great regret, after long soul-searching, that I must inform you that I cannot in good conscience support your decision to pardon former President Nixon even before he has been charged with the commission of any crime. As your spokesman, I do not know how I could credibly defend that action in the absence of a like decision to grant absolute pardon to the young men who evaded Vietnam military service as a matter of conscience and the absence of pardons for former aides and associates of Mr. Nixon who have been charged with crimes—and imprisoned—stemming from the same Watergate situation. These are also men whose reputations and families have been grievously injured. Try as I can, it is impossible to conclude that the former President is more deserving of mercy than persons of lesser station in life whose offenses have had far less effect on our national well-being.

If TerHorst had only given me some warning of his intention perhaps I could have altered the Presidential statement to meet his arguments more directly. Instead, unbeknown to anyone, the press secretary went to the Oval Office shortly after Ford returned from early Communion and handed him the letter. The President read the resignation thoroughly, without showing the emotion or astonishment he must have felt, then said evenly, "Well, Jerry, I'm sorry you feel this way."

After TerHorst left the room, however, the enormity of what his old friend had just done to him began to work on the President. His quitting in protest would be the second line in every account of the pardon announcement, overshadowing the President's own prayerful reasoning. He summoned Jack Marsh and asked him to try and persuade TerHorst to take it back, at least for the day. Jack was the in-house conciliator and soother of injured egos throughout Ford's Presidency and Vice Presidency. Despite his great talents of gentle persuasion, however, Marsh was unable to do anything but delay leakage of TerHorst's walkout for a few hours.

The President, with less than an hour left before the media people had been summoned for the Sunday-morning announcement, vacated the Oval Office so that the cameramen could set up their equipment. He stuck his head in my door and said he was ready now to go over the final script. He pronounced it "fine." Almost as an afterthought, he turned to the paragraph which stated "It is common knowledge that serious allegations and accusations hang like a sword over our former President's head as he tries to reshape his life."

The President took his felt-tip pen and inserted three words that were to cause trouble later on. He made it conclude "threatening his health as he tries to reshape his life."

I started to protest that adding the "health" element at the last moment was like writing it in neon against a midnight sky, besides screwing up the whole carefully developed basis for the pardon. But there was no time. The President impatiently cut off my misgivings and headed for the Oval Office door and the end of his honeymoon with the American press and public.

He was not, on such short notice, on live television. A single videotape camera was set up, a baker's dozen of the White House "regulars" were on hand to hear the President's surprise announcement, and the documents were handed them as they filed into the Oval Office.

Considering that everything that could go wrong had gone wrong (although I was still blissfully unaware of TerHorst's bombshell), the President did a magnificent job. We could faintly hear the church bells pealing their 11:00 A.M. summons as he began to read the pardon statement.

As reporters rushed to their phones, the President capped his pen, murmured, "Thanks, fellows" to the camera crew and popped into his hideaway.

"Well, you sold me," I said, more cheerily than I felt. "You did it perfectly. Now we'll all do our best to make it fly."

"I'm glad I did it, Bob. It was the right thing to do."

He still didn't tell me about TerHorst. Afterward, when I reproached him about it, he admitted he deliberately kept me in the dark that morning because I had a short fuse and he was afraid I'd get so mad as to create another problem. He was probably right.

TerHorst's abrupt exit immeasurably compounded the damage done by Ford's pardon decision. Whether or not designedly, TerHorst had made his break with the President a matter of conscience, on the pattern of Elliot Richardson's break with Nixon. Publicly identified as a longtime Michigan friend of Ford's and never a certified Nixon man, TerHorst had the confidence of the Washington press corps as a symbol of the new and open Administration. It was he who spearheaded the first clashes with the Praetorians. With his defection the tiny phalanx of Ford people was weakened and Ford's own shining image was dimmed.

On Monday we flew to Pittsburgh, where the President was to address an urban-affairs meeting. For the first time hostile signs appeared among the sidewalk crowds, protesting the pardon. The press had turned sour, and Ford heard himself booed.

Nasty rumors began to bust out all over. There was a secret "deal." There was a "secret reason" for the pardon which the public didn't know. Clearly, only the President himself could handle these suspicions, and we scheduled his second news conference for September 16, one week and a day after the pardon announcement.

The first question came from Frank Cormier, tall and gentlemanly in manner, the senior AP correspondent at the White House. Frank's inquiries were always fashioned with considerable care.

"Mr. President, some Congressional Republicans who have talked to you have hinted that you may have had a secret reason for granting President Nixon a pardon sooner than you indicated you would at the last news conference, and I wonder if you could tell us what that reason was," Cormier began.

The President responded by categorically denying there was any secret reason and saying he didn't recall ever telling any Republicans that. He then went on to review the chronology of events from his August 28 news conference to the September 8 pardon. For a while the press seemed content.

Some days after the pardon the President told me that he was even more convinced that it was the right course to have taken because he had received some very shocking news. Nixon had been staying at the Walter Annenberg estate in the Palm Springs, California, area and somehow managed to give his Secret Service guards the slip late one night. Accompanied only by his faithful valet, Manolo Sanchez, the former President had presumably been driving around on back desert roads for several hours, his whereabouts unknown, before returning to his frantic keepers.

The compulsion to get away from everybody affects all Presidents

267

and is understandable enough to anyone who has witnessed a normal citizen suddenly enveloped in round-the-clock surveillance. In the context of Nixon's resignation and self-banishment from the power and glory of Washington, however, his breakaway took on ominous overtones. Ford was obviously worried. We had all heard rumors that Nixon took unnecessary risks with his phlebitis on his trip to Cairo; his last days in the White House had included some bibulous and bitter cracks about loaded pistols. It was not like Nixon to crack; in fact, he carried off his last hurrahs with more self-control than most of his tormentors expected. But who knew what pressures converged on him now?

"If anything happened to him, and I hadn't granted the pardon— even though I'd already made up my mind it was the right thing to do but was just waiting around for a better time to announce it—and if anything happened to him, I'd never be able to live with myself," Ford told me soberly.

It was a complex sentence but it answered, to my satisfaction, the main question of why Ford pardoned Nixon.

Whether the Nixon pardon was wholly or primarily responsible for Ford's failure to win election in his own right in 1976 is at least arguable. Certainly it was a factor, and it was exploited both by Reagan and the Carter–Mondale camp.

But if this one irrevocable exercise of Presidential power at the zenith of the American public's infatuation with Gerald Ford was, as I believe, the key to much of what happened during the remaining twenty-nine months, it deserves careful attention by historians.

Historians are not reporters but artists. Much of what we believe about the past—even the fairly recent past—is the legend of oft-told tales. So I shall draw some conclusions of my own.

The "real" reasons why President Ford pardoned Richard Nixon are four in number.

1. Because he was becoming so fed up and frustrated with the legal legacy of the Nixon White House—the mountains of tapes and papers, the subpoenas and endless litigation involving not only the former President but also his associates, the prospect that the press and politicians would continue to harass and hammer away at these unresolved issues as long as he was President—he wanted to sweep it all into the ashcan of ancient history with one bold stroke.

2. Because he truly believed it was the right thing for the country and that nothing less would really close the book on Watergate, reunite Americans and reorient their attention and energies toward pressing problems of the present and future. This was his stated reason at the time, and a sincere one, but it was a projection of his own personal paralysis within the new parameters of the Presidency. With Nixon gone, was the country *really* still wallowing in Watergate? Were ordinary people all that polarized and preoccupied with the past? Or was it merely Washington, his *de facto* home town for twenty-five years, his own White House staff, his own friends in the Administration and the Congress and the national media, in truth, his own innermost self and sense of values, that still writhed and wrestled with dying demons?

3. Because he secretly—despite his denials—did fear for Nixon's mental stability and dreaded the prospect of the former President ending his own life. I cannot explain why someone habitually so honest with himself and others went to such lengths to deny that this motive had anything to do with the pardon. But I am perfectly certain that he recoiled in horror from a recurrent vision of Richard Nixon's blood on his hands. Had he waited only a few weeks until Nixon lay at death's door in Long Beach Memorial Hospital and then pardoned him, Ford might have been acclaimed for both courage and compassion. But he would have condemned himself as a coward for not having acted sooner.

4. He persuaded himself that the flak he would have to take for pardoning Nixon would be no less if he waited and might be worse.

Ford usually moved slowly to a decision, but he had an impatient streak. It came out when he suddenly took the lead in denouncing Justice Douglas. It came out when he got fed up with what he termed the "shocking mismanagement" of the Vietnam war. It came out later when he fired not only Jim Schlesinger but combined it with a fast shuffle of Cabinet posts and the dumping of Nelson Rockefeller. Gordian knots were normally his specialty. He would confer endlessly and patiently untangle them strand by strand. But every so often out flashed the sword and "Wham!" The hell with the consequences.

Finally, was there a "deal"?

As the word is commonly understood, in horse-trading or politics, a deal differs from a formal contract only in the fact that no binding consideration need be given and received. But it is a meeting of minds, a mutual agreement from which both parties expect to get something they want.

If what Ford wanted was the Presidency and what Nixon wanted was a pardon if he gave up the Presidency, there was no deal. Forget any elements of honor and virtue and stick to common sense. By the time Nixon began to entertain the idea of resigning, he had no chips. In due course, Ford would gain the Presidency whether Nixon gave it up voluntarily or after impeachment and conviction. All accounts agree that until Nixon himself was convinced of this, he had no intention of resignation. By then, Ford had nothing to do but wait; no reason to deal with anyone.

Still, it is possible that Nixon believed he had a deal before he resigned. Who knows what Haig reported back to Nixon (and others) after his private talks with Vice President Ford on August 1 and 2? Considering that Haig was trying every trick in his considerable bag to get President Nixon to resign, it is inconceivable he would not at least convey the impression that Ford was amenable to the idea of a future pardon. And it would be equally inconceivable to Nixon that any Vice President was not panting to become President, at any price. For my part, I believe that President Ford was right to pardon Nixon and that his reasons, stated and unstated, were honest and understandable. Our long national nightmare is indeed behind us, and the demons of Watergate have been exorcised. Perhaps time, the great healer, would have accomplished this in any event. No one can say now.

Richard Nixon has suffered the ultimate punishment for a public figure: People are becoming bored with him. The implacable Nixon-haters may complain that he was never convicted by legal process. But neither was he ever acquitted, which might well have been the end result of a legal process that insists upon an unbiased jury not one member of which has been influenced by pretrial publicity or formed any prior opinion as to the guilt or innocence of the defendant.

I believe the cloud that hangs over Ford's pardon was largely of his own making. If he had been more candid and more articulate with his close advisers—and ultimately with the American people—about his real reasons, it would now have faded to a footnote in history.

That is all it truly deserves.

Is there a lesson to be learned here? If there is, perhaps the episode shows that those "lonely decisions" that Presidents and Presidential scholars love to cite are a lousy way of doing business. Bold, dramatic action by a President has its place, but it works best when there has been plenty of preliminary game-planning and ground-breaking. If a President cannot trust the judgment of his closest coun-selors, he should get new ones. But the voice of conscience, or gut feel-ings, are often inadequate guides. Even with the most elaborate of preparations, things sometimes go wrong at the launching.

Life is full of Snake Rivers.

12

RUMMY'S RUN

★★──────────────★★

Fortune often favors those who have the rare gift of being in the right place at the right time. Even rarer, however, is the knack of being somewhere else.

Donald Rumsfeld possessed both.

When the rising murk of Watergate began to muddy the shoes of almost everyone at the White House, Rumsfeld had already flown. He was perfecting his experience quotient as U.S. Ambassador to NATO in one of Europe's most elegant and expensive capitals, Brussels, adding the usages of diplomacy and military geopolitics to his considerable attainments in government at age forty.

When Vice President Ford and his handful of close advisers faced the awesome task of taking command of the Executive machinery of the demoralized and disintegrating Nixon Administration in a few frantic days, Rumsfeld happened to be home in Washington and was tabbed with Morton, Scranton and Marsh to chart the basic transition course.

But when President Ford and his neophytes, struggling to hold that course, faced fanatic Praetorian resistance and smashed onto the shoals of premature pardon, Rumsfeld was back at his NATO post, untouched either by Watergate or its painful postlude. Then, he came a-running to the rescue. His credentials were impressive. He had won four terms in the Congress, almost as soon as he was Constitutionally old enough. He had been one of the brightest rising stars of the early Nixon Administration, as director of the Office of Economic Opportunity, of the Cost of Living Council and as a Presidential Counsellor with Cabinet rank.

Rummy was an Eagle Scout. In high school he was Illinois state wrestling champion. At Princeton, Don studied hard and upon graduation married his high-school sweetheart. He served his obligatory three years as a Naval Reserve aviator and flight instructor in the period between Korea and Vietnam. He went to Washington for brief apprenticeships in Congressional offices and returned to a Chicago investment banking firm, which evidently bored him.

In 1962 he ran for a vacant House seat from Illinois' North Shore. It was an affluent suburban district, traditionally Republican, and he won handily.

Rummy incurred the gratitude of Jerry Ford by helping to line up votes among younger House Republicans when Ford took the Minority Leadership away from Charles Halleck (R–Indiana) in 1965. If he was hardly the architect of that narrow victory he later let on, he was a loyal Ford lieutenant in numerous legislative skirmishes. I liked him.

Rummy's abrupt acceptance of Nixon's invitation to join his new Administration surprised people on Capitol Hill, including Ford. His ambition to move onward and upward was thought to point toward the U.S. Senate or the House leadership. OEO was believed marked for early extinction.

But Rumsfeld astonished everyone by fighting hard to keep the poverty program alive. His politics had been predictably pro-business and conservative, but now his Republican critics—not without twitches of jealousy—began complaining that Rummy had "gone liberal" like Charlie Goodell.

At the White House, Rummy was similarly stigmatized by hard-rightists such as Pat Buchanan, but a more balanced view was that he belonged with the younger activists of the Moynihan–Finch school. President Nixon gave him high marks and more assignments. Rummy's explanation of why he left Washington in early 1973—that he was ready for a change—was fully consistent with his job-hopping career.

In due course he was back in the White House on October 1, 1974, to claim Haldeman's and Haig's old "corner pocket" suite with the formal title of Assistant to the President, Cabinet rank, and the job of "coordinating" the chaotic Nixon–Ford staff.

To function with any degree of effectiveness, the person who is generally perceived as being a President's first lieutenant or "chief of staff" must have, and be constantly reassured that he has, the 100 percent backing of the President. Any indication that this is not the case is fatal to his imperative function of protecting the President from the trivial, the painful and the damaging consequences of his own mortal mistakes.

So long as this relationship is unimpaired, he can deflect a great

273

deal of heat away from the President. But he will not, in the process, accumulate any popularity among the power brokers of Washington, the Congressional and Cabinet politicians, the entrenched bureaucracy, the media, the leaders of his own or the opposition party, or even—perhaps most especially—the other Presidential aides who rank officially equal or a cut below him. Nor with the President's wife and family. The effective White House "chief of staff" has a constituency of exactly one.*

As Ford's Vice Presidential chief of staff and official SOB, I experienced and even enjoyed a taste of this lightning-rod function. But I had no burning desire to carry such a martyr's role to the White House. I wanted swiftly to sweep the decks clean of the debris of the old regime, beginning with Haig. I was confident—too confident, perhaps—that this was also the firm purpose of the new President and all his realistic and unselfish friends. Rummy, one of the architects of the Ford takeover blueprint, would surely carry on this campaign, I felt certain.

Everything in Rummy's life seemed to come early and easily. But this was deceptive. He was a cool and careful planner. As a politician, he recognized and respected fate; as a wrestler, he was ever alert for an opening to take fate by the forelock.

I once asked him, half in fun, if his ambition really was to be President of the United States. Half in fun, he answered that his ambition had been trained to one step at a time, to do each job well without neglecting to watch for the next, better one. It seemed a good formula—indeed, a lot like Jerry Ford's.

They hit it off well; in fact, Rummy started off as "staff coordinator" with warm good wishes from almost everyone in the White House, including me. To the Ford folks he was an old Congressional friend. To the Nixon Praetorians he was the prodigal returned.

I turned up bright and early in the Roosevelt Room for Rummy's first 8:00 A.M. meeting with the senior staff. It was the first I had attended since early August, when Haig's brassy presumption of primacy—as if nothing had changed—became insufferable. I terminated my boycott deliberately as a show of confidence in Rumsfeld.

* Hardly anyone had kind words for Wilson's Colonel Edward House or for Harry Hopkins during Roosevelt's long reign, or for Governor Sherman Adams in Eisenhower's or for Bob Haldeman in Nixon's. Truman took most of his own heat, to his credit; Brother Bobby absorbed most of the resentment of Kennedy's "Irish Mafia"; and LBJ permitted no lesser performers on center stage, to his undoing.

It was a good thing I did, because the President himself popped in to introduce Rumsfeld.

"The White House is an intricate and complex operation," Ford said, "and the job I want Don to do is to coordinate and organize all your activities, and to do these things he has to know what is going on in your various departments. It is your responsibility to keep him informed at all times and to work through Don so that we have an orderly operation and maximize the time I have to deal with various problems."

The President went on to say that although Rumsfeld would regulate access to the Oval Office, "my door will always be open" to senior staff members who had "significant" matters requiring his attention.

This rather equivocal mandate left everyone happy, except perhaps Rummy, whose acute antennae immediately picked up the fact that the President had substantially restricted the authority given him privately. The crucial decision as to what was indeed significant enough to intrude on the President's time had just been tossed back to a score of people.

But Rummy wisely bit his tongue and bided his time. He was all humble pie as he thanked Ford for his confidence. He assured the rest of us that he was too new to know exactly how he'd go about his job, but he did know one thing he'd never do—block or lock the door to the open Oval Office.

He got off to a good start. But before his chair was warm, rumors began to appear in print that hobbled Rumsfeld's effectiveness. Exactly one week after the love fest in the Roosevelt Room, Jack Anderson's column was headed "Rumsfeld Slated for Pentagon Duty" and asserted:

> President Ford's new staff chief, Donald Rumsfeld, won't be around the White House more than six months. Sources in the President's confidence say he needed someone in a hurry to replace Alexander Haig [who] held too tight a rein on the White House staff, which looked to him instead of Ford people for their orders.
>
> The President therefore summoned Rumsfeld, whom he actually had in mind to be the next Secretary of Defense. Our sources say Mr. Ford still intends to send the able Rumsfeld to preside over the Pentagon. . . . The President's plans for Rumsfeld, of course, means [sic] Secretary Schlesinger will be dropped from the Cabinet. This will be a victory for Secretary of State Henry Kissinger, who has been feuding with Schlesinger over foreign-military policy.

275

PALACE POLITICS

In the Byzantine ways of Washington news leaks, it is quite impossible to trace a bit of mischief like this. It could plausibly have come from the embittered Haig camp, or from Kissinger, or perversely from the Pentagon, to evoke a Presidential denial. Rumsfeld himself was no novice at the calculated leak.

Variations on the theme that Rumsfeld contemplated only a short stopover in the White House continued to surface. Some said it was Secretary of the Treasury Bill Simon's job he was shooting for. Others had him coveting Kissinger's. The most persistent version was that Rummy agreed to serve temporarily as Ford's *de facto* chief of staff only after the President promised him the first vacancy in the three top Cabinet posts—State, Treasury or Defense—and that Rumsfeld proceeded on his own to expedite the exit of the incumbents.

Obviously, Rummy's very presence in Ford's inner circle stimulated extreme insecurity among high-ranking appointees. Rumsfeld's self-confidence and long-range ambition were too conspicuous to conceal.

The *New Republic*'s John Osborne, who seemed to have talked to the same confidential source as Jack Anderson, wrote on October 5: "Rumsfeld preferred either to retain his ambassadorship in Brussels or to head a major Federal department. He wanted an assignment with a political future and White House staff positions, however exalted, seldom offer that."

I was one of the few people in Ford's inner circle who didn't see Rummy as any threat. He certainly wasn't after my job; he understood my long-standing relationship with the President and knew Ford well enough to accept that he would never rely solely on any single counselor. Rummy would, I figured, try to cut me down to size but not cut me completely out. I accepted the necessity—even the desirability—of a reduced role when Ford became President. Far from clinging desperately to my former unique intimacy, I was more joyous than jealous about having some of my burden lifted.

There are only two types of executive organization. From the time of the pharaohs the most common form is the pyramid, the ruler at the apex, all power delegated by him and descending to ever more numerous echelons below. Authority flows down and responsibility up. That is the way armies, corporations and most organizations are run.

The "spokes of the wheel" organization that Ford favored and Rummy endeavored to fashion sounds a lot more reasonable and republican (or democratic, as you prefer). At the hub is the head man.

276

But lines of authority and reciprocal responsibility run outward, on the same plane, each connected directly to him without passing through any other. Nobody knows where the wheel is going except the hub, but all the spokes are equal.*

Rumsfeld's reorganization charts, approved by Ford, showed nine senior officials within the White House staff as spokes in the wheel with direct access to the Oval Office. They were his two Counsellors, Marsh and I; Buchen and Rumsfeld, also with Cabinet rank; Press Secretary Ron Nessen; Presidential Assistants for National Security (Kissinger), Domestic Affairs (Cole, succeeded by Cannon), Economic Affairs (Seidman); and Management and Budget (Ash, succeeded by Lynn).

Each of these senior staff members would have operational responsibilities. Counsellors would not serve simply as advisers and trouble-shooters across the board of Presidential concerns but also would manage specific subdivisions of the staff.

Marsh was given oversight of legislative liaison and of public liaison.

My areas, Rummy proposed, would be editorial and political. The latter was his idea, or perhaps the President's, certainly not mine. I was never shy about offering political advice, but I didn't think anyone should be labeled and singled out as the "political expert in residence." The President is that.

Also Rummy regarded himself as something of a political genius, and I couldn't imagine him keeping his nose out of it. So I protested.

"But we have to have some sort of liaison with the National Committee, Republican Governors and so forth," Rummy argued. "Dean Burch is doing that, but he'll be leaving soon. People have to have someone here they can call, somebody they know, and they all know you."

"How about you?" I asked innocently.

"I'm not interested in politics," he said, grinning.

A few days before August 9 I had put in an SOS call to Bob Orben in New York City.

* King Arthur did not sit in a doughnut hole at the middle of Camelot's Table Round, but that was the same idea. The theory has formidable antecedents. There is the Roman Catholic doctrine of the equality of bishops, with the Pope at the hub. In 1787 the Founding Fathers seriously deliberated a multiple Presidency. The collegium principle survived in the Supreme Court. And the Soviet Union is ruled, in theory, by a Presidium of equals.

277

PALACE POLITICS

"Can you come down and give us a hand?" I asked.

"Sure," Bob replied. "When?"

"Like tomorrow?" I said.

Orben nearly fell out of his chair, but he knew the call of duty when he heard it. The next day he was there. Eventually, after much foot-dragging by the Praetorians, Bob got his commission as Special Assistant to the President.

President Nixon had a speech-writing staff averaging about eight. Under President Ford's (and Rumsfeld's) personnel cut this was reduced to six. They were supported by thirty-five research and clerical personnel.

Suiting my action to my advocacy, I brought in Paul Theis as head of the editorial department, superimposed him on Dave Gergen and his whole Nixon speech-writing crew. I told Theis to replace them as soon as he could recruit substitutes. The holdovers were not to be flatly fired if he could avoid it, since their only fault had been to serve President Nixon faithfully. But Ford's speaking style was not Nixon's, and I didn't want the familiar Nixon clichés popping up in Ford texts where the press and public would immediately recognize them. Moreover, Gergen's people were physically and emotionally spent.

If any further justification is needed for my clean sweep, let us take the worst example, a very hard-right fellow whose forte was stem-winding speeches for Vice President Agnew. He was fired for publicly disparaging not only President Ford but also the First Lady one time too often. Subsequently he authored a book confirming his contempt for the new regime, including this revealing passage:

> I had a four-martini lunch with a group of former Nixonites that noon, and in the afternoon I found that I couldn't hit the typewriter keys well enough . . . and so, for the first time, another writer had to pick up my assignment. Nor did I care in the least. . . . With Ford in the White House, it didn't seem to make any difference.

In the editorial area we established an important precedent from the first day of the Ford Presidency, reconfirmed in Rummy's reorganization. This was that I had to approve every single word that went out of the White House in the President's name—with the exception of statements he authorized the press secretary to make.

This was a much broader responsibility than simply drafting or editing Presidential speeches. It embraced all written statements, messages to Congress, Executive proclamations and orders, reports, congratulations and condolences to private citizens or foreign dignitaries, political appeals, all official correspondence bearing the President's signature, other than notes he personally dictated or wrote by hand.

As the first new Counsellor, I simply asserted this right to General Haig and his Praetorians. They fumed, but Ford backed me up. I approved (and often edited) every word purporting to be Ford's own until the end of his term of office. I could not, of course, do anything about extemporaneous comments for which there was no prepared text—such as in the Ford–Carter debates, his news conference responses or after-dinner toasts.*

But there was never a Presidential statement or speech prepared in advance that got Jerry Ford in really serious trouble or embarrassment. This was an immense bonus from the Atlantic City fiasco in our Vice Presidential age of innocence. Every President, in this era of endless verbiage, ought to have a censor.

Rumsfeld's reorganization plans also involved reduction of the White House staff. All Presidents promise this, before they know what they're doing, and subsequently resort to all sorts of hocus-pocus to prove they've done so.

The President's opening-day invitation for all the Nixon people to stay on, obtuse and open-ended as Haig's Praetorians intended, was still operative. Some had left, but most couldn't be blasted loose with dynamite. Survival is, first of all, the nature of the bureaucratic beast. The ability swiftly to switch allegiance—to appear to embrace new masters enthusiastically—is Washington's commonest character trait. But with the Nixon Praetorians there was another, more powerful compulsion.

They sincerely felt that it was *their* White House, not Ford's. They honestly believed the new President needed them more than they needed him, that he was incapable of running the place without them.

By October 1, only Buchen, Marsh, the press secretary and I, together with the President's personal secretaries and official photographer Kennerly, had managed to find cubbyhole offices in the West Wing. The rest of Ford's Vice Presidential staff were still in the old Ex-

---

* The most memorable of these was his state-dinner toast to Egypt's President Sadat and "the great people of the government of Israel." Ford quickly corrected himself. Sadat never blinked, but the guests choked on their chocolate mousse. Try it yourself sometime at the end of a fifteen-hour day, eleven meetings and dumping your Vice President.

ecutive Office Building and not yet on the White House payroll. Some could not even get passes to enter the premises.

There had been some other minor purges. Circumstances prior to the pardon forced Buchen to clean out the upper echelon of the President's legal office. TerHorst had tried, without pruning very deeply, to reshape the press office. He was unable to get rid of two of Nixon's last-ditch defenders, the Reverend John McLaughlin, a Jesuit priest, and Ken Clawson, a defector from the Washington *Post* whose "communications" section had been put under the press secretary's wing. They simply refused to be fired.

Rumsfeld very adroitly left it to each department head to determine who should go and who should stay. (So far as I know, the only holdover staffers Don fired personally were Mrs. Nixon's social secretary and press secretary, which cleared the First Lady's East Wing enclave for the advent of one Sheila Rabb Weidenfeld, for whom Betty Ford must herself atone.)

Rummy, the coordinator, conferred with each of us nine "spokes" and set a deadline of mid-December for completion of the reorganization. He imposed a 10 percent personnel cut across the board. In an excess of zeal I would later rue, my staff wound up with ten fewer people than Nixon left behind, saving the taxpayers $199,403 a year.

When Rumsfeld unveiled his new staff setup on December 19 he proclaimed that it was now "President Ford's White House" and that "his approach and working style is reflected in this organization."

Don deftly sold the idea that an "open" White House had at last been structured and the Haldeman–Haig iron curtain was a relic of the past. For example:

Q: Can you tell us whose authority has been enhanced and whose authority has been diminished?

Rumsfeld: Yes, the President's authority is enhanced.

Q: Mr. Rumsfeld, I see your name in more boxes than anyone else's. Does this mean that you are the chief aide, the first among equals?

Rumsfeld: No, it means exactly what the President said when I was announced. He wanted me to be in charge of the administrative part, and he also wanted me to serve in a coordinating responsibility—and he does a great deal of the coordinating himself.

Q: Why would Hartmann move to a new office?

Rumsfeld: The answer is fairly simple. The President decided he would like to have an office next to his [Oval] office, as a study and more relaxed environment, which happened to be the one Bob was in. If people are trying to read things into that, don't.

Rummy's answer was straightforward. New West Wing office assignments had been made, and I would take over retiring Bill Timmons' suite, the second most spacious (after the President's) in the West Wing. It was between Rumsfeld's and Kissinger's, twenty paces from my previous cubbyhole, and I was delighted to inherit it from such good friends as Bill Timmons, Clark McGregor and Bryce Harlow.*

But the Praetorians gleefully leaked the lie that I had been downgraded and banished to the old EOB under Rumsfeld's iron regime. Of more concern to me, Rumsfeld fully cooperated in getting most of the Ford Vice Presidential staff into the White House.

Another of Rumsfeld's administrative innovations was the "deputy" principle. Sensibly, he pointed out that none of the President's top advisers could be expected to be available twenty-four hours a day. Each of us needed to get away from the White House once in a while, get reacquainted with our wives and children or just sit and think. Each principal, therefore, was to have a deputy who could work with the President, attend meetings and make urgent decisions in his absence.

I had felt this need for weeks. When Ford first became President I begged him to let me have Benton Becker. He refused; he was using Becker himself in the Nixon negotiations. Temporarily, Marsh had Commander Howard Kerr and I had Lieutenant Colonel Bob Blake as confidential assistants.

Rumsfeld decreed that career military officers couldn't be involved in White House political functions. After all my howling about General Haig, I couldn't disagree. With my added political chores I proposed—and Ford agreed—to bring on Jack Calkins as my political deputy.

Jack was a widely respected Republican Party pro, for the past five years executive director of the National Congressional Campaign Committee. The President and I had worked closely with him. Ford once asked Jack to be his administrative assistant, but Calkins knew little about Michigan and declined. He was from upstate New York,

---

* Earlier occupants of that office were Joe Califano and Bill Moyers in the LBJ years; Ted Sorensen in Kennedy's; General Wilton Persons in Ike's; General Harry Vaughn, Charles Murphy and Clark Clifford in Truman's; and Judge Samuel I. Roseman, FDR's speech writer.

PALACE POLITICS

Syracuse University and George Washington University Law School and served from 1949 to 1970 as administrative assistant to three New York Congressmen.

I called a staff meeting to introduce Jack, break the good news that their White House status was finally official and explain the reorganization.

"The new system is the way the President wants it," I told them. "It is untried. I urge everybody not to regard this as Rumsfeld's structure or anybody else's but as the President's. It is our business to serve him and to make things work better than they have in the past.

"I'm deeply grateful for the great loyalty to me represented here. I know it will continue. However, there's a great danger in any White House—this one is no exception—and that's the development of factions.

"We haven't taken the lead in this, but we have tended to react to it. People always coalesce around certain leaders, but to the extent possible, I think we all ought to forget the old Nixon people versus Ford people idea."

Rummy's reorganization was well planned and executed. Everyone thought he knew where he stood and what he was supposed to do. Essential access to the President seemed assured; morale and efficiency improved and internecine warfare tapered off. Yet a good deal was there that escaped the immediate notice of the press and those of us who believed that a Ford Administration was at last a reality.

First, while ostensibly carrying out the "spokes-in-the-wheel" concept, the wheel that emerged was not really round. Of the nine spokes, the one designated as the "White House Operations Office" and directed by Rumsfeld turned out to be much bigger and stronger than the others. The asymmetry was further exaggerated by Rumsfeld's claim of a nebulous "coordinating" authority over everything within the purview of the Presidency.

It was all spelled out in the open, right there in the mimeographed press handouts. Rumsfeld would run the Office of the Cabinet Secretary, the Office of the Staff Secretary and the Presidential Personnel Office, as well as providing military assistance to the President.

Rumsfeld placed four of his own dependable lieutenants in each of these critical slots, and every one of them—except the military careerist—was a Nixon holdover or retread. Not one of them owed the slightest personal allegiance or obligation to Jerry Ford. In the key spot of staff secretary he retained Jerry Jones, a CREEP alumnus and Haig's deputy commander of the Praetorian Guard.

Over them Rumsfeld set his own tried and trusted deputy, Richard B. Cheney, thirty-four, a conspicuous example of what George Reedy meant when he declared that "no one should be permitted to enter the gates of the White House until he is at least forty and has suffered major disappointments in life."

Cheney's adult life had been devoted to the study of political science and the service of Donald Rumsfeld. The study occurred at the Universities of Wyoming and Wisconsin and in apprenticeships with Governor Warren Knowles (R–Wisconsin) and Representative Bill Steiger (R–Wisconsin) on a Congressional fellowship. His only stint in the "private sector" was with an investment counsulting firm while his mentor was in Brussels.

Cheney had been Rumsfeld's assistant in the Nixon White House, an admirer of the Haldeman system and Rummy's alter ego at OEO and the Cost of Living Council. He returned to the Ford White House with the august title of Deputy Assistant to the President. He was, in fact, the second most powerful person on the staff.

Cheney was a serious student of political power and derived both his employment and his enjoyment from it. Whenever his private ideology was exposed, he appeared somewhat to the right of Ford, Rumsfeld or, for that matter, Genghis Khan.

Rumsfeld and Cheney were a rare match. Their differences reinforced the team. Rummy was darkly handsome, like Tyrone Power. Cheney was a presentable young man who could easily be lost in a gaggle of Jaycee executives. His most distinguishing features were snake-cold eyes, like a Cheyenne gambler's. Rummy was expansive and, when it suited him, all smiles; Cheney's demeanor was low-key and even dour. He was tough, tireless, book-smart, with a touch of sarcasm occasionally overcoming studied subordination. Rumsfeld was more secure, more sensitive of others' feelings, more sophisticated and, when crossed, more passionate. But Don had some class; he was ruthless within the rules.

The deputy device that Rummy introduced enabled him to bring Cheney instantly into the inner circle of President Ford's confidants. This reinforced the initial suspicion that Rumsfeld regarded his White House stopover as a short-term steppingstone to something bigger and better.

Rummy also moved to insinuate subordinates of his own selection into every department of the senior staff—except Kissinger's and mine. He provided lawyers for Phil Buchen; pushed Max Friedersdorf to succeed Timmons as Jack Marsh's principal legislative deputy; man-

283

aged the switch of Nixon's Secretary of HUD, Jim Lynn, to Director of Management and Budget (a demotion in protocol and pay but not in power); installed his old OEO press aide, Bill Greener, as Ron Nessen's No. 1 deputy; promoted Dr. James Cavanaugh, Rockefeller's *bête noire,* to second place on his Domestic Council staff. All were postgraduate Nixon Praetorians, like Rumsfeld himself.

This is not to accuse, or imply, that they were not able and attached to Ford. But they were creatures of the Nixon–Haldeman–Haig system. Nothing could be more natural than to work within it, with the new commander of the old palace guard.

In short, *plus ça change, plus c'est la même chose.* The highly touted Rumsfeld reorganization at the end of 1974 was more cosmetic than real. There still was no Ford Administration.

The Nixon–Ford Administration continued.* The Praetorian Guard was not disbanded, as by the bold stroke of Septimus Severus, but merely transferred its allegiance to Rumsfeld and Cheney.

There were doubters and isolated pockets of resistance. When the press persisted in asking how many of the 500-odd people on the Nixon White House staff were still there after Ford's reorganization, Rumsfeld doubled-talked adroitly. Only about 112, he explained, were permanent professionals. Since Ford became President, about seventy of these had departed and fifty new people had come aboard, he surmised. By and large, the media bought it.

The *New Republic's* John Osborne didn't. There is, after all, a distinct advantage in being able to count. He observed on October 12:

> Eight of the 13 assistants who attended the first senior staff meeting that Donald Rumsfeld (himself a former Nixon Counsellor) presided over were Nixon appointees.

Two weeks later he reported:

> Rumsfeld moved fast to form his own temporary staff, lay the basis for a permanent central staff, and establish his primacy over the White House staff at large. . . . Four lawyers and a political scientist who were associated with Rumsfeld in early 1969 comprise his temporary staff. . . . [One of] the lawyers,

---

* In the organizational chart distributed by Rumsfeld on December 13, only fourteen of the eighty-two top staff positions had been filled with Ford people. The *U.S. Government Manual,* as of May 1, 1975, listed sixty-six persons in the White House Office. Some forty of them worked in the Nixon Administration. The ratio never changed much thereafter.

William Walker, is Rumsfeld's appointee to the powerful post of White House personnel chief.

A lively question was whether and to what extent Robert Hartmann, a longtime and valued associate of the President and his principal speechwriter, would subordinate himself to Rumsfeld. . . . Hartmann turned up at a few of Rumsfeld's morning staff meetings, so that nobody could say he refused to attend, and not often enough to acknowledge that he had to be there. . . .

After about a week of chairing them, Rummy invited suggestions from the senior staff on how to improve the meetings. My response had at least the virtue of brevity.

MEMORANDUM TO: DONALD RUMSFELD

FROM: ROBERT T. HARTMANN

1. Have no more than two per week, say Monday and Thursday, except in major crises.
2. Get the President to preside at least every third meeting.
3. Most meetings of more than two people are a waste of time for all.
4. For special projects, let the guy in charge set up his own meeting with all who need to know.
5. Set a more civilized hour.

Not much came of this, except that the President did show up from time to time to get something off his chest. These sessions were far and away the most valuable in terms of the staff getting Ford's thoughts for guidance.

Jerry terHorst, who had returned to his first love as a syndicated columnist, wrote on December 28 that "President Ford has found a way to head off a potentially calamitous clash of authority between two of his oldest aides . . . a very difficult decision and a Solomonesque one. While some of his associates pushed hard for a Ford choice between Hartmann and Rumsfeld, the President in effect chose both.

"Instead of saying precisely who will sit at his right hand, Mr. Ford has divided their authority in ways that will permit him to use both men to the fullest and in a way that should also satisfy them.

"Those who speculate that Hartmann has lost the power struggle with Rumsfeld are not speaking from knowledge of the President's *modus operandi* or the strength of the Ford–Hartmann relationship," TerHorst concluded.

I sent the column to the President, who returned it with a handwritten note: "Very interesting—good."

Ford had a considerable hand in perfecting Rumsfeld's plan. The original proposals of the transition team underwent some modification. I'm certain that Henry Kissinger and I, at least, wound up with a good deal more freedom and scope in our special areas than would otherwise have been the case.

The trouble with these special areas of responsibility was that, like liberated serfs subdividing the deposed lord's lands, nobody was content to hoe within his own plot. Everybody wanted to tell his neighbor how to cultivate his.

Ford's reliance on Kissinger was almost complete in the field of foreign affairs, and Henry made the most of it. The transition advisers made it a point of principle that no one person should be both Secretary of State and Assistant to the President for National Security Affairs. Henry had won this double-edged eminence after a long and bloody war within the Nixon camp, creating a fearsome aura of indispensability and invincibility. When all else failed, he was a cry-baby *par excellence.* He would not tolerate any encroachment on his turf. Neither, I have to confess, would I. Some complex personalities you can either admire or hate. With Henry Kissinger it's easy to do both at the same time.

Nobody, least of all Kissinger, doubts his brilliance. His sense of humor delights detractors as well as defenders. He can also be frighteningly in earnest. In both modes, it is hard to tell whether he is acting or not. The moment you believe you have caught a glimpse of the real Henry, he disappears. His ego is enormous, as he boasts. He suffers little from peer rivalry because he acknowledges so few peers. Yet he frequently exhibits the most acute symptoms of insecurity, buttering up superiors and bullying subordinates.

Calculating, cruel, conceited—those are some of the nicer adjectives applied. But to whom did President Nixon turn for human comfort in his direst despair? And Henry prayed and wept with him. Nor did he turn his back on the Shah of Iran. Kissinger *can* be sympathetic, considerate and kind.

Our first close encounter in the Ford White House came with startling suddenness only a day or two after the President named me his Counsellor with Cabinet rank. Evidently I had upset the Secretary by my temerity in altering some of the Germanic cadences of his composition for a Ford address.

Henry came stomping into my office, practically trampling over my fragile secretaries in a fine, Teutonic fury.

"I chust vant you to know," he spat, "I haf survived Haldeman, and I vill survive Hartmann too!"

For once I kept my cool. I really wanted to laugh.

"Well, Mr. Secretary, you're so much younger than I am, I surely hope so," I said. "Now, if you'll tell me what the hell is bugging you, we will see what can be done about it."

He smiled and I smiled, and we were both more intrigued than infuriated. He was just kidding, of course. We had a pleasant exploratory chat, in which I learned that I was, in fact, only five years his senior. And he learned that I had knocked about seventy countries from prewar student carousings in Munich's Hofbrauhaus and Paris' Left Bank to covering the global crises of the Fifties and Sixties as a foreign correspondent. I wasn't exactly the international ignoramus Henry expected, but, I hastened to assure him, I wasn't the genius of twentieth-century diplomacy that President Ford, fortunately, had in Henry Kissinger.

"You are the expert of politics," he said, beaming. "And I have admired your speeches immensely. I myself know nothing about politics."

That was the first but by no means the last time we said sweet nothings to each other. French may be the language of diplomacy, but nothing compares with English in variety of meanings and interpretations. It can be the most precise or imprecise of tongues. Kissinger is immensely gifted and pardonably proud of his mastery of its nuances and subtleties. But his English was not Ford's, and we had many confrontations over my translations, not of substance but of style.

Be that as it may, Henry Kissinger is a dedicated American, unquestionably the ablest diplomat I have seen in my lifetime and probably as good a politician—internecine or international—as all but a formidable few: Churchill, Roosevelt, Chou En-lai, De Gaulle, Nehru, Khrushchev, Golda Meir and Richard Nixon.

Certainly Henry was the most fascinating fellow in the Ford Administration. And that was his problem. On me does not devolve the duty of delineating the Ford–Kissinger relationship. Ford himself has never been able to do other than smother Henry in the most effusive adulation. By his account, Kissinger should be a candidate for beatification. One assumes Dr. Kissinger will modestly corroborate that view. Subsequent developments in the world suggest that together they did not do at all badly by the United States of America.

In the first hectic days of autumn 1974, most of us shared Ford's recognition that Kissinger was an imperative of continuity and stability. We grumbled resentfully about his monopolizing the President's time, but we were really too busy to care.

Somewhat inconsistently, perhaps, I did not see in Henry what I saw in Haig, though they were professor and pupil, proctors of the same wiretapping school of White House security. Nor was there any drumfire from the media for Henry to lead the purge parade. He kept them too well fed, and, let's face it, Kissinger always makes news. Call it charisma or *chutzpah,* Henry has it.

The fact is that the initial resistance to Rummy's new regime and all-pervading powers of "coordination" came not so much from Hartmann, as the media gossip continued to insist, but from Kissinger and his former boss, Nelson Rockefeller.

Kissinger suspected me of being in league with Rumsfeld to weaken his authority with the President. Vice President Rockefeller accepted the more conventional wisdom that Rummy and I were natural enemies. Heeding the Arab maxim that "the enemy of my enemy is my friend," Rocky looked to me as a potential ally.

I was neither. On the strength of recent history and common sense, I agreed with Rumsfeld, Laird and others that a President needs foreign-policy input from a variety of sources.

On the strength of my own experience in Ford's short-lived Vice Presidency and my observation of others, I was certainly more sympathetic to Rockefeller's needs and sensibilities than the Nixon holdovers and less worried than Rumsfeld about Ford being eclipsed, or his staff being bypassed, by a strong-willed Vice President. Presidents just aren't outshone, and their aides' egos need periodic shrinking.

My position was very simple. I wanted what the President wanted. As near as I could tell, he wanted Rocky to be an integral part of his policy-level inner circle, a Vice President in the full meaning of the term. I also understood that he wanted Kissinger's stellar status undiminished.

One thing Rockefeller, Kissinger aN I all quickly discerned was that, Rumsfeld aside, Ron Nessen was the lajor mouthpiece for our mutual detractors. Nessen certainly was not, in the beginning, Rumsfeld's fault. It behooves me now straightforwardly to confess the greatest single disservice I ever did Gerald R. Ford.

When TerHorst suddenly jumped ship on the very day of the Nixon pardon, nothing was more urgent than to replace him rapidly. I was afraid the President would stick me with the job, on an interim basis I would never escape. So I recommended, and finally pushed hard, for Nessen's appointment.

There are three essential requirements for a Presidential press secretary.

One, he must have, and continuously earn, the respect and confidence of the President and his principal subordinates. He may not, among the latter, play factions or favorites.

Two, he must have, and continuously earn, the total respect and confidence of the media representatives with whom he deals, particularly those permanently assigned to the White House. He may play favorites among them only if he is clever enough not to get caught at it.

Three, he must be able to sublimate completely his own judgments, his own prejudices, his own emotions and his own ego in the interest of the President for whom he speaks many times daily. The opinions of most Americans about their President are formed to a great extent from the words and the demeanor of his press secretary. This may not be right, but it is true.

It is, plainly, the second most difficult and never-ending responsibility in the White House, and few who have held it approach perfection. In my book, Jim Hagerty and Pierre Salinger were the best, but perhaps I was more tolerant then. I cannot fault Jody Powell on performance. Jerry terHorst rated high in the first two categories but failed the third. As it turned out, Ron Nessen flunked all three.

I boiled my recommendations down to five names: Dave Broder of the Washington *Post,* a fair, perceptive and highly respected political pundit; Bonnie Angelo of *Time,* one of the best Washington reporters of any sex for more than a decade; Bill Roberts, then an assistant White House press secretary and deputy during Ford's Vice Presidency; Jerry Friedheim, veteran Pentagon spokesman and reportedly Mel Laird's candidate; and Ron Nessen, who covered Ford as Vice President for NBC and moved with him to the White House.

I was intrigued by the idea of shattering precedent by naming (1) a woman or (2) an electronic journalist as the top White House spokesman. I reminded the President that TerHorst had been unanimously acclaimed because he was chosen directly from the White House press room.

"But look what happened," the President said. "Why risk it again?"

289

"When you crash in an airplane," I said, "the first thing they make you do is get into another plane and fly. If you don't pick someone right out of the White House press room, they'll all say you're frightened and falling back on a career Federal press agent to protect you."

The President, apparently convinced, marked my five names in order of his preference. I was to sound them out discreetly.

They were flattered even when they politely declined.* When I got down to Nessen on the President's priority list, something told me that if it sounded halfway like an offer, the story would be on NBC before I awoke the next morning. So I pretended to be calling to ask Ron's advice. Would he or she accept? I'd ask. If Ron were in their position, would he accept?

Nessen lives only a block and a half up my street, and I could almost hear his eagerness without the phone. The President called Nessen and me into the Oval Office the next day and the deed was done. TerHorst had always appreciated me as an ally. The very next thing Ron did was to pay his respects to General Haig. Haig not only vented his bile on me but put down Ford as well, criticizing the way the new President wanted to reorganize the White House, scorning his loyalty to longtime associates. Nessen was Haig's last recruit to the Praetorian Guard but one of the aptest.

Rumsfeld's reincarnation as a Presidential assistant coincided with several simultaneous crises: the beleaguered new President's efforts to calm the storm over the Nixon pardon that sent his popularity polls plummeting from 72 to 49 percent; a rapidly worsening economy in which energy shortages, rising unemployment, recession and runaway inflation all combined; and the personal trauma of his beloved wife undergoing surgery for breast cancer.

It was eerie the way the dread thunderbolt of cancer struck twice into the President's consciousness shortly before it hit him directly. These examples of Jerry Ford's innate compassion have been known only to a handful of people. Though both cases proved fatal, I have since pondered the question: Because Ford genuinely cared for and consoled others, were his prayers for Betty better heard?

One beneficiary of the President's secret good works was a twenty-five-year-old Seaman Recruit in the Coast Guard named Stephen Sugg. The other was one of the most celebrated heroes of all time, Charles A. Lindbergh.

* Bonnie Angelo told me she had already turned down a similar feeler about being Mrs. Ford's press secretary. Too bad.

Soon after Ford became President, I got a long-distance call from Sam Pryor, a Washington vice-president of Pan American Airways in the Fifties who was retired and living in Darien, Connecticut. In the utmost confidence he told me that the Lone Eagle of 1927, whom I had worshipped as a boy, was about to make his final solo flight.

Pryor, his friend and neighbor, explained that Lindbergh had known for several weeks that he was dying of lymphatic cancer. Concerned over privacy ever since his infant son was kidnapped and slain, Lindy expressed a wish to see his seaside home in Hana, on the island of Maui, and to be buried there in a simple wood coffin built by his Hawaiian cowboy friends.

Pan American, many of whose global routes were pioneered by Lindy, flew him and his wife incognito to the island. No reporters recognized his frail figure at seventy-two. But Sam said it would boost Lindbergh's spirits to receive a get-well message from President Ford. He had not always been well treated by the White House: FDR sarcastically proposed that he be awarded the Iron Cross for trying to warn of Hitler's growing airpower. Pryor cautioned that there was no telephone at the Lindbergh hideaway and that air-mail delivery might come too late.

The President sat down immediately to pen a personal note. He hoped Lindbergh would recover and add to his many contributions to the country. We had it transmitted by military communications to Pearl Harbor, in secret code, and the decoded message carried by small plane to Maui by an officer courier. It was delivered a few days before Lindbergh lost consciousness on Sunday, August 23, and the President later was assured he read and deeply appreciated it.

Ford issued a public eulogy and sent personal condolences to Anne Morrow Lindbergh when her husband died, but the private note was never disclosed.

There was also another cancer tragedy that came to us. Early in September I received a letter from Mrs. Marion Sugg, a friend of a friend, who lived in a small city in central Missouri. Her son, Stephen, a schoolteacher and coach, always had a yen to fly, she related. On April 29 he had enlisted in the Coast Guard, passing both the regular and flight trainee physical examinations with flying colors. A little over two weeks after reporting for duty in Alameda, California, Stephen had difficulty breathing. The base doctors sent him to the U.S. Public Health Service Hospital in San Francisco, and there a fortnight of diagnostic tests disclosed a rapidly increasing dysfunction of the lungs. Stephen's parents and young wife were summoned, lung surgery

291

was performed on June 3, revealing metastatic melanoma, cancerous lesions spreading like a prairie fire. A medical board recommended Stephen be given a total disability retirement from the Coast Guard. Their prognosis for recovery was extremely poor.

A review board in Washington also recommended retirement but ruled that the cancerous condition was presumed to have existed prior to Sugg's enlistment and was not, therefore, "service-connected."

Sugg, perfectly lucid mentally, requested that he be transferred to a new Veterans Administration hospital in Columbia, Missouri, where—though nobody acknowledged it aloud—he would die near his loved ones and lifetime friends. Coast Guard officials in California were agreeable until advised by Washington that, according to the regulation book, the patient would have to be discharged without any disability pension or medical benefits. Stephen had not yet served the 180 days on active duty required to be legally eligible as a veteran.

All he would be entitled to as a retired Seaman Recruit, USCG, would be severance pay of $688.20, and his $20,000 government life-insurance policy would expire in six months.

Mrs. Sugg's letter was not a sob story. It was factual, precise, full of praise of the people who had been trying to help. Still, however intelligently she faced her inevitable loss, her mother's heart asked why the government Stephen volunteered to serve—in the apparent prime of health and life—could not somehow soften this tragic twist of fate. I thought of all the draft dodgers in Canada and Sweden denouncing the earned amnesty offered them by President Ford, and I wondered too.

I talked to the President about it, and his eyes moistened as he read Mrs. Sugg's neatly typed letter.

"What's the use of being Commander-in-Chief if you can't help a good kid like this?" he asked. "Get me all the facts, and if we have to bend a few rules we will. But there's to be no publicity, understand? I don't want anyone to think I'm grandstanding on this poor family's heartache."

We did bend some rules and were able to assure the Suggs that the Coast Guard would keep Stephen on active duty and immediately fly him and his wife to the VA hospital in Missouri, paying all his expenses pending final disposition of the case.

I called the Vice Commandant, Admiral E. L. Perry, to thank him and suggest, not very subtly, that they just sit on the matter to see if Sugg could pass the 180-day mark before the finish line, which he did, though not by much. But he enjoyed his last weeks as an outpatient with his family and died still in the service of his country.*

President Ford wrote the parents a warm personal note, which they still treasure: "My prayers will be added to yours for his recovery, and I am assured that the Coast Guard will handle its administrative procedures expeditiously and fairly and with full consideration for your son," he assured them. "I hope this will relieve any concern he may have and help him in his courageous fight."

The letter was dated September 26, the day before Betty's cancer was found.

There isn't much I can add to the story of Betty Ford's cancer and her courageous conduct, which encouraged millions of women to seek preventive exams and endeared her to people everywhere. Less widely recognized but memorable to me was the President's remarkable display of self-control and sustaining faith during his hours of anguish.

At his first appearance as President on August 12, Ford had told the Congress of his concern for the rapidly worsening economy. He accepted the suggestion of Senate Majority Leader Mike Mansfield for an "economic summit conference" in which spokesmen for Congress, the Administration, business, labor and consumer groups would all participate. Bill Seidman had done a superb job of organizing eleven preliminary meetings around the country, and the President himself was to chair the final two-day "summit" on Friday and Saturday, September 27 and 28.

The staggering news of his wife's suspicious lump hit him Thursday evening; he had not known beforehand of her routine check-up. He concurred in the doctors' recommendation for immediate surgery. Betty insisted on going ahead with her Friday plans for a Salvation Army benefit and entertaining Lady Bird Johnson and her daughters at a White House tea after she and the President attended ground-breaking ceremonies for the LBJ Memorial Grove along the Potomac.

Both the First Lady and the President carried on that day in the best "show must go on" tradition. Not until that evening, when Susan stood in for her mother at a White House reception for the 1,000 summit participants, did the delegates—and the rest of the nation—learn that Betty had just checked into Bethesda Naval Hospital and would undergo surgery the next morning. Their expressions of sympathy

* Mr. and Mrs. Sugg graciously gave me permission to tell this sad story.

made it doubly hard for the President to maintain his stoic composure.*

Those of us around him didn't quite know how to help or what to say. So we followed his example and went about our work, unable to conceal our lesser shock as successfully as the President. All of us, I guess, found duty the best therapy.

Ford went ahead with a breakfast meeting Saturday morning with Kissinger and the French Foreign Minister, Jean Sauvagnargeus. He was waiting for me in the Oval Office at nine to make final changes in the speech he was to give at noon to close the economic summit. Betty had been in the operating room about an hour.

"Any news?" I asked. A dumb question, since I could see from his set lips that there was none. He shook his head and glanced at his watch.

"Why don't you cancel this?" I said. "Everybody will understand. Seidman or somebody can read it for you."

"No," the President said. "They told me there was nothing I could do out there; they didn't want me in the way until she is conscious and knows it's me. Here, give it to me. Let's get it finished."

I handed him the final draft of his address, and we began to go over it. Suddenly the phone on his desk buzzed. I knew no other call would have been put through, and as I watched his face I prayed silently. He didn't say much except an occasional "yes" but I could read the bad news in his eyes. He hung up with a hoarse "Thank you very much" and started to turn back to the typed pages before him. Then he said; "That was Dr. Lukash. It's malignant, and they're going ahead. Excuse me a minute."

The President got up abruptly and headed for his private toilet off the Oval Office. When he returned, his eyes were red and he was noisily blowing his nose. He picked up the speech text, cleared his throat and tried to say something—but words wouldn't come.

"Go ahead and cry," I said gently. "Only strong men aren't ashamed to cry. You're among friends."

The President of the United States—my friend—cried like a baby for a minute. So did I.

"Bob, I don't know what I'd do without her," he said, choking. "I just don't know what I'd do. . . ."

"Boss," I said, forgetting the "Mr. President," "you've got twenty

---

* Though her eyes misted, Susan played her hostess role like a trouper.

or more years to worry about that. Betty'll be all right. Except for skin cancers and prostates in men, it's the safest kind of operation. Just thank God they found it so soon."

"I will, I will," he said. "She's a strong girl, she'll be all right."

It was over. We went back to work, and when we finished, he said, "I'm going out to the hospital, to be there when she comes out of it. Then I'll come to the conference. Tell Bill [Seidman] to filibuster a little if he has to, but I'll be there. You bring my final text."

As he headed for the door, he stopped and stuck out his big All-Star center's hand.

"Thanks, Bob," he said, and both our tear glands started up again.

Neta retyped the speech, and I headed for the Washington Hilton. John Saar, in the Washington *Post,* described the scene there more movingly than I can:

> In a way no one could have wished for, Gerald R. Ford showed his remarkable mettle yesterday. All morning long the chairman's empty seat at the economic summit was a departure point for thoughts that even then the President's wife was undergoing major breast cancer surgery.
>
> Word spread among the delegates that an early morning biopsy indicated malignancy and Senator Hubert H. Humphrey (D–Minnesota) drew conference participants to their feet for a half-minute of silent prayer. Few expected the President to show up for his closing address.
>
> When he was announced and strode pale and taut of face into the harsh television lights, Senator Mike Mansfield (D–Montana) clasped him by the hand and elbow and then led the conference in a standing ovation.
>
> Biting his lip and struggling for a smile that would not come, the President launched into a prepared speech on the need for leadership and arousal of the American spirit in the struggle against inflation, a spirit which was dramatically underlined by his own courage in the face of personal adversity.
>
> In a brief reference to his wife's condition, the President said he had seen her after the operation. "Dr. Lukash assured me that she came through the operation all right," Mr. Ford said.
>
> Then in a few choked, terse phrases the President said; "It has been a difficult thirty-six hours. Our faith will sustain us; Betty would want me to be here."

PALACE POLITICS

Among the substantive announcements in the President's closing speech were the creation of a sixteen-member advisory committee, equally composed of labor and business leaders; a Council of Wage and Price Stability; a new Cabinet-level Economic Policy Board with Bill Simon as its mouth and Bill Seidman as its muscle; and a promise to send specific proposals to Congress in ten days.

The economic summit was also the birthplace of the "WIN" program, which may well be the last noble experiment at volunteerism on a national scale. It still evokes ridicule, but the true story of its beginning and ending has never been told; even President Ford's recollections are faulty.

Either I or Paul Theis, my editorial deputy at the White House, are usually cited—disparagingly—as having fathered "WIN." I would be proud to claim paternity, but the truth is we were merely midwives. The fact is "WIN" was sort of Siamese twins, one fathered by William J. Meyer, president of the Central Automatic Sprinkler Company in Pennsylvania and the other mothered by Sylvia Porter, the popular financial writer who was an economic summit delegate. Their philosophically disparate concepts were forcibly joined together by the President himself and christened by Madison Avenue.

At the end of August, Theis told me over lunch that he and an old friend, Bill Meyer, had been pondering the runaway inflation and came up with an idea that might at least slow its savage pace. It was partly the NRA "Blue Eagle" Depression remedy of the New Deal, a national morale booster, but it also resembled the Army-Navy "E" (for Efficiency) awards of World War II, which aimed at increased production.

They proposed to call it the "IF" program—for "Inflation Fighters"—and to extend it from manufacturing plants to retail outlets, allowing those who pledged to hold prices for one year to display a distinctive emblem which the President would present. Unions who took a similar pledge to hold the line on wages would get the award and attendant publicity. Individuals could wear INFLATION FIGHTER lapel pins. Consumers would be urged to patronize only "IF" stores and buy only "IF"-labeled products.

I was intrigued and asked Paul to put it all in memo form for the President. Ford thought the idea was terrific and asked where it came from. I brought Theis in and we kicked it around. The President, typically, wanted to kill two birds with one stone. Inflation was intricately hooked up with the energy crunch. So why not make it "INFLATION FIGHTERS AND ENERGY SAVERS"? he said.

There the matter rested until the economic summit began. On the opening day Sylvia Porter gave a rousing speech advocating a nationwide campaign to reduce waste and lower consumer pressure on prices through victory gardens, recycling of paper, cans and bottles and voluntary energy conservation by both businesses and individuals. Hers was a consumer-oriented approach to the inflation problem to bring down demand. Meyer's, as a businessman, was to improve productivity while freezing both labor costs and prices. Both relied on voluntary action with moral support from the President.

President Ford pricked up his ears during Ms. Porter's presentation. Right afterwards he instructed me to dig out the month-old IN-FLATION FIGHTERS AND ENERGY SAVERS memo and sound out Ms. Porter to see if she'd be willing to head up a voluntary citizens' campaign. Her only caveat was that the effort remain nonpartisan and nonpolitical. Ford agreed.

The President thereupon appealed to the conferees: "Let's do as Sylvia Porter suggested" and announced she would organize a nationwide mobilization of Inflation Fighters and Energy Savers.

"I know that all across our country the question everyone asks is 'What can I do to help?' " Ford told the television audience. "I'll tell you how we can start. Right now make up a list of ten ways you can save energy and fight inflation."

Two days later a remarkable cross-section of Americans assembled under the gavel of Sylvia Porter to plan their strategy. If that high-powered bunch couldn't mobilize and energize the vaunted spirit of self-help in America, who could? But at least half of them were anathema to the Nixon people and, even worse, liberal Democrats. We had not counted on the resistance and subtle sabotage of the entrenched Praetorians.

Milt Friedman very expertly wove together in speech form the main conclusions of the economic summit and the program fashioned by the President and his economic experts, foreign and domestic.

On October 8, President Ford went before Congress in midafternoon and outlined a ten-point program for joint Legislative and Executive action to meet the economic and energy crisis. It was a masterful marshaling of the economic facts of life, adopting at least half of the Democratic House and Senate leaders' proposals at the summit conference and stressing "There is one point on which all advisers have agreed: We must whip inflation right now." Pointing to the red-and-white WIN button on his lapel, he concluded by speaking directly "to your constituents and, incidentally, mine."

PALACE POLITICS

"Unless every able American pitches in, Congress and I cannot do the job. Winning our fight against inflation and waste involves total mobilization of American's greatest resources—the brains, the skills, and the willpower of the American people.

"Here is what we must do: to help increase food and lower prices, grow more and waste less; to help save scarce fuel in the energy crisis, drive less, heat less. Every housewife knows almost exactly how much she spent for food last week. If you cannot spare a penny from your food budget—and I know there are many who can't—surely you can cut food you waste by five percent.

"Every American motorist knows exactly how many miles he or she drives to work or to school every day. If we all drive at least five percent fewer miles, we can save—almost unbelievably—250,000 barrels of foreign oil per day. Most of us can do better than five percent by carpooling, taking the bus, riding bikes, or just plain walking. We can save enough gas by self-discipline to meet our one-million-barrels-per-day goal.

"There is one final thing that all Americans can do, rich or poor, and that is share with others. We can share burdens as we can share blessings. And it will strengthen our spirits as well as our economy."

The President promised more details on the WIN program a week hence in Kansas City. Pointing to the red-and-white WIN button on his lapel—one of the only two hand-made samples in existence*—he turned back to his audience of former Congressional colleagues.

"Only two of my predecessors [Wilson and FDR] have come in person to call upon Congress for a declaration of war, and I shall not do that. But I say to you in all sincerity that inflation, our public enemy No. 1, will—unless whipped—destroy our country, our homes, our liberties, our property, and finally our national pride, as surely as any well-armed wartime enemy.

"I concede there will be no sudden Pearl Harbor to shock us into unity and to sacrifice, but I think we have had enough early warnings. The time to intercept is right now. The time to intercept is almost gone."

Five years later with inflation soaring over 13 percent, I cannot see how President Ford could have said it any better. His warnings, how-

---

* Veteran House doorkeeper William "Fishbait" Miller deftly relieved the President of his WIN button as he left the rostrum. Ford, informed of the rarity of his souvenir, dispatched a high-level emissary to implore Fishbait to give it back. Miller let him have it strictly "on loan."

ever, fell on deaf ears in the Democratic Congress. Ford's appeal for sharing failed to inspire the blasé editorial writers in their ivory towers. Their liberal cartoonist counterparts came up with starving black children eating WIN buttons as their scathing commentary.

But the American people were listening. Over the next nine days a record 101,420 citizen volunteers mailed WIN enlistment papers to the White House, and this number doubled by the end of the year. Each received—eventually, I hope—a facsimile-signed thank-you from the President and a WIN lapel button.

The Associated Press reported that twelve million WIN buttons were in production, and we never could keep up with the demand. Eastern Airlines pinned all their stews with WIN buttons. A popular variant went on sale in Florida—SIN—for Stop Inflation Now.

Meredith Willson, the music man, composed a stirring WIN marching song blessed by ASCAP. The Navy Sea Chanters and the U.S. Marine Band recorded it; every disk jockey got a copy. In Tennessee, the country-western people came up with their own WIN ballad.

An overwhelming majority of the nation's governors, mayors and county executives responded affirmatively to the President's telegram urging enforcement of the 55-mph speed limit and other energy-saving, anti-inflation measures.

In his Future Farmers address in Kansas City, President Ford read a dozen or more letters from individual citizens, selected by Sylvia Porter's committee. None was faked; they were the real voice of America. The most memorable was from Luette Drumhiller, eight years old, of Bristol, Virginia, who wrote, "Turn off lights when not needed, and if you are scared when you go to bed without the light on, tell your mother or father, and they will do something about it."

Edward Block, vice-president of Illinois Bell, signed on as executive director of the Citizens Committee after designing a comprehensive public-relations blueprint. Patrick J. Healy, recently retired as executive vice-president of the National League of Cities, surveyed WIN's administrative setup and recommended valuable improvements. Donald Regan, board chairman of Merrill Lynch, helped with volunteer financing; Hobart Taylor, a distinguished D.C. attorney and former LBJ aide, served without fee as WIN's legal counsel.

With all this great talent and general enthusiasm, why did WIN lose?

1. Lack of money. Even a volunteer army needs office space, typewriters, telephones and postage stamps. The White House WIN

PALACE POLITICS

Coordinator Russell Freeberg, proposed a modest $450,000 annual budget including a paid staff of five. But both the President and the Porter group were ideologically adamant about WIN's independence of any Federal strings, so it depended on sporadic private contributions, mostly in the five-dollar range. Any other Administration with its President's prestige on the line would have silently tapped some contingency fund in the $300 billion Federal budget.

2. Internal dissension. The policymaking WIN committee was, predictably, loaded with prima donnas. Further, their fundamental convictions clashed. When they got around to the original idea, voluntary pledges to hold the line on both prices and wages, they waffled on wages.

3. Deliberate sabotage. Led by William Simon, Nixon's last and worst Secretary of the Treasury, the economic cohort of the Praetorian Guard who despised the WIN idea employed every dirty trick in their considerable bag to make it fail.

In his 1978 book *A Time for Truth,* Simon proudly confesses that "every time the WIN issue came up, we at the Economic Policy Board would hide our heads in embarrassment." He fails to mention the scorn and ridicule he assiduously relayed to the media which severely embarrassed and undercut the President of the United States. Rightly or wrongly, Ford himself made WIN a conspicuous symbol of his leadership. Nobody who ate his salt should have scuttled it.*

Ultimately, it was not the American people but the Praetorian Guard who lost their taste for volunteerism as a facet of economic recovery. Late in January I learned that Jerry Jones, the holdover staff secretary, had simply pigeonholed 25,000 Presidential form letters promised to new WIN volunteers.

The nonstop internal barrage against WIN eventually got to Ford. WIN didn't exactly die; it just sort of melted with the winter snow. The President himself lost interest after presiding over a few White House meetings of Sylvia Porter's steering committee. He disliked dissension and wouldn't bring himself to be President and put his foot down on

---

* To give the economist devils more than their due, there was an abrupt strategy switch as recession, rather than inflation, became Ford's primary concern. Consumer demand fires inflation but needs encouragement in recession. But the WIN concept was flexible enough to make the change. When Ford finally brought the annual inflation rate down below 5 percent, how nice it would have been for him to declare WIN over because the American spirit had WON.

one side or the other. In a mixture of disappointment and disgust, the WIN committee disbanded. To their credit, the volunteers did it quietly, saying their emergency duty was done. Ford sent them all personal thank-you letters.

In the wake of Watergate, Republicans in the 1974 campaign were handicapped from the start. The pardon made it worse, and the failing economy foretold a Democratic triumph. Our main hope was to keep it from turning into a referendum on President Ford's performance, and mercifully our losses were less than we expected. We were kidding ourselves, however, to think this would be our final penalty for the past.*

After the Republicans lost forty-three seats in the House, three in the Senate and four Governorships in November, despite Ford's strenuous campaigning, Bill Simon continued to advocate austerity and inaction. Within the Oval Office or Cabinet Room this was proper, but when he publicly described Ford's own proposed $51.9 billion budget deficit as "horrendous," he was way out of line. Privately, the President wished aloud that "Bill would shut up."

Simon's own version is that "a Republican campaign to drive me from government began. My clash with a certain type of Republican partisan was inevitable. . . .

"Quivering with an indignation based on everything but concern for principle, certain White House aides—most notably chief of staff Donald Rumsfeld—argued that I was 'betraying' the President. News was leaked . . . that I would leave before or just after the end of the year. When I declined to take the hint, the leakers used UPI's Helen Thomas to report that my resignation was imminent," Simon wrote.

The most enduring effect upon me of the WIN episode was to become the scapegoat of the Praetorians for its failure. As Ford knew the facts better than anyone, I wasn't sufficiently alarmed. Over the Christmas–New Year holidays, however, the warring Rumsfeld and Simon camps put together a new coalition. Their aim was to dominate the construction of the forthcoming State of the Union message, Ford's first, which he had assigned to me.

---

* Of the forty-seven Republicans Ford campaigned for as Vice President, thirty-three won. But as President he concentrated on the thirty-three toughest contests, risking the blame. There was plenty. After a twenty-state blitz, the best we could claim was that the Presidential coattails helped Governors Milliken (Michigan) and Rhodes (Ohio) and probably tipped the Senate scales for Bob Dole (Kansas) and Jake Garn (Utah).

PALACE POLITICS

Ron Nessen describes a disconsolate huddle at the end of 1974 in Rummy's corner office, also attended by Cheney, Greenspan and Marsh. Marsh, who might have been expected at least to warn me, kept his mouth shut and a foot in both doors. Nessen quotes Rumsfeld as being discouraged because he could not get the President to take "an intellectual approach about his goals and aspirations, the changing relationship between Americans and their institutions." Instead, he said, Ford insisted on a practical list of legislative recommendations and budget cuts. He recalls Rummy's pessimistic view that the President was tottering on the brink.

"At the end of three months, the Ford Administration will either have the smell of life or the smell of death," Ron quotes Don as predicting. "If it's the smell of death, this White House is going to be torn to pieces by the press, by the Democrats, even by other Republicans who will challenge the President for the nomination."

But before the smell of death clung to Rummy, he would be off again and running, running for . . . ?

13

ROCKY'S LAST HURRAH

Nelson Rockefeller's last hurrah in American politics was characteristically audacious, magnanimous and foredoomed.

It began early in 1975 with a blunt warning to President Ford that there were people in the White House he thought were friends but who really wanted to see him fail as President and lose the forthcoming nomination.

It reached a dramatic denouement in mid-1976 when Rockefeller, having taken himself off the ticket at Ford's personal request, boldly volunteered to take charge of the White House as the President's deputy.

It almost sputtered out in a backstage blow-up at the Republican convention in Kansas City with an angry declaration that the Vice President was walking out and would have no part in Ford's campaign against Carter.

It ended with the Rockefellers sharing the Fords' last night in the White House and Rocky, the good soldier, seeing the former President off to California with a warm bear hug.

It is one helluva story, as my old city editor used to say.* If it were televised as a prime-time Washington soap opera, nobody would believe it.

Congress finally confirmed the former New York Governor as Vice President under the Twenty-fifth Amendment on December 19, 1974, by the ample margins of 90–7 in the Senate and 287–128 in the House, with ultraconservative Republicans joining liberal Democrats in opposition. President Ford attended his swearing-in in the Senate chamber.

* The material in this and later chapters is a mixture of my contemporary observations and conversations, two long interviews with the former Vice President in December 1977 and February 1978 and talks with other members of the Ford and Rockefeller staffs. The suppositions and conclusions are my own, except where Rockefeller and others are quoted.

303

It was the first time the United States ever had an unelected President and an unelected Vice President at the same time. (So far as I can determine this situation was not anticipated by the amendment's framers.) It was also the first time the U.S. Senate's proceedings were ever telecast.

In their preliminary talks, Rockefeller understood that President Ford wanted him to serve as vice-chairman and *de facto* head of the Domestic Council, in Rocky's own words, "to do in the domestic field what Henry [Kissinger] was doing in the international field." Ron Nessen, already relaying Don Rumsfeld's thoughts as often as Ford's, seemed to cut this sweeping authority down by telling the press that the new Vice President's duties would involve "explaining the President's programs" around the country.

By no stretch of the imagination could Rockefeller be considered naïve about the awkward role of the Vice President. Philosophically, he told reporters immediately after his confirmation that he didn't intend to be a problem to anybody.

"I want to be helpful and only do that which is appropriate and helpful to the President and the people of this country," he said modestly.

But real modesty was not Rocky's forte. He had a deservedly high opinion of his own abilities and experience in national politics, in the exercise of executive powers and in attracting excellent subordinates. The worst thing Congressional inquisitors found to charge him with was his generosity toward loyal and dedicated aides.* He felt that the President really needed and wanted those talents and came to Washington ready and anxious to supply them.

Following the Christmas and New Year's lull, Rocky brought to his regular weekly meeting in the Oval Office a draft memo for the President to send to his Cabinet heads and other members of the Domestic Council and a draft for an Executive Order Ford would sign putting it into effect.

In Rockefeller's draft the President would have cleanly defined the jurisdictions of the Domestic Council and the Office of Management and Budget. The former, representing a broad spectrum of Administration agencies with primarily domestic concerns, and the OMB,

* Henry Kissinger received a modest $50,000 in 1969 after leaving Rockefeller's employ and before joining Nixon's. Other gifts ranged as high as $625,000, on which Rockefeller paid thousands more in gift taxes. The IRS found nothing amiss.

strictly an adjunct of the White House staff but with enormous power of the purse strings, had been warring throughout the Nixon years. Ehrlichman dictatorially ran the Domestic Council and was survived by several lieutenants, while Roy Ash zealously guarded and expanded the prerogatives of the Director of Management and Budget. As a result there were duplications and government-wide dismay over who was running domestic programs in the latter days of the Nixon Administration.

Rockefeller proposed that Ford order "the Domestic Council to coordinate policy formulation in the domestic area. In this activity the Council will concern itself with policy and the Office of Management and Budget will be concerned with the fiscal side.

"Because of the complexity and interrelationship of domestic policies and programs, I believe the broadest perspectives must be brought to bear in the Domestic Council's deliberations," the key paragraph stated. "For this reason I have asked the Vice President to serve as Vice Chairman of the Council and to *oversee the work* of the Domestic Council. I have requested that the Executive Director of the Council and Assistant to the President report to me *through him.*" (Emphasis mine.)

According to Rockefeller, the President quickly agreed to his proposal. But he did not initial it immediately, tossing it into one of the baskets on his desk. This was Ford's time-tested way of ensuring himself of time for reflection and further counsel.

Ford's transition team, reflecting Rog Morton's and Rumsfeld's separate concerns, had pinpointed the feud between the Council and OMB, which was frequently conducted by press leaks to pre-empt a Presidential decision. But they were inclined to blame the conflict on Ash's prickly personality rather than an organizational flaw. Ash was targeted for early replacement, and Rummy already had recommended Jim Lynn, Nixon's Secretary of HUD, to be OMB's director.

After Rockefeller left, figuring he had carried the day more easily than he expected, the President discussed his draft with key advisers.

When Ford showed me the Vice President's proposal, I supposed that it represented—as Rocky said in a covering note—"your wishes relating to my role." The President had indicated in our earlier talks that he wanted Rockefeller to really make something of the Domestic Council—not simply receive weekly briefings from its staff as Ford had while he was Vice President. The charter was very broad, I said, but since the President was chairman of the Domestic Council and the

Vice President only vice-chairman, he'd always have the last word. Ford didn't disagree. I, too, went away convinced the thing was as good as done.

But Rumsfeld went up the wall. He had joined the Ford White House with what he considered a mandate to restructure the White House staff, and part of his plan was to bring both the Domestic Council and OMB under his control, coupling their considerable authority to his own. Now here was the new Vice President, on virtually his first day at work, proposing to be the sole conduit between the Domestic Council and the President, at the same time cutting OMB down to the size of a bookkeeper.

Furthermore, Rumsfeld's only previous experience with Vice Presidents had been with Agnew, who was held in ill-disguised contempt by the Nixon Praetorians. I was anxious from the outset to see that that did not happen with Rockefeller.

What Rumsfeld told the President remains between them, but I know what he told me and what Rockefeller told me. Rummy told me that Rocky's proposal for the Domestic Council amounted to abdication of Ford's authority in the domestic field. If Ford consented to it, Rockefeller in a few months would become a sort of Acting President for domestic policy. In the process the Republican Party would be bifurcated, the right wing claiming that by trick and device the liberal New Yorker had achieved what they had denied him for decades. Ford, an unelected President, dared not give such a sweeping mandate to any subordinate, not even his Vice President.

At this point I had no feeling that Rummy's misgivings were prompted by anything but Ford's best interests. At this point, also, Rumsfeld had need of my support. I listened, and agreed there was some risk. But, I told Rummy, this was something the President, rather than either of us, would have to decide. If Ford wanted his Vice President to have extraordinary authority, though it ran against the grain of previous Presidencies, that was his right and it might work. Nobody in the past, despite their rhetoric, ever really tried making the Vice President a true deputy.

Rumsfeld took Rocky's draft memo and sent it to the Staff Secretary, Jerry Jones, to be circulated to the President's senior staff for comment. This process, central to the Praetorian system of control, was known as "staffing it out." The person who decides to whom a paper should be circulated can almost always control what the preponderance of opinion on the matter will be.

Jones sent this document to five people: Ken Cole, Ehrlichman's successor as director of the Domestic Council staff, who was about to leave at his own request; Roy Ash, who was about to be ousted as director of the overextended OMB by the Ford forces; Jim Lynn, Ford's newly enlisted OMB boss, whose job would be relegated to mere mathematics by the Vice President's proposal; and to Marsh and me. I don't know what Marsh's reaction was, but I had no serious misgivings. I had Neta call Jerry Jones and say that the President and Mr. Rumsfeld were already aware of my views.

When Rocky learned through the grapevine that Rumsfeld was trying to derail his Domestic Council plan, he characteristically marched into Rummy's office to confront him. According to Rockefeller, Rummy sagaciously argued in organizational terms. He did not oppose Rocky's plan on merit but said that momentous changes of this magnitude should be "coordinated"—should not be shoved at the President for a "yes" or "no" decision without preliminary "staffing out." That, said Rummy, was his job and his concern, to ensure that the President weighed all his options before making a considered decision.

"Look," Rockefeller heatedly interrupted, "the President asked me to give him my recommendation as to what should be done and that I have done."

"We don't do things that way around here," Rumsfeld retorted with a coolness close to insolence. "We give him options."

"Look, let's not kid ourselves," the Vice President shot back. "You don't give him options. You give him three alternatives, two of which are absurd and the other is the one you want. And you try to make him think that *he* is making a decision.

"To me this is avoiding responsibility—the responsibility of saying what you think *should* be done, so he can judge the merits by the people who recommend various choices. You're putting the President on the spot by forcing him to make a decision on a phony basis."

"Well, this is the way we do it," Rumsfeld reportedly countered. "I want to be in on all these things. They have to be taken up at our morning staff meeting. The person who's the head of the staff has to know all the details. How can you, Mr. Vice President, possibly do all that paperwork?"

"The President didn't ask me to come down here to do paperwork," Rocky retorted with rising wrath. "He wants advice and help on the major issues that face this country. He was on my Critical

307

Choices Commission—in fact, he was the only guy from Washington who came to the meetings. He understands the issues—and he wants me to help him on them. And what I'll do is organize this thing so the paperwork is run smoothly by people who are competent to handle paperwork," the Vice President concluded.

"That isn't the way we work around here" was Rumsfeld's last word.

Rocky stomped out and later told friends, "It was very clear to me Rumsfeld was not an executive or administrator. He had a legislator's background. He refused to take responsibility for a decision. He'd go in to see the President alone and then come back and say 'the President says.' He just couldn't see how a Vice President could simply do what the President wanted him to do.

"What really was the case was that Rumsfeld wanted to use the Domestic Council as *his* staff to do *his* paperwork for him. But *he* would take the decisions in to the President—not the Domestic Council. We would just be paper shufflers."

Still in a state of high dudgeon, Rockefeller called for Ann Whitman, his longtime executive secretary whom he had designated to head his Vice Presidential staff. Ann had forgotten a lot more about the White House than most of us ever learned. She had been President Eisenhower's Girl Friday for a decade, so she also knew something about VIP tempers. Rocky began to dictate: "Mr. President, I cannot be useful to you unless your staff is enthusiastic and supportive of what you want me to do. You will have to make that decision. I will be happy to drop the whole thing, if you wish, or happy to go ahead if your staff will support it. . . ."

"Mr. Vice President," Ann interrupted gently, "I think you ought to cool down before you do this. It isn't fair to the President to put him on such a spot, especially in writing."

Rocky cooled down as easily as he warmed up. But he did bring the subject up at his next private session with Ford in the Oval Office. He had somewhat revised his original approach after conferring with two of his trusted aides, Jim Cannon, a personable, politically astute ex-newsman, and Dick Dunham, his New York State budget director and trouble-shooter in Albany.

Instead of revamping the Domestic Council's structure by having its top staff director report to the President via the Vice President, Rocky would be content to select the key people involved. There would be two—one who served as Assistant to the President for Domestic Affairs (Ehrlichman's previous role, then held by Ken Cole) and a deputy, who would administer the substantive work of the Council staff. This was currently being done by Dr. James Cavanaugh, a deceptively mild-mannered Ehrlichman disciple with doleful spaniel eyes that never directly met his quarry's. Cole wanted to get out. Rocky would replace him with Cannon in the political–public relations slot; order Cannon to fire Cavanaugh and put Dunham in his place as the substantive issues deputy. The Vice President was also eager to get rid of another Domestic Council holdover, Michael Raoul-Duval, a thirty-seven-year-old lawyer and one of the slickest of Haldeman's advance men turned policymaker. ("Anybody with that kind of arrogance and lack of sensitivity has no place around a President.")

With the top places on the Domestic Council staff manned by Rockefeller loyalists Cannon and Dunham, backstopped by others from his New York coterie—Art Quern and Dick Parsons, a brilliant black attorney—Rockefeller was confident he could dominate domestic programming for Ford. This was what he believed the President wanted him for; hadn't Ford said, "I want you to be a partner in this thing"?

Which was fine—except that Rumsfeld also thought that was what the President wanted *him* for, and he resisted Rockefeller's plan to carve out an autonomous fiefdom in domestic policy in both direct and indirect ways. The Vice President's acute sensors soon felt the heat, and he headed for a showdown with Ford.

"Mr. President," Rockefeller began as he settled into a chair alongside the Oval Office desk, "you remember not long ago sitting right here I told you that I wanted to have a relationship in which I could feel free to say to you everything I think and feel, politically speaking. I didn't want you to comment on all my observations, or feel obliged to, because you shouldn't sometimes. But I want you to know at all times. And you agreed."

Ford pressed his forefingers against pursed lips and nodded.

"You gave me a number of things to do at our first meeting, and one was to take the vice-chairmanship of the Domestic Council and come up with a structure so that we can do a job in the domestic field. So I worked up a plan. I studied the White House structure. You have set up an energy board and an economic board with your friend, Bill Seidman—a very able guy—as head of it. But already it's obvious to me there's fractionalization of responsibility in the domestic field.

309

PALACE POLITICS

"In domestic policy you can't separate the economic side from the social side, you can't separate energy from economics. They all have to be pulled together somewhere and that is what this Domestic Council was supposed to be. I went back to the original order approved by Congress. Now I have two people who could organize it and do it properly. But Rummy, no matter how I set it up, is opposed to it," Rockefeller's account continued.

The President listened intently, and Rockefeller went on, handing him a revised Domestic Council memo and draft executive order. He said the original paper he'd discussed with Ford had been "staffed out" by Rumsfeld and came back totally changed.

"Mr. President, I can't do it on that basis—it won't work for you. I've been through bureaucratic infighting ever since nineteen-forty when I started with Roosevelt. I really understand infighting—the whole gamut of it—and how this stuff works. I'll never involve myself in White House infighting—it isn't fair to you and that's not what I came for. So I'll tell you what the situation is and give you my best judgment and if you want to do it, that's fine. If you don't, that's fine. I'll support whatever you want."

As the Vice President reconstructed their meeting, Ford studied his memo and after some discussion said, "This is what I want. I want you to do this." The President would sign the Cabinet memo and executive order the way Rockefeller wanted them in the first place. He agreed to name Cannon his Presidential assistant and Dunham deputy director of the Domestic Council staff. He also added his economic and energy "czars" to the Council's membership, ostensibly subject to the Vice President's oversight and coordination.

Rumsfeld's candidate for the top Domestic Council job was widely believed to be Philip Areeda, who was waiting in the wings as one of Phil Buchen's two principal legal aides. Understandably, when word reached him of Rocky's breakthrough, he sent a terse resignation to the President on February 7 and returned to Harvard.

In announcing his decision to assign the Domestic Council to his new Vice President, Ford chose a convenient and appropriate forum, an "appreciation" banquet honoring Rockefeller at the Waldorf-Astoria the evening of February 13. These Manhattan rituals, whether conducted by Republicans, Democrats, the Archdiocese or the Zionists, are remarkably alike. There are almost as many people on the multitiered dais as at tables on the ballroom floor; everybody, but everybody, of the New York establishment shells out to be seen there, and the introductions are interminable.

310

In his address to the enthusiastic New York audience, Ford waxed even more expansive than the generous bounds of Rocky's own draft. "Tonight we pay tribute to a man of unlimited talent, outstanding accomplishment and boundless enthusiasm," he began. "I am here to tell you that one of the best ideas this Ford ever had was nominating Nelson Rockefeller to be Vice President of the United States.

"When Nelson tackles a project, he gives it everything he's got. I have never known him to apply a half-nelson to anything. (Laughter.)

"I want the Domestic Council to undertake the following responsibilities: First, assessing national needs and identifying alternative ways of meeting them; second, providing rapid response to Presidential needs for policy advice; third, coordinating the establishment of national priorities for the allocation of available resources; fourth, maintaining a continuous policy of review of our ongoing programs and, as we look down the road, proposing reforms as we need them.

"That is why I personally, with the deepest conviction and support, have asked the Vice President to serve as Vice Chairman of the Council and to personally and vigorously oversee its work," Ford declared as Rocky beamed.

As the President went on to announce his appointments of Cannon and Dunham, the audience, White House reporters in the room (who had been given the texts earlier to meet Eastern time-zone deadlines) and Rockefeller's own inner circle had reason to believe Ford was making history. For once, a President was really in earnest about giving his Vice President a meaningful role in government and the authority to match.

"Putting Rockefeller to Work" was *Time* magazine's verdict, quoting me. " 'This is an ongoing experiment and unique policy in having complete harmony and complete concord between the President and his Vice President,' observes Presidential Counsellor Robert Hartmann," *Time* reported. " 'A great many around this town [Washington] believe this is impossible. But the President believes that you trust your Vice President and you trust your Vice President's men.' "

The *National Observer*, discoursing on "Rocky's Growing Role," anonymously quoted other officials with mixed reactions. "This is one President who believes in giving a man a job to do and letting him have a long leash," said one. But another cautioned: "The big question is what happens when Rocky starts giving advice that runs counter to what Ford is hearing from his economic advisers and the Rumsfeld crew. There's a potential here for real conflict."

311

PALACE POLITICS

It didn't take long for that potential to develop. But instead of erupting as a bare-knuckle battle royal, it festered and suppurated, sapping the strength and self-confidence of the President's bold and clear-cut decision. Nor would he ever lance it, bearing the temporary pain. Like so many of Ford's early initiatives, the revitalized Domestic Council under Rockefeller never really got off the ground. It was sabotaged and strangled by his own Praetorian Guard, and I wonder if he knows yet what really happened.*

What happened was what always happened in the Ford White House whenever the Praetorians lost an argument. Behind the President's back they set out to prove to him that he had made the wrong decision, relied on the wrong adviser and that it just wouldn't work. This was the same technique whether the immediate winner of the debate was Rockefeller, Hartmann, one of Ford's Congressional pals or anyone with enough independence and influence with the President to challenge the way the palace guard had programmed he should decide. It was usually accompanied by a torrent of subtle badmouthing and press leaks aimed at the offender, not at his views so much as his motives, his mental competence and his moral character—a standard weapon of the Nixon Praetorians that Ford could neither comprehend nor curb. Invariably, he suspected the wrong person.

By the form books Rockefeller, armed with virtual *carte blanche* from the President, should have been more than a match for the pygmy Praetorians who stood in his way. But the Vice President made several simultaneous mistakes. He failed to follow the second law of the battlefield**—mop up fast; destroy the demoralized and scattered pockets of remaining resistance. Rocky's victory was so spectacular in

* My hunch seems to be confirmed by Ford in his autobiography. He saw the whole thing as a gentlemanly difference of organizational opinion which he thought he had resolved. He wrote: "Rumsfeld bore no animosity toward Rockefeller or Cannon personally. He simply opposed what they wanted to do organizationally. Unfortunately, the end result was that tension developed between Nelson and Don. I could see both sides of the argument. Nelson felt that he knew more about domestic policy and politics than Don, and he was probably right. On the other hand, Don was the man responsible for organizing and managing the West Wing. To do so effectively he had to have control. Finally, after three or four unhappy meetings, I made the decision to go along with Nelson. The paper would have to flow through Don . . . but Nelson would be in charge of domestic policy. . . . To his credit, Don didn't complain. I'm sure he was disappointed, but the only comment he made was: 'Fine, we'll try to make it work.' "
** The first law, of course, is General Stonewall Jackson's "Git thar firstest with the mostest."

his first Oval Office skirmish that this battle-scarred veteran of countless political wars laid aside his sword and went off to ponder more grand-scale plans, leaving his lieutenants to consolidate the high ground he had won. And if Rumsfeld, Simon Greenspan, Lynn and all the surviving Nixonians were separately no match for Rockefeller, together they quickly subdued his subordinates.

Using familiar techniques perfected by Haldeman and Haig—of which Rummy claimed to have been himself a victim—disemboweling the newborn Rockefeller apparatus was a pitifully easy exercise. Since it would take a little time, the first phase was the pretense of complete acceptance of the President's decision and utmost cooperation in the new order.

Jim Cannon was quickly sworn in as Assistant to the President and loaded with the perquisites of the White House senior staff, including a handsome office in the West Wing.

There was one small hitch. Cannon found himself with two deputies instead of one. Cavanaugh had been doing the job for months and showed no sign of resigning with the outgoing Ken Cole. Dick Dunham had just been named a deputy director but hardly knew what it entailed. He would have to learn the ropes from Cavanaugh. Ditto for the other new Rockefeller appointees.

It made sense, and Ford himself had set the example of tender solicitude for the Nixon holdovers. So right from the start Cannon was half encircled by the Praetorians. As between the veteran Cavanaugh and the neophyte Dunham, there was no question whose direction the rest of the Domestic Council people would heed.

Also, in his lofty disdain for "paper-pushing," Rockefeller readily accepted Ford's insistence that the Domestic Council's paperwork continue to flow through the White House secretariat, which Rumsfeld tightly controlled. The President himself grossly underestimated the importance of paper-pushers, since he had never before in his life had to depend on them. Actually, it was not a compromise but a contradiction to say that Rockefeller would be in charge but the paper would flow through Rumsfeld.

Whoever determines which papers are pushed up to the President, which are pushed under the rug, which are sent back for revision until they are gutted and which are heavily reinforced can preordain Presidential decisions about 90 percent of the time. Whenever a President lets down his guard just enough to show which way he is leaning, the chief paper-pusher's score approaches 100 percent.

The second phase of the Praetorian game plan to reverse Rockefeller's ascendancy was to eliminate Dunham. They whispered it about that he was some kind of Rockefeller "spy" in the Ford camp—even insinuated as much to his face. He found himself unable to get anything done without Cavanaugh. In Albany he had been the boss. When Rumsfeld's personnel office proposed Dunham for a vacancy in the chairmanship of the Federal Power Commission, he was glad to get out of the White House neighborhood. So Cavanaugh remained deputy director of the Domestic Council, moving Mike Duval up to a new post as "associate" director.

As Rockefeller recalled the episode, he told Cannon in March of 1975: "To fire whatever that fellow's name is, the old Nixon guy—Cavanaugh—and to fire Mike Duval. Cavanaugh was one of those guys who's a competent bureaucrat who always hung around the halls. Whenever the President was coming out of his office he just happened to be there, and Duval was the same way. They were very suave, smooth White House bureaucrats but not guys who understood substance or were devoted to seeing that the President got what he needed to make a proper decision.

"Jim [Cannon] came to me about two weeks after he was in and I said, "Why haven't you gotten rid of Cavanaugh?" Rockefeller related. "And Cannon said, 'Rummy says this would be a disaster. I have a commitment to him that I will keep him and have two deputies and Cavanaugh would do the papers.' "

Cannon recalls that Rumsfeld offered to replace Cavanaugh with another deputy of his or Rockefeller's own choosing but says he made the decision to keep Cavanaugh on the basis of discussions with the President. He took full responsibility with Rockefeller, since he was now working for the President, although the Vice President was clearly unhappy about it. Cannon was correct, certainly, that no man can serve two masters; Rockefeller was unrealistic in thinking things could be otherwise.

"Cannon said he couldn't undo his promise to Rumsfeld without a major internal fight breaking out in the White House. My alternatives were to tell him he had to do it or to fire him. Jim said he could handle it and I made the mistake of not doing anything.

"And a few months later Dick Dunham said, 'I cannot handle this thing this way' and resigned," Rockefeller recalled. "So now we are back with the whole organization in the same hands as it was before, under Rummy through this fellow—Cavanaugh."

Why did Rockefeller abandon the field? Perhaps he was simply battle-weary from past wars. He was sixty-seven, and this was really about all he had expected the Vice Presidency would be. But he was a compulsive doer; neither his mind nor his body could sit still. So he did what all his predecessors, including Ford, had done, made up work to his own liking to while away the Vice President's idle hours. His own explanation, after it was all over, was: "I didn't want to make a fight. I wanted to work and not cause the President trouble. My usefulness in this area—and I told the President—was really finished. The President was really interested in the reaction of the country, so I suggested there be a series of town meetings around the country on the problems we faced as a nation. This I could run and preside over and take Cabinet members with me. And Rumsfeld couldn't control this."

Gerald Rudolph Ford was born (and christened Leslie Lynch King, Jr.*) in Omaha, Nebraska, on July 14, 1913. Some years earlier, on the one hundredth anniversary of the fall of the Bastille, my father— Miner Louis Hartmann—was born in Hutchinson, Kansas.

On Easter Sunday, April 8, 1917, little Bobby Hartmann was born in Rapid City, South Dakota. One year later, though it wasn't Easter, little Betty Bloomer (eventually Betty Ford) was born in Chicago.

The coincidence and intersecting influences of these memorable dates I hope some day to find time to pursue with a reliable astrologer. I relate them now because on my fifty-eighth birthday, and Betty's fifty-seventh, the President of the United States threw a surprise double birthday party aboard Air Force One.

We were returning from an Easter recess break in Palm Springs, the fun of which was dampened by South Vietnam suddenly going to hell in a handbasket. This required the presence of Henry Kissinger, who was also aboard. Just after midnight Air Force crewmen brought in two huge cakes, pink and red for Betty, green and yellow for me. They set them on the two staff tables on opposite sides of the aisle, candles flickering.

Everybody was summoned, but as soon as the press photographers appeared, Henry Kissinger slipped into the seat behind my cake

---

* As almost everyone knows, Ford was adopted as an infant by his step-father, Gerald R. Ford of Grand Rapids, and took his name. He was nick-named "Junie," for junior, which may account for his spelling of "Jerry" with a "J." Whenever people purporting to be old friends wrote him as "Gerry," his staff knew they didn't know Ford all that well.

and posed with the cutting knife. The President had to order Henry to let me have my momentary place of honor before the festivities could proceed.

Kissinger wasn't being rude; he automatically assumed that if anything was going on worth photographing he should be front and center in it.

Henry is pretty hard to beat at one-upmanship. Once Roberta did it beautifully. Whenever she greeted the Secretary of State, who is a real charmer with the ladies, Kissinger would reply with a twinkle in his eye, "Oh, how nice to see you again, Mrs. *Rumsfeld.*"

This was pretty hilarious the first couple of times. But after a while Roberta told me she'd really had enough of it. Next time what could she say to stop him?

"Don't wait for the next time," I said. "Beat him to it."

So the next time they met Roberta smilingly stuck out her hand and said sweetly, "Oh, how are *you* this evening, Secretary *Richardson?*"

The champagne fizz of the dual birthday party aboard Air Force One quickly turned to flat beer when we got our feet back on the ground in Washington. Despite the leafy greenery and lovely blossoms of spring, Washington's mood was surly and downcast.

Whatever positions they had taken in the past, official Washingtonians were in a guilty funk about the impending military collapse of South Vietnam. It had been inevitable ever since the pull-out of a massive American expeditionary force, when the hawks became as sick as the hippies of our longest war. But now we had to face the unpleasant consequences of being on the losing side. Outside of the old Confederacy, Americans had never lost a war.

Furthermore, Americans had never before had to live with the consequences of abandoning an ally. Korea was hardly a triumph, but it was a draw on the same line where it began. The situation in Saigon was deteriorating so rapidly there was a very real danger the few remaining Americans might have to fight their way out against the embittered South Vietnamese defenders.

The American conscience was wracked by the certain fate of hundreds of thousands of South Vietnamese who collaborated with us over a decade, their wives and children pledges to our assurance of protection.

The grim situation was complicated even more because the President was not completely sure he was getting the facts. The fog of war thickens when rout begins. The Pentagon was pressing for early evacuation, while the American Embassy was seized of a sort of Custer's Last Stand syndrome. There was grave peril both in doing too much too soon and too little too late. Congress had put severe restrictions on the President's traditional authority to act.

Before he left for California and Congress scattered for the Easter recess, the President had dispatched General Frederick C. Weyand, Army Chief of Staff, to Saigon and instructed him to return with a firsthand, professional assessment of the situation.

In the midst of all this, Kissinger arrived at Rancho Mirage, where the Fords were staying in the handsome hillside home of Fred and Vonnie Wilson. There is an interesting aside which, while it has no bearing on the Vietnam situation, tells something about Kissinger's personality. At a farewell cocktail party the President told me that Henry was giving a small dinner that night and one of the guests was to be Frank Sinatra.

"You're not going, are you?" I asked.

"Of course we are," the President replied with some surprise. "Why not?"

I reminded him that Sinatra had been a close Kennedy and Agnew pal and was often linked with unsavory types by Hollywood rumormongers. I just didn't think it would look good, with Saigon going up in smoke, for the President to be partying with Kissinger's swinging show-biz friends.

"Well, I promised Henry, and that's that," he said with finality.

I told Ron Nessen to be prepared for another blast from the traveling White House press. They had been potshotting all week at the President's playing golf with millionaires. Nessen agreed that the Sinatra dinner would be a disaster.

"Why don't you call Henry and ask him to disinvite Sinatra or let the President off the hook?" he suggested.

"Henry wouldn't listen to me," I said. "I've done my part. *You* call Kissinger."

Ron picked up a library extension phone and called Kissinger. He told me the Secretary of State, after pondering the probable press reaction, said he'd explain to Sinatra that he and Ford had to discuss urgent confidential matters that had come up.

"What will you bet Henry's on the phone to the President right this minute?" I said as we returned to the party. Sure enough, Ford was off in a corner taking a call.

He always shouts on the phone, and we heard him say with feeling, "Well, *he* is not the President. *I* am."

(Others heard this fragment, too, and assumed Ford was talking *about* Henry rather than to him.)

The President hung up, shot a withering glance at Nessen and me huddling there and muttered, "I'm *going.*"

He did. But Sinatra didn't. Kissinger, after proving that he could influence Ford better than both of us together, disinvited his controversial guest.

Back in Washington all attention was riveted on Vietnam. General Weyand had come back with a grim, but, as it turned out, optimistic estimate. There was a chance—not a very good one—that the South Vietnamese Army could regroup and hold a defensive perimeter around Saigon, at least long enough for some kind of negotiated settlement. They might need U.S. air support, which would have been justifiable in view of gross North Vietnamese violations of the 1974 accords, and could have been furnished from offshore carriers without a risky recommitment to land bases. But Weyand was well aware even this might be politically impossible.

His recommendation was for quick Congressional appropriation of another $722 million, ostensibly to supply the South Vietnamese with desperately needed ammunition and supplies. Actually, as everyone who really wanted to understand could deduce, it was high-stakes poker in an effort to buy a little time to ransom the remaining Americans and as many blacklisted South Vietnamese as we could get out.

Earlier, the President had asked for $300 million extra for South Vietnam and $222 million for Cambodia. But Americans had already poured $150 billion into Southeast Asia and suffered 57,000 dead and twice as many seriously wounded. The Congress wouldn't buy even an emergency extension of it. They knew Ford's unspoken reason, but they were chicken. Let Ford take the blame.

Kissinger argued eloquently for the one final gesture of nobility and responsibility President Ford proposed. It was useless. Americans felt vaguely ashamed, but their will to fight for the freedom of faraway people was exhausted.

The President himself, known in Congress as the hawk of Vietnam hawks, realized that the time was long past for decisive American action to change the course of history on that strategic peninsula.

Ford, in fact, had come to that agonizing conclusion in 1967. A friend of unimpeachable authority, who must still be anonymous, brought to him secret maps and statistical summaries that proved that President Johnson's Administration had imposed bombing restrictions that put seven out of every ten significant targets in North Vietnam out of bounds. At that time we had already lost 636 planes over enemy territory. Yet most of Hanoi's air control centers, three-fourths of their petroleum storage depots, 60 percent of their transport network (including all seaports and canal locks), five out of six industrial targets and one-third of their power-generating capacity had never been attacked and could not be attacked under Presidential orders. Except for ammunition dumps, only one-third of all Hanoi's Air Force, Army and Navy installations in the North had been damaged. With this inside information, the Minority Leader stopped and thought.

"Why are we pulling our best punches in Vietnam?" he demanded in a watershed speech to a surprised, spellbound House of Representatives on August 8, seven years before he inherited the legacy of a losing war. "I am troubled. Why are we talking about money when we should be talking about men?

"This is not an academic exercise with computers. This involves the finest of our future leaders. The essential question is not whether every American should live better, but whether hundreds and thousands of Americans are going to live at all. This is a question crying for bold leadership and political courage of the highest order—even the courage to admit past policies have been woefully wrong," Ford declared.

Now, as President, Ford found himself facing a situation crying for even greater political courage, and he measured up to it. He flung open America's door to "the wretched refuse" of Vietnam's teeming shore and dramatized it by making an unscheduled dash to San Francisco personally to carry some of the first three hundred orphans and homeless children off a rescue plane from Saigon.

As the clock ran down on resistance in Saigon, I watched the President move calmly and confidently through the evacuation minefield. In my innermost thoughts, I had sometimes wondered about his decisiveness in personality clashes. But now, when the lives of multitudes and the international image of America hung in the balance, Ford acted as if he'd been President all his life. He met for hours with the National Security Council, with Congressional leaders, with Vice President Rockefeller, with his senior staff. The advice he got was pretty much the same: get out and get all the Americans out alive. But that, as Britain learned with only a narrow Channel to cross from Dunkirk, is the trickiest of all military maneuvers. The President announced his moves, neither stalling nor stampeding, always saying simply that he accepted full responsibility for the consequences.

On April 17 the Cambodian capital of Phnom Penh fell to the Khmer Rouge. The eighty-two remaining Americans were lifted by helicopter to the U.S.S. *Hancock* and U.S.S. *Okinawa* offshore, without casualties. The fate of the Cambodians left behind is a grisly story still being told.

One week later Saigon was encircled. The Situation Room in the bowels of the West Wing was humming with messages. Evacuees could no longer reach the sea by road. The tempo of landings and takeoffs of our giant C-130 transport planes was stepped up. Then the enemy opened devastating rocket and artillery fire on the airport. One plane was hit on the ground and two Marines killed.

The gutsy pilots of the evacuation planes kept coming, but soon the landing strip was crowded with hordes of frantic South Vietnamese. There were still a thousand Americans inside the U.S. Embassy walls, protected by only a few hundred Marine guards. Refugees hammered on the gates.

Ambassador Graham Martin for days had resisted hauling down the Stars and Stripes. But now or never was the time for the choppers. A vast U.S. naval armada had gathered offshore, with both helicopter and attack carriers. President Ford, through Kissinger, ordered Martin and the remaining Americans to leave. Through the Pentagon, he personally directed the final evacuation plan to be set in motion. It was about 11:00 P.M. Washington time on April 28.

Covered by jet fighter bombers, the first wave of choppers carried Marines to secure the evacuation sites at the Embassy and airport. In about sixteen hours, miraculously without loss of life, the remaining Americans and about six thousand South Vietnamese were lifted out. Martin, after destroying secret files and equipment, was the last to leave from the rooftop of the Embassy. At least that's what we thought when Nessen announced the completion of the operation.

Incredibly, the commercial transpacific telephones were still working. Even more incredibly, nobody had ordered the Marine guards to leave, and one hundred twenty-nine of them were still at their posts in the deserted Embassy compound. They called Washington and asked what to do next. The choppers were ordered back for one more run and got them all out safely. The President went over to the Residence to change into his tuxedo for a State Dinner honoring

Jordan's King Hussein, the last of his eighteen scheduled appointments for that day.

President Ford, often unfairly accused of having no forward vision, was already looking to the future. He saw it not in roseate dreams but in tangible things. He thought of the young people in America. Tragic as the final agonies of Vietnam were, there was an opportunity to be seized.

An entire generation had grown up with this war, fighting in it or fighting against it, their attitudes indelibly colored by it. Now the intelligence, the energy, the idealism and the passion of these young Americans must be turned and committed to the pressing problems of tomorrow.

A week before Saigon fell, the President had met with Paul Theis, Milt Friedman and me to talk over a major speech he had to make at Tulane University in New Orleans.

"What I want to get across," Ford began, "is the idea of all the challenges awaiting college students today. I want to give them a feeling of purpose, of being needed. They should think about the future, stop arguing about the past. Vietnam has been going on ever since any of them can remember. Well, the war's over."

"Why don't you just say that?" I asked.

Ford's brow furrowed. "I'm not sure Henry would approve," he said.

"He's been saying the same thing, in a long roundabout way," I went on. "Even Barry Goldwater is saying it now. But *you* have to say it to make it official. A lot of people suspect you're trying to get us back in. You're not. Nobody declared this war, but you can declare the end of it."

"It's not quite finished yet, Bob," the President cautioned. But he obviously liked the idea. "I agree, there's a lot of misunderstanding. See what you can come up with, but don't pass it around until I decide."

We went to work with only two days to go. Milt sweated over his typewriter almost all night. He was still fussing with the draft when we met aboard Air Force One early the next morning. The President called us into his cabin and marked up his final text.

In the Tulane fieldhouse, the floor and grandstands were packed and the band played "Hail to the Chief" with gusto. Ford recalled America's humiliation in the War of 1812 when the British captured and burned the National Capital, and how American pride was restored by General Andy Jackson's illustrious victory at New Orleans.

"Today, America can regain the sense of pride that existed before Vietnam," the President said. "But it cannot be achieved by refighting a war that is finished as far as America is concerned."

His final words were drowned out as soon as the students heard the word "finished." They almost literally raised the roof with whoops and hollers. They jumped up and down on the narrow bleachers, hugging whoever came up next. Pandemonium lasted for several minutes and continued to erupt through the remainder of Ford's speech.

"Jesus, I can't believe it!" I heard one tall, bearded boy yell to nobody in particular. "We finally got a President who tells it like it is!"

"It's over, it's over," a nearby group chanted, linking arms.

The jaded White House press corps had read nothing very exciting in the phrase "refighting a war that is finished" in the advance text distributed to them. Suddenly they came to life. This *was* a story.

"To the standing ovation and cheers of six thousand Tulane University students in New Orleans, President Ford called the Indochina conflict 'a war that is finished as far as America is concerned,'" UPI bulletined.

On the return trip, Ford didn't need Air Force One; he could have flown home unaided on Cloud Nine. Friedman and I would have been right behind him. Nessen told the President the media people would like him to come to their aft compartment for a visit, as he often did at the end of a journey.

"I wouldn't go," I said. "You can't make tonight's story any better."

He was in no mood to miss any more praise, especially from the press. So I tagged along to hear what the President said. The first question was predictable, but his answer was a shocker.

"Mr. President, did Secretary Kissinger have anything to do with the preparation of your speech or approve it in advance?"

"No!" Ford practically shouted over the jet noise. "Nothing at all."

I could see there'd be hell to pay. So I shouted too, "Mr. President, I think you should explain that a draft of this text went through the regular system, including the NSC office, so we assume Dr. Kissinger or his deputy saw it."

The President said yes, of course. He wasn't really pleased by my interruption. He was asked if he had been aware that his words ended an era of American history.

"Yes—after all, it's been a pretty long era," he replied with a note of sadness in his voice. "I had mixed emotions. It's not the way I wish it had ended, but you have to be realistic. We can't always achieve perfection in this world."

For once the press was filled with praise. Henry Kissinger was filled with something else. Bright and early the next morning, the buzzer on my direct Presidential phone sounded off like a smoke alarm.

"Will you come right in—and bring Milt with you?" the President said. Milt evidently was still sleeping, so I summoned Theis. Misery wants company.

The Secretary of State was pacing up and down the Oval Office, while Ford puffed on his pipe. The President greeted us warmly and invited us to sit down. Kissinger kept on pacing.

"This we don't need, Mr. President," Henry expostulated, glaring at us. "How is it I knew nothing about this? How can I explain it all to the people who are calling me to ask what it means?"

The President looked at me. I looked at Theis. Henry waited, hands on hips, for his satisfaction.

Paul explained that we'd sent the first draft to General Scowcroft but that Milt carried the second aboard Air Force One to finish without leaving a copy behind. I added we had no idea that one innocent phrase was going to be a blockbuster until the Tulane students detonated it. Neither of us said a word about that being the way the President wanted it from the start. Obviously what Kissinger was really mad about was the President's comments on the plane. He felt it had all been prearranged to humiliate him.

"Well, we *were* a little pressed for time," the President said. Turning to me, he added—did I detect a tiny wink?—"Just be sure it doesn't happen again."

At a news conference on May 6 Ford did his best to answer all the leftover inquiries about the final Vietnam evacuation, his legal authority to commit U.S. armed forces and the rescue of some 120,000 refugees. He turned aside Helen Thomas' request for a philosophical post-mortem on how we got into the Southeast Asian quagmire.

"It seems to me that it's over. We ought to look ahead. I think the lessons of the past in Vietnam have already been learned—learned by Presidents, learned by Congress, learned by the American people. And we should focus on the future."

Indeed, the media questions mainly focused on his campaigning plans for 1976, the CIA probe, gun control, housing, unemployment and other domestic issues. It seemed to all of us our troubles halfway around the world were over, and we had plenty more at home.

But on the morning of May 12, at a meeting in the Oval Office, Ford announced, "I think we've got a little problem. I have some bad news."

Quickly he related that Brent Scowcroft, Kissinger's tireless and unflappable NSC deputy, had just learned that the S.S. *Mayaguez,* an old container cargo ship bound for Thailand out of San Francisco Bay, was in trouble.

The U.S. Embassy in Jakarta, Indonesia, had been informed by a shipping office that they had picked up a distress radio message from the *Mayaguez* stating "Have been fired upon and boarded by Cambodian armed forces at 9 degrees 48 minutes north and 102 degrees 53 minutes east." That was all. The ship did not respond to further calls.

Brent had managed to gather a few details. The ship was of U.S. registry and had a crew of thirty-nine, mostly American or Philippine citizens. Her last port had been Hong Kong. The position radioed put her about sixty miles off the coast of Cambodia, well in international waters, but near a small island called Poulo Wai, jointly claimed by Cambodia and Vietnam. Both now had Communist governments less than a month in power. Neither the United States nor the United Nations had any direct contact with the new Cambodian regime.

Ford called a National Security Council emergency meeting at noon. Though it was nighttime in the Gulf of Thailand, he told Scowcroft he needed more facts. He instructed Nessen to skip his morning news briefing until more facts were available.

It could be another *Pueblo* incident, or it could be a drunken Khmer Rouge lieutenant playing hero without orders, or there could be a dozen other explanations. One thing was certain: It was President Ford's first acid test as Commander-in-Chief.

Crisis always tended to calm Jerry Ford. He had superbly trained himself to contain any inner feelings of agitation or alarm. But he knew, as we all knew, that the United States had just been run out of Indochina like a dog with its tail between its legs. We had, despite assurances by Nixon and Kissinger, run out on a wartime ally. All our other allies—in NATO, in Israel, in Japan, in Iran, South Korea, Formosa, the Philippines, even Australia and New Zealand—were watching to see whether America was indeed a helpless giant.

Was this a provocation premeditated in Moscow? Never mind,

the result of weakness and indecision would be the same. Did the United States of America, torn internally and with a novice, little-known leader, still have any guts? The world was waiting for the answer.

Buchen, Marsh, Rumsfeld and I all marched into the NSC meeting. Nobody invited us, and nobody—including the President—told us to leave.* But we were seized with the transcendant importance of the moment and wanted to share it with our President, to lend him whatever support we could.

President Ford's dilemma was complicated, ironically, because after the Saigon exodus, all U.S. units had been ordered to stay clear of a wide area around Vietnam to avoid provocations.

We may be the mightiest power on earth, but on the day the *Mayaguez* was bushwhacked, the only American military forces within range of the scene were pitifully few: in Thailand, some Air Force police units not combat-equipped, a few jet fighters, some antisubmarine reconnaissance planes; and far away, on Guam, a small armada of B-52 strategic bombers, capable of blasting Cambodia off the map. There was nothing else around on land or sea.

The first and most fundamental decision made by the Commander-in-Chief was that an effort must be made to rescue the *Mayaguez* crew and that the presence of an attack aircraft carrier was essential to cover such a rescue operation if we were to avoid recommitting U.S. forces on the Southeast Asian mainland. A historic principle as well as human lives were at stake. From the War of 1812 onward the United States had asserted freedom of the high seas for the innocent passage of merchant shipping. This doctrine might be the key to the free nations' survival in the future.

The fast carrier USS *Coral Sea,* headed for Australia to take part in a commemoration of the crucial World War II battle for which she was named, was ordered to turn around and race toward the Gulf of Thailand.

But waiting for the *Coral Sea* to arrive on station took precious time; the longer Ford waited before taking some forceful action to free the captive Americans, the worse the chances of their rescue became.

* Some media criticism later surfaced about the presence of "political" counselors. I recall none when Robert Kennedy managed the Cuban missile crisis for his brother. Why not? Von Clausewitz correctly defined war as "not merely a political act, but also a political instrument, a continuation of political relations, a carrying out of the same by other means."

PALACE POLITICS

The first solid reports from circling U.S. spotter planes indicated that the *Mayaguez* was anchored off a small island, Koh Tang, about thirty-four miles from the mainland. The President ordered the planes to keep the ship under day-and-night observation and to prevent any Cambodian boats from moving between her and Kompong Som harbor. But in fact, there was nothing to stop them but aerial gun and rocket fire.

Some of the early rescue scenarios were right out of Rube Goldberg. One was that Air Police from Thailand be landed by helicopters on top of the metal containers on the deck of the *Mayaguez* and then storm the ship. A container expert turned up to explain that they were not strong enough to bear the weight of a loaded chopper. They would crumble like a cardboard box. O.K., said the brass, the helicopters can hover over them and lower combat-equipped assault troops by rope ladder.

"While the Cambodians spray them with Russian burp guns as they climb down?" one of the civilian participants asked sarcastically. The President quickly decided the assault would have to be made from U.S. destroyers with sufficient gunfire to cover a boarding party, and the assault troops would be seasoned U.S. Marines airlifted from Okinawa and the Philippines. But this would take more time.

As the days passed, Ford kept to his regular schedule. He was anxious that Washington not be gripped with a crisis atmosphere, which it dearly loves. Virtually nothing was given out by Nessen to the press. He tried to muzzle the State and Defense departments, too—a virtual impossibility—though Kissinger did better at it than Schlesinger. The Pentagon was eager to portray the military, and the Defense Secretary especially, as advocates of restraint and minimal force while Kissinger was some kind of mad Dr. Strangelove.

In fact, the debates within the National Security Council in the Cabinet Room were never all that polarized.

We were all haunted, of course, by the *Pueblo* affair, when eighty-three Americans were ignominiously imprisoned by North Korea for eleven months in 1968 because there was no swift response by the United States. Ford wasn't sure at the outset what he would do, but he was sure he had to do *something*.

Kissinger's concern—in fact, everybody's—was the same. Henry knew that the whole world was watching, and his ferocity was affected by what he knew our allies and our enemies would conclude from Ford's course of action. I never heard him, as was later alleged, urge that the B-52s from Guam blast Cambodian cities to rubble. He would have used the big bombers if it were either do that or nothing, and he was right. In the end it was the fear of continued precision bombing by the carrier-based jets that caused the Cambodians to free their captives.

There was, by the time all options were explored, substantial unanimity. The President listened, asked probing questions and issued precise instructions without hesitation or room for appeal. He had thoroughly learned the lesson of World War II, forgotten in Vietnam, that it is far better to have too much force than not enough.

Although naval tactics have come a long way since World War II, Ford, the old carrier navigator, was the only one who remembered that after steaming at flank speed several thousand miles, ships must replenish fuel before going into action.

At one point I passed a note to him, saying, "Mr. President, has anyone given you an estimate of minimum and maximum casualties for this operation?"

Nobody had. The uniformed chiefs put their heads together for a few minutes and then responded: twenty minimum; forty maximum. (As it turned out, they came pretty close in their grim guess. Thirty-eight Americans lost their lives, including a whole helicopter load of twenty-three airmen who crashed in Thailand before the shooting started, and three Marines who were missing when the survivors pulled out of Koh Tang Island. Twenty to forty American lives to rescue thirty-nine other Americans. Was it worth it? Or course it was. Protecting unarmed U.S. citizens in their peaceful pursuits is why we have police and military forces. It's what organized society, as opposed to anarchy, is all about.)

The night of May 14, I was waiting in the Oval Office, along with Kissinger, Marsh, Rumsfeld, Scowcroft, Friedersdorf and Nessen, when the President returned in his tuxedo from a dinner for the Netherlands Prime Minister. Less than two hundred Marines were heavily engaged on Koh Tang by an unexpectedly strong and effective Cambodian garrison. The *Mayaguez* had been boarded without resistance and found to be deserted. Two nights before, a pilot flying low over a boat headed for the mainland thought he saw "Caucasian faces" on the deck. Ford gave him radioed orders not to strafe or sink it, but it was a long chance.

The whereabouts of the American captives was now completely unknown. They could be on the island or in Kompong Som, or anywhere in Cambodia, or dead. Covering strikes from the *Coral Sea* on selected targets around the harbor had been launched. A local Phnom Penh radio broadcast was intercepted and translated, indicating the Cambodians might release the ship. But nothing about the *Mayaguez* crew was revealed except that some of them might have been killed by American bombs.

While we were talking gloomily about the unfolding violence in the Gulf of Thailand, the "hot line" on the President's desk buzzed like a doomsday alarm.

The President answered and listened intently. Then he let out an old-fashioned Indian war whoop.

"Thank God! We got 'em all! They're all safe!"

Rumsfeld prudently insisted on calling Schlesinger back to make doubly sure every last man of the *Mayaguez* crew had been accounted for. He also tried to get firm casualty figures, but the operation was still going on and the Pentagon stalled.

Next, Nessen learned that Schlesinger's press spokesman, Joseph Laitin, had scooped him by announcing the rescue to Defense Department reporters. This was contrary to Ford's explicit orders that all developments, good or bad, would be announced at the White House.

While Nessen summoned the White House media (it was now midnight) the President returned to the Residence to change into business clothes. Then he walked over to the press room and announced the rescue, in five sentences, concluding with "My deep appreciation and that of the entire nation to the men who participated in these operations for their valor and for their sacrifice."

He was weary, and the strain of four long days and short nights was beginning to show. He was thinking of the sacrifice still going on. Over the years he had exhorted other Presidents to take firm and decisive action against such provocations. Now he knew the awful burden of having sent young Americans to their deaths. It is a special, unquenchable agony that goes with the glory and high office of the Presidency.

I walked with him through the portico by the Rose Garden and over to the elevator of the Residence. I sensed his need for companionship, not conversation. Sometimes I am capable of silence.

If Jerry Ford has one ability above all others, it is turning his conscious mind off one subject and immediately onto another. The crisis over and the *Mayaguez* crew safe, the President turned to his Army aide, Major Bob Barrett, following close behind with his battered briefcase.

"Say, Bob, how did Baltimore do tonight?" he inquired. Ford, for the first time since the pardon, was perceived as the kind of President the people want. *Mayaguez* wasn't the only reason; there was his careful evacuation of Saigon, his candid admission that the war was finished, along with other developments in his duel with Congress. The Gallup Poll put him over the 50 percent approval line in June, and the media pundits as if by signal all took new note of Ford's prescience.

But there was no diminution of their fascination with the question of where Henry Kissinger stood in the President's graces, a question that was eternally dangled before them by Kissinger's own paranoia.

On the overseas trips Ford undertook in 1974, to Mexico, Japan, South Korea, Vladivostok and to meet French President Giscard on the Caribbean island of Martinique, the Secretary of State thoroughly dominated and monopolized the President, sharing the news spotlight and sometimes shouldering him offside.

Except for the SALT talks in the Soviet Union, these trips were largely ceremonial. Nobody was quite so bilious as to think Henry should be anywhere but at Ford's right hand during his first meeting with Leonid Brezhnev.

It is a tragedy, really, that the ex-Harvard professor never considered taking the time to enroll and enrapture Ford's other principal aides, as he had so many students. We did not like him publicly putting the President of the United States in a pupil's role. Perhaps he didn't really mean to, and Ford may be faulted for permitting it. But most of us would have gladly gathered at Kissinger's feet to better understand his grand design.

Henry never disguised his contempt for "politicians"—particularly those who had not been elected, from whom he required Constitutional sanction for his schemes. In his own vision of a new world order, President Nixon and certainly President Ford were only incidental. It was a brilliant though not necessarily Divine revelation. I'm still sorry he proved incapable of assuming human form to make disciples out of doubters.

Jayne Brumley Ikard put her finger on it in the Jacksonville (Florida) *Times Union:*

> The Secretary of State, who has had it all his way through two Presidents, is more and more enchanting people in Washington less and less.
>
> Kissinger's own personal hangups are endless. When

things go wrong, they don't just go wrong. As far as Henry is concerned, they go *personally* wrong.

While Henry Kissinger may well be a genius in foreign policy and diplomacy, he is a high school dropout on domestic policy and the mood of the American public.

14

FUN WITH RON AND HENRY

★★————————————★★

In February 1975 Dom Bonafede of *National Journal Reports*—one of the ablest reporters in Washington—interviewed me for an early political prognosis. I told him:

"The American people are not going to hold [Ford] accountable for the mess, but they are going to hold him accountable as to how far he can get them out of the mess. It all depends on how well he assumes the role of leader in the face of economic developments.

"It's not what he does to turn the graphs up or change the figures, but what he does to the hearts and minds of the people. When you say our unemployment rate of 8.2 percent is the worst since 1940, people forget that was after eight years of FDR. What cured the Depression was not governmental action but the war. Obviously we don't want that solution.

"But what FDR did was to boost the nation's morale and promote confidence—that's what President Ford must do now. He believes the best politics is to do a good job as President rather than spend time thinking about his election."

A sticky political point came up in February when Ford flew to Houston and agreed with Senator John Tower to meet privately with Texas Republican leaders. The state party chairman submitted a list of those to be invited, and of course John Connally was among them. Connally was then under Federal indictment for his alleged part in the "milk fund" scandal of the Nixon years. Most of the President's advisers urged him not to meet with the former Texas Governor and Nixon's Treasury Secretary.

There was no way to cross his name off the list and no way such a put-down could be kept secret. A Presidential snub, I argued, would in itself be making a premature and improper judgment that Connally was guilty. It could even affect a jury. Ford, who admired Big John, agreed and overruled the others. They promptly leaked the story of the

Oval Office debate and blamed Hartmann for steering Ford into "another bonehead blunder."

Governor Connally was in Canada but jetted home for the meeting. He got there just as it was breaking up but stayed and chatted with the President for forty-five minutes—with Cheney sitting in. When Connally was acquitted, everybody agreed that Ford had made a courageous and correct decision. Nobody could be found who had ever been against it. The Governor campaigned for Ford valiantly in 1976.

Soon after becoming President, Ford authorized Jerry terHorst to say that he "probably" would be a candidate in 1976. He confirmed this at his first news conference August 28, but the same question kept popping up as reporters tried to substitute "definitely" for "probably."

This was essentially a silly exercise, and Washington newsmen ought to have known better. Nobody really believed for a minute that Ford would not run. They all knew, if the public did not, that under the new Federal campaign reform law a formal declaration of candidacy subjected a candidate to numerous restrictions and stringent financial limitations. None of the other Presidential hopefuls in either party was harassed the way the incumbent was.

On March 24 I took the President a succinct three-page memo from Jack Calkins urging that he promptly authorize a campaign finance operation outside the White House, name an American of stature to head a President Ford Committee and personally clarify a single direct link between the White House and the Ford campaign organization.

Calkins was not the only one urging the President to get off to an early start, since others were gearing up,* but for some reason he kept procrastinating.

After a full month elapsed without Ford doing anything about our urgent memo, or other proddings, I told Jack that if the President took our advice and asked what was the next step, we'd better be prepared. I suggested that he and Gwen gather together a small group of their campaign-experienced friends and brainstorm a specific list of "things-to-do-today" in setting up a Ford organization.

Working all weekend, they came up with twenty-six pages of practical, step-by-step recommendations for launching a pre-primary

---

* That same evening the President met with his transition team—by now transformed into a "Kitchen Cabinet." Byrnes, Harlow, Laird and Scranton bore down hard on Ford's urgent need to "leave no doubt as to who's head of the Republican Party" and warned him the Reagan threat was real.

drive to clinch the Presidential nomination long before the convention. The effect of the new law limiting campaign spending to $10 million before and $20 million after the convention was brilliantly analyzed. The bottom line was that "the 1976 Presidential campaign will require the most *careful* expenditure of monies in history. Regardless of the timing of the President's formal announcement, it is imperative that preparations start as soon as possible."

When I laid this document on Ford's desk Monday morning, April 28, however, the current issue of *Newsweek* was already there. It created a one-day sensation by reporting the President had made a secret, "irrevocable" decision not to run at all.

The Calkins–Anderson blueprint for 1976, had it been followed, might have changed history. But what shook the President out of his political paralysis was this mysterious magazine piece.

Tom DeFrank, *Newsweek*'s White House man, had phoned Ron Nessen just before the story went to press and asked for comment. The report was attributed only to "a well-connected source" who admittedly got it secondhand from one of "a small handful of Ford confidants." Allegedly, the President met with them within the past fortnight, swore them to secrecy and confided that he would not be a candidate for a full term.

What made *Newsweek*'s report ridiculous on its face was that it went further. The President was supposed to have revealed his intention of going through the motions of setting up a campaign committee and entering the New Hampshire primary, but vowed he eventually— like LBJ—would withdraw from the race. Even if Jerry Ford were Niccolo Machiavelli and plotted such a shameful masquerade, he would not have needlessly enlisted a half dozen "confidants" to share his secret.

Everybody, including the President, denounced the rumor with varying degrees of vehemence. Cheney called it "absolute bullshit." I suggested to DeFrank that *Newsweek* was being gulled by somebody, perhaps in the Reagan camp, who was out to do Ford in. Others accused various members of the Kitchen Cabinet of trying to pressure Ford into action. But *Newsweek* insisted its source was unimpeachable, and it probably was. Ford had secretly promised Nixon not to be a candidate, and the Praetorians would never forgive him for changing his mind.

Bill Baroody was organizing "White House Conferences" in various parts of the country, a series of "town meetings" with regional television and news coverage. He'd pack about 1,000 citizens into a hall, representing a cross section of local interests, and let them fire questions at the President and members of the Cabinet.

I arranged for Dick Wirthlin's pollsters to go into Houston, Texas; Topeka, Kansas; South Bend, Indiana; and South Florida a few days before these events. Then they'd ask the same questions immediately afterward. The results showed that Ford was most effective in such personal face-to-face encounters with people—far better at selling his policies than he was in nationally televised speeches.

We also got some free opinion polls. They were worth all they cost. Midway in 1975, a year before the 1976 conventions, Louis Harris found Ford leading Reagan 40 percent to 17 percent among Republicans and independents; Democrats and independents favored Kennedy (31 percent) and Wallace (15 percent), with ex-Governor Jimmy Carter ranking twentieth with less than ½ of 1 percent.

It wasn't until June 20 that the President authorized the legal creation of a "President Ford Committee," with Dean Burch (who had gone back to practicing law) as its temporary head. Don Rumsfeld's hand-picked candidate, Army Secretary Howard (Bo) Callaway, soon was approved by Ford as chairman and given the kamikaze mission of holding his native Georgia and the rest of Dixie in the Ford fold for a reprise of Nixon's 1972 "Southern strategy."

Whoever concocted this strategy was either (1) dumb or (2) disloyal to Ford. Reagan was the obvious favorite of the Sun Belt, as far as the Republican nomination was concerned. There was no way the President could get around to the right of him—and trying to just made Ford look silly. As soon as Jimmy Carter was chosen by the Democrats the South was lost for *any* Republican. By then the President had jettisoned much of the strength he could have had in the North.

Ronald Reagan was the subject of a lot of wisecracks around the White House in mid-1975, though Ford usually spoke of him respectfully in public. But neither the President nor most of his advisers took Reagan seriously enough soon enough. Though some of us (Parma, Packard, Harlow, Marsh and me) were more vocal about the "Reagan problem" than others, we didn't push hard enough—and there was a personal chemistry between Ford and Reagan that complicated everything.

It was very much Ford's style to take a political rival off into a corner and make a man-to-man appeal for his counsel and cooperation. As President, the worst prima donnas found him hard to refuse. He perceived no ego threat from a Rockefeller, a Connally, a Kennedy or even a Kissinger.

Why would he never butter up Reagan, even a little bit? I had sat in on a number of their meetings over the years—while Ford was Minority Leader, Vice President and President. In these encounters both men were usually uptight, unnatural, pathetically polite and acutely on guard. Betty Ford and Nancy Reagan hit it off even worse.

As early as August 24, 1974, a curious comedy of errors occurred in Washington. Reagan, still Governor of California, had come to a meeting with some conservative crusaders in nearby Maryland but stayed a country mile away from the new President's much-touted "open door" at the White House.

Ford felt that Reagan, who'd always found time to call on President Nixon, was showing discourtesy. Reagan, I'm told, was equally miffed that the President didn't invite him over. You don't just barge in on a President as you would a Congressman. Nixon's staff would have set it up before he ever left Sacramento.

Of course, Ford put Reagan on his public list of five "finalists" for the Vice Presidential nod. It's interesting to speculate what a different course we might have taken if Ford had moved to embrace the Republican right by an appropriate Reagan appointment at the same time he announced Rockefeller's.*

At one point I suggested that the President might want to name Reagan to head a new Hoover-type commission to slenderize the bloated Federal bureaucracy, since he prided himself—deservedly or not—as an authority in that area. Ford also had toyed with the thought of offering Reagan a prestigious ambassadorship, such as London.** Instead, the President subordinated him to Rockefeller on the CIA Investigating Commission. Reagan did his duty like a draftee, but it must have grated.

Would Reagan have taken a Ford Cabinet post? At the outset I

* For hindsight, how about Reagan for Defense, Rockefeller for State and George Bush for Vice President? This combination could have made Ford unbeatable.
** I learned Reagan was going to London to address the Pilgrim Society, one of Ike's launching pads. The President sent word to Ambassador Elliot Richardson to extend him every courtesy, which he probably would have done anyhow. I made sure the Reagan people knew, however. They said "Thanks."

suspect he would have accepted Defense, where Ford wanted to replace Schlesinger. Reagan would have sold the Defense budget to Congress with a whole new Panama Canal thrown in. Ford did sound Reagan out about the possibility of being Secretary of Commerce, but instead of asking him personally, the President had Rumsfeld—whom Reagan hardly knew—call him on the phone. If Ford had only picked up the telephone himself and said, "Ron, I need your help—"

But he didn't. The fact of the matter is that they just don't like each other.

Ford thought Reagan was a phony, and Reagan thought Ford was a lightweight, and neither one felt the other was fit to be President. If Ford and the Twenty-fifth Amendment hadn't intervened, Reagan had reason to believe he could have beaten Connally and all other comers for the 1976 GOP nomination. Within hours after Nixon's resignation, Reagan's political operators were phoning Congressional conservatives with sneering asides on Ford's ability and acumen. When the President named Rocky and proposed amnesty for the same kids who razed California campuses, the Reaganite whispering campaign became a shout.

Reagan is a virtuoso of the political double-entendre, and you never really caught him taking a personal swipe at the President until a good deal later. But Jerry Ford could read his radar, and he didn't like it.

He didn't like the fact that Reagan never seemed to be able to get to the airport to greet the Vice President or the President of the United States when either arrived in California. He also didn't like the fact that Reagan for years charged five thousand dollars to speak at Republican fund-raisers. Ford had been knocking himself out all over the country for years doing it for nothing. Knowing he wasn't in Reagan's league as an orator or drawing card didn't soften his distaste. Ford usually wasn't one to harbor mean feelings, but Reagan brought out the worst in him.

Nowadays it's fashionable among Monday-morning quarterbacks in Republican circles to say, "If Ford had only taken Reagan as his running mate, we wouldn't be stuck with Carter." And in Reagan circles they swear Ronnie would have accepted, despite his protests. No way, I say. They just weren't made for each other.

Normally, an incumbent President dictates where his party's convention will be. But Ford wanted to let the site committee of the Republican National Committee survey the possibilities and make its recommendations before he showed his hand.

Basically, what we were up against was a very clever Reagan ploy to get the convention for Los Angeles, in Reagan's own heartland. The President didn't want to oppose this openly but authorized me to pass the word to Mary Louise Smith, the National Chairman, that we would prefer someplace other than California or New York.

Most of the Nixon Praetorians wanted to go back to Miami Beach, scene of their triumphs in 1968 and 1972, and it was also the favorite of two of the committee veterans. Kansas City claimed two first choices, including Mrs. Smith's. But it was almost everyone's second choice.

The President was leaning strongly to a Midwest location, either Kansas City or Cleveland. San Francisco and New Orleans were, surprisingly, last among the contending cities, proving conclusively that politicians are not gourmets.

It seemed to be all cut and dried when Dick Herman, a Rumsfeld ally who had stage-managed Nixon's 1972 production in Miami Beach, launched a final effort to torpedo Kansas City and Cleveland. He scared Mary Louise into acute twitters and ran to Rumsfeld, who, after keeping it a week, noncommitally passed Herman's appeal along to me. By this time the President was traveling and the deadline for decision was three weeks away. Calkins* was with Ford, so I fired off a powerful plea for Kansas City for Jack to hand the President personally. Miami Beach, I warned, was crawling with Watergate ghosts, too luxurious, run by Democrats and now Wallace and Reagan country. Kansas City was midway between Ike's Abilene and Truman's Independence, in Ford's natural habitat and constituency, surrounded by attractive GOP Governors in Missouri, Kansas and Iowa. Ford agreed, and nobody afterward regretted the choice.

One of the hottest convention battles that would develop there was over Reagan's demagogic charges that Ford and Kissinger had been "soft" toward the Soviet Union.

Kissinger gets a bum rap, I think, for urging the President not to meet with Aleksandr I. Solzhenitsyn in July 1975. Maybe I say that because I did too. But Ford himself didn't cotton to the idea from the start.

Kissinger and Scowcroft, it is true, cautioned that the Soviets would not take kindly to such a gesture toward their most celebrated

---

* Calkins and Anderson justified their political liaison jobs by arranging for President Ford's participation in Republican fund-raisers in twenty-five states during the warm-up year of 1975, bringing in more than $6 million and all but erasing the party debt.

dissident. Solzhenitsyn was a deadly foe of détente, which might affect the SALT II agreement begun in Vladivostok. That warning was their duty, though I doubt that Brezhnev & Company assigned that much throw-weight to exiled literati in their strategic plans.

What happened was that the President, for good and sufficient reasons unrelated to the Russians, declined an invitation from George Meany to an AFL-CIO dinner honoring Solzhenitsyn in Washington on June 30. The press seized upon this as a "snub."

Ford, who had no such intention, was next presented with what amounted to an ultimatum by Senators Jesse Helms (R–North Carolina) and Strom Thurmond (R–South Carolina). The two ultraconservatives asked to bring Solzhenitsyn to the Oval Office, but, they said, it had to be done on or before Friday, July 4; the exiled author was leaving Washington the next day.

Marsh, Rumsfeld, Friedersdorf, Nessen, Scowcroft and I discussed the request with the President on July 2. Kissinger was out of town, but Ford was aware of his feelings. About a month earlier, our former colleague Dick Burress telephoned me from Stanford, where he'd returned to his post at the Hoover Institution. Solzhenitsyn had been named an Honorary Fellow by Hoover, which has the world's foremost archives on the Russian Revolution. Dick told me the renowned Russian would be coming to Washington and wondered if the President could grant him a few minutes of his time. I relayed this to Ford, whose attitude was "Sure, why not?" But I heard nothing more of it and assumed Kissinger had vetoed it in view of the President's plans to meet again with Brezhnev at the end of July.

The message that Marsh brought from Senator Helms came on very short notice. We were going to be gone all the next day to Cincinnati and Cleveland, and Friday was the Fourth of July, start of a much needed three-day holiday. It smelled to me very much like someone was trying to force Ford either into boosting Helms' stock with the far right or, by refusing, giving the rightists and their hero, Governor Reagan, something else to gripe about.

Curiously, no direct request from Solzhenitsyn for an appointment with the President was ever received, then or thereafter. I felt that both men were being used.

"Why does he have to leave Saturday?" I asked. "It seems to me that if somebody is given an appointment with the President of the United States, he gets his ass on an airplane and comes wherever and whenever the President is able to see him."

The pros and cons of the politics involved, domestic and international, went round and round. The President pretty much settled it by wondering if perhaps Solzhenitsyn's primary purpose wasn't to sell some more books. After he got back from his European trip, he said, maybe there would be time on his schedule.

Most people now, including Ford, think this was a major political mistake. Reagan certainly made the most of it. I'm not so sure—I'm as stubborn as Jerry Ford sometimes. I think Solzhenitsyn sees himself as a Biblical prophet crying in the wilderness; surely he has the credentials for a modern martyr. He doesn't like the Soviet system but, aside from the asylum and affluence it offers him, he doesn't think much of ours, either.

There are only two ways to handle tormented prophets, endure them or cut off their heads. We settled this question two hundred years ago in this country, but there's nothing in the Constitution that says a President is obliged to kiss their aspirations.

The Solzhenitsyn affair was no great big deal at the time, the New York *Times* judging it worthy of page 5. But interest was compounded a few weeks later when the President took off for the Conference on Cooperation and Security in Europe, in Helsinki, Finland. This was seen by some American ethnic groups and anti-Communists as a betrayal of the captive nations of Eastern Europe.

In this episode Henry Kissinger's excessive secretiveness, combined with Ford's concurrence in it, must be severely faulted for painting the President into a corner. Not only was the political fallout damaging at the time, but Helsinki became a code word for the right wing. It set the stage for gross distortion of President Ford's rhetorical liberation of Eastern Europe in the second campaign debate.

Ford's ten-day tour was to take him first to Bonn to meet with Chancellor Helmut Schmidt and review NATO troops in West Germany, next to Warsaw and Cracow, Poland, and then to Helsinki, Finland. During the European Security Conference, Ford would meet privately with Brezhnev, the Greek and Turkish Premiers and other NATO leaders. Afterward he would visit Rumania and Yugoslavia—the two most autonomous Iron Curtain countries.

It seemed like a balanced itinerary, but the flak soon began, encapsulated in a leading *Wall Street Journal* editorial titled: "Jerry, Don't Go." The White House was deluged with mail, ten to one opposing the trip. Americans of Estonian, Latvian and Lithuanian descent, whose cause Ford had championed for decades, denounced his decision. Ronald Reagan on the one hand, and Mr. Solzhenitsyn on the other, charged into the fray. The Russian snarled that President

PALACE POLITICS

Ford "will shortly be leaving for Europe to sign the betrayal of Eastern Europe, to acknowledge officially its slavery forever." The Californian, with commendable simplicity, said, "I'm against it."

If Kissinger had briefed the other senior people in the White House as to what Helsinki was all about, we might have been able to build some backfires before the blaze of criticism was roaring out of control. The reasons for Ford's going, quite apart from the opportunity to iron out some SALT difficulties with Brezhnev, were valid. The Presidents or Prime Ministers of thirty-four nations—all of Europe (save Albania) plus Canada—would be on hand for the biggest "summit" since the Congress of Vienna. Should Ford abandon the news spotlight to Brezhnev and abdicate America's rightful place as the champion of the West?

Symbolically, Helsinki had to be weighed for the Moscow triumph it would have been if President Ford had *not* gone. And the declaration signed there was by no means all bad. It was the product of three years of hard negotiations. The free European nations and our NATO allies had wrung unprecedented human-rights concessions (on paper) from the Soviets. After two decades of U.S. preoccupation with the Far East, they wanted assurance that we had not forgotten Europe, our first love.

But the White House was put on the defensive by Kissinger's lack of early warning, and the defense the Administration made was pretty feeble. The State Department line was that the East–West boundary provisions weren't really legally binding, anyway, ignoring the fact that the most critical of these had been settled since 1970 by the German treaties.

The anti-Kissinger cabal renewed efforts to clip his wings. Somehow they imagined it was flattering to Ford to spread the word that Henry led him to Helsinki by the nose. Or that this would at least make Ford mad enough to deprive Kissinger of his White House hat. They misjudged their man. The President decided to go. I never detected any sign of his having second thoughts.

I felt the best contribution I could make was to ensure that the President's major address in Helsinki was of such caliber and clarity that it would be hailed at home as well as in Finland. Milt Friedman was at work on the preliminary draft, but Kissinger and the NSC people were exasperatingly evasive about rendering substantive help.

A brief digression may serve to shed more light on Kissinger's penchant for secrecy—as well as his resolve always to be front and center. Rummy and Nessen had tangled repeatedly with Kissinger about his fetish of withholding vital information from everyone except Ford himself. During their daily briefings Ford made important decisions, but by the time the President got around to mentioning them to one of us, they often became an embarrassment or worse, reflecting on the whole White House operation.

Returning from California back in April, Kissinger had confronted the press secretary, who was abundantly guilty, about a speculative CBS report that Ford, drawing on a broader spectrum of foreign-policy advisers, sometimes overruled the Secretary of State. To appease him, Nessen summarily fired one of his assistants, Louis M. Thompson, Jr., as the culprit. It was quickly determined by White House reporters that Thompson was an innocent sacrifice and Nessen's credibility, never very high, plummeted as low as it could.

Nessen and Rumsfeld got their revenge when we went to the NATO summit in Brussels at the end of May. Kissinger had gone on ahead to an energy meeting in Paris. Over the Atlantic, Rummy strolled back to the press section of Air Force One to chat with reporters. He was returning to the Belgian capital where he had served as U.S. Ambassador to NATO. It would do no harm to remind them that he was quite as well informed on this subject as the absent Secretary of State.

His comments would be "for background," Rumsfeld said, but he could be identified as "a senior American official" traveling with the President. I will let Aldo Beckman of the Chicago *Tribune* tell the rest:

> It all started the day before Ford left for Brussels when "senior White House officials" leaked a story to the *New York Times*—the U.S. newspaper most widely read by NATO officials—that Kissinger's role in planning American foreign policy was diminishing.
>
> The plan was that this would subsequently be proven because Kissinger would be forced to maintain a low profile during the trip.
>
> To add spice to their already simmering relationship, Rumsfeld grabbed Kissinger's coveted role as a "senior American official" during the flight on Air Force One.
>
> Every head of government in the world had known from the beginning that the "senior American official" who is often quoted as he shuttles around the world is, in fact, Kissinger himself, talking "background."

341

PALACE POLITICS

But the egotistical Kissinger has become possessive of the title and enjoys wisecracking about the escapades. So when Rumsfeld insisted on being referred to as "a senior American official," Kissinger predictably was angered and became more determined than ever to exert himself publicly during the NATO sessions.

Predictably, Henry threw another series of tantrums, but Rumsfeld's complicity was so open this time I was spared my share of his generous abuse. In fact, flying home,* he leaned over to me and confided: "I want to apologize for suspecting you of shafting me, because now it is perfectly clear who has been doing it. But we have ways of dealing with these clowns."

It sounded pretty scary, but I knew who was really scared. I felt a little sorry for Henry—and that is always a grave mistake.

But to return to the Helsinki matter: The day before the President was to leave, a score of leaders of U.S. organizations representing Eastern European communities were hastily invited to the Cabinet Room. Ford spoke feelingly and frankly about his reasons for undertaking the journey. We had worked hard on his remarks, and Scowcroft had approved them. Apparently Henry had not, and it was too late to do anything about it.

Kissinger flailed the mild-mannered general unmercifully in the anteroom of the Oval Office, in front of a handful of startled aides.

"You will pay for this! I tell you, heads will roll!" he raged and stalked out. Ford had planned to make the same points in his departure talk at Andrews Air Force Base. Kissinger, fearing it would offend Moscow, persuaded him to drop the key sentence "The United States has never recognized the Soviet incorporation of Lithuania, Latvia, and Estonia and is not going to do so in Helsinki."

Nessen had already distributed the full text to the media. The President's conspicuous omission made it look as if he was being muzzled by his Secretary of State and bent on appeasing Brezhnev.

Not until we got to the Finnish capital did Milt and I get a good

* In the lounge section of Air Force One there are two huge reclining chairs and a number of sofa-type seats. When the Secretary of State was not aboard, which was most of the time, I always had the big chair on the outboard side to take photographs out the window. It was really the President's and when he came in to chat with his guests, I popped out of it and sat on the floor. The first few overseas flights Kissinger claimed it according to protocol. Eventually he ceded it to me and took the inboard throne. Didn't I say Henry was capable of great courtesy and consideration?

342

FUN WITH RON AND HENRY

look at what Kissinger wanted Ford to say. Henry was always suspicious of Friedman, possibly because of Milt's previous association
with Jewish organizations. His own stable of writers tended to be Ivy
League WASPs whose six-bit vocabularies drove the President right up
the wall.

Because the thirty-five heads of governments spoke in alphabeti-
cal order and the protocol was in English, U.S.A. came during the last
of four plenary sessions, while the Soviets, C.C.C.P., were among the
first. Ford insisted on being in his front-row seat in Finlandia Hall for
the entire conference. It pleased the spokesmen of the smaller countries to see the American section filled. My seat was just behind the
President's, and toward the end of the first six speeches I began to get
nervous about the President's address.

When the conference wasn't in session, Ford had a nonstop round
of meetings, not to mention official receptions put on by the hospitable
Finnish hosts. I'd tried some translating and editing of Kissinger's
proposed speech, but it wasn't much improved. I couldn't get a minute
in edgewise to talk with the President about *his* ideas.

I passed a note over the President's shoulder.

"When can I talk with you briefly, but privately, about Henry's
latest draft of your speech?"

All the time listening intently through his simultaneous-interpre-
tation earphones, the President scrawled this on a sheet of scratch
paper: "The first six speeches were all high-level and good quality. We
are up against *tough* competition. It requires we do our very best. You
and Milt Friedman must consecrate [he meant "concentrate," of
course] so that ours is ready as soon as possible. Ask me when meeting
ends today. State and NSC substance but *my words.*"

Rumsfeld had prudently taken himself off this trip. It was a test of
Dick Cheney's ability to manage one of these moving medicine shows,
but it also left me the most visible target for Kissinger, who had to be
fed at least one dragon per journey. Cheney worked Milt and me into
an hour with the President at the American Embassy, while he was
supposed to be dressing for President Kekkonen's dinner.

It was obvious he was thinking how his words would sound at
home, as well as to the delegates. He didn't like Henry's diplomatic
gobbledygook any better than we did, except for an exceptionally fe-
licitous final sentence: "History will judge this conference not by what
we say today, but what we do tomorrow; not by the promises we make
but by the promises we keep."

We toiled most of the night and the next two days to fashion the

343

kind of speech Ford wanted. After paying compliments to Finland and its freedom-loving people, the President proposed to start off by reaffirming the interdependence of Europe and North America and the effect of that relationship on peace in the postwar world.

Next he wanted to answer bluntly the question of why he came, "as a spokesman for a nation whose vision had always been forward, whose people have always demanded that the future be brighter than the past.

"I am here simply to say to my colleagues: We owe it to our children, to the children of all continents, not to miss any opportunity, not to malinger for one minute, not to spare ourselves or allow others to shirk in the monumental task of building a better and safer world."

And finally he wanted to deliver a lesson from the two-hundred-year-old history of the United States. The representatives of the Colonies had met in 1776 full of noble ideals and brave hopes to assert their independence. Cynics and doubters scoffed. But eleven years later those principles were embodied in the Constitution, enforceable as legal rights by all Americans, rights which still give hope to millions around the world.

To this speech, more than any other of his Presidency, Jerry Ford himself contributed some of the most trenchant phrases:

"Peace is not a piece of paper."

"There is not a single people represented here whose blood does not flow in the veins of Americans and whose culture and traditions have not enriched the heritage which we Americans prize so highly."

"The people of all Europe—and I assure you the people of North America—are thoroughly tired of having their hopes raised and then shattered by empty promises. We had better say what we mean and mean what we say, or we will have the anger of our citizens to answer."

Ford's address was a bell-ringer, delivered with impressive assurance. In my memory book this was one of his finest hours. He looked Brezhnev right in the eye and told him "the United States considers that the principles on which this conference has agreed are a part of the great heritage of European civilization, which we hold in trust for all mankind. To my country, they are not clichés or empty phrases. We take this work and these words very seriously. It is important that you recognize the deep devotion of the American people and their government to human rights and fundamental freedoms."

When the American President concluded, he got the only really enthusiastic standing ovation of the conference. Kissinger joined in it and even congratulated me.

344

"Your words were better," he said and smiled.

The Secretary of State's euphoria was short-lived, however. Ford's Helsinki declaration didn't get the attention it should have back home. The timing was bad for U.S. television. Editorial writers from the *Wall Street Journal* to the Los Angeles *Times* proclaimed it "one of the best speeches of [Ford's] tenure," but UPI—with a much wider circulation—had a piece by their number-two White House reporter, Dick Growald, entitled: "Backstairs Battle Over Kissinger."

It stated that "some Presidential senior advisers" were critical of Kissinger's presence on the ten-day tour, worrying about his involvement in Watergate, charging he gave bad advice to Ford on Solzhenitsyn and tried to persuade the President to cancel a pilgrimage to Auschwitz,* the Nazi death camp in Poland. Growald's piece concluded:

"The White House critics argue that Kissinger is a poor team player. They say he shuns the chummy togetherness in which such Ford lieutenants as Chief of Staff Donald Rumsfeld and Counsellor Robert Hartmann exchange memos in staff work, despite any personal differences."

As soon as we returned to Washington, Henry angrily told the President he was sure Milt Friedman was the culprit of this latest outrage. Ford, uncomfortable and not too certain where the blame lay, told me to find out if Milt did it.

I asked Milt, and naturally he denied all. I believed him, but how do you prove what you didn't say?

In any case, the President's leadership at Helsinki had not come across at home. Ronald Reagan ignored his noble words, which he might himself have been proud to use in his lucrative column. He continued to lambaste the head of his own party for softness toward Moscow. Ford decided to give the Helsinki speech over again, but accented for Americans, and the earliest and best forum would be the annual convention of the American Legion in Minneapolis on August 19.

This time, with Milt's fate still in limbo, I undertook to do the Legion draft myself. But I wanted Friedman to help, lest word got around that he was being shunned. I solicited input from Jim Schlesinger, Henry Kissinger, Bryce Harlow and Mel Laird, who had gone

---

* This charge was false. Kissinger's counsel on the Auschwitz visit was wise. I find it impossible to describe the impression this place makes on seeing it for the first time. A strange mixture of shame and pride—shame for belonging to the species that conceived it, pride for having been part of the generation that annihilated its architects. "Never again!" really says it all.

through his own purgatory with the paranoic Secretary of State.

Mel advised that the President should clearly define what "détente" meant to him and to most Americans, as well as what it did not mean.

"Détente," Mel said, "is something carried on between adversaries, to relax tensions that develop with those who are not our friends. It is a process of exploration of ways to reduce or ease political and military confrontations. It rests, therefore, upon maintenance of an equilibrium of force, or balance of power, without which changes might be brought about that would be destructive to us.

"Thus, as we pursue détente, we must maintain our strategic defenses," Laird argued. "We are prepared to reduce strategic arms, but a worldwide balance must be maintained so there will be no temptation for an adversary to take advantage of our inferiority."

Preparation of this important post-Helsinki pronouncement was complicated by the fact that the Fords had gone off to Vail, Colorado, for their August vacation. Cheney was with them, and I sent Theis along.

Kissinger was in a frightful tizzy that I would totally repudiate his accomplishments in Europe. He came storming into my office on August 12 as Milt and I were working.

Sitting down without being asked, Henry shouted, "I am putting you two guys on notice, if there are any further leaks on the process of speeches, blood will be in the streets."

After having witnessed the first half dozen of these histrionics, they had begun to wear a little thin.

"Oh, stop the shit," I said. "Spend a little time over in your own State Department and you'll find your leakers. Now, for the past couple of days we've been trying to get some help from your people on this American Legion speech. We're busy trying to write something and getting no cooperation whatsoever from you or from them. Yeah, I know, when it's done you'll go running to the President and say you weren't consulted. Well, I'm consulting you now, and I have a witness."

Henry still wanted to rave about the UPI leak in Helsinki. He again accused Friedman of inspiring it and a later variation by André Marton of AP.

"Mr. Secretary," I said as calmly as I could, "do you ever read the New Republic?" I handed him the current week's copy.

Thank heaven for John Osborne. He owed us nothing, but he told it like it happened. In a round-up on Helsinki, Osborne related that Helmut Sonnenfeldt, the State Department counsellor, had called in reporters at Helsinki for a "background" session in which he related all the wicked things the White House bullies were saying about his boss.

I sent a copy of Osborne's exoneration of Milt by courier to Vail for the President, along with this sealed personal note: "I must say, Mr. President, that Milt was as hurt by my questioning as I was by yours. I think our loyalty to your interests both antedate and presently surpass Dr. Kissinger's. His paranoia is so advanced that he must have somebody persecuting or trying to 'get' him. First it was Nessen. Then, on the NATO trip, it was Rummy. Last time it was me. I just shrug off his temper tantrums and hope he feels better afterwards and succeeds in getting peace in the Middle East pretty soon."

The President never again brought the subject up. His Legion speech in Minneapolis was a great success, dampened only by the fact that Kissinger had already said substantially the same thing in Birmingham a few days earlier.

And darned if Henry didn't go ahead and get a cease-fire in the Middle East. Three guesses who got the credit for it. If Ford or Nixon had been hereditary monarchs Henry would have been a perfect Foreign Minister. But Ford had the minor problem of getting elected in 1976, and Kissinger never understood. People who employ geniuses, as Michelangelo taught several Popes, have to pay a price.

We didn't spend all our waking hours warring over politics and palace power. There were some laughs, even on serious questions.

Bryce Harlow opened the first transition alumni meeting after Rumsfeld's anointing by saying, "I am told by Don that we are free to accuse anybody, except you, Mr. President, of being a jackass."

"I don't know why I'm being excluded," Ford replied.

We held a long, solemn Cabinet session with the President over the burning question of whether Federal restrictions should be lifted on the use of poison bait to kill coyotes. Packs of coyotes were ravaging herds of Western sheep during the fall lambing season. Eastern environmentalists wept not for the slain lambs but for the noble wolf-dog so dastardly destroyed. After enduring an hour of technicalities, the President rose as if he were Speaker, rapped the table and announced, "On this question, the lambs are eleven votes, coyotes zero. The lambs have it."

PALACE POLITICS

Rockefeller's experience with the Praetorians by no means ended with his defeat in the Domestic Council power struggle. The third phase of their plan was to eliminate the real object of their disaffection, the Vice President himself. The chosen instrument in this epic was Rummy's (and Ford's) former House colleague, Howard "Bo" Callaway, who resigned as Secretary of the Army on July 3, 1975, to become the first chairman of the President Ford Committee and to launch Ford's election campaign.

Callaway, scion of a wealthy Southern family, attended the Georgia Institute of Technology and then West Point, afterward serving with distinction in Korea. Then he dropped out of the military to pursue a political career, highlighted by one term as a Republican Congressman and an unsuccessful but very close race against Lester Maddox for the Georgia Governorship in 1966. He was named Army Secretary by President Nixon, did a good job inaugurating the all-volunteer Army but was unhappy at the Pentagon, where in recent decades the service secretaries had become so overshadowed by the Secretary of Defense, and even the military chiefs, that they are little more than exalted lobbyists and public-relations spokesmen.

Almost the first time Bo opened his mouth as Ford's campaign spokesman, however, he said bluntly that Rockefeller on the 1976 ticket would be a liability in the South.

Rocky, naturally, was livid. Moreover, he was convinced that Rumsfeld and his handyman, Cheney, had put Callaway up to it. Rumsfeld wanted to replace him on the ticket as Ford's running mate, the Vice President felt, first by downgrading his role in the Administration and finally by persuading Ford, with selective polls and calculated leaks to Washington pundits, that Rocky had to be dumped as a matter of the President's political survival.

The Vice President was, as a matter of fact, the only member of Ford's inner circle who had ever conducted a national Presidential campaign. True, he never got past the primary season, but that was what we were heading into. And he had been a rousing success as a statewide candidate, which was more than Ford or any of his other lieutenants had been. Rogers Morton had been Republican National Chairman but not in a Presidential year. Mel Laird had an astute and agile political sixth sense but had campaigned only for the Wisconsin state senate and the U.S. House from Republican districts supposedly as safe as Ford's.

Politics was Rocky's vocation and avocation. He loved it, like an

348

aging toreador, however many times he had been impaled. Politicking is something you do, like playing chess, not merely to prevail in the end game (though it's always more fun to win) but because the infinite variety of moves and countermoves affords a continuing satisfaction in itself. There is always a lot of nonsense around the White House about what things are "political" and "nonpolitical." *Everything* an effective President does is political. There are occasions when he should not be unduly *partisan,* but that is quite another adjective.

When a grand master at the game of politicking, such as Rockefeller, first settled into the number-two position in the Ford Administration, he felt a vague uneasiness around the White House. The reason was not immediately clear to him. The trouble was that Jerry Ford was really a novice at that game, despite his quarter century in Washington. Ford didn't think the same way a conventional President thinks, or make the same conventional moves, or size up his opponents—and his allies—with the same jaundiced eye. Ford was a different kind of player, from another school of politics.

The reason is simple. Congressional politics is a completely different game. Except for his first fling in 1948, when he upset a veteran Congressman in a Republican primary, Ford never waged a really tough campaign. The worst he ever did was win 60.5 percent of the vote.

His battles were all within the walls of the House of Representatives, and there he was truly a champion. But the game there is strictly the end game. Scoring points along the way through masterful moves means little if you lose when the roll is called. Being the star is not the goal; being the center of the winning team is far more important.

Leadership in legislative politicking requires making more friends than enemies, a willingness to listen and sometimes to embrace another's argument, the ability to compromise for five-eighths of a loaf and hail it as a glorious victory. Success is not planting your battle standard on a remote hilltop and rallying a majority around it; rather it is the knack of discerning and taking your position at the point where the sight of your standard will turn the battle.

In Congressional competition, as in sports, the same players face one another time after time, sometimes choosing up different sides. The fury of combat is forgotten as swiftly as the sound. One soon learns not to nurse grudges, or probe too deeply into motives. Power, to be enjoyed, must also be shared. Trust is a commoner coin than suspicion; bitter personal feuds are really very rare.

PALACE POLITICS

Rockefeller—and indeed most politicians whose careers bring them within sight of the Presidency—played a completely different game. They are inherently wary not only of their declared rivals but perhaps even more of their supposed supporters. They instinctively examine motivations and analyze actions in terms of their own ambitious drive. Like the gunslingers of the Old West, they never sit with their backs to the door.

Presidents Kennedy, Johnson and Nixon had, like Ford, served in the House, but none was cut out to be a true "man of the House." They soon moved on to the Senate. Nor were they content there, though it honed and polished their political intuitions and skills. Truman, Johnson and Nixon patiently endured normal Vice Presidencies. Ford's prep school for the Presidency was no more than eight nightmarish months on a high wire without a net. In this balancing act his Congressional habits of compromise and conciliation served him well. The Presidency, though, was another league with unfamiliar rules.

At one of their first Oval Office sessions, Rockefeller told President Ford something that would have shocked a Truman, a Kennedy, a Johnson or a Nixon right through the six-inch bulletproof windows.

"Mr. President, I have lived in a very tough political climate in New York," the Vice President began. "It is a rough place. I have a reasonable understanding of politics. Although I love people and am a positive thinker, I am a very suspicious person in the sense of being aware of what is going on. I am watching all the time what's going on—and I'd like to share with you what I think."

Ford nodded his agreement. "Fine, I'd like to have it," the President said.

"All right," Rockefeller continued. "I want to start out by saying that there are people you think are friends of yours who want to see you fail in this Administration; who, if you run, don't want to see you get the nomination; and if you get the nomination, they want to see you lose the election."

Rocky named no names. Incredibly, Ford didn't demand them. He didn't even seem very interested in what amounted to a charge of high political treason from his brand-new partner. He reacted with neither annoyance nor alarm. To Rockefeller's amazement, the President simply said he didn't believe that could be the case and went on to another topic.

The initial reason for Rockefeller's warning was a report from Nixon's last days, relayed to him by Secretary Kissinger at one of Henry's show-and-tell sessions with his former boss. Toward the bitter end, Ziegler, Kissinger and Haig were among the few White House aides Nixon saw regularly. To some degree they got used to his extreme and emotional outbursts. What set Nixon off this time is unclear, but after coming to his decision to resign, the President reportedly raged that appointing Jerry Ford was the worst mistake he ever made and that the Ford Administration was going to be a disaster.

Then, according to a responsible source, Nixon turned to Kissinger and said, "Tell your friend Nelson not to have anything to do with this Ford administration—just keep away from it. And if he does I will support him for the Presidency in nineteen seventy-six."

This might easily have been dismissed as the ravings of a troubled mind, but as time went by the Vice President observed that certain of the Nixon holdovers made no secret of their low opinion of Ford. The same extreme characterization—"a disaster"—kept popping up. Rockefeller did not tell the new President of the Nixon–Kissinger exchange because he felt Ford was still fond of Nixon and would be hurt by Nixon's harsh judgment.

But Rockefeller's low opinion of the political acumen of the Nixon holdovers was no secret either. Even before Ford formally declared his candidacy on July 8, 1975, the Vice President was worried that the President was not getting the right mix of political realism in his daily decision-making. I was concerned, too. My long-dormant California ties persuaded me that Ronald Reagan was no idle threat, that he was not being properly handled by the Rumsfeld Praetorians who had inherited Nixon's distaste for a former Democrat who made it to Sacramento. I believed that Governor Reagan, prodded by an ambitious wife and staff, was quite capable of challenging an incumbent President if convinced he had an even chance to win. He was not getting any younger; he had not worked his way up from the ranks as a Republican "party man," but his easily understood politics and evangelistic platform style evoked an emotional response long missing from Presidential campaigning. He was a George Wallace with a little more polish.

The Vice President, who had scars aplenty to show the peril of underestimating the right wing, took Reagan seriously. He was as conscious as Callaway that his presence at Ford's side was a drag in Dixie, but he believed the President would need some support in New York and the Northeast as well. So did I.*

Rockefeller began to drop into my office when he was in the West

* Only three Presidents in this century have won without New York's electoral votes—Wilson in 1916, Truman in 1948 and Nixon in 1968.

Wing, to the delight of Gail and Neta, for whom he always had charming compliments. We would shut the door and talk politics, going back to the campaigns of the Fifties and Sixties and drawing the conclusion that Ford, while acting *Presidential,* had pretty soon better start thinking like a Presidential *candidate.*

He ventured the opinion that the only people close to Ford who had any sense politically were Rogers Morton and me. This was flattering, but there were others—my deputies Jack Calkins and Gwen Anderson, Bill Baroody, Jr., members of the transition group, such as Laird, Harlow, Byrnes and Scranton, some of his Capitol Hill cronies such as Rhodes, Scott, Griffin, Michel and Quie.

"I told the President in my opinion Bob Hartmann has the best political judgment in the White House and you need it when substantive issues are discussed," the Vice President said. "And we ought to set up a group of the best people—whoever you have confidence in—and meet regularly and start focusing on the issues and your campaign.

"Well, he always agreed with that and said, 'We've got to do that,' " Rocky concluded wearily, "but he never did it. He just listened to those little -----." And then he would take off on Rumsfeld and Callaway and the likes of Cheney, Cavanaugh and Raoul-Duval, who he was sure were not only giving the President bad political advice but badmouthing him to boot.

It may seem surprising, but I often defended Rumsfeld in these bull sessions, explaining the way Ford liked to work. "He doesn't like big meetings around a table, with everybody taking notes on what everybody else says. He thinks they're a waste of time, and I sort of agree. You notice I never say much because if the President takes my position, the others will all try to make it a flop. If he rejects it, it will be in all the papers the next day that Hartmann was put down. But I do try to give him my honest opinions, when we're alone, whenever he asks me and even when he doesn't. He collects a lot of counsel that way, in person on on the phone. You can't really level with a President in a group," I said.

Rockefeller continued talking politics with Ford whenever they met, and he patched up his initial row with Callaway after an angry confrontation and soothing words of reassurance from the President.

Ford told a press conference that the new campaign law made it mandatory that candidates for the Presidency and Vice Presidency conduct separate operations prior to the nominating conventions. He contended that was all Callaway was trying to say about the "President Ford Committee" not being a vehicle for Rockefeller. But he insisted that Rocky was his personal preference and that when convention time came "I am confident that both of us can convince the delegates that individually and as a team we should both be nominated."

The President, of course, was not quite all that confident; his was an expression of affection and hope. Unwilling to blame the President himself, Rocky became increasingly convinced that Rumsfeld was egging Callaway on and pressuring Ford to dump Rockefeller in order to win the Vice Presidency for himself the second time around.*

The Vice President's worst suspicions seemed to be wondrously confirmed a fortnight later when Callaway met again with reporters and opined that the President might be thinking of "a younger man" as his 1976 running mate. Rocky was then sixty-seven; Rummy had just turned forty-three. For good measure Bo added that Rockefeller was Ford's "Number One problem" and that it would help win the nomination if the New Yorker "took himself out."

It was impossible for anyone to believe that Callaway, however dumb, would say something that explicit the second time without explicit instructions—but from whom? The press was certain they came from the President; hadn't Eisenhower tacitly encouraged Harold Stassen's tragicomic dump-Nixon drive in 1956?

---

* Rumsfeld was one of the three finalists on Ford's list checked out with the FBI in August 1974, along with Rockefeller and George Bush. I know this firsthand but never knew why he was eliminated. Harry Dent, Nixon's White House political operator who learned the South Carolina brand of *Realpolitik* at the knee of Senator Strom Thurmond, offers this version in his 1977 book (*The Prodigal South Returns to Power*): "In spring, 1975, Rumsfeld invited me to visit with him. . . . When I walked into the old Haldeman office, Rumsfeld was very hospitable. I had assumed he wanted my advice about the President's political strategy. Instead, I soon realized I was there to be politicked in favor of Rumsfeld's vice-presidential hopes. . . . I might be a link to southern GOP conservatives to pave the way for acceptance of Rumsfeld as Rockefeller's replacement. Rumsfeld told me how close he had come to being selected by Ford as vice president. . . . Rumsfeld left me with the impression he was Ford's choice, but 'Operation Townhouse' questions had caused him to be passed by, and also Bush." (I must add that nothing of this nature derogatory to either Bush or Rumsfeld surfaced during their respective Senate confirmation hearings as CIA Director and Secretary of Defense. But Dent, who worked hard for Ford in 1976, does corroborate some of Rockefeller's suspicions. Rumsfeld categorically denies them.)

PALACE POLITICS

Rockefeller chose to believe they came from Rumsfeld and so angrily informed Ford. The President assured him that this was ridiculous—that Rumsfeld was just as upset as he was about Bo's big mouth. Together Ford and Rumsfeld had given Callaway a stern lecture never to do it again. But Callaway was not sacked on the spot—so Rocky had his answer. His old combative instincts came alive. He would not oblige; he would fight back and force Ford to renominate him. He still had a few convention votes in his pocket. He would save Ford from himself.

With the President's encouragement, the Vice President threw himself into a vigorous stumping tour of the South—"to show 'em I don't have horns." Southern audiences are almost always hospitable, but their hearts belonged to Reagan and Wallace, and Rocky's late conversion to conservatism could never atone for turning his back on their true Messiah in 1964.

Much more significantly, when Ford needed an early show of strength in a preemptive but futile attempt to freeze Reagan out of the race, the New York State Republican Committee (still heavily laden with Rocky loyalists) was among the first to declare for the President. The message was plain: What New York can giveth, New York can taketh away.

What happened next were two essentially unrelated events that shattered the Ford–Rockefeller axis more permanently than Callaway's clumsy potshots.

The first was an unannounced huddle in the Oval Office at which the President finalized his budget decisions for fiscal 1976, to be submitted to Congress the next January. He met with his loquacious OMB Director, Jim Lynn, and his holdover chairman of the Council of Economic Advisers, Alan Greenspan. Neither Rockefeller, who was supposed to be "overseeing" domestic policy, nor any of his Domestic Council people were invited; only afterward did they find out what had been decided.

In 1975, his first full year, Ford had faced simultaneous inflation and recession and, striving to restrain the built-in growth of Federal expenditures, declared a moratorium on any new domestic programs except those intended to conserve or increase energy. The upshot of his October session with Greenspan and Lynn was to continue this freeze for 1976.

It was a courageous decision and probably correct economically. But politically it was suicidal. In election years Presidents—even Republican Presidents—normally come ablooming with all sorts of popular new domestic programs. By forswearing any in 1975 most of us assumed Ford was positioning himself to launch his own "new agenda" for uplifting America's spirits in 1976.

Instead, over national television on the evening of October 6, 1975, the President prescribed Simon's and Greenspan's old-fashioned recession remedy, a $28 billion tax reduction for individuals and corporations coupled with a $28 billion cut in Government spending programs already on the books. This was suppsed to be as simple as Simon, and in fact Ford's speech was largely the handiwork of David Gergen, the head of Nixon's speech staff to whom Simon had given sanctuary.

It did not take Rockefeller long to realize that the high honor he had of planning and proposing bold new domestic initiatives for the Ford Administration wouldn't amount to beans without any money to fund them. And it rankled badly that he wasn't even allowed to argue the political folly of a premature "no new spending" pledge.

About the same time, after decades of spending more than it raised in taxes and borrowing the difference, New York City found itself on the verge of bankruptcy.

Ford took a very hard line. As the day approached when the city would not be able to meet its obligations, Mayor Abraham Beame and Governor Hugh Carey came running to Washington for emergency funds. The President, relying on his economic advisers—Arthur Burns, Alan Greenspan, Bill Simon and Bill Seidman—said New York had far from exhausted other ways of balancing its income and outgo and sent them away emptyhanded. Rockefeller strongly supported Ford in that tense Cabinet Room confrontation, reminding Carey that he could bail Beame out from Albany as well as from Washington if the city were as good a credit risk as the Governor seemed to think. Rocky knew where all the state funds were stashed.

In public, however, the Vice President wanted Ford to take a softer line toward the nation's largest metropolis. It was poor politics, he argued, to appear cold and indifferent to the plight of eight million Americans, even though their fiscal predicament was partly of their own making. His unspoken concern, of course, was that Ford's hardnosed response to New York's pleas undercut his own standing at home.

The President's political advisers, myself included, saw Ford's tough stand as a plus. Here was a perfect example—much closer to home than Great Britain—of what happens when people year after year elect officials to run their affairs on the basis of getting more and more benefits and free services without being willing to pay commensurate taxes. There are millions of Americans, moreover, who don't give a damn about New York City. They pay high taxes to their own cities and see no reason why their Federal tax dollars should be subsidizing New Yorkers.

The polls confirmed this, as did the mail on Capitol Hill. Nobody, it seemed, wanted Washington to bail New York City out of its difficulties except New Yorkers and the holders of tax-exempt New York municipal bonds who were, in the main, the big banks and investment institutions. Largest of these was Chase Manhattan, and the Vice President's brother, David Rockefeller, was out front rallying support for the city's plight.

Nelson's role, however, was preeminently political. Late in September he entertained the Republican chairmen of sixty-two New York county committees at luncheon at his Pocantico Hills estate, as he had done annually when Governor. This group generally enjoyed the spectacle of Democrats Carey and Beame sinking deeper into their own fiscal quagmire. But there was a consensus of grave concern over a growing perception of President Ford, Secretary Simon, *et al.,* as being "anti-New York." They felt this would rub off on Republican political prospects throughout the state and should be countered by some high-level Administration expression of compassion for the people of New York City.

Rockefeller reported this to the President on October 2, concurring with his chairmen. He told Ford that perhaps he could handle it, preventing the impression that the President was backing off. The thing to do was shift the onus to the Democratic Congress, which would have to approve Federal funds for New York anyway. They didn't want to, but were happy to have the President take the heat.

Ford didn't react strongly to this proposition or forbid Rocky from pursuing it. He was, in fact, already working with me on a major speech on the New York City situation, which had been simmering along all summer without any real resolution. Simon was grimly standing pat, but Seidman, Lynn and others were becoming persuaded that the President had to show leadership by proposing to *do something* and to show sympathy for the frightened citizens of New York, who were being told there soon would be no money to pay policemen, firemen, teachers or garbage collectors—and that municipal hospitals would be shut down.

So Rocky spoke out. He sent up a small trial balloon in Oregon the next day. When it was not immediately shot down by Ron Nessen, he went on to a Columbus Day speech in New York City and gave it all he had.

More in tone than in specifics, the Vice President's conciliatory words seemed to depart from the President's stern and steadfast line. Rocky termed the city's situation "crucial" and asked whether "the Congress can act in time to avoid catastrophe."

True, Rockefeller tried to explain Ford's economic logic, agreed that the essential first step was for New York State and City to restore their fiscal integrity, but he also was confident this would happen and Washington would then come to the rescue—the President included.

This was an amazingly accurate prophecy, but Ford wasn't yet ready to show his hand. He wanted to keep the heat on Carey and Beame until he saw something more than pious promises. He understood what Nelson meant—but would they? He was troubled but not, at least it seemed to me, really teed off.

The Praetorian Guard closed in on Rockefeller for the kill. There is no more continuous thread in the history of our Republic than White House wrath when Vice Presidents speak out of turn in public. Now they said Rocky was really off the reservation, sabotaging the President's careful and nearly successful strategy, feathering his own New York nest, furthering his family's banking interests, fueling conservative rebellion in the South, West and mid-America.

Simon and Rumsfeld temporarily buried their old blood feud. The President was inundated with polls and polemics with a single theme: Rockefeller's gotta go. Ford was reminded of the Vice President's presumption of independence in the CIA flap, of his antagonizing key Senators in the cloture debate, of his power grab for the Domestic Council and other real and imaginary transgressions. The Praetorians reserved for the Vice President their most devastating (and, for Ford, most telling) indictment: He just was "not a team player."

I defended Rocky whenever I could, which did not further endear me to the Praetorians. I had become genuinely fond of the Vice President and his wife, Happy, whose shyness in Washington belied a warm and supportive partner with a keen judgment of people. Nelson certainly was not shy, but for a lifetime politician he was remarkably real. He had so much fun from life I wonder if he would really have needed all that money. (At one of our last meetings he was getting a huge kick out of a new pocket camera, snapping tourists on the dock at Caneel

PALACE POLITICS

Bay in the Virgin Islands before they recognized him and grabbed for their own cameras.)

Still, I wish he hadn't made that New York speech. It had exactly the opposite effect of what he intended. The President's plan, which was to be unveiled October 29 at a National Press Club luncheon in Washington, was to ask Congress to amend the Federal bankruptcy law as it applied to municipalities, enabling New York to default on its bonds and avoid further staggering interest payments. Then the Federal courts, instead of the politicians in the city, Albany or Washington, would administer the orderly and equitable relief of creditors. And in return the Treasury would guarantee funds to prevent the interruption of essential public services to New York residents.

Working with the President, Simon, Greenspan and other advisers on innumerable drafts, I tried with minimal success to soften the harsh rhetoric of some of the best economic minds of the eighteenth century. Rockefeller had provoked them into an even more righteous denunciation of Babylon's sins. While the result was one of the most lucid and logical dissertations Ford ever made, it was also hard-nosed and harsh in a way foreign to the President's good-tempered nature. The voice was the voice of Simon, and the hands were the hands of Greenspan.

Lost were most of my mollifying phrases such as "none of us can point a completely guiltless finger at New York City. None of us should now derive comfort or pleasure from New York's anguish."

What stood out were strident sentences like these:

"The people of this country will not be stampeded; they will not panic when a few desperate New York City officials and bankers try to scare New York's mortgage payments out of them.

"I can tell you, and tell you now, that I am prepared to veto any bill that has as its purpose a Federal bailout of New York City to prevent a default."

Following his National Press Club speech on New York City, the President rushed off to Andrews Air Force Base, where we boarded Air Force One for Los Angeles. The reporters rushed off with a big story, which played great in Peoria and assured Ford a rousing reception in Reaganland. There he replayed portions of it at a Republican fund-raising dinner from which the former Governor was conspicuously absent.

The New York *Daily News* capsulized it with a classic headline: "FORD TO CITY: DROP DEAD."

358

However the New York City crackdown was received, it was seen by almost all political observers as a severe put-down by the President of Vice President Rockefeller, the first major break in their idyllic partnership—perhaps a prelude to Ford's picking another running mate in 1976.

15

NEW MODEL FORD

★★────────────────★★

On October 16 the "Kitchen Cabinet" of transition alumni met in the Cabinet Room with the President. The charter members of this inner circle were Phil Buchen, John Byrnes, Bob Griffin, Bryce Harlow, Bill Scranton and Bill Whyte and from the White House Rogers Morton, Jack Marsh, Don Rumsfeld, Bill Seidman and I. The group expanded to include Mel Laird, Leon Parma, Dave Packard and Dick Cheney.

The "outside advisers" sometimes complained about the presence of White House staff people because they felt inhibited about criticizing the President's performance in front of the help, but Ford overruled them. This time Bryce, who usually started the round-table discussion, pulled no punches.

"Mr. President, your image is holding up well, your vitality continues to amaze everyone, you have done a tremendous amount of good for the party, and your leadership is affecting public attitudes more than you thought possible a few months ago. You haven't put your foot in your mouth—*yet.*"

Thus ended the good news. Next Bryce ticked off eight criticisms the team members had heard, but the one he really bore down on was the appearance of "internal anarchy" at the top of the Administration.

"Every day you pick up the paper and read about Nelson Rockefeller's feud with Don Rumsfeld, Rumsfeld's feud with Bob Hartmann, Hartmann's feud with Henry Kissinger, Kissinger's feud with Jim Schlesinger, Schlesinger's feud with Bill Clements, Clements' feud with Bill Simon, Simon's feud with Alan Greenspan, Greenspan's feud with Fred Dent, Dent's feud with Earl Butz," Harlow said. "Now, Mr. President, if you have to fire 'em all, you have got to put a stop to it."

Ford blanched at the bitter truth that he was not yet master in his own house. But he pretended to understand that Bryce was talking about the perennial problem of false White House "leaks." He denounced leaks for the umpteenth time. Nobody had nerve enough to tell him this missed the mark. The leaks were only symptoms of a sickness that was real; the feuds were fact.*

The third week of October, the President came down with a bad cold. For the first time anyone could remember, he failed to show up at the Oval Office. Rumsfeld explained that Dr. Lukash had recommended he stay in the residential section of the White House and nurse his voice for his upcoming talks with Egyptian President Sadat and other public appearances.

Rumsfeld was running back and forth to the President all the time, like a modern Moses with orders from the top to relay to the rest of us. "It's just like the good old Haldeman days," one Nixon holdover growled.

Presumably echoing the President's concern, Rumsfeld scolded the staff at a meeting on October 21 about a couple of nasty foul-ups in which Kissinger's National Security office and Simon's and Seidman's economists had issued important policy statements without clearing them in the usual way, either with Jack Marsh's Congressional liaison people or with me for final editing.

"Some people seem to think it's to their private advantage not to work with others," Rummy declared. "The President has Cabinet officers and senior advisers because he values their judgment. It hurts the President when they are bypassed.

"Nobody should covet a particular area and keep others in the dark," he went on. "There's still a tendency on this staff to think some things are too important for others to know about. When people are cut out of the deal, White House morale is destroyed."

Though he hadn't been singled out, Simon felt the shoe fit. "It's always been that way," he snorted. "It's dangerous for some speech writer to monkey with the meaning of our words."

"I was the one who gave your words to Bob Hartmann," Rummy retorted with some heat. "That's what the President has Bob Hartmann here for. He wants Bob to see that his statements are written for the American people and not just for your considerations. He wants Marsh and Friedersdorf to participate, same for the Counsel's office, and he wants everything in writing coordinated with the speech office. He also wants the Vice President involved and informed, to have an option to be present."

Being of a fairly curious nature, I wondered why Rumsfeld was

* Not necessarily in the exact pairings Harlow rattled off for rhetorical effect.

making this speech. What he said was right, but it was about a year overdue, and nobody had been more guilty of bypassing me and the Vice President than Rummy.

Then came the clue, though I didn't catch its significance until later. It was his farewell, his apologia.

"The President doesn't have a deputy. He does have eight or nine key people. It's hard to make this system work, but from the President's viewpoint it's better that way. *It isn't the way I would operate but the way President Ford operates,* and I respect that. I think you all ought to think about that." (Emphasis mine.)

Rumsfeld was never given the authority he thought he had been promised to "coordinate" the prima donnas within the White House walls. Whenever he tried to assert it, the Rockefellers, Kissingers, Simons and, yes, the Hartmanns went directly to the President and usually got their way, then gossiped gleefully about it.

One of the Washington *Post* columns Harlow referred to, under a not-very-flattering caricature of Rumsfeld, reflected this continuous internal hemorrhaging. The column began:

> The fact that a 34-year-old presidential aide named Dick Cheney is increasingly taking charge of the day-to-day White House business is a fascinating manifestation of backstage intrigue with far-reaching implications.
>
> The reason Cheney is handling so much of the White House routine today, say knowledgeable insiders, is that his boss and mentor, Donald Rumsfeld, is quietly deepening his involvement in the management of President Ford's election campaign. And that is widely viewed in upper reaches of the administration as a means to one end: putting Rumsfeld on the 1976 ticket as Vice President.
>
> All this creates a tableau worthy of the Byzantine palace. Mr. Ford, typically open and straightforward, clearly wants to reward Rockefeller's loyal service the past year with a full term as Vice President. But constantly at the President's side advising is Rumsfeld—secretive, clever and no friend of Nelson Rockefeller.
>
> While the Ford campaign is technically removed from the White House, Rumsfeld actually runs it. What's more, anti-Rockefeller conservatives get this private message from Rumsfeld: I can't do anything about it right now, but I agree that Rocky should go.

As the President pondered these things (he never missed reading the papers or riding his exercise bike every morning), he must have

362

concluded that Henry Kissinger was also a focal point of "internal anarchy."

Indispensable as Henry was, Ford would not be human if he hadn't been piqued at times by Kissinger's proprietary attitude toward him and his habit of regularly saying the things the President planned on saying a day or so before the President said them. Henry's popularity polls regularly ran higher than either Nixon's or Ford's; Henry's picture appeared with greater frequency on the front pages and the social pages; Henry's *bon mots* were the ones quoted at Georgetown dinner parties; and Henry, of course, dearly loved every minute of it.

Kissinger was and is a congenital celebrity. His compulsion to crow is as natural as a rooster's, his propensity to preen as normal as a peacock's. Ford was wiser than most about this. He knew it was hopeless to fool with Mother Nature. Henry's vanity was part of his total ability to perform well. If he needed more reassurance than the rest of us, Ford gladly gave it.

Most of the tales that were told about Kissinger losing favor with the President were more wishful than real. Going far beyond the internecine squabbles of the White House, Henry's foes included a lot of politicians too cowardly to take a straight shot at the President but who found a convenient scapegoat in his Secretary of State.

In this respect, Kissinger's situation was similar to that of Dean Acheson taking right-wing brickbats actually aimed at President Truman, or John Foster Dulles drawing left-wing fire away from President Eisenhower.

With the collapse of anti-Communist resistance in Southeast Asia, Kissinger became the special villain of the reactionary right. In the haunted minds of ultraconservatives, Henry was not a hardliner (as he really felt he was) but a soft touch, the apostle of détente, the appeaser of Panama, archagent of the international Rockefeller conspiracy.

Kissinger embarked on a strenuous campaign to polish up his image. He worked the backwoods and the bayous, the corn belt and the cow towns, and his erudite writers did their best to make him sound like a combination of John the Baptist, John Birch and John Doe. Alas, Henry was never what you'd call a domestic political plus. It's in the nature of American politics for a foreign-policy adviser to be either obscure or suspect. Henry couldn't be obscure.

As President Ford pondered what to do to tidy up his team and tamp down the tumult raging around his Oval Office, the question surely crossed his mind: Does Henry really need that corner office in the West Wing? Why can't he just be Secretary of State, my senior Cabinet officer? Scowcroft, who thinks like Henry, gets along with everybody and makes no waves.

The speculations gain credibility from events. After a week of communing with himself while nursing a cold, the first persons Ford admits taking into his confidence about his proposed shuffle were Kissinger and Rumsfeld. This, all three agree, was on Saturday, October 25.

Despite the President's insistence, at the time and later, that he reached his decisions entirely alone, he did discuss them in the process of formulation with at least two and possibly three persons, not counting his family circle. Rumsfeld was most certainly privy to Ford's original intention to name George Bush as Secretary of Commerce and Washington Attorney Edward Bennett Williams, an establishment Democrat, as head of the CIA. Williams declined, and Bush was switched—over the objections of one of Ford's most valued political advisers.

The President started from the premise that he wanted to get rid of Secretary of Defense James Schlesinger. They never really hit it off, as Ford incautiously revealed as Vice President. Since then Schlesinger had annoyed and antagonized him for even more reasons.

Rumsfeld, Kissinger and Bill Clements, Schlesinger's deputy, continuously called Schlesinger's shortcomings to Ford's attention. Clements clearly wanted Schlesinger's job and might have been Ford's early choice.* His working knowledge of the Defense Department, however, was needed to augment Rumsfeld's almost total lack of it.

The President didn't like Schlesinger's resistance to his budget cuts and Jim's scarcely concealed airing of their policy differences in the media. Though Bill Simon used the same techniques to advertise his own fiscal differences in the opposite direction, Ford respected Simon's convictions. He suspected Schlesinger of hypocritically sounding more hawkish than his record showed, just to align himself against Kissinger and détente.

But the main thing Ford didn't like about Schlesinger was Schlesinger. Whenever they talked, even alone, Schlesinger gave him the

* Clements was also suggested as a White House replacement for Rumsfeld as a really tough manager who would impose order where Rummy had failed. Ford rejected this, primarily because he didn't really want a hard-boiled straw boss. He wanted someone he could handle, and Cheney seemed ideal.

impression of a bored intellectual saying, "I know you're pretty dumb, but I'll do my best to explain it simply." Ford didn't like the fact that a Cabinet officer couldn't remember to button his shirt collar and cinch up his tie when he came to see the President of the United States. He held Schlesinger responsible for several foul-ups in which his direct orders were disobeyed and incorrect information was given the Commander-in-Chief. He couldn't trust the man, and they could no longer communicate. He had to go.

According to those involved, both Rumsfeld and Kissinger protested the firing of Schlesinger. Kissinger knew he would be blamed for it. He had already taken Schlesinger's measure and won. He could afford to be charitable and may have felt Jim was the best Defense Secretary available at that stage of global negotiations. Why have to Indian wrestle with a new one?

Rummy was fed up with the White House. He had not created a whole new Praetorian Guard but took over the old Haldeman–Haig legions and placed his key lieutenants in command. Don had been a dominant, if not decisive, influence in many of Ford's major appointments. But the President would not abandon his untidy administrative habits, and Rumsfeld's role was now making him far more enemies than friends.

At this point it is unclear whether Kissinger or Rumsfeld knew of the central Rockefeller piece in the President's jigsaw puzzle.

Alone in the Oval Office, Rockefeller and the President had agreed that the Vice President would write a letter requesting that he not be among those considered by Ford for the number-two spot on the 1976 ticket.

That this was the upshot of Rocky's regular weekly meeting with Ford at 4:30 P.M. on October 28, 1975, is about all that can be stated with absolute certainty, even now. The preponderance of evidence, though, is that the President, on the advice of unidentified "advisers," first proposed that Rocky withdraw, ostensibly voluntarily, and that the Vice President, his pride deeply but not yet mortally wounded, readily agreed.

Thereafter the retrospective accounts differ. Rockefeller's recollection, first given me shortly after the President's election defeat in November 1976, was that "I didn't take myself off the ticket, you know—he asked me to do it." I didn't want to believe him, because the President himself, in strictest confidence, had told me soon after the October 28 meeting that the Vice President "wanted" to withdraw his name from consideration and that Rocky would announce it sometime the following week.

When Presidents play with hypothetical situations, their suggestions can easily be construed as veiled commands. When two politicians sit down to shoot the breeze alone, they converse in a kind of code in which each one understands perfectly what the other is *not* saying—and will publicly deny he ever said. So I felt that the Vice President simply inferred that the President wanted him to get off the ticket and had obligingly done so. I could not bring myself to believe Ford had literally asked it, though it was obvious he was going along.

When Ford told me I responded, "I'm sorry to hear that, Mr. President. I don't think you'd win over Jesse Helms or Clarke Reed or any of those Reagan-lovers in the South if you personally pulled out the Vice President's fingernails one by one with a pair of pliers. Don't you see, it's not Rocky they're after—it's you. You're never going to appease them, and now you're going to lose all of Rockefeller's friends, too."

The President sighed. He wasn't mad, but he looked a little pained. "Well, it's done," he said, turning to another subject.

Why did the President confide in me about Rocky's "decision"? Was he wanting, masochistically, someone to berate him for what he had done, knowing I was one of the few people who would dare? Or was he testing the cover story Rockefeller and he had agreed to, knowing my suspicious nature, to see if anybody would buy it when it came out?

Whatever his motive—maybe he just needed someone to talk to—I failed him. I simply accepted his story, sadly ventured a mild dissent and kept my mouth shut. And the astonishing thing was, most of the press and public bought it.

In their fascination with the President's fast shuffle, the normally cynical and suspicious White House watchers rolled over and let Rockefeller's early "dumping" pass for a fit of frustrated Vice Presidential temperament.

Rockefeller played his part to the hilt. Except for his one cryptic aside to me, he stuck to the story that he got off the ticket of his own free will and without a Presidential shove. Even under the probing inquiries of John Osborne, in December of 1976, all the Vice President would say was that Rumsfeld, wanting to be Vice President himself, had engineered his exodus and that Ford pliantly "allowed it to happen."

OSBORNE: "Did he [Ford] try to discourage you, ask you to withdraw the letter, reconsider?"

ROCKEFELLER: "No."

OSBORNE: "After your announcement, did he ever express any regrets to you?"

ROCKEFELLER: "Well, considerably later, I said to him one day, just out of a whimsical thought, I said: 'You know, Mr. President, I think I made a mistake.' He said, 'What's that?' I said, 'I should have said in that letter . . . when Bo Callaway delivers to you the Southern delegations, *then* I'm off the ticket.' And he [Ford] very graciously said, '*You* didn't make the mistake. *We* made the mistake.' "

When Osborne then asked President Ford whether Rocky's recollection was correct, he reported the President replied: "There may be some credence to that. It in no way undercuts my admiration and affection for Nelson Rockefeller. We were in a tight situation. In retrospect, I probably let it go further than I would if I were doing the same thing today."

Pressed further, Ford couldn't remember the precise details.

Almost a year after Osborne's interview, throughout which the premise that Rocky's withdrawal was voluntary remained unscathed, I had a long conversation with the Vice President in his Rockefeller Center office in New York. I brought up the disparity of his statement to me, which I regarded as having been made in confidence, that Ford had in fact *told* him to remove himself from consideration.

"I think it was our regular meeting, the week before the massacre—and by this time he really wanted to be re-elected," Rockefeller recalled. "Up to that point the President had always said 'We are a team' and, you know, he was wonderful. And then this day he said to me, 'I really feel, it's very important that I get this nomination. And I have been talking with my political advisers and I think it would be— as much as personally I feel badly about it—it would be better if you were not on the ticket and if you would withdraw.'

"And so I said, 'Fine,' " Rockefeller continued. "Listen, I understand completely. I came down here because you asked me to help and I have no problem at all—you have got no problem at all—and I will write you a letter. I will just say that I can't do it.' And he said that would be wonderful."

According to some of Rockefeller's close lieutenants, there was no particular urgency to this understanding. In due course, at the politically advantageous moment, the Vice President would hand the President his letter and the deed would be done. According to what the President told me immediately after their meeting, he expected Rockefeller to act within a week or so.

As I was totally in the dark regarding the other changes Ford planned, I cannot say authoritatively which revelation was supposed to come out first—the Vice President's withdrawal or the Cabinet and White House shuffle. Rockefeller told me in December 1977 that he knew nothing about the so-called Monday-night Halloween Massacre when he agreed to get off the ticket on the previous Tuesday. According to Rockefeller, his first inkling came when the President called him from Florida on Sunday, November 2. Rockefeller was weekending in Tarrytown, New York.

"Do you think you can have that letter by Monday?" he quoted Ford as saying, "because I've got some other changes I am making and the story has leaked."

Rockefeller recalled that the President then told him about the imminent replacement of Schlesinger with Rumsfeld and implied that one of his reasons was that Kissinger complained of Schlesinger's constant press leaks against him. Kissinger may also have briefed Rockefeller about the upcoming changes. He was upset to the point of threatening resignation over loss of his National Security Council post, Rockefeller said.

The Vice President said the President merely told him about his decisions, without asking his opinion about them. But Rocky's decision was already made. He agreed to be back in Washington on Monday with his withdrawal letter, which he and Hugh Morrow, his press secretary, had already been drafting.

The Vice President met with the President in the Oval Office the next morning and handed him his letter. The President read it in a cursory way and said it was fine.

Earlier that morning the President had met with Rumsfeld, Marsh, Nessen, Friedersdorf and me and decided to announce all his changes at an evening news conference in the East Room. Just prior to that he would brief the bipartisan Congressional leaders.

I was waiting for my scheduled appointment with the President, which Rockefeller had preempted. They emerged from the Oval Office and Ford told an aide to summon Nessen. Meanwhile, he showed me Rockefeller's letter and a joint statement the two of them had worked out on foolscap. It said: "The President and the Vice President have a complete understanding between them regarding the Vice President's decision. The letter speaks for itself. *The initiative was the Vice President's.*" (Emphasis mine.)

Nessen arrived and was given the two documents. We both urged that they be released immediately before being clouded by rumors and incomplete leaks. Ford and Rockefeller agreed, and the stories thus made the late editions of the afternoon papers and the early-evening television news, prior to the President's press conference.

Though I did not notice it at the time, the "joint statement" was curious. Obviously Rockefeller's letter did not "speak for itself." It did not state the crucial point: Whose idea was it? Evidently Rocky refused to alter his letter, but Ford extracted his consent to the statement. Both were, essentially, false.

They were no more false than the white lies which accompany almost every regretful Presidential acceptance of a subordinate's facesaving resignation. But this was one of the major crossroads of the Ford Presidency. In it, I must conclude, he fudged his pledge of openness and candor with the American people. It was a serious, perhaps fatal, blow to his unsought Presidency in which truth was to be the glue.*

The Halloween Massacre, when it unfolded, completely convinced Rockefeller that Rumsfeld was his nemesis. He reconstructed a not implausible scenario. Rummy was possessed of an overpowering drive to be President—a condition Nelson would readily recognize. One of the major Cabinet jobs—State, Treasury or Defense—would give him both experience and exposure. From such a platform Rumsfeld would be ready to be Ford's running mate, or his successor, in 1976 or 1980. He could wait, being only forty-three.

In the meantime, Rockefeller reasoned, Rummy had to eliminate from serious consideration his foremost potential rivals for the Vice Presidential nod—namely, the incumbent and George Bush.

The Vice President saw such a game working out precisely as planned. Everybody around the White House, except (apparently) the President, knew Rumsfeld was using Nessen and others to plant rumors of Ford's disenchantment with Simon, Kissinger and Rockefeller. All three confronted Nessen and complained to the President about this obvious undercutting, which Nessen blithely denied.

* In his memoirs the old Jerry Ford plows through all this and admits that, putting his arm around Rocky to bid him goodbye, "I was angry with myself for showing cowardice in not saying to the ultraconservatives: It's going to be Ford and Rockefeller, whatever the consequences."

PALACE POLITICS

Simon and Kissinger survived their ambushes, but Jim Schlesinger was a far more vulnerable target. And, according to Rocky's thesis, efforts to oust the Defense Secretary would certainly be blamed on Henry.

When Rumsfeld went over to the Pentagon, he took along Nessen's deputy press secretary, Bill Greener. This was fine with Nessen, who had long suspected Greener was eagerly waiting for him to slip—even strewing some of the banana peels. Rockefeller, by a curious convolution of logic, chose Greener's departure from the White House as a way to denounce Rumsfeld's alleged self-seeking to the President. And also to settle an old score with Nessen.

"Mr. President, Donald Rumsfeld has no right to take the man who, in my opinion, is your best contact with the press," the Vice President informed Ford. "This is evidence of what I have felt and hesitated to talk very much about.

"But I'm now going to say it frankly: Rumsfeld wants to be President of the United States. He has given George Bush the deep six by putting him in the CIA, he has gotten me out through his guy Bo Callaway. He was third on your list and now he has gotten rid of two of us.

"You are not going to be able to put him on [the 1976 ticket] as Vice President because he is Defense Secretary, but he is not going to want anybody who could possibly get elected with you on that ticket," Rockefeller's account continued. "And I have to say I have a serious question about his loyalty to you."

Rockefeller said that thereafter he kept telling the President his misgivings about Rumsfeld but that Ford neither agreed nor got angry.

For as long as anybody cares, people will argue whether dumping Rockefeller gained Ford the nomination or cost Ford the 1976 election. Certainly it did not accomplish what was apparently intended—to discourage Reagan's entry into the race and appease his right-wing supporters. Nor did it bring him a less controversial running mate. Did it cost Ford the electoral votes of New York, Ohio or other urban-industrial states? How much did merely the impression of waffling, of flinching from the first rebel yell cost him even among conservatives?

The neat theory that Rumsfeld engineered the simultaneous elimination of his leading Vice Presidential competitors, despite his and Ford's denials, remains a strong suspicion among those who still muck about in old palace plots. It does have some holes in it. The surest way to rule Bush out was to leave him in the Forbidden City. Bringing Richardson back into political visibility was no boon to Rumsfeld. The combined enmity of both Rockefeller and Bush admirers would not be an auspicious start for an Illinoisian's bid for either the Vice Presidency or the Presidency later on.

Further, it was Bush himself who wanted the CIA assignment and persuaded the President, against his better instincts, to promise the Senate committee confirming him that Bush would be ruled off the 1976 GOP ticket. Lastly, I don't think Ford ever really meant to set Rumsfeld up for the Vice Presidency, though he may well have led Don to think so. He had a wonderful knack of leaving people thinking what they wanted to think about his plans for their future.

What was it, then, that Ford saw in his jigsaw puzzle when "all the pieces fitted together perfectly"? The preordained departure of Jim Schlesinger and Bill Colby but, more important, their replacement by two of his protégés from House days who seemed destined for greater political roles *if* they did as they were told and mastered their respective challenges.

Simultaneously, removal from the White House of two controversial and high-powered personalities, Kissinger and Rumsfeld, halting their running battles with each other and with other noisy rivals for his ear—at least reducing the volume and frequency of these rhubarbs to polite interdepartmental exchanges. Their successors, Cheney and Scowcroft, would be low-key, typical staff types he could easily control. Both, he thought, would work comfortably with Buchen, Cannon, Hartmann, Lynn, Marsh, Nessen and Seidman.

Rockefeller's purportedly voluntary withdrawal from consideration would leave Ford's future Vice Presidential nod an open option and thus ensure the subordination to the President of everyone interested in it—in the rebellious ranks of statehouse Republicans, in the Congress and in his own Administration—even so far as reconsideration of Rocky himself.

Almost as an afterthought, it occurred or was pointed out to Ford that there was nothing in his perfect plan that would appeal much to liberal Republicans. They would surely be distressed by Rocky's fate. Who might appease the Northeastern, urban, liberal establishment of press and party?

What else but the rehabilitation of Elliot Richardson, currently composing his memoirs in London? And the vacancy thereby made in the most prestigious of diplomatic posts could come in handy later on. Elliot's ambition, still not fully requited, was for Secretary of State or better, but the President correctly figured he would settle for anything that brought him back on center stage in Washington.

So why not Secretary of Commerce? A good spot for a liberal Republican to mend his fences with conservatives.

I was privy only to the Rockefeller piece of the jigsaw puzzle and, at the end, to the Richardson-for-Morton plan. It was no reproach for Rog, who wanted out of the Commerce job and into Ford's campaign. He had a slow but steady cancer problem, not much of a secret, to which he succumbed in 1978.

Rogers Morton was everything a Kentucky gentleman* is supposed to be. He was one of the biggest men in Washington, not only in physical stature but in every respect. He was loyal, tough-minded and tenderhearted at the same time. He loved Jerry Ford.

For different reasons than Rockefeller, Rog was deeply troubled that somewhere within the White House was a Trojan horse, determined to prevent President Ford's success, his nomination and his election. He had seen what the Praetorian Guard did to Nixon and knew its power. As one of the original transition advisers, he knew the recommendations on which Ford temporized until the proper time had passed. As a former Republican National Chairman, he knew that a divided minority party was foredoomed to defeat. Long before it happened, he believed that the dumping of Nelson Rockefeller would be a fatal error.

On Wednesday, October 29, the President had gone directly from a National Press Club speech (declaring he was not going to make Federal taxpayers go bail for New York City) to California. There he addressed receptive Republican groups in Los Angeles and San Francisco. I dropped off Air Force One after the Bay City luncheon on Thursday and flew back to Pasadena, where I was to receive the Distinguished Eagle Scout award.** President Ford and his party re-

---

* Born in Louisville, the younger brother of Senator Thruston Morton, one of his predecessors as Republican National Chairman, Rogers Clark Ballard Morton moved to Maryland's Eastern Shore, where he told inquisitive neighbors his middle initials stood for "Chesapeake Bay," and was elected in 1962 to the first of four terms in Congress.

** The President thoughtfully sent sponsors Bob Finch and Ed Butterworth a personally dictated letter congratulating "my Counsellor and friend, Bob Hartmann. . . . During the decade he has been at my side, Bob has abundantly proven how well he learned the second Scout law—a Scout is loyal."

turned via Milwaukee to Washington. I had no hint of the momentous events I was missing during one of the few times I played hooky from my job.

After I got home late Saturday night the phone rang. It was Jim Schlesinger, very agitated. He had been trying to reach me all evening.

"*Newsweek* has it that I'm going to be fired," Schlesinger said. "And I've just been told the President wants to see me first thing tomorrow morning—no reason given—though I just talked with him for an hour this morning and everything seemed O.K. Is *Newsweek* right?"

"I've talked with the President several times today," I said. "Surely I'd know if he were plannning any Cabinet changes of that magnitude. Don't worry about it."

"Then why does he want to see me at eight-thirty on Sunday morning?"

"I imagine it's just something he wants to get straight about arms aid before he talks to Sadat," I said. I thought Schlesinger was imagining things.

At eight the next morning I was in the reception room off the Oval Office waiting to fly in the President's helicopter to Andrews and thence to Florida. Sadat had been resting there, after an earlier official visit in Washington. They were to meet again informally.

Jim didn't tell me (there is such a thing as playing your cards *too* close to your vest) that Jack Marsh was the one who had relayed the President's summons. Saturday, Ford told Marsh to bring Schlesinger and Colby in for their marching papers. He was specifically instructed not to tell me, though he urged the President to do so. His remonstrations about certain aspects of the plan were overruled. The die was cast.

I watched Bill Colby leave the Oval Office and Schlesinger enter. There was nothing unusual about the President getting an update from his intelligence chief, and Colby's demeanor betrayed nothing amiss. Schlesinger shot me a nervous glance which seemed to ask confirmation of our midnight conversation, but I still knew nothing. After an hour he strode out without looking left or right, and I dashed off to the waiting chopper.

It was a little strange that Marsh came along; he wasn't manifested for this trip. Rumsfeld had been scheduled to go to Florida but was replaced at the last minute by Cheney.

Upon our arrival at Jacksonville Naval Air Station, however, I got my first hint that something was up. The President, Kissinger,

PALACE POLITICS

Marsh, Cheney and his Praetorians were all put on a Navy motor launch to proceed to the Sadat meeting. But I was assigned to the First Lady's motorcade and routed with several White House secretaries to a private home volunteered for the use of the staff.

I was accustomed to being excluded by Kissinger from negotiations with foreign dignitaries but never this pointedly. When I protested, to Red Cavaney—a veteran Praetorian—I was told the Navy launch was full, which it obviously was not.

Thereafter, things got mysteriouser and mysteriouser. I settled down in the staff house, constantly interrupted by press calls, asking about a big shake-up that the President was about to announce. I had been sworn to secrecy about Rockefeller and knew nothing more. But I remembered Schlesinger's anguished call. I told the newsmen I could neither confirm nor deny the rumors. Then all the electricity went out. There were no staff cars to be found. I put in an urgent call for Jack Marsh. By now it was dawning on me that I had been deliberately isolated from more than the Sadat meeting.

Marsh wasn't there. I said to hell with it, let's see what's going on. In the 90-degree Florida sun, I walked the mile to the President's house. I didn't think the Secret Service agents would bar the door to me. They didn't.

The Praetorians were glued to the color TV watching the Washington Redskins vs. the Dallas Cowboys. The President was in a bedroom trying to get through to Richardson in London and finish his jigsaw puzzle. Everybody knew what was going on except me. I called Jack Marsh into a corner and lit into him with more passion than I'd ever displayed.

"Jack, don't try to talk me out of this. I am resigning as soon as we get back to Washington. I am going to tell anybody who asks me why I am resigning. I have never taken this kind of ---- before and I am never going to take it again."

"What's the matter, Bob?" Jack pretended and then saw his old hoe cakes and honey wouldn't work. "Now, come on, Bob, simmer down. I know the President has been wanting to talk with you. Give him a little time."

"I have given him a little time—the best ten years of my life," I countered bitterly. "In fact, the best ten years of my wife."

"Well, promise me to wait until we get back aboard the plane," he begged. "Don't say anything you'll regret. I don't think you've been treated properly, but I can't tell you any more now. I'm sure he will."

The President emerged from the bedroom and joined in the jollity around the television set. He greeted me warmly as if wondering where I'd been all day. We talked about the football game and drank martinis until it was time to go to dinner.

Neither the terminable martinis nor the interminable dinner did anything for me. I felt used, abused and totally disenthused. I had had it.

Once on Air Force One, the President sent for me. He told me the whole story—most of which I had picked up meantimes except for the Richardson bit. Elliot would call back with his answer in the morning. Meanwhile—a trifle late, it seemed to me—he wanted my advice on how the formal announcement should be made.

I sat there on the blue sofa in his cabin and looked at this good man who was obviously writhing within himself. What he had done was done. I couldn't change any of it, and I probably couldn't have if he had consulted me at the outset. I didn't know who had counseled him, but I did know Jerry Ford. When he was right he was very, very right; and when he was wrong he was horrid.

I fell back on technical specifics. I said that in view of all the leaks the whole plan should be disclosed personally at a news conference the very next day. I refrained from reminding him that the Rockefeller part he *had* confided to me was the only part that had not been leaked.

We got home in the early-morning hours. I was too uptight just to crawl quietly into bed. I woke Roberta and spilled it all.

"Honey," I concluded, "how would you like being the wife of a private citizen again?"

"Bob, you can't do it," she said, now wide awake.

"Why not? I *can* and I'm going to tomorrow. I'll go away quietly, just like that. We'll go to the islands."

"Nobody will believe you resigned. They'll say you were fired, that you were the foremost offender, while Rummy and Cheney were promoted. Not one of your dear old newspaper friends will say a word in your defense. Don't you see, you'll be doing exactly what they want you to do?" Roberta countered.

"Well, isn't it what the President wants me to do?"

"I'm not so sure," she said. "What would he do without you? Did you ever think that maybe he left you out of it on purpose? You weren't told, but you weren't touched. So be thankful for small favors."

The sun came up the next morning as usual. The bathroom scales told me I was just as large as I had been twenty-four hours before. The morning papers were more interested in President Ford raising a welt on his forehead by bumping the side of the Florida swimming pool, a tidbit Nessen had obligingly supplied them.

Welt and all, the President summoned his senior aides to go over the day's mechanics of announcement. Vice President Rockefeller would bring his withdrawal letter in that morning. Nessen was to set up an evening press conference on prime time. Meanwhile, Marsh, Friedersdorf and the President himself would alert selected Congressional leaders about what was coming.

Rumsfeld professed to be surprised by the whole business. He had reluctantly—he said—yielded to telephonic importunings by Marsh and Cheney and accepted Ford's decision to pack him off to the Pentagon.

"In your press conference tonight, Mr. President, try to act 'Presidential,' " Rummy urged. "Don't go into long explanations of why you did this or that. Whenever you can, answer the question 'Yes' or 'No.' Be decisive, in command. Be crisp and concise. Don't let them nickel and dime you to death."

Nessen seconded Don's advice. The President turned to me.

"Be yourself," I said.

He knew this had always been my bottom line. But for once he tried the other route. As a result, it was more like a Nixon or Johnson news conference than a Ford one. Reporters were startled by the change.

Ford's nationally televised news conference on the evening of November 3 in the East Room was symptomatic of the contrived, tense atmosphere of what was dubbed the "Halloween Massacre."

The President was not at his best that night. He was not, as I advised, being himself. He looked and sounded defiant and defensive all the way. His cursory, curt answers were conspicuously out of character. He also resorted at least seven times to responses he could not himself have believed.

Dick Growald of UPI asked the first question: "Has the Vice President, by his action today, sacrificed himself on your political behalf, and have you in any way urged him to do so?"

The President: "The decision by Vice President Rockefeller was a decision on his own. . . . Under no circumstances was it a request by me. It was a decision by him."

Later, Godfrey Sperling of the *Christian Science Monitor* asked:

"Mr. President, how do you make a high-level personnel shift of this kind, such a fast shift? Did you ask for suggestions, or did you do this largely on your own?"

The President: "I did it totally on my own. It was my decision. I fitted the pieces together, and they fitted excellently. It was my decision."

Sperling again: "With Mr. Rumsfeld, who is involved in your decision, would he have had any input into the overall decision?"

The President: "He did not."

The questioning then veered briefly to the New York City financial crisis, in which Rockefeller had been deeply involved. The President was asked: "Did he talk to you at all about the effect of your position against aid to New York City and other cities on your campaign for next year?"

The President: "He has not."

Finally, for the last question, John Osborne returned to an earlier Ford answer, which he found unsatisfactory and incredible on the basis of what everyone had heard directly from Kissinger and Schlesinger.

"Are you saying, and intending to be understood to say, that neither personal nor policy differences between Dr. Kissinger and Mr. Schlesinger contributed to this change?"

The President passed up Osborne's generous and open invitation to qualify, or weasel out of, his previous answer.

"That is correct," he snapped, and the press conference mercifully ended.

Since the big news was out before Ford announced it, the media had a field day dissecting the President's demeanor and ulterior motives. Most of this analysis was not at all flattering, portraying Ford as secretive and calculating, just another sneaky politician playing pre-election games, trying to fool all the people after all.

The manner of making the announcement revived memories of the Nixon pardon, complicated by the President's curious insistence that he consulted no one before making such a major move. With unconscious irony the Washington *Star* reported that "to avoid leaks, only four men at the White House were involved in the planning: Ford, Rumsfeld, Scowcroft and Rumsfeld's deputy Richard Cheney. Top White House aides like Robert Hartmann, John Marsh and Ronald Nessen were kept in the dark."

If there is one axiom that should be written large and pasted in every new President's hat it is that the American public does not like to be taken by surprise. The "leaks" that give most Presidents so much pain serve a useful purpose by preparing people to accept sharp shifts in Presidential policies and dramatic personnel changes.

The pundits gave him a terrible time. They were divided as to who came out the big winner but unanimous that Ford was the big loser.

"Gerald Ford had obviously grown weary of reading pollsters' reports of voters' doubts that he is tough enough and cold-blooded enough to run a huge government," wrote Charles Bartlett in one of the sharpest columns. "When politicians react against their images, the results can be explosive. Schlesinger . . . was apparently sacrificed so the President would look like a leader, so Kissinger could expand his dominance and Rumsfeld could have a big desk of his own. By choosing this moment to withdraw, Rockefeller softened the vehemence of the right wing's reaction."

Newsday predictably hailed Richardson's rehabilitation but added: "Ford tried hard to project the image of a new team, his team. Instead, he has given the country an image of confusion. In his haste to fire Schlesinger and Colby, Ford seems to have forgotten Bush can't leave Peking until after the President's visit there. Colby was already cleaning out his desk when word from the President reached him asking him to stay."

"Why now? Why not? And why in such an abrupt and clumsy manner?" asked the Washington *Post*. "The removal of Mr. Schlesinger at this moment sends all the wrong signals from Mr. Ford's point of view to everyone from the Republican right wing to the Soviet military to the members of Congress chewing over his defense budget. Our best guess is that the decision of Vice President Rockefeller . . . is all part of a general refurbishing of the Presidential image with Ronald Reagan and the 1976 election clearly in mind. The point, it seems to us, is that the President was trying to will or wish away problems and conflicts he has been unable to cope with or resolve.

"The effect of this inability has been to present the unfortunate image of a weak caretaker, presiding over a divided and unruly government . . . [but] the President with this drastic and summary treatment of his problem managed to confirm both the degree of disarray he had allowed to set in, and his own inability to deal with it except by the most abrupt and heavy-handed means."

One might have thought John Osborne would be happy that his

nineteen-month-old scoop in the *New Republic* foretelling Schlesinger's fall was finally confirmed. But he hit Ford hardest of all, concluding that the President's explanations "and the events they concern show Gerald Ford to be intensely egotistic behind that humble facade of his, capable of an inhuman cruelty stupidly evinced, and desperately anxious to establish and prove himself as a national leader in his own right."

16

NICE GUYS FINISH LAST

★★————————————★★

About a year before the Presidential election of 1864—possibly the most crucial in our history—some of Abraham Lincoln's closest political friends worried that he was not sufficiently concerned about the coming campaign. They warned him that many Republicans thought he was not tough enough, not showing dynamic leadership, that he might lose unless he changed his ways.

Others in his own party—even his own Cabinet—politicians like Chase and popular generals such as Fremont and Butler—no longer bothered to conceal their desire to replace him as President, they told Lincoln. Why did he let them get away with it?

"No man knows what that gnawing is until he has had it," the President replied.

Gerald R. Ford, as 1976 approached, knew that gnawing.

The country was about to observe its 200th year of independence, but its unelected President had yet to mark two full years in the White House. He had grown to like the job he never sought. He was not only comfortable in it but confident of his ability to handle it. Ford, unlike many Presidents, never soliloquized about the terrible burdens and lonely decisions of the office. He unblushingly admitted he enjoyed them and very badly wanted four more years to finish what he had begun.

He was the ninth Vice President to succeed to the Presidency for the balance of a predecessor's term. Of the others, the first four (John Tyler, Millard Fillmore, Andrew Johnson and Chester Arthur) failed to gain the next nomination of their parties. The four more recent inheritors of the Presidency (Theodore Roosevelt, Calvin Coolidge, Harry Truman and Lyndon Johnson) went on to win full terms in their own right and certainly were not the worst Presidents of the twentieth century.

Upon the death or assassination of a popular President, their successors have usually benefitted from an initial surge of sympathetic emotion. In a backhanded way, so did Ford. His contrasting character and conduct upon assuming the Presidency won him an almost idyllic honeymoon with potential political rivals as well as the American public.

It was too good to last, even if he had not cut it shorter with his premature pardon. But the fact remains, and is fundamental to any analysis of the Ford years, that he had only a scant two years to master his job, demonstrate his leadership and compete for his own party's nomination and the nation's mandate to continue. It was either a year too many or a year too few.

The final year of any Presidency finds the incumbent preoccupied with perpetuating himself in office, if he can, or with ensuring his policies and his place in history if he cannot. In short, with campaign politics.

Understandably, President Ford's inner security and innate confidence, which enabled him to take over the Presidency with easy and visible assurance, did not suffice for the unfamiliar role of national candidate. He was thus more vulnerable to challengers and more dependent on advisers as the gnawing to be a duly nominated and elected President grew within him. The so-called Halloween Massacre was evidence of his awareness of this, but it was in large measure the wrong move.

Its net effect was to put outside his inner circle of White House advisers those with relatively more campaign experience, ability and dependence on Ford's success—Rockefeller, Rumsfeld and Bush; to place in highly visible and semiautonomous Washington positions those who might be inclined to consider their own futures before Ford's; to surround himself with pliable technicians like Scowcroft and Cheney; to alienate simultaneously Republican conservatives with his dismissal of Schlesinger and Republican moderates with his dumping of Rockefeller; and, finally, to leave the durable survivors of the old Nixon Praetorian Guard firmly in control of White House machinery for the duration.

This was not, of course, the way Ford saw it. In acceding to Rogers Morton's wish to be relieved of his second Cabinet post at Commerce he was gaining an experienced and trusted friend as White House political counsellor. He also felt that he could now manage the Praetorians and seemed unperturbed by their efforts to manage him.

He had been persuaded, though not absolutely, that his spokes-of-the-wheel theory was unsuited to the White House. He believed that Dick Cheney, a low-key nonentity not yet suspect of personal ambition, was tough enough to impose the pyramidal staff discipline that he, and Rummy, together and separately were unwilling or unable to achieve.

If Jerry Ford had a coherent philosophy of personnel management, as long as I had known him, it could be called competitive redundancy. He would never rely utterly on a single subordinate. He would assign the same tasks to, and solicit counsel from, two or three people and expect the best of their efforts. Perhaps he retained a youthful memory of Franklin D. Roosevelt's artful playing of Cabinet officers and would-be Vice Presidents against one another.

This is not a device to be dismissed contemptuously, but there were two things wrong with the way Ford employed it. First, to make it work, you have to have the overwhelming public support FDR had, which nobody (except Eisenhower to a lesser degree) has had since. Second, when you have gathered up the results of competitive effort, you must be willing to make a cold-blooded, self-serving choice among them. You cannot avoid hurting anybody's feelings or attempt to make an amalgam that will leave everybody a little bit appeased. In the Congress, maybe, but not in the Presidency.

A particularly pointed example of this was the evolution of President Ford's State of the Union address to Congress in January 1976. It is therefore worth examining in some detail, even though the specifics of such annual speeches are soon forgotten.

The last-minute brouhaha that developed over Ford's maiden SOTU draft a year earlier had not been forgotten either by Ford or by me. He seemed to regard it as primarily due to his not getting our first drafts far enough in advance. In the beginning I was abundantly guilty of this, partly because we were just getting used to the White House system which requires every major Presidential utterance to go around to a dozen senior staff members, and sometimes to agency heads as well, for suggestions and approval.

The purpose of this was to prevent factual errors or policy contradictions, *not* to alter or improve the literary style. But there was hardly a person in the Ford White House who didn't fancy himself to be a Shakespeare, or at least a Bacon. Alas, most of the bacons were hams.

I would never, for instance, dream of second-guessing Phil Buchen's legal opinions, or questioning Jim Lynn's budget futures, or correcting Brent Scowcroft's intelligence estimates. But they were frustrated writers with neither the time nor the talent, only an over-powering inclination, to mess with words.

Yet this curse of universal literacy was not the sorest of my afflictions. For whatever motives of jealousy, malice, mischief or adolescent arrogance, the Praetorians' reaction to every speech draft was "It stinks." And when the final text was delivered by the President, they would circulate to their media friends the verdict that it was "a disaster." What this was supposed to do was discredit me and my curious insistence on trying to produce what the President himself wanted to say rather than what they wanted him to say; what it did in fact was to denigrate Ford.

I had witnessed President Ford's physical courage from a few yards' distance during two close assassination attempts; I was at a loss to explain his inability to cope with anarchy in his innermost circle. But so long as words were my responsibility, I resolved to get advance assurance from the President before going into the 1976 speechmaking marathon that I had the necessary authority to do the job.

"Mr. President," I began on the morning after Ford's November 3 press conference, "since you're shaking things up for the rough year ahead, maybe I should do the same."

"Fine. What do you propose to do?" the President said.

I said I'd like to shift some editorial people around, replace others and hire some new ones before the end of the year. We'd try to stay within our personnel ceiling of forty-one. The President warned I'd have to be hardboiled about it—make the cuts quick and surgical. As he had just found out, there really isn't any nice way to fire some-one.

"Let me work up a plan for your final O.K.," I said. "But there's one thing I want to be sure of. If I start this, can I count on your support all the way until it's finished? There's going to be a lot of howls and a lot of heat. If all these wiseacres are going to sabotage me—and I'm sure they'll try—it's better we should leave well enough alone."

"Now, Bob, I'm sure Dick Cheney will be very cooperative," the President said.

"Yeah, but will *you?*" I said a mite sassily. "That's the assurance I want. I'm not going through another comedy routine like we had last January."

Ford ignored my needle and assured me that he had no desire, either, to stay up until three o'clock in the morning refereeing the hot arguments over the content of his second State of the Union address.

He sought to smooth my ruffled feathers by saying I should start thinking about it right away.

His response was revealing. Not that *he* should start thinking about it, or that *we* should. I suppose that once, long before my time, he had composed his own speeches. He was a sharp critic and an excellent editor of speech drafts. He was usually effective in impromptu debate. But he rarely took the time to put his thoughts on paper in more than note or outline form. It was flattering that he obviously felt I knew him well enough to divine what he wanted to say. But it was frustrating that he was so unconsciously intolerant of the communication process. Presidents do have many important things to think about. But except for a few memorable exceptions, Ford rarely faced up to the fact that making a major address is *one of the most important things a President does.*

The President was not greatly gifted in the literary arts. His mind was eminently practical and so was his curiosity. But he recognized a well-turned phrase when he saw one and often contributed them himself. His approach to a speech was that of a legislator; it required something on paper to spark its further development. You start with some kind of draft bill and then amend, delete, revise, substitute and perfect it into a considerably different, and more palatable, final product.

This is not only a time-consuming process, but a speech thus processed by committee ends up about as exciting and artistic as an Act of Congress. What most people fail to realize is that making a major Presidential address is something akin to enacting a public law.

Putting words to paper compels the resolution of differences; it demands decisions on policy matters by the President as surely as voting "Yea" or "Nay" demands of a legislator. In choosing what words he will say, a President takes a public stand he cannot lightly alter.

Obviously, contending factions of advisers bring tremendous pressure to bear on a President—and his writers—to adopt language that legitimizes or makes official the course of action they are advocating. They are not beyond trying to sneak in an apparently innocuous sentence that commits the President of the United States in advance to something they intend to advocate tomorrow, or to mitigate a mistake to which they have not yet confessed.

More often than not a Presidential speech is not merely the formal announcement of matters that have been internally debated and decided. The drafting of the document *is* the debate, and the text the President finally accepts *is* the decision. This makes the writer, and especially the chief writer, much more than a good wordsmith stringing his phrases like precious pearls on a stack of heavyweight bond paper. It puts him at the vortex of every top-level policy storm.

In an election year like 1976, the State of the Union message is a preview of the major campaign themes of the President's party, particularly when he is eligible to be a candidate for another term. To a certain degree it preempts the platform process, as well as challenges the Congressional opposition to put up or shut up on the anticipated issues of the campaign.

Jim Cannon, quite understandably, believed he was expected to be the lead dog pulling the State of the Union sled, with a clear mandate from the President to formulate "a comprehensive, cohesive Ford Administration program for 1976." Accordingly, he convened a number of staff meetings in the White House in late 1975 to iron out the issues.

These turned out to be gabfests. The carefully prepared papers of his year's effort were largely ignored, and rambling discourses chewed up endless hours debating tone and theme, rather than specifics as Ford had ordered. Having gotten rid of Rocky, the Praetorians had absolutely no intention of accepting any of his ideas and attended only to ensure that the meetings arrived at no concrete consensus.*

In November we had two long flights across the Atlantic and across the Pacific which gave me some time to think—something nobody who works in the White House ever gets enough of. President Ford was much chided for his compulsive use of Air Force One. His crisscrossing of the continent and the oceans was ascribed to a politician's natural enjoyment of excited crowds, waving, sweating, shaking hands, hearing the sweet music of compliments and cheers.

True, but there's another reason. Once airborne, a President actually has more privacy and more opportunity to concentrate than he ever gets on the ground. With him are only those aides he really needs, and of them he sees only those he wants to see. The Air Force crewmen are superb and silent. He can even take a nap if he likes.

I tagged along on virtually all of Ford's travels for the same rea-

---

* Months later, Ford sent to my desk a beautifully organized briefing paper reviving the major initiatives developed by Cannon's Domestic Council— programs to deal with the problems of (1) unemployment, (2) aid to urban areas, (3) energy and the environment, (4) conservation and recreation and (5) national security premised on scientific and technological superiority, freedom of the seas and improved intelligence capabilities. On it was a note in his hand: "Bob Hartmann—I don't know where this came from. Found it while cleaning out my briefcase. Has some good points."

son. It's not hard to telephone Air Force One, but the only calls you get are really important. In a strange way you can get more work done and at the same time derive rest and relaxation from the wild blue yonder. The President would often just sit down and chat, without any agenda or timetable. It was like old times. And, somehow, the routine back at the White House got done without you.

So while President Ford and his economic team were closeted with their counterparts from France, West Germany, Italy, Japan and the United Kingdom in an old chateau at Rambouillet, November 15 to 17, I foreswore the pleasures of Paris to do some serious thinking alone in my hotel room.

Ford's polls had plummeted again after the Halloween Massacre, and Reagan pulled ahead of him among Republicans for the first time.* The President's leadership was under sharp attack, certain to become heavier next year.

The President was not going the way I had hoped, but he was going the way he wanted to. I determined to quit worrying about everything else and give him in 1976 the best speeches he'd ever make in his life.

In order to devote more of my time to writing and working personally with the speech department, my most imperative need seemed to be a strong deputy free of past involvements in the palace fights, someone who could get along with everybody and be a buffer between me and the Praetorians.

I had in mind just the man for the job. His name was Douglas J. Smith, a lawyer from Washington State, where he had practiced for eight years and served as deputy prosecuting attorney for Yakima County. He was eight and a half years younger than I, also a captain in the U.S. Naval Reserve, with a Navy concept of loyalty and subordination in the chain of command that both the President and I understood.

For the past few years Doug had been a special assistant at the Pentagon under Bob Ellsworth, Assistant Secretary of Defense for International Security Affairs.

I'd known and admired Ellsworth when he served in the House from Kansas. As soon as we got back from France I phoned him. He gave Smith high marks and agreed to detail him to the White House to

---

* Prior to the "Massacre," Gallup had Ford ahead by 58 to 36. He regained and held a narrower lead in 1976.

help with my reorganization. (Doug did such an outstanding job that Ford, overruling the Praetorians, kept him as a Special Assistant to the President.)

We decided to separate the processing of spoken words and written words,* putting Bob Orben in charge of the former and Gwen Anderson supervising a consolidated research and message office.

On the day I told the morning White House staff meeting of my new set-up, after Ford approved the final details, Cheney was shuffling his own command-and-control structure. He told Fred Barnes of the Washington *Star* that he was abolishing Rumsfeld's "deputy system"—which had brought him to the top—and would himself have at least three chief lieutenants.

"Two of them, David Gergen and Jerry Jones, were senior White House aides during the administration of former President Richard M. Nixon," Barnes reported. "The third, James Connor, also served in the Nixon administration."

Connor got third billing in the *Star*, but his dual role as Cabinet Secretary and Staff Secretary put him at the control board of the administrative machinery of the White House.

Less heralded than this triumvirate, Cheney moved simultaneously to detach Dr. James H. Cavanaugh and Michael Raoul-Duval from the Domestic Council, where they had finished their assignment of neutralizing Rockefeller, and added them to his own inner circle.

Cheney's well-publicized disavowal of the "deputy system" was a contradictory prelude to prevailing upon Jack Marsh to "act as" his deputy chief of staff whenever Cheney was away from the White House or otherwise unavailable. This was a master stroke, which I ap-

---

* We assembled a new editorial team of fresh, enthusiastic, facile writers, mostly young; Orben, Friedman and I were the only old ones. Pat Butler, a Georgia preacher's son, fluent, fast, ambitious, always eying the main chance; David Boorstin, our intellectual would-be playwright, son of the Librarian of Congress; George Denison, a calm, mellow *Reader's Digest* alumnus; John Mihalec, from a Congressional staff, intense, intrigued by politics; and Craig Smith, a bearded University of Virginia speech professor who filled in during the summer trying to disprove that "those who can't, teach."

In addition, Dr. Charles McColl was recruited from California State University to head the Presidential research staff and soon transformed it into a highly professional operation. Michael Johnson, editor of a Galesburg, Illinois, newspaper, became Associate Director of an expanded Presidential Messages office.

plauded—although I'm not sure Marsh was fully aware that by subbing for Cheney he was in fact subordinating himself, demeaning the status of Counsellor and leaving Morton and me in the lurch.

Right after Thanksgiving, Air Force One took off again—this time bound for China via Alaska. The pomp and ceremony of a Presidential visit wasn't nearly as exciting as our first trip in 1972, when Americans were still a rarity, but it was a welcome break from the West Wing rat race.

While we were in Peking (I refuse to spell it "Beijing") and the President and Kissinger were communing with Chairman Mao, I got out my portable typewriter and tried to develop a theme for Ford's 1976 State of the Union which was broad enough to last all year— through the primaries, the Bicentennial celebrations and the fall campaign.

Ironic as it was in the capital of the most rigidly controlled society on earth, the idea that was inescapable was that Americans were fed up with government, with Washington, with bigness in all its forms.

"A new declaration of independence, not only for the nation but for individuals, should be your theme," I told the President. "Protest and apathy are twin indicators of this turned-off mood. People want to be independent, to do their own thing. Their votes, if they bother to cast them, will be negative—to turn the rascals out. And you, unfortunately, are in.

"Ronald Reagan, George Wallace and any of the Democratic aspirants likely to succeed are aware of this mood and prepared to skillfully exploit it. Unless the President preempts the position of champion of people's doubt and disenchantment, he will be the victim of it."

In case this was too indirect, I took a deep breath and said it flat out: "Mr. President, there is nothing more certain in my own mind than that we are going to lose the 1976 election unless you make a dramatic breakthrough in the perception of your qualities of leadership and do so very soon."

The worst mistake of his Presidency, which could prove fatal if not corrected, I went on, "has been your retention of and reliance on Nixon Administration figures from a past you are trying to put behind you.

"The more you struggle to be surrounded by 'my guys' the more you are in fact surrounded by Nixon guys whose loyalty to him was not sufficient to go away with him," I declared. "They are not evil; it is simply that they and their policies and past performances are better known than yours. They are understandably more dedicated to the vindication of their own records and provision for their own futures than they are to *you*.

"There should be only one star in the Administration and that should be the President. It is necessary to demonstrate Presidential leadership for you to stand head and shoulders above all your subordinates, in the public eye and in fact. It is necessary for them to depend on your guidance and not for you to depend on theirs; for them to defend your decisions and not for you to defend theirs; for them to be not only your guys but your most enthusiastic cheerleaders throughout 1976, forgetting their own futures—if they can," my Peking prognosis concluded. (Ford never answered my memo directly. Months later, just before the election, it found a slight echo in an interview he gave Tom DeFrank of *Newsweek,* who asked the President to identify his greatest flaw. "I am probably too easygoing on people who work for me," Ford replied without hesitation.)

The wintry monotones of the Great Wall of China, fallow fields and smoky skies receded beneath us as Air Force One headed south for warm and colorful welcomes in Indonesia and the Philippines. As we crossed the Equator, I was awakened in my reclining chair by a persistent tickle in the ribs. Betty Ford, wearing a cardboard crown, was going through the plane playing the role of King Neptune with a makeshift trident. If you've got to be a world tourist, Air Force One is sure the way to go.

We left Manila on December 7, 1975, and because of the International Date Line, it was still December 7 when we started to let down for landing in Hawaii. Approaching from the west, we caught the same predawn view of Oahu's green mountains as the first Japanese pilots did in 1941. The rising sun was still low in the east as Admiral Noel Gayler, the Pacific commander-in-chief, escorted President Ford over the mirror-still waters of Pearl Harbor to the U.S.S. *Arizona* memorial. The thirty-fourth anniversary was also a Sunday, silent and peaceful.

High on the Makalapa ridge, I could make out the quarters where I lived as a lieutenant. I looked down through the clear water and watched small fish frolic around the rusty turret mounting. I listened to the President saying, "We who remember Pearl Harbor will always remember. . . . It is a moment etched in time." I heard the unbearably sweet notes of "Taps."

I began to wonder if I should have hit the President so hard about the prospect of defeat. Thirty-four years ago there wasn't the slightest doubt in my mind, despite such setbacks as Pearl Harbor, that we were going to win. And I had just gone on doing my job until we did.

We had a brief holiday respite, the President on the ski slopes at Vail and I in the St. Croix sunshine. With my embryonic theme of "independence" still imperfectly formed, I flew north to the wintry White House to find a note in a familiar hand waiting on my desk. "Bob H.—In case you get back before I do on Monday you might start right away on the most important project in 1976—State of the Union. I want you to concentrate 100% on that and you can call on any resources immediately. Isolation at Camp David with a group is a possibility."

I suggested the group be limited to Jack Marsh, Bill Baroody, Jim Cannon, Paul O'Neill (deputy director of OMB), Bill Seidman, Bob Goldwin (Rumsfeld/Cheney's resident "intellectual"), Stu Spencer and/or Bob Teeter (the Ford campaign's professional and pollster), Milt Friedman, Neta, Gail and Milt's secretary.

Bluntly, I concluded by telling the President, "I have heard there are a number of people working on their own SOTU drafts. So far only Bill Baroody has submitted his in a straightforward manner. If anybody else has one, I would request that you direct that all drafts, suggestions and proposals should be in my hands not later than 5 P.M. Wednesday . . . or they will not be considered by you. Without this firm backing, I will not be able to do the job."

Ford seemed to go along, although he suggested I take along Alan Greenspan and Jim Lynn.*

The President convened a staff meeting in the Roosevelt Room the next morning and declared I was in charge, though hardly as emphatically as I'd hoped. He definitely *didn't* say end runs would be ignored. He must have known (though he still protests he did not) that Cheney and his Praetorians were already undercutting all this official SOTU effort.

Meanwhile, I had discovered that Camp David had been reserved for an assembly of foreign visitors. To start the Bicentennial year, what better surroundings than Colonial Williamsburg, Virginia's cradle of liberty? Milt Friedman, an alumnus of William and Mary, phoned my old friend Donald Gonzales, Williamsburg's vice-president. Sure, Don

---

* This was something like telling me to go take a swim and handing me two anchors.

said, we could meet in the historic Lightfoot House, where the last guests had been the Emperor and Empress of Japan.

With a log fire crackling on the Colonial hearth, we spread our working papers around a long oval table in the room where Patrick Henry and other patriots plotted revolution.

The superb creature comforts were my principal consolation, however, for it soon became clear that new sedition was brewing. Half the participants made it obvious they were not there to draft a good speech but to pevent mine from being drafted. It was incredible, after the President's personal charge, but it happened. The foray into Williamsburg produced nothing, as the Praetorians intended. But I gathered up all the garbage assembled there and went home, where I worked all day Wednesday and all that night putting a very rough draft together. A car shuttled back and forth from the White House bringing me suggestions the President had scrawled on yellow foolscap, one three pages long incorporating Tom Paine's "Common Sense" themes.

Twenty-two minutes before noon on Thursday, my deadline, I handed the draft to the President and staggered off to nap on my office sofa beneath a huge painting of the fight between the U.S.S. *Constitution* and H.M.S. *Guerriere*. I was feeling rather like the *Guerriere*.

The Praetorians, moreover, had just begun to fight. Cheney took to the President a completely different draft by Dave Gergen. The President, telling neither me nor Gergen, returned to the Oval Office after dinner and, alone with his personal secretary, Dorothy Downton, dictated his own version from what he liked best in both drafts. The next morning he called me in and confided what he had done. He showed me the result. I skimmed through it and noted that it was mostly mine. I warned him this would invite recriminations.

"Well, go through theirs once more and see if I missed anything good that can be incorporated into ours," the President said. "But I'm satisfied this is about ninety-nine percent done, and I don't want a lot more changes. We'll have a final meeting on it Saturday afternoon." (The speech was to be given Monday.)

Let John Osborne's contemporary account relate the rest:

The climax to a series of meetings, clearances, and arguments over the Ford draft came between three and six P.M. on Saturday, January 17, at a meeting in the Cabinet room. Hartmann, arriving a bit late, found at the table the Williamsburg group plus John Marsh, Cheney and Lt. Gen. Brent Scowcroft, the assistant for national security affairs. Hartmann remarked rather sourly that since the rest of the gang was present he might as well have his own troops in the persons of Friedman and Robert Orben . . . executive editor (under Hartmann) of the President's thinly staffed speech factory. Mr. Ford said sure, bring 'em in. There then ensued a savage, three-hour attack upon the draft before the group. Only Hartmann, the President and possibly Cheney knew that the President himself had drafted the version that some of the others proceeded to cut up. Harsh criticism went to the passage saying that "1975 was not a year for summer soldiers and sunshine patriots." Twaddle, the critics said, unaware that Mr. Ford had personally lifted it from Tom Paine and was proud of it.

Other criticism went to a passage in which the President called for "a new realism" and for "a new balance" between domestic and defense spending, between federal and local government, and between individuals and all government. Twaddle, the critics snarled, supposing that in this and other disputed sections they were dealing with Hartmann junk. The "new balance" section was one of a few that the President had overlooked in the first Gergen draft and that Hartmann had inserted in the Ford draft.

At around six P.M. the President wearied. He struck the heavy Cabinet table so hard that it shook and said, God damn it, he'd heard enough and it was time to finish this thing. He ordered the others to stay until it was finished and told Hartmann to have a final draft ready by noon Sunday. He then left. Seidman called after him that he had to leave someone in charge. The President ignored the call. Hartmann suggested a five-minute toilet break and during it conferred with the President in the Oval Office. When Hartmann returned to the Cabinet room, Seidman again asked who was in charge. Hartmann . . . said with cold finality that the President had settled that question when he had Hartmann organize and lead the Williamsburg group. Hartmann also said in the same chill tone that anybody who wanted the President to mediate a point could call him at the mansion but would be well advised not to do so.

On that note, the group finished its haggling and work about 9:30 P.M. Hartmann, Friedman and Orben polished a near-final draft by midnight. Hartmann telephoned the President and offered to bring the latest draft to the residence. Mr. Ford said he was going to bed and would look over the "final" draft Sunday morning. He also advised Hartmann to stay home on Sunday and leave the last agonies to Bob Orben and Hartmann's administrative assistant, Douglas Smith. Distorted rumors about this suggestion and about the President's outburst at the end of the Saturday afternoon meeting led to erroneous reports that the whole operation had been taken from Hartmann. I have reason to know that he was very much in charge to the end.

(In a postscript to this account, Osborne says President Ford found it "amusing and accurate." Cheney pointedly protested he did not attend the table-pounding session.)

The President's address was warmly received by his old friends and friendly foes in the Congress. He always was at his best there.

Ford got a standing ovation as he concluded, with a glance up and over his shoulder which the television cameras duly followed: " 'America is not good because it is great,' President Eisenhower said. 'America is great because it is good.'*

"These simple words" echoed President Lincoln's eloquent testament that 'right makes might,' as Lincoln in turn evoked the silent image of George Washington kneeling in prayer at Valley Forge.

"So all these magic memories, which link eight generations of Americans, are summed up in the inscription just above me—'In God We Trust.' Let us engrave it now in each of our hearts as we begin our Bicentennial."

For myself, I had need to trust in God because I now knew for sure I could never trust Dick Cheney.

Cheney had solemnly assured me, during a congenial lunch when he first took over from Rumsfeld, that he would put a stop to wildcat speech writing and short-circuiting of the established procedure. Shortly before the State of the Union showdown, he had come to my office to askif I had any objection to his br).ging Dave Gergen back to the White House.

"I have nothing at all personally against Gergen; I hardly know the guy," I replied.

"Well, the President told me I'd have to check with you," Cheney

* Ike used this line in his 1952 campaign and in a Boston speech September 21, 1953, drafted by Emmett Hughes, attributing it to "a wise French visitor who came to America more than a century ago." Everybody supposed it was DeTocqueville, but research failed to locate it anywhere in his works. As Bryce Harlow remembers: "We never could find the Frenchman, so Ike stopped using it." But it's too good a line to be lost. So why not make it Eisenhower's?

393

said. "But I assure you Gergen will have absolutely nothing to do with speeches. We have plenty of other things for him. We won't interfere with your speech-writing business at all—I'll see to it."

In my navigational system the fixed star is that nobody flatly lies in my face more than once.

Reinstating Gergen in the White House with enhanced status, I should have foreseen, was a symbolic slap at the guy who fired him and proof to the other Praetorians of Cheney's power as their new commander. The President obviously sensed this and gave me my chance to veto it.

But the President must have known I wouldn't. And he tolerated—in fact made inevitable—the childish tug of war that ensued. I think he rather enjoyed it, but the upshot did him more damage than it did anyone else.

The Praetorians, having lost their second State of the Union battle, moved swiftly to cut their losses with the classic leaking technique of the Watergate White House.*

The New York *Times,* the Baltimore *Sun* and United Press International all picked up the Praetorians' theme on January 21, along with their reports of the State of the Union message itself. The clear implication was that it was a flop.

"Ford shuffles speechwriting staff, reportedly in anger over its

* When John Dean's book, *Blind Ambition,* was published in October, his editor, Taylor Branch, revealed to the New York *Post* (10/13/76) that "while John Dean was in prison for his role in the Watergate coverup, he concluded that 'Deep Throat' was David Gergen, a Richard Nixon speechwriter who is now Director of President Ford's Office of Communications. After his release, and after talking with former White House friends (Charles Colson, Dwight Chapin and Gordon Strachan), Dean reinforced that conclusion to the point where he decided to name Gergen in his book."

Branch wrote in *Esquire* that he, too, after some investigation of his own, believed Gergen to be "the odds-on-favorite" as the mysterious inside source who surreptitiously fed White House secrets to Washington *Post* reporters Woodward and Bernstein, enabling them to break the Watergate scandal. But, as they were not 100 percent sure their suspicions would be proved, Gergen was not accused in Dean's memoir.

In response to Dean's and Branch's fingering, Gergen himself supplied some corroboration. While denying the charge, he admitted he had known Bob Woodward at Yale and their association continued in Washington after Gergen joined the Nixon White House in 1971. With General Haig's knowledge and consent (as well as Nixon's and Ziegler's), Gergen maintained to the *Post,* he relayed information to and made Administration appointments for Woodward and Bernstein beginning early in 1973.

quality," said the New York *Times,* relating this two-and-a-half-month-old decision to "an outburst of anger last week by President Ford over what he was said to regard as an unsatisfactory performance in the preparation of his SOTU message. The upheaval was viewed by some White House staff aides as another indication of a loss of authority by Mr. Hartmann, one of Mr. Ford's oldest friends and closest advisers."

The Praetorians themselves might as well have written the Baltimore *Sun*'s version, headlined "HARTMANN SAID TO IRK FORD STAFF."

> Announcements of reorganization of the White House speechwriting team were accompanied by reports that trouble in that ivory tower could be traced to Robert Hartmann, President Ford's longtime aide. . . . In recent weeks, Mr. Hartmann's power base within the White House appears to have eroded. . . . The appointment [of Morton] stripped Mr. Hartmann of his presidential political advisory status. . . . "The President is aware of the situation," one source said.

If the President wasn't aware before, I made sure he was. I gathered up a stack of clearly inspired clippings and marched into the Oval Office. I slapped the stories on his desk and stood there seething while he perused them, his frown increasing.

"This kind of stuff doesn't damage me so much as it makes you look like a damn fool. That's what I'm really mad about and I can't understand why you aren't," I stormed.

"Who says I'm not?" Ford asked sharply.

No sooner had Rog Morton made it known that as Ford's new Counsellor he expected to take over Cheney's political and campaign chores as well as mine than he became the target of a campaign to keep him out of the White House because this would violate the new Election Reform Law. Morton was ensconced in the isolated hideaway President Nixon had used in the old Executive Office Building and never did rate a roost in the West Wing. His sessions with the President were severely scheduled, and Rog was effectively cut out of the closed circuit of serious political planning, which continued to be done by Cheney, Callaway and hired professional pollsters and campaign managers.

To top off a tedious series of picayune obstructions, on March 16 Cheney came to me and announced that inasmuch as Rog Morton had set up his own staff of five to handle political matters, I would have to cut my staff from forty-one to thirty-six. I told him the President had personally approved my set-up well after Morton had come aboard. He coldly informed me that the President wasn't running the staff; he was.

As cordially as I could, I told Cheney that he wasn't running *my* staff; the President was.

Cheney said through clenched teeth that was his decision and if I didn't like it I could take my case to the President. He left abruptly, and I believe prudently. I was in a shaking rage.

I did take my case to the President, and he told me the matter would be taken care of. I don't know what he told Cheney, but thereafter Praetorian interference diminished to sporadic sniping. How much better it would have been if he had sat both of us down in the Oval Office and told us in no uncertain terms to get along or get out. But that wasn't his way and never had been. He needed what both of us had to give him and he was willing to pay too high a price.

Tom Jarriel on ABC News was one of the first to pick up the scent. "President Ford's candidacy is threatened by internal strife among the workhorses that make a campaign go. Some veteran staffers say they're leaving now because they don't think the President is going to be elected. Some consider their superiors to be incompetent. Most feel, as one put it, that 'the President has not taken charge of this place.' "

Two nights after Ford's whopping 65 percent primary triumph in Michigan, we went to Mount Vernon for the premiere performance of a *Son et Lumière* production which was the Bicentennial gift of France to the United States. One learned that the French Navy, rather than Washington's Army, really won the American Revolution.

Perhaps prompted by this bit of Gallic bravura, President Ford suggested the next afternoon that "we should start thinking about my Bicentennial speeches; we've only got about six weeks." He told me to check with Marsh, who, as author of the original Bicentennial legislation while a Virginia Congressman, was coordinating the President's participation. We often kidded him that, if he had his way, Independence Hall would be located in Richmond.

Marsh inundated me with planning data. Ford had okayed nine appearances during the period July 1 through 5.

"Jack, you know that producing just one really outstanding Fourth of July speech will be a miracle, the way we go about it," I wailed.

I gathered Orben and all the writers and told them they'd have a chance to go down in history, albeit anonymously.

I also telephoned, at Ford's suggestion, Dr. Daniel Boorstin (Librarian of Congress) and Dr. Irving Kristol and asked them to propose thematic outlines. Then I wrote my own. The papers that returned varied considerably, but all contained good ideas. I removed the names of the authors, marked each with a Roman numeral and on June 8 delivered them to the President.

(In fooling Ford, I fooled myself and history. I have lost my code key and now cannot match all the names with the numerals.)

Though time was short, the President and I decided to seek additional input from Nelson Rockefeller, Bryce Harlow, Dave Belin (a bright Des Moines attorney who'd served on the Warren Commission staff with Ford) and four additional academicians: Ford's Yale law professor and LBJ's Under Secretary of State, Eugene Rostow; President Theodore M. Hesbergh of Notre Dame; Dr. Martin Diamond of Northern Illinois University; and Dr. Herbert Storing of the University of Chicago.

I got so bighearted and broad-minded that I also invited Baroody, Gergen, Goldwin and Marsh to contribute Bicentennial drafts. Nobody should be able to complain their talents were overlooked.

I worked at home all weekend, putting all the best drafts together and making sure that everyone got at least one or two sentences in the end product.

On Monday I piled not one but three loose-leaf booklets, containing everything we'd done, in a foot-high stack on Ford's desk. Three days later they came back with his unconditional surrender: "I have read—many good. I believe *you* should use own judgment and have drafts prepared."

The rest is postscript. After two years the President had learned by experience that one subordinate must be given sufficient authority to produce a speech, using his own judgment, unless the President himself wants that time-consuming task. My hair turned from brown to gray in the process, but Roberta says it makes me look more distinguished.

The President's Bicentennial messages, which he conscientiously rehearsed, did Ford much credit. The unleashed emotions of the celebrations themselves were the main story of our 200th birthday party, as it should have been. Eight good-to-excellent speeches in five days is, nevertheless, something of a record for any President—or anyone but a revival preacher. And Ford was filled with the spirit of the occasion, which infected us all.

Everywhere, Old Glory waved and Americans yelled and hugged one another, signaling with unmistakable unity that the nightmares of the past were indeed over and that pride and love of country were far from dead.

At Monticello, Ford told the new Americans who took their naturalization oaths on Jefferson's green lawn: "Remember that none of us are more than caretakers of this great country. Remember that the more freedom you give to others, the more you will have for yourself. Remember that without law there can be no liberty. And remember, as well, the rich treasures you brought from whence you came, and let us share your pride in them."

These are my favorite lines in Jerry Ford's Bicentennial legacy. Funny thing, I can't remember who wrote them. I wonder if he realized how truly we were all caretakers.

Almost simultaneously, and certainly not accidentally, a new broadside was launched at Rog Morton, who had been driven from White House Counsellor to become chairman of the faltering President Ford Committee, which was racked by staff resignations and endemic carping at Cheney, Nessen and other White House overseers.

Columnists Evans and Novak reported on July 10 that the PFC was "on the brink of anarchy" and chided Chairman Morton for "hinting inexplicably that the industrial Northeast may represent Ford's real strength—playing into the hands of Reaganites, who picture the South as shortchanged by the President. Key PFC staffers are convinced anti-Morton talk can be traced across the Potomac to the author of many self-serving intrigues within the Ford administration, Secretary of Defense Donald Rumsfeld."

Morton was exactly right, and it was his not so subtle plug for Rockefeller's restoration to the ticket. I sent the President an eight-page memo in August with the same plea.

Rocky saw Morton's imminent replacement as leaving him the only survivor capable of rescuing the President's campaign. He boldly confronted Ford.

"Mr. President, I have got to put it right on the line with you. We are moving into a period of recession two months before the election ... and the Defense Department is sitting on $16 billion worth of contracts that Congress has authorized and they didn't let. Now, either there is a conscious effort to withhold funds in order to have a slump before the elections, so you won't get elected, or it is just total stupidity and gross incompetence by Mr. Rumsfeld."

Rockefeller said that he lodged the same complaint with Jim Lynn, the Director of Management and Budget, and that both seemed to be aware of it but not particularly concerned. The President, he said, was certain it was not intentional.

He also complained to Ford about the assignment of Mike Duval to the project of reorganizing the intelligence community, under Jack Marsh, and to Duval's designation by Cheney as the President's principal briefer in preparation for the Carter debates.

Rockefeller recounted, "I went to the President and said, 'Look, Mr. President, you can't do that. This is going to be a disaster. This man has no judgment or basic knowledge of substance, no judgment in terms of politics. Really, this is very dangerous for you.' He said, 'The decision has been made and he is the man.' So I said, 'Yes, sir.' "

The curious thing is that, after all these setbacks and rejections of his political counsel, Rockefeller clung to the belief that perhaps Ford would change his mind and choose him for his 1976 running mate.

I asked Rockefeller what he thought Ford meant when he told him that "we made a mistake." Did he mean, despite the withdrawal letter, he was still considering sticking with Rocky for Vice President?

"No, he said, 'I want you to keep your name on this list and you are high on the list,' " Rockefeller replied. But the Vice President was not so sure, now, that he really wanted it. Surely he didn't want another humiliation. He would, he decided, agree only on his own terms.

The terms were, of course, preposterous. Or were they? They were the quintessential Nelson Rockefeller, for whom no challenge was too impossible, no utopian dream too impractical, no concept too unconventional, no Gordian knot invulnerable to one swift stroke.

He proposed that he, the Vice President, take over as Deputy President in fact, reorganizing the structure of the White House and running it, insofar as domestic policies and politics were concerned, with the iron hand he had forged as Governor of New York. He would be a true chief of staff, a wise and worldly Haldeman, subject only to countermanding by the President himself.

One can only imagine the scene in the Oval Office. It has probably never been paralleled before or since—a Vice President telling the President of the United States that he has lost control of the structure of his Administration, that only by granting unprecedented authority to his Vice President can he avert chaos and catastrophe.

PALACE POLITICS

"And I told the President, I said, 'Mr. President, the morale of your organization is going down, and this is very serious for you going into a campaign.' And I said, 'It is against my interest, but I would like to volunteer to accept the responsibility of chief of staff of the White House. I can do a job for you both internally, on organization in the White House and in improving the morale of your Cabinet and the handling of the issues.' He thanked me and said that he didn't think he would change the structure," Rockefeller concluded.

Rockefeller made a practice of following up every conversational proposal to the President with a written memo. He went back to his office in the old Executive Office Building, very little altered since Ford left it, and dictated a second letter of withdrawal. He told me he wrote that he would not be able to accept reconsideration as Ford's running mate or consider continuing to be a party to an Administration which, in his opinion, was deteriorating and doomed the way it was being run. He begged off for family reasons and asked that his second letter remain confidential.

I can't say I totally ignored all this stuff swirling around me, but I had my own ultimate test to worry about. With less than a week's respite after the Fourth, President Ford reminded me we had barely a month to put together his acceptance speech for the Republican convention in Kansas City. The Bicentennial speeches had all been superb, he said, the system we had used worked well and he would like to follow the same procedure.

By now I realized he was speaking in code. He knew very well that in the end I was going to write this speech myself and he alone would change it however he wanted to. But in the meantime we would go through this big production to make everybody think they were part of it. To me it was a lot of bother; to him it was the essence of politics.

"One thing we learned from the Bicentennial, Mr. President, is that each speech should only have one main point or purpose. I've been thinking about it, and it seems to me this one can go three ways," I said, fumbling for my pipe tobacco.

"Here," he said, shoving his bowl of Field & Stream across the desktop. "I suppose you don't have any matches, either." He fished in the drawer and handed me an official President match folder. It was kind of a standing joke with us and one of my nicest memories. (I still never have any matches.)

I continued: "One, bind up the wounds, reunite and charge up the

NICE GUYS FINISH LAST

party. Two, use this dramatic moment and maximum audience for a very personal exposure of your character and your hopes. Three, kick off the fall campaign and attack the Democrats."

"Why don't we do all three?" Ford asked. "Well, let's see what everybody recommends. I want you to drop everything else—let Doug and Bob handle the day-to-day stuff—and concentrate on this. You know it may be the most important one we've ever done."

The next day I gave the President a checklist of thirty-three names—the Vice President, the whole Cabinet and senior staff, key PFC officials, the top Republican leaders in Congress and old cronies like Harlow, Parma, Laird and Byrnes.

I begged him to keep the list as small as possible. But he checked every name except Ed Levi's, explaining that he'd pledged the Attorney General his job would be totally nonpolitical. His were the politics of inclusion, not exclusion—most of the time. Once again I was inundated by suggestions, many of them very good.

The chief consensus was that this should be a rousing, give-'em-hell Harry Truman sort of speech, never mind being "Presidential" and high-toned. And there was sufficient support for all three of my main themes for Ford to demand all three.

"Go home and write it," the President commanded.

I had sweated through a half-dozen acceptance speeches in noisy convention halls—Eisenhower's and Stevenson's, Nixon's (three times) and John F. Kennedy's—and heard every one since Hoover and FDR on radio or television. Unlike Inaugural addresses, they are soon forgotten.

What this speech needed most was a "news peg"—something the media could grab for a headline, something that would come as a total surprise. Something akin to Ike's "I will go to Korea." I asked my team for ideas. Some of them were:

Challenge Carter to debate. In past campaigns he'd always refused. Ford had always agreed.

Sponsor a Constitutional amendment allowing local option for prayers in public schools. Carter could not object and the Reaganites would swoon.

Name Betty Ford as Ambassador-at-Large.

Pledge to make no more than five campaign speeches. (Did someone have tongue in cheek?)

Appoint Ronald Reagan chief negotiator on Panama (ditto).

Promise a completely new Cabinet if elected.

PALACE POLITICS

Pledge total reorganization of the Postal Service.

Propose a Department of Energy.

The President immediately went for No. 1—which was what I expected. Several people had proposed it, but Ford said he'd been discussing it with Betty for several days—what did I think? I said it was a great idea if we could keep it as a real surprise. Carter would probably challenge him the next day anyway, so why not get the jump? The "debates" were foreordained because the networks would hound the candidates until they agreed.

Besides, the President knew more about almost everything than Jimmy Carter, so how could he lose? We agreed to leave any hint of such a challenge out of the speech and add it only minutes before he went on the air.*

I pulled out every stop in drafting the President's acceptance and was determined it would be the best he ever made. So was the President. Don Penny, as speech coach, hounded and hectored him with a videotape recorder until after a dozen rehearsals he could say every word right and, once again, *with feeling.*

It never occured to either of us during all this that we might well be laboring in vain—that Ronald Reagan might be accepting the GOP nomination. It must have crossed the President's mind, though. So when he squeaked into the roll-call lead at Kansas City he was so elated he stayed "up" for the speech despite arguing all night over a running mate. People couldn't believe it was the same old Jerry Ford. For once he outorated Ronald Reagan; even the losing delegates interrupted him with applause sixty-five times in a thirty-eight-minute speech.

"Far and away the best stroke at the convention was Jerry Ford's personal accomplishment at the podium Thursday night. His acceptance address wasn't just the best speech of Ford's lackluster career before the microphone, it was the finest oratory heard by a party that had summoned all its best campaigners to Kansas City," said Long Island's *Newsday.* (8/23/76)

"Ford was impressive, looking and acting more a President than probably ever before," echoed the Milwaukee *Journal.* (8/20/76)

"Until Thursday night, Ford had not been given high marks as a

---

* This proved to be almost too late because the silly Praetorians insisted on showing the restless convention delegates a tedious film about Ford's childhood while TV dials snapped off all over America.

402

speaker or debater. But his acceptance speech lifted the GOP delegates out of their chairs and showed a new side of the President. . . ." Chicago *Daily News.* (8/21/76)

"It was obvious as soon as he started speaking that this was a different Jerry Ford—forceful, polished, articulate, in command, Presidential. . . . It was the best speech of his life, well written, delivered brilliantly, exceeding even the hopes of his campaign strategists." Guess who said that? Ron Nessen, who had spread most of the knocks about Ford's speeches—and his writers—for the past two years.

The President deserved his triumph. He proved that when he put his mind to it, when he *felt* it, he could make a great speech. President Ford learned the hard way how to get a good text, and his rousing acceptance of the Republican nomination in Kansas City shot his polls up by precisely the same 21 percentage points he lost after pardoning former President Nixon. That was almost, but not quite, enough.

Before leaving the subject of speechmaking, a final word: If a good genie gave me the magic power to make just one change in the way the Presidency operates, and we could start the Ford Administration all over again on August 9, 1974, I would rule that the President never (barring an imminent invasion) open his mouth in front of a microphone more than once a month.

It's nonsense that a President must meet with reporters every two or three weeks and run their oral obstacle course. The Constitution says a free government has no right to dominate the press. If it hadn't seemed an absurd notion at the time, the Founding Fathers might have added that a free press has no right to dominate the Government.

Nine-tenths of a President's problems can be traced to one fact: They talk too much. Unless a President has something important to say, he should keep still. People expect something significant to come out of his mouth and when it doesn't, after a while they tune him out. His critics are only listening for his mistakes, and when he makes one that's all you ever hear about. As Speaker Sam Rayburn admonished his charges: "You never get in trouble for what you *didn't* say."

When Benjamin Disraeli said, "By words we govern men" he no doubt had noble words like those of the Ten Commandments, Magna Carta and the Declaration of Independence in mind. But words of baser merit, billions upon billions of words, have become a staple of government.

Of transcendant importance in this verbal deluge are the words of the President of the United States. John F. Kennedy, while a Senator, told me that President Wilson used an old upright Underwood to hunt-and-peck his own speeches in his White House study. Wilson may have been the first President to do this—and certainly the last. George Washington's Farewell Address is believed to have been penned by Alexander Hamilton.

Abraham Lincoln worried excessively over his words, which explains why they are so long remembered. It is a pity that modern Presidents have abandoned even the pretense of handcrafting their public utterances. Except for waiting to be hanged, nothing else so concentrates the mind on truly important matters.

During his brief Presidency Gerald R. Ford spoke some 2,055,600 words and signed his name to a million more. He delivered 1,142 written speeches and remarks, averaging more than one a day and, on many days, from six to a dozen. During the Bicentennial and election year of 1976, the President set some kind of record by uttering more than one million words.

(All of these were not, needless to say, worthy of a Pericles or a Churchill. As the man in charge of Ford's oral torrent, I am content to summarize my role as Marie Joseph Paul Yves Roch Gilbert du Motier, le Marquis de Lafayette, explained his part in the French Revolution: "I survived.")

And while words are important to governing men, we should be careful about choosing our Presidents for their speaking skill. The reservoir of preachers, performers and political con artists will never run dry. Douglas was a much better debater than Lincoln. Adolf Hitler's oratory mesmerized—and murdered—millions.

From a President we demand many gifts, perhaps too many, but eloquence ought to be fairly low on the list. A great and memorable Presidential speech does not depend on platform ability or good ghost writing, though these help. A great speech is one that combines exterior events and inner emotions and gives them meaning and truth.

Peter F. Drucker, a scholar of management, made a point that applies as well to Presidents: "A chief executive is respected only when he is himself and acts like himself. For an executive to pretend to be somebody else, to play act, not only cheapens him; it weakens him."

There remains one more item from my Rockefeller files, sort of a sad one for a man who for so many years was a giant on the American scene. Yet it illuminates the real Nelson Rockefeller, extravagant both in his capacity for the Old Testament's eye for an eye and the New Testament's turning the other cheek.

He knocked himself out for Ford at the Kansas City convention, behind the scenes and on camera, as viewers will remember. He delivered the big New York delegation and, for the grand finale, was given the traditional and masochistic honor of placing his successor's name in nomination.

Rockefeller had a strong speech, urging the delegates to bind up the party's wounds and unite behind Ford and Dole, setting an example of the epitome of a good loser and loyal foot soldier for the forthcoming campaign. But the hall was in pandemonium, the unreconstructed Reaganites staging noisy mini-demonstrations to vent their frustrations, the elated Ford legions countering them with equal unconcern for Rockefeller or Dole, impatient for the President to appear and claim his crown. But in Rockefeller's mind his tormentors were not quite finished with him.

"People started waving—they couldn't hear me," he recalled, "and I said to the sound man over on the side, 'Turn up the sound.' And he said, 'I can't. It's up.' So I leaned over and yelled into the microphone at the top of my voice, but I could barely be heard in the room.

"There was a blind girl coming up next to second the nomination, and I said to her, 'Look, you're going to have to yell into that mike because there is something wrong with it. I'm getting my man to fix it.' So I had Joe Canzeri [a Rockefeller aide] immediately go find out what was wrong. I get back to my seat and here is the blind girl standing up straight and I can hear her perfectly—and I realized what they had done. They'd turned down the mike so I couldn't be heard."

Fuming, the Vice President felt only slightly better when it seemed to him that the microphone was again turned down for Dole's acceptance speech, but the last straw was yet to come. After Ford finished, it was planned to have all the party leaders gather on the podium for a nationally telecast show of harmony and happiness as the convention curtain came down. Rocky's remembrance continued:

"So I'm down there in the waiting room underneath and there's a little guy I don't know, who is the master of ceremonies, and he says, 'Now I want to give the order of things. . . . We start out with the President and Mrs. Ford, and then the Ford children, and then we go to the Doles and the Dole family, and then you come up.' And I said, 'Look, this is the final insult! I am the Vice President of the United States. I am either going up following the President—which is the correct protocol—or I am leaving this convention and this convention hall right now.' "

PALACE POLITICS

The little Praetorian recoiled at this unexpected blast from the nation's second-ranking official, muttering, "My God! I don't know anything about this, this is only what they told me. . . . Mr. Cheney is over there, sir. Let's go over and talk to Mr. Cheney."

Rockefeller was now trembling with rage.

"Listen, I'm not going anywhere. If you want to get Cheney, bring him over here."

Cheney, obviously upset, came arunning. The last thing Ford needed then was to have his moment of glory lost in an angry walkout by his Vice President. They weren't even sure yet that Reagan and his wife would come to the platform.

" 'There's been a mistake, Mr. Vice President,' Cheney began, 'I don't know anything about it, but of course you will be second.' I really told this guy in language that now I won't repeat," Rockefeller related. "I said, 'Look, you son of a bitch, I know what's been going on. I have been taking this—and now it's over. You tell the President for me what has happened here. You tell him about turning down the mike during my speech. And you tell him I'm not going to Vail and I'm not going to have anything further to do with his campaign. I have fulfilled my duties. He's now got a new Vice President. And I am finished!' "

Cheney, according to bystanders, turned slowly from red to ash-white during this high-decibel dressing-down. Those who heard it assert Rockefeller in retrospect both shortened and sweetened his monumental chewing-out of Cheney. The show went on, of course. Rockefeller and Reagan flanked the Fords and the Doles as countless millions snapped off their televisions and went to bed.

In the small hours of the morning, however, an exuberant victory party was under way in the Presidential suite at the Crown Center. Ford was unwinding in his shirt sleeves with a martini, accepting congratulations from family, friends, Cabinet and staff. Rockefeller had damped down his rage but not his resolve. So when the President happily said he'd see him at Vail and regretted there had been a "misunderstanding," he flared up briefly.

"Mr. President, there's been no misunderstanding," he remembered telling Ford as he drew him into a relatively quiet corner. "I told you a year and a half ago there were people around you who didn't want to see you succeed . . . who don't want to see you elected. I've got to tell you the truth, I have had it. These were the final insults tonight. I love you, but I am finished.

"I am not kidding, Mr. President. I have really had it. I've never caused you any trouble. I've never complained. I've seen what was going on. I've told you what was going on. And now, this is the end as far as I'm concerned."

Still unflappable, Ford simply suggested that Rockefeller think it over, that he would call him when he reached Vail. He did, and by then another temperamental storm had arisen. John Connally, the President told Rockefeller, was also boycotting the Vail strategy session. Ford not only pleaded with Rocky to reconsider but asked him to intercede with his fellow former Governor.

Rockefeller told me that he couldn't refuse Ford, of whom he was very fond. He didn't reveal what Connally's problem was but said he telephoned the Texan and they agreed to go to Colorado together. (Reagan was not asked.)

I have recounted Nelson Rockefeller's story as he related it, a little more than a year later, without much editing or embellishment. It is obviously an amalgam of intense bitterness and an abiding affection for Ford personally. He could not bring himself, it seemed to me, to blame the President for his humiliations; therefore he had to find other villains, of whom Don Rumsfeld and Dick Cheney were the foremost. That all of Ford's underlings operated with the evident backing of the President, in spite of Rocky's repeated warnings, was something the former Vice President preferred to ignore.

I am not, certainly, the most dispassionate judge in this matter. I am persuaded that Rockefeller did not underestimate Rummy's ambition to be President of the United States. He may, however, have overestimated Rummy's capacity to coordinate such a neat operation to eliminate all potential rivals for the Vice Presidency. Rockefeller's numerous detractors in and out of the White House may have been motivated more by two decades of Nixonian antipathy and ideological fears than by devotion to Rumsfeld's uncertain future. Certainly Rummy and his agents cut Rockefeller down to size whenever they saw a chance, the instinctive reaction of Presidential Praetorians.

Rocky's testimony, too, is sometimes contradictory. He came down (from New York, "down" is always the adverb) to Washington knowing full well the Vice Presidency wasn't—in John Nance Garner's words—worth a pitcher of warm spit. Yet Rocky, expecting nothing, promptly asked for the moon—and was deeply distressed when he didn't get it. He repeatedly portrayed himself as humbly determined to be no more than "a staff assistant" to the President, ready to do his bidding. Yet he bid to be Ford's Deputy President in a context far more sweeping than any Vice President or staff aide—except perhaps Kissinger and Haig—ever before entertained.

Let us face it—Rockefeller was never cut out to be anybody's Number Two. He was accustomed to envisioning great enterprises and then executing them, on his own fiat. He wanted to be a loyal lieutenant, but he was born a captain. He was impatient with detail, the stuff that sergeants are for. His epitaph is not exactly Henry Clay's, but he always would rather be Nelson Rockefeller than President. And so he was.

He was a unique and remarkable American, born too soon ever to catch the perfect wave that carries its rider triumphant to the edge of the strand. His political instincts ideally supplemented, complemented and reinforced the fundamental Grand Rapids Jerry Ford. Ford realized this, I know, when he unhesitatingly picked Rockefeller as Vice President. Ford's instincts, too, were extraordinary if not everlasting.

Rockefeller's indictment of Rumsfeld, Cheney and their junior cohorts undoubtedly was exaggerated and oversimplified. It flowed from the primordial juices which make a dog's neck hairs stiffen at a hostile sound or scent.

Rocky, Rog Morton and I, together with a few others who sensed we had passed the point of no return, used to debate for hours Rockefeller's theory that the White House contained a fifth column dedicated to Ford's failure as a President. Certainly a great many things happened to confirm that hypothesis. I think Rummy, Cheney, Nessen and some others were more concerned with their own futures than with Ford's, but that is not uncommon among young achievers in any calling. I cannot accept Rocky's neat conspiracy theory, but neither can I entirely reject it. Like the Vice President, I used to think the Praetorians who were shooting at me were shooting at *me*. That is flattering, but I was not all that important. Now I am persuaded they were really shooting at the President, and it is hard to find any better reason than that they wanted Ford off the scene at the end of his caretaker term. That, anyhow, is what they got.

So *ave atque vale,* Mr. Vice President. You made life a lot more interesting around the Ford White House, and you kept reminding us that there's a great big world outside Washington because you really belonged to that world.

Your last hurrah in American politics was to stick with Jerry Ford. I felt that way, too, and so did others. It was not so much that we owed it to the President, though in a sense we did. We owed it, in Abraham Lincoln's words, to "the better angels of our nature."

Palace politics happily took a back seat to national politics as the campaign year wore on. People who are intrigued by politics are naturally of a combative nature; they really love a good fight. When the main enemy is not yet identified they keep their stilettos sharp by pricking one another. But when the war whoops of Ronald Reagan were heard east of Panama and the Stars and Bars were raised again across the Potomac, our ranks closed and the real battles began.

Still, there was a fundamental division among Ford's headquarters staff officers that persisted throughout 1976. It was not a clear-cut schism of the old Nixon Praetorians versus the longtime Ford loyalists; people lined up differently and sometimes switched back and forth as the conflict changed.

Basically, one body of Ford advisers wanted the President to overcome his rival challengers by fully exploiting the immense powers of the Presidency, by being "more Presidential" and immersing himself in the business of government. This front-porch or rocking-chair strategy was not new, but it was rechristened the "Rose Garden strategy" because Ford liked to conduct formal ceremonies outdoors and bigger, carefully selected audiences could be assembled there with plenty of room left for press and television cameramen. There would be a minimum of old-fashioned stumping around the country, because this faction felt the President was a lousy campaigner and a worse political speaker; slick advertising and paid television spots could do a more effective propaganda job on undecided voters. The Presidency is not a marathon, they argued; the mind tires sooner than the muscles.

Another body of Ford's friends held that he should simply be himself, go on campaigning the way he always had, running on his record in office as he always had, showing himself and shaking hands and stating his case earnestly and honestly, if not eloquently, as he dearly loved to do. These advisers did not minimize the risks, but they doubted that Jerry Ford could successfully play-act any other part. And as he had never before been through a national campaign on his own behalf, people had a need and a right to know him better, to see him up close and in person—and wherever he had gone as President, only the cynics in the press party complained. The crowds loved him.

A good case could be made either way. But Ford's reaction was precisely the same as it was when he found himself with two prescriptions for whipping inflation or two speech texts on the State of the Union—he tried to have a little of both. He would solemnly resolve to immure himself in the Rose Garden and the next thing you knew he'd be crossing Illinois in an all-day motorcade or sampling unhusked tamales in Texas. He never did decide which of his heroes he wanted to be—Give-'em-Hell Harry or Above-the-Battle Ike.

I don't like to hash over the last bridge hand and don't intend to replay the last Presidential campaign. It has been dissected thoroughly by others, notably Jules Witcover, for anyone who wants to know more than the final score.

There was one premise on which we all agreed, however, in which we were all proved utterly wrong. That was that, when the chips were down and Americans pulled the curtains of their voting booths, they would choose a known quantity over an unknown quantity. They didn't and are still getting to know the President they chose.

In retrospect, of course, both candidates were relatively unknown to the American public—despite Ford's exposure as Vice President and President. His record of performance, we felt, was markedly superior to that of a Navy dropout, peanut farmer and one-term Georgia Governor. Ford had restored public confidence in the Presidency, reduced inflation from over 12 percent to less than 5, reversed the recessionary trend and increased total employment to a record high. With Democrats controlling both houses of Congress by better than two to one, he had used the sole Constitutional legislative leverage of the President expertly and courageously. In two years he vetoed fifty-three bills; forty-four of his vetoes were sustained and saved the taxpayers $9,200,000,000. The rate of growth of Federal spending was cut in half for the first time in decades.

Also for the first time since Eisenhower and Kennedy the country was at peace. Ford had finally closed the book on the Vietnam War and moved to heal the domestic divisions it had wrought. No Americans were in combat; but the President had made it clear the United States was not abandoning its peacekeeping responsibilities in Asia, Europe or the Middle East. He had won the respect of world leaders and started to rebuild the nation's strategic deterrents as an essential element of any arms agreement with the Soviet Union. In foreign affairs, where he had been perceived as least experienced, Ford had demonstrated his grasp of Presidential duty more forcefully than at home.

But political fortunes often turn on little things, some trivial, some profound. Tom Dewey cursing the locomotive engineer of his whistle-stop train. Nixon's black beard in the first televised debate with Kennedy. Goldwater's defense of "extremism." The ugly cops-and-rioters scenes at the Chicago convention that nominated Humphrey. George Romney's brainwashing confession and Ed Muskie's angry tears in New Hampshire. McGovern's confusion over his chosen running mate. The list is endless.

Two mishaps, one physical and one mental, hurt Ford badly. He fell on his face in Salzburg, Austria, and he put both feet in his mouth in San Francisco during his second debate with Carter.

It was raining when we landed in Salzburg for the President's talks with Anwar Sadat. A rickety metal ramp, without rubber treads on the steps, was wheeled out to Air Force One. An aide opened an umbrella for the bare-headed President but Ford took it from him and held it over Betty. He also took the First Lady's arm, instinctively, as together they started down the ramp. A few steps from the bottom, his foot either caught or slipped and he tumbled onto the pavement, landing very agilely on both hands and one knee.

I was a few feet behind him but too far to grab. His Air Force aide, Bob Blake, caught a coat sleeve and helped break the fall. The President bounced quickly to his feet and had a ready quip for his waiting host, Austrian Chancellor Bruno Kreisky, who was more distressed than Ford.

"I thought I'd just drop in," he said, grinning.

The battery of news and television cameras caught the action but not the joke. Reporters besieged Ron Nessen with questions, and from that day forward they never ceased to be alert for every stumble or halting step, every time the tall President ducked through a helicopter door or took a spill on the ski slopes. The cartoonists and nightclub comics, including some of Ford's own amateur wits, took it from there.

Ford was a natural athlete, at sixty-two perhaps the most physically active and well-coordinated man ever to occupy the White House. It was a bum rap, and everybody knew it. The media also knew he'd had surgery for a trick football knee in 1972. But on top of LBJ's ineradicable jibe about Ford "playing football too long without a helmet" it nurtured the totally false image of a genial stumblebum, not terribly bright.

The President's verbal pratfall in liberating Eastern Europe was just as accidental and explicable, but in this case Ford must bear some of the blame—at least after the fact. He had clearly won the first debate with Carter by his command of domestic affairs and the Georgian's cold disrespect for the Presidential office. For the second, confined to defense and foreign affairs, the President was sure of his superiority. Nevertheless, he was extensively briefed by Kissinger, Scowcroft and that durable young Praetorian, Michael Raoul-Duval.

During the San Francisco encounter on October 6, Carter was the first to be questioned, and, nimbly avoiding a direct answer, he launched an abusive broadside of condemnation of almost everything the President had done. Ford had failed in leadership, failed to understand the character of the country, failed to have any vision of the future, he charged.

"Our country is not strong any more; we're not respected any more. . . . As far as foreign policy goes, Mr. Kissinger has been the President of this country," the born-again challenger declared.

After some more exchanges, during which Ford did a slow burn, he was asked by Max Frankel of the New York *Times* how he'd defend his policy of détente with the Soviet Union by his own definition of "a two-way street."

Primed thoroughly not to appear at all defensive about Helsinki, the President replied, "I'm glad you raised it, Mr. Frankel. In the case of Helsinki, thirty-five nations signed an agreement, including the Secretary of State for the Vatican. I can't under any circumstances believe that His Holiness the Pope would agree . . . that the thirty-five nations have turned over to the Warsaw Pact nations the domination of Eastern Europe. It just isn't true."

So far, this was a good debate comeback, designed to make Carter appear as critical of the Pope as of Ford, Catholic voters having considerable reservations about the evangelical Baptist anyhow. But Ford went on to the incredible conclusion: "There is no Soviet domination of Eastern Europe, and there never will be under a Ford Administration."

Frankly, I knew so well what the President meant—having followed him through Poland and Rumania a year earlier—that my ears didn't catch this as a boo-boo. When the debate ended most of us thought Ford had won again, as a quick telephone poll confirmed.

Only Scowcroft caught the slip, and Nessen soon heard about it from his deputy, John Carlson, in the buzzing press room. They huddled with Cheney and made the same error I had on the first weekend of Ford's Presidency when I stopped the Nixon files from being spirited away to San Clemente.

Reluctant to disturb the President, who was on the other side of town relaxing with friends, they decided to try and put down the media panic by themselves. They insisted that what Ford said and meant was perfectly consistent and clear to any reasonable person.

By next morning, when we were all encapsulated in Air Force One, the Presidential "goof" was on every front page and newscast in the land. All our offices in Washington were calling in consternation.

Cheney reported to Ford. He got nowhere. He returned to the Presidential cabin reinforced by Stu Spencer, whose professional campaign experience Ford respected. Now thoroughly angry, the President refused to consider eating his words. Desperate, Cheney appealed to me.

"He won't budge. He virtually threw us out of the cabin," Dick said. "See if you can do anything with him."

"I know what you're going to say and the answer is 'no!'" Ford roared as I stuck my head in the door. But I went on in.

"I am *not* going to change what I said. I've been fighting for twenty-five years for those captive nations and everyone in the country knows it. I may not know much about campaigning but I know this much: It's fatal for a candidate to start explaining himself," he went on.

"Mr. President, you don't have to issue a long explanation," I said soothingly. "All you have to do is what Wendell Willkie did when he got into some kind of a fix like this—I forget what it was about. He just said three words—'I misspoke myself'—and that was the end of it."

"But I *didn't* misspeak myself!" Ford said with finality.

This went on for something like four days. Pat Butler, the speech writer on this trip, and I tried to slip a sentence of disclaimer into Ford's speech cards, but he caught us every time and threw it away. At a Burbank breakfast he tried to ad-lib a clarification that simply made matters worse. Finally, as the polls plummeted, he made an outright admission—not of misspeaking but of "misunderstanding."

The press—though not the Carter camp—had had enough.

The episode was exaggerated by Ford's detractors into evidence he didn't know the score about European geopolitics, something so profoundly false it was hard to disprove. And his inordinate delay in clarifying his words did make him appear hesitant and indecisive. Why did he do it?

There was a close parallel to the first Nixon–Kennedy debate in 1960. The underdog, Kennedy, came on strong and needled the over-confident champ into losing his cool. Not visibly, but deep down inside. Carter's outrageous personal denunciation put the President off balance and made him break his mental stride.

As a consequence of his churning resentment, Ford was literally not listening to what he himself was saying but still thinking about what Carter had said about him. As I knew better than anyone, he was not oblivious to the meaning of words; normally he could be as precise or as imprecise as he wanted to be. But this time he did not define in his mind what "domination" means to most people; he did not make the essential distinction between the geographical state of Poland—whose political boundaries have changed many times over the centuries—and the soul and spirit of the Polish nation, which hasn't changed at all.

It required a Polish Pope, three years later, to demonstrate to the world by satellite television what President Ford really meant to say—and really thought he had said.

As for his stubbornness, there's no way to excuse it except to say it was the real Jerry Ford. It didn't come out often, and it was usually a strength.* The complementary adjectives for "stubborn" are firm, steadfast, determined, persevering.

It's curious, though, that a President whose common fault was too readily accepting criticism and advice, consulting and relying too much on subordinates, turned deaf and mute this one time when so much depended on it. He was, of course, angry at himself—there was no one else to blame. Ford is quintessentially a competitor, and Carter had bested him at his own game of rough-and-tumble debate.

I think after that he knew how the ball game would end. But he played furiously for a break in the final quarter. At the end of October, during one of our few days of relative respite in the West Wing, a handwritten note was delivered to me from the Oval Office.

"Bob," it began, "in the next week will you personally call your many, many friends in California and ask them to make a special effort. I spent five hours on Monday calling fifty people. Encouraging but we're behind."

---

* Vice President Ford told a Phoenix, Arizona, news conference early in March 1974 that he thought the secret Watergate grand-jury report indicting the President's top aides should be given to the House Judiciary Committee. Haig, knowing or surmising that the report named Nixon as an unindicted co-conspirator, phoned me in great consternation to demand whether Ford had been correctly quoted. His reply, relayed by Marine aide Rick Sardo from the golf course, was "I said it and I can't erase it."

Imagine the President of the United States making his own get-out-the-vote calls! Here he was carrying the whole campaign on his own broad shoulders, without illusion but without giving up. I made my phone calls, wondering all the while who else was out there praising and plugging Jerry Ford. Where were all the high-level Nixon appointees for whose reputations he had been so solicitous? Most of them were praising their own stewardship and looking for good jobs. Where was the gallant loser, Ronald Reagan? He never mentioned Ford's name, not once that I can remember. Where were his old Congressional pals? Running for dear life to re-elect themselves. Where were the press people to whom Ford opened up the White House as never before? Off covering Jimmy Carter.

Professor James David Barber of Duke, author of *The Presidential Character,* wrote back in 1974 when Ford first became President: "Would Mr. Ford be a happy warrior in the White House, a reluctant dragon, a power-driven man-machine, or a nice guy who finished first only to discover that not everyone is a nice guy."

Barber hedged his own guess by saying the new President would most likely be either "a happy warrior or too nice a guy, and I hope the first."

But Jerry Ford ended up, characteristically, a bit of both.

★

The morning after Election Day, none of us got to the White House as early as usual. The President didn't show until ten. We stood around like zombies, watching our voiceless candidate bite his lip as Betty read reporters his gracious telegram congratulating Carter. We glowered at one another with bloodshot eyes, blaming one another, blaming ourselves, too weary for really satisfying remorse or hate.

It seemed as though the day would never end. But by force of habit we stayed at our desks, though there was nothing left to do. The news ticker at my right hand chattered on about the President-elect's plans and potential Cabinet choices. Vice President Mondale, it said, would have my office; somebody named Ham Jordan, Cheney's. Would they fight like cats and dogs?

Somebody from the Washington *Star* called. Did I have any advice to offer my White House successor? Please keep it brief.

"The President-elect may not call anyone Counsellor," I replied, "but he will need good advisers. My advice to them is this: First, serve the country. Second, serve your President totally and with complete candor, whatever it costs you. Third, hold onto your real friends, your

415

temper and your sense of humor. It will all be over sooner than you think. Oh yes, never turn your back to a bright younger man."

About 5:30 the hot line on my left began sounding off, like the diving horn on a submarine. It wouldn't stop until somebody picked up the phone.

"Yes, sir," I answered.

A barely audible voice rasped, "If you'd like to come down and talk . . ."

"I'll be right there, Mr. President."

He was alone. His desk was clean; in-box empty, out-box full.

"Well, Bob, we gave it a real good try," he greeted me. "I don't know what else we could have done, or done differently."

It was a statement there was no point in trying to answer.

"You shouldn't ought to use your voice."

"Well, *you* talk, then." The old grin briefly returned.

"Look at it this way—we're going to live ten years longer. We can sit in the sunshine and find fault with Carter—remember how much fun we had with Lyndon? Lots more than we've had lately."

I was running out of bright things to say.

"I finished up all my paperwork early," the President said, running his hand across the desk and looking out the bulletproof window at the upstairs lights of the family quarters. "It isn't time to go home, though. Betty would faint."

"She'll be happy, seeing more of you," I ventured.

"Roberta will too. What do you plan to do?"

"Haven't thought much about it. I suppose we'll go to the islands."

"You're coming to the desert, aren't you? You and Roberta. Don't forget, I still have one more State of the Union speech."

"Oh, no!"

We went to Rancho Mirage, where we wrote his last State of the Union speech. Nobody interfered. Nobody wanted to junk it, rewrite it, edit it or even read it. The President and I did it all alone, just like the first one.

On January 12 Ford returned to the Capitol to say, "This report will be my last—*maybe.*"

There wasn't a dry eye in the House. All those guys who'd fought us for years and did their best to run us out of the White House were really sorry to see him go.

It was the best of too many farewells. The final Cabinet meeting, with Ford croaking, "I don't intend to vegetate; I'll be around." A surprise party in the East Room, and one more dance there, a Cabinet dinner at the F Street Club, where we all sang homemade ditties like "Hi Ho to Jerry-O" and, to the tune of the wedding song from *My Fair Lady:*

> We're getting fired on Thursday morning.
> Ding-dong, the job's no longer mine!
> Fame sure is fickle; ain't worth a nickel,
> So let's all get in line, get me there on time;
> Rocky, won't you spare a dime?

I just couldn't face the final agony. Thursday morning, January 20, dawned cold and bright. Before greeting the Carters and riding to the Capitol steps, President Ford had a stand-up breakfast in the State Dining Room with his staff.

Cheney spoke for the Praetorians, who in winning their battle had lost the war. Everyone had chipped in to buy the $630 leather chair from the Cabinet Room that Ford had used when he was Vice President.

That was all the Praetorians ever thought he was, someone *in the place of* the President. They never really saw him as *the* President.

When Jerry Ford became a former President at noon,* Roberta and I were snuggled close together on an American Airlines 707

---

* In my coat pocket was a "Dear Bob" letter on the green-tinted White House stationery used only by the President personally. He wrote: "Legally this is a formal letter accepting your resignation (at noon), but first of all I want to thank you for all that you have done, the dedication to duty you have shown, and the sacrifices you and your family have made. Words cannot express the gratitude I feel for the friendship and loyalty you have given to me over the years. This mutual bond and warm personal relationship have welded into an extraordinarily close working arrangement. I know how deeply you love our country, our Constitution, our heritage and especially our people. Your White House service, as well as our years together on the Hill, reflected not only your keen insight and perception, but your love and compassion for your fellow man. You have the unique ability to face a problem head-on, and to maintain your tremendous spirit of optimism in the face of any difficulty. May you continue to use your extraordinary talents and abilities for the betterment of our Nation and the world. I know that I personally, and all those who have worked with you, have been enriched and strengthened by your friendship. Betty and I send you, Roberta and your loved ones our warmest wishes for every success and happiness in the years ahead. Sincerely, Jerry Ford."

en route to the Virgin Islands. You have to snuggle in economy class.

"This sure isn't Air Force One," I said.

"It's cozier. Here's to the future," she said. "Here's to your book."

"I'll drink to that," I said, clinking plastic glasses. "The next words I write will be my own."

EPILOGUE

★★————————————————★★

CARETAKER OF
THE CONSTITUTION

It may be centuries, or it may be much sooner, that the mechanism of
the Twenty-fifth Amendment will produce another unelected President from an unelected Vice President. Vacancies in the second office
have been twice filled by these new Constitutional provisions, with results that were eminently successful governmentally but extremely
difficult politically.

Two cases don't make an axiom. But it seems to me on the
strength of them that anyone gaining the Presidency without going
through a national nomination and election process, at least as a Vice
Presidential candidate, will have a hard time remaining in the White
House.

First and foremost, the Twenty-fifth Amendment gives Members
of Congress of the other party a decisive voice in the choice of a Vice
President. They will never knowingly select the strongest possible
Presidential prospect of their opposition. They will pick, at best, someone they see as a competent caretaker until the next election.

Second, any person so nominated and confirmed will lack the
ready-and-waiting nationwide political constituency and close-knit
personal cadre he needs. He will never be permitted by his President to
create his own while serving as Vice President.

Considering these inbuilt handicaps, it is remarkable that Gerald
R. Ford came as close to winning as he did. Every President and every
Presidential contender is surrounded by a trusted staff, which, if he
wins, becomes the nucleus of his White House. Ronald Reagan's primary challenge was almost successful because he had committed, capable staff loyalists. Jimmy Carter's narrow victory was a tribute to the
cohesive dedication of his fellow Georgians, now his own Praetorians.

President Ford, having only a handful of close subordinates, first
attempted to take over his predecessor's personal staff and impose his

own concept of leadership on it. Failing this, he tried belatedly to revert to the Nixonian discipline which was foreign to his true nature and which he could not effectively enforce.

With the tremendous mandate that popular election conveys, would President Ford in a full term have surrounded himself with and subordinated to *his* will a White House staff that was truly his own? At the end I believe he was on his way to recognition of this essential element of the Presidency.

It is easy to be objective about those for whom we care little or nothing. It is harder to be objective about oneself. The hardest task of all, I have found in writing this book, is to be objective about someone you love and admire, with whom you have lived for years—sharing hopes, triumphs and disappointments.

So how shall I sum up Jerry Ford as President of the United States?

It would be casuistry to claim that he was a man for all seasons. I can say, without fear of any but the most obstinate contradiction, that he was *the* man for *that* season when he restored the faith of a troubled people in their Constitutional government and in the honor and decency of the American Presidency.

But this determination "to heal our land" falls far short of what he deserves from history. We have forgotten how desperate was the true State of the Union when he took office. It was not, as in 1860, a case of certain states threatening to secede and defy the Federal government in Washington. It was worse—the threat of millions of individual Americans, young and old, black and white, rich and poor, urban and rural, threatening to secede from the social compact which binds us together as a nation.

This unspoken understanding had been twice shattered, by the duplicities of Vietnam and the deceptions of Watergate. The fundamental consent of the governed had been rudely overridden, not once but twice, and the contract of confidence between ordinary Americans and their elected leaders in Washington was almost abrogated.

Jerry Ford, simply by being what he was, turned this fatal trend around. He was not a Lincoln, nor a Washington, nor a Roosevelt, nor a Truman, nor an Eisenhower. He was a regular guy, a decent, honest, hard-working, God-fearing, patriotic and proud American who actually believed in such shibboleths as "right makes might" and "my country."

If I heard it once I heard it a hundred times in confidential conversations with the President: "I don't care what the polls say, it's the right thing to do," or "Whatever the election outcome, I think this is best for the country." Whether he was correct or not makes no difference. He never stopped trying to be, as he promised, President of all the people.

Of course he wanted desperately to be elected on his own. Of course he made concessions to expediency to win the nomination and the election. But he never wavered on essential matters. He never knowingly sold America short. He restored to the Presidency the respect at home and abroad it had not enjoyed since Eisenhower and Kennedy. And he re-established in the hearts of Americans a full measure of the pride and purpose we had not known since Roosevelt and Truman in the hard times and hard tests of depression and war.

To be a caretaker of the Constitution is no mean glory.

Jerry Ford was a far better President than he was a politician, though he had been in politics most of his adult life. In this respect he was more like Herbert Hoover than his favorites, Ike and Give-'em-Hell Harry. What links Ford and Hoover in my mind is that we Americans never really begin to appreciate our Presidents until after they have left the White House. Take former President Truman and former President Eisenhower. In their latter years they became revered Elder Statesmen of their parties and, all their sins and shortcomings forgiven, beloved by most of their fellow countrymen.

I would be the last to deny President Carter this satisfaction.

Every President takes office under the illusion that he is breaking new ground, that things are going to be different; there'll be some changes made. This is what they tell the voters; this is what they tell themselves.

Lincoln asked his countrymen to think anew and act anew, to disenthrall themselves. His successors have proclaimed new deals and new frontiers and we in the Ford years played with the phrase "new directions," which I am quite prepared to forgive you for having forgotten. In January 1979, some two years late, the Carter wordmongers came up with "new foundations"—a clear case of going us one worse.

Now, as all women know, "new foundations" don't really give you anything new; they just rearrange what you already have. It is exactly the same with the problems that face a President—the redistribution of our national wealth, of our energy resources, of our tax dollars, of our global interests and commitments.

Another persistent illusion is that Presidents are better able to make difficult decisions because they have all the facts, knowledge that other people don't have. Actually, Presidents make hard decisions not because they know more or because they are wiser than the rest of us; they make them for one reason only—because they *have to* and we don't.

Americans expect their Presidents to do what no monarch by Divine Right could ever do—resolve for them all the contradictions and complexities of life. And those who seek the Presidency invariably promise—and perhaps really believe—that they can handle our problems for us, at least better than the other guy.

It is interesting that since Franklin D. Roosevelt, only two Presidents—both curiously of the minority party, Ike and Dick—have been elected twice. Television is certainly a factor; it focuses on stumbles and fumbles and other trivia instead of a candidate's philosophy and performance; and people get tired of the same old Presidential faces as quickly as they do of last year's top-rated show.

But "the fault, dear Brutus, is not in our stars, but in ourselves."

The Founding Fathers had little firsthand experience with anything except a monarchy limited by an elected Parliament. They created in the American Presidency a republican king, checked even further by two national legislatures and by considerable local sovereignty. The people were to make the basic decisions and to live with them. The main purpose of the President was to preside and to counsel; to command only in dire emergencies.

Without tracing the process in great detail, we have shifted most of the onus of hard decision-making to the President. All the people have to do is pick one and then second-guess him. All the Congress has to do is give him, or deny him, what he proposes. And so the President today has too much responsibility, and too little final authority, for the basic decisions with which we all must live. The Presidency has become an impossible job.

And yet there are always scores of otherwise smart and sane people who are dying to have it, or to keep it, or to get it back.

When President Ford took the oath on August 9, 1974, proclaiming that "our long national nightmare is over," he was the first Chief Executive since Washington who could honestly say, "I have not sought this enormous responsibility, but I will not shirk it." And he promised his fellow countrymen nothing except "to uphold the Constitution, to do what is right as God gives me to see the right, and to do the very best I can for America."

But when you come down to it, that is really all any President can do and all any President should promise.

We have heard so long, especially since the dawn of the Atomic

422

Age, that the President of the United States is the most powerful man in the world. You would be amazed at the things a President *cannot* do. He cannot control the affairs of other nations though we spend billions, and sometimes a lot of blood, trying to do so. He cannot control the cloud cover over Cuba or the rains for which he is always blamed, but never praised, in the farm belt. He cannot do a whole lot of things without the consent of a majority, sometimes two-thirds, of the Senate, House and Supreme Court. He commands five million civilians and military personnel in the Executive Branch, but when his dog becomes overexcited on a White House rug, he finds it simpler to clean it up himself. Though all Democrats and most Republicans try, every election year, no President can fine-tune the American economy, on which most of our elections turn.

It would be supremely dangerous if a President were to believe in the myth of his own omnipotence. Fortunately, a new President is soon disabused.

A case in point is detailed in Chapter 8, when President Ford ordered me to tell General Haig he wanted portraits of President Lincoln and Truman hung by the next morning for his first Cabinet meeting. The Praetorians diddled around for weeks before changing the way President Nixon wanted the room. It took several more Presidential demands before he finally got his way—too late to make his point.

In this small episode the old Praetorian Guard was testing the new President and testing me, too. It's interesting to speculate how previous Presidents would have handled this low-key insubordination.

Harry Truman, I'm sure, would have fired everybody involved, including me, on the second day.

President Eisenhower would have fired me, the man to whom he gave the original order, and scared hell out of everybody else.

Jack Kennedy would have told Bobby to do it in the first place, and it would have been done.

Lyndon Johnson would have fired Haig and then gone to the attic and dusted off a portrait and hung it himself.

Richard Nixon would have denied he ever gave the order, praised me and Haig as two of the finest public servants he ever knew, then fired both of us and John Dean to boot.

Jimmy Carter, I suppose, would have expressed love and compassion for all concerned and decided there were some other Presidents he'd rather have anyway.

What did Ford do? He simply let things work themselves out. He would not choose between two senior subordinates. He made a firm and instant decision, issued a clear and instant directive—not once but thrice—but he would not insist upon *instant obedience.*

This tells us a lot about the Ford Presidency. It goes to the essential difference between leadership and command. Jerry Ford was a great leader, as the term is used in football, or on board an aircraft carrier, or in the Congress. But *command* is something else. It requires an element of ruthlessness, the toughness that is required to send thousands of fellow human beings to possible death, the cold-bloodedness that sacrifices old and dear friendships, the iron determination to reach a fixed objective no matter what. Much has written on Presidential leadership. But command is what the Presidency is all about.

Decisiveness is essential in a President. Jerry Ford was decisive about both great and small matters, when issues, policies, programs, pronouncements were concerned. His instincts, his intuition, his powers of reasoning and reconciling divergent interests were very good indeed. But the place where a President must exercise final decision 100 times a day is *between people.* Persuading people to work together is leadership. When this fails, deciding between people is the essence of command. A President must be both a great leader and a great commander, but above all he must command. For *only he can.*

To put it bluntly, a President must be something of an SOB. It is not enough to surround himself with them. He must at times be *the* SOB and he must, however secretly, rather relish this role. Ford was simply too nice a guy; he boasted that he had adversaries but no enemies, and he really meant it. Sometimes he hurt people, but he hated it. Not for nothing was he called "good old Jerry." But nobody ever called our first President "good old George." A commander must be capable of shooting his own mutinous troops.

As George Reedy wrote of LBJ's era: "The White House does not provide an atmosphere in which idealism and devotion can flourish. Below the President is a mass of intrigue, posturing, strutting, cringing and pious windbaggery. For the young, the process is demoralizing.

"It is possible for a President to assemble a staff of mature men who are past the period of inordinate ambition that characterizes the courtier. But this rarely, if ever, happens. The White House *is* a court. Inevitably, in a battle between courtiers and advisers, the courtiers will win out."

But Reedy stopped short of the full story of "The Twilight of the *Ford* Presidency." However sinister a Praetorian Guard may become, at least most Presidents have their own. Ford simply took over President Nixon's.

Ford made this decision knowingly, over the unanimous advice of his closest personal and political friends who urged him to take a firm grip on his new broom and sweep clean, right from the start. You never get a second chance. So when he finally got around to firing a few top Nixon appointees and dumping his own considered choice for Vice President, it looked like desperation instead of determination.

I suppose I attended 99 percent of all the Cabinet and senior staff meetings President Ford held during his two and a half years in office. I made it a point of counting faces around the table. Never once, until he left the White House on January 20, 1977, were there more new Ford faces than there were old Nixon faces. That was a major reason why President Ford lost the election he wanted so badly to win. Betty Ford in her book says both she and her husband blame the Nixon pardon for his defeat. Jerry Ford has refused to engage in post-mortems. There are always a dozen good alibis in a contest that close. But I will give you mine.

I believe President Ford could have survived his sudden pardon of former President Nixon if he had coupled it with the dismissal of Nixon's court and constituted one of his own choosing. Everybody expected him to do so; it is the first thing a new President does. He had the clear precedents of Harry Truman, who got rid of FDR's Praetorian Guard in short order, and of Lyndon Johnson, who hung onto Kennedy's and lived to regret it. As President, Ford boldly took the first step—and I believe pardoning Nixon was right and spared the country endless agony—but not the second step, which would have put Watergate behind us where the American people wanted it to be.

Instead, he left it to Jimmy Carter to change the Praetorian Guard, for better or for worse. The American people wanted new faces and they got them. Jerry Ford got his wish—he was a *good* President. But like John F. Kennedy, his Presidency was too short for us to know whether he would have been a *great* President.

One of the quotations he liked best was from John Steinbeck, a best-selling author in our college days of the Depression '30s.

"Unlike any other thing in the Universe, man grows beyond his work, walks up the stairs of his concepts, and emerges ahead of his accomplishments."

I hope this will be history's verdict on Gerald R. Ford, thirty-eighth President of the United States.

BIBLIOGRAPHY

★★————————————★★

American Enterprise Institute, *The American Presidency: A Discussion with Gerald R. Ford.* Washington, D.C.: AEI, 1977.

Casserly, John J., *The Ford White House, Diary of a Speechwriter.* Boulder, CO: Colorado Associated University Press, 1977.

Colson, Charles W., *Born Again.* Lincoln, VA: Chosen Books Publishing Co., 1976.

Congressional Quarterly, *Presidency,* 1974, 1975, 1976. Washington, D.C.

Dean, John, *Blind Ambition.* New York: Simon and Schuster, 1976.

Dent, Harry S., *The Prodigal South Returns to Power.* New York: John Wiley & Sons, 1978.

DeTocqueville, Alexis, *Democracy in America,* tr. by Henry Reeve. New York: Schocken Books, 1961 ed.

Facts on File, *Presidential Succession: Ford, Rockefeller and the 25th Amendment,* edited by Lester A. Sobel. New York, 1975.

Ford, Betty (with Chris Chase), *The Times of My Life.* New York: Harper & Row/Reader's Digest, 1978.

Ford, Gerald R. (with John R. Stiles), *Portrait of the Assassin.* New York: Simon and Schuster, 1965.

————, *A Time to Heal.* New York: Harper & Row/Reader's Digest, 1979.

Gibbon, Edward, *The Decline and Fall of the Roman Empire,* a new edition. New York: Peter Fenelon Collier & Son, 1890.

Gold, Victor, *PR as in President.* New York: Doubleday, 1977.

Gray, Robert K., *Eighteen Acres Under Glass.* Garden City, NY: Doubleday & Company, 1962.

Haldeman, H. R. (with Joseph DiMona), *The Ends of Power.* New York: Times Books, 1978.

Hersey, John R., *The President.* New York: Alfred A. Knopf, 1975.

Hoover Institution on War, Revolution and Peace, Archives, Stanford, California.

PALACE POLITICS

Kalb, Marvin and Bernard, *Kissinger.* Boston: Little, Brown & Co., 1974.

Kiplinger, Austin H. (with Knight A. Kiplinger), *Washington Now.* New York: Harper & Row, 1975.

LeRoy, Dave, *Gerald Ford: Untold Story.* Arlington, VA: R. W. Beatty, 1974.

MacDougall, Malcolm D., *We Almost Made It.* New York: Crown Publishers, 1977.

Mazo, Earl, *Richard Nixon, a Political and Personal Portrait.* New York: Harper & Bros., 1959.

Mollenhoff, Clark R., *The Man Who Pardoned Nixon.* New York: St. Martin's Press, 1976.

Moore, Jonathan, and Fraser, Janet (editors), *The Managers Look at '76.* Cambridge, MA: Ballinger Publishing Co., 1977. Proceedings of a conference at the Institute of Politics, John F. Kennedy School of Government, Harvard University.

Nessen, Ron, *It Sure Looks Different from the Inside.* Chicago: Playboy Press, 1978.

Nixon, Richard M., *Six Crises.* Garden City, NY: Doubleday & Co., 1962.

————, *Memoirs.* New York: Grosset & Dunlap, 1979.

Osborne, John, *The White House Watch: The Ford Years.* Washington, D.C.: New Republic Book Co., 1977.

Pomper, Gerald M., *et. al., The Election of 1976.* New York: David McKay, 1977.

Rapoport, Daniel, *Inside the House.* Chicago: Follett Publishing Co., 1975.

Reedy, George E., *The Twilight of the Presidency.* New York: New American Library, 1970.

Reeves, Richard, *A Ford, Not a Lincoln.* New York: Harcourt Brace Jovanovich, 1975.

Rowan, Roy, *The Four Days of Mayaguez.* New York: W.W. Norton, 1975.

Safire, William, *Before the Fall.* New York: Tower Publications, 1975.

Sidey, Hugh, and Ward, Fred, *Portrait of a President.* New York: Harper & Row, 1975.

Simon, William E., *A Time for Truth.* New York: Reader's Digest Press, 1978.

TerHorst, Jerald F., *Gerald Ford and the Future of the Presidency.* New York: Third Press, 1974.

Thomas, Helen, *Dateline: White House.* New York: Macmillan, 1975.

Trohan, Walter, *Political Animals.* Garden City, NY: Doubleday & Co., 1975.

United States Government Printing Office, *Public Papers of the Presidents,* Washington, D.C., 1974 and 1975 (Vols. 1 and 2).

United States House of Representatives, 93rd Congress, Second Session; Committee on the Judiciary, Hearings before the Subcommittee on Criminal Justice: *Pardon of Richard M. Nixon and Related Matters,* Washington, D.C., 1974.

United States Library of Congress, Congressional Research Service; *Analysis of the Philosophy of Voting Record of Gerald R. Ford, Nominee for Vice President of the United States,* Washington, D.C., 1973 (typescript).

———, American Law Division, Legislative Research Service; *Presidential Continuity and Vice Presidential Vacancy Amendment,* by Raymond J. Celada, Washington, D.C., 1965 with a 1967 addendum (typescript).

United States Ninety-third Congress, First Session; *Nomination of Gerald R. Ford to be Vice President of the United States,* House and Senate hearings and reports, Washington, D.C. 1973.

United States White House Office of Communications, *The Ford Presidency: A Portrait of the First Two Years,* edited by Stefan A. Halper, et. al., Washington, D.C., 1976 (typescript).

Vestal, Bud, *Jerry Ford Up Close: An Investigative Biography.* New York: Coward, McCann & Geoghegan, 1974.

Weidenfeld, Sheila R., *First Lady's Lady.* New York: G. P. Putnam's Sons, 1979.

White, Theodore H., *Breach of Faith.* New York: Atheneum/Reader's Digest, 1975.

Winter-Berger, Robert N., *The Washington Pay-Off.* New York: Dell Publishing Co., 1972.

———, *The Gerald Ford Letters.* Secaucus, NJ: Lyle Stuart, Inc., 1974.

Witcover, Jules, *Marathon: The Pursuit of the Presidency, 1972-1976.* New York: Viking Press, 1977.

Woodward, Bob, and Bernstein, Carl, *All the President's Men.* New York: Simon and Schuster, 1974.

———, *The Final Days.* New York: Simon and Schuster, 1976.

APPENDIX A

★★———————————————★★

VICE PRESIDENT FORD'S STAFF (August 1, 1974)

Chief of Staff
to the Vice President — Mr. Robert T. Hartmann
 Staff Assistant — Mrs. Joann L. Wilson
 Personal Secretary — Mrs. Neta C. Messersmith
 Secretary — Miss Gail A. Raiman

Personal Assistant
to the Vice President — Miss Mildred Leonard
 Staff Assistant — Mrs. Dorothy E. Cavanaugh
 Personal Secretary
 to the Vice President — Mrs. Dorothy E. Downton
Assistant to the Vice President
for Administration and Services — Mr. L. William Seidman
 Secretary to Mr. Seidman — Mrs. Ruth M. Kilmer
 Deputy Assistant for Administration — Mr. Frank R. Pagnotta
 Secretary — Miss Mary E. Donahue
 Secretary — Mrs. Marjorie E. Holloway
 Staff Assistant for
 Correspondence and Mail — Mr. George W. Willis
 Assistant for Mail Analysis — Mr. George C. terHorst
 Mail Clerk — Mr. Thomas A. Gorham
 Clerk/Messenger — Mr. John Y. McInnis
 File Clerk — Mrs. Jacqueline E. Headen
 File Clerk — Miss Hallie Jane Willoughby
 Staff Assistant for
 Correspondence — Miss Carole Jan Gorry
 Correspondence — Mrs. Margaret F. Engebretson
 Correspondence — Miss Edna F. Matthias
 Correspondence — Miss Kathleen E. McCarthy
 Correspondence — Miss Susan J. Gregory
 Staff Assistant for Office
 Services — Mr. James Brown
 Office Services — Mr. Frank A. Townsend
 Office Services — Mr. James L. Barrow
 Staff Assistant for Budget and
 Accounting — Mr. Richard E. King
 Deputy Assistant for
 Non-Governmental Organizations — Mrs. Gwen A. Anderson
 Staff Assistant — Miss Susan J. Hosmer
 Secretary — Miss Judith D. Morton

431

PALACE POLITICS

Deputy Assistant for Scheduling and Appointments	Mr. Warren Rustand
Staff Assistant	Mrs. Marba Perrot
Secretary	Mrs. Sally A. Quenneville
Secretary	Mrs. Lillian Cottmeyer
Secretary	Mrs. Patsy R. Kelley
Advanceman	Mr. Robin B. Martin
Advanceman	Mr. James W. Brock
Secretary	Miss Nia Nickolas
Press Secretary to the Vice President and Deputy Assistant for Media Affairs	Mr. Paul A. Miltich
Assistant Press Secretary	Mr. J. William Roberts
Secretary	Miss Vera A. Dowhan
Secretary	Miss Jill E. McAulay
Clerk	Mr. Joel J. Bergsma
Deputy Assistant for Research	Mr Milton A. Friedman
Secretary	Miss Patricia G. Petrone
Assistant to the Vice President for Defense and International Affairs	Mr. John O. Marsh, Jr.
Secretary to Mr. Marsh	Miss Nancy C. Chirdon
Military Assistants	
Army	Col. Jack A. Walker
Navy	Cdr. Howard J. Kerr
Marine Corps	Lt. Col. Americo A. Sardo
Air Force	Lt. Col. Robert E. Blake
Secretary	Miss Sue Cockrell
Secretary	Miss Barbara I. Martin
Staff Assistant for Travel, Transportation and Communications	Mr. Ralph E. Martin
Staff Assistant	YNC (SS) Richard J. Williams, USN
Driver	M/Sgt. Ulysses A. Owens, USAF
Driver	T/Sgt. Ralph S. Hopkins, USAF
Driver	Sgt. Darrell S. Riffle, USAF
Assistant to the Vice President for Legislation and Domestic Affairs	Mr. Richard T. Burress
Secretary to Mr. Burress	Mrs. Margaret O'Neill
Legal Counsel to the Vice President and Deputy Assistant for Executive Branch Liaison	Mr. William E. Casselman, II
Staff Assistant	Mr. Barry N. Roth
Secretary	Mrs. Brenda K. Wilson
Assistant to the President of the Senate	Mr. Walter L. Mote
Legislative Assistant	Mr. H. Spofford Canfield
Legislative Secretary	Mrs. Josephine E. Wilson
Staff Assistant	Mrs. Charlene C. vonPawel
Receptionist	Miss Anne F. Kamstra
Secretary	Mrs. Elizabeth L. Macbeth
Clerk/Typist	Miss Susan E. Stover

432

Mrs. Ford's Staff

Staff Assistant	Mrs. Nancy M. Howe
Staff Assistant	Mr. Richard D. Frazier
Secretary	Mrs. Carolyn K. Porembka

APPENDIX B

PRESIDENT FORD'S STAFF (May 1, 1975)

Underscore denotes Nixon Administration appointees

✶ With Ford before His Presidency

Counsel to the President	PHILIP W. BUCHEN ✶
Counsellor to the President	ROBERT T. HARTMANN ✶
Assistant to the President	HENRY A. KISSINGER (underscored)
Counsellor to the President	JOHN O. MARSH, JR. (underscored) ✶
Assistant to the President	DONALD H. RUMSFELD (underscored)
Assistant to the President for Management and Budget	JAMES T. LYNN
Press Secretary to the President	RONALD H. NESSEN
Assistant to the President for Economic Affairs	L. WILLIAM SEIDMAN ✶
Assistant to the President for Domestic Affairs	JAMES M. CANNON
Assistant to the President for Public Liaison	WILLIAM J. BAROODY, JR. (underscored)
Assistant to the President for Legislative Affairs	MAX L. FRIEDERSDORF (underscored)
Counsel to the President	RODERICK M. HILLS
Deputy Assistant to the President	RICHARD B. CHENEY (underscored)
Deputy Press Secretary to the President	WILLIAM I. GREENER, JR. (underscored)
Deputy Press Secretary to the President	JOHN W. HUSHEN (underscored)
Deputy Assistant to the President for National Security Affairs	LT. GEN. BRENT SCOWCROFT, USAF (underscored)
Counsel to the President	WILLIAM E. CASSELMAN II (underscored) ✶
Special Consultant to the President	ROBERT A. GOLDWIN (underscored)
Deputy Press Secretary to the President	GERALD L. WARREN
Deputy Assistant to the President for Legislative Affairs (Senate)	WILLIAM T. KENDALL
Deputy Assistant to the President for Legislative Affairs (House)	VERNON C. LOEN (underscored)
Secretary to the Cabinet	JAMES E. CONNOR (underscored)
Special Assistant to the President for Hispanic Affairs	FERNANDO E. C. DEBACA (underscored)
Staff Secretary to the President	JERRY H. JONES (underscored)
Special Assistant to the President for Consumer Affairs	VIRGINIA H. KNAUER (underscored)

PALACE POLITICS

Military Assistant to the President	CAPT. LELAND S. KOLLMORGEN, USN
Associate Counsel to the President	KENNETH A. LAZARUS
Associate Counsel to the President	JAMES A. WILDEROTTER
Special Assistant to the President for Women	PATRICIA S. LINDH
Special Assistant to the President for Human Resources	THEODORE C. MARRS
Special Assistant to the President for Minority Affairs	STANLEY S. SCOTT
Executive Editor, Editorial Office	PAUL A. THEIS
Special Assistant to the President for Labor-Management Negotiations	W. J. USERY
Director, Presidential Personnel Office	WILLIAM N. WALKER
Assistant Press Secretary to the President	MARGARETA E. WHITE
Deputy Executive Assistant to the Counsellor to the President	GWEN A. ANDERSON ✚
Special Assistant for Legislative Affairs (House)	DOUGLAS P. BENNETT
Executive Assistant to the Counsellor to the President	JOHN T. CALKINS
Director, Advance Office	BYRON M. CAVANEY, JR.
Assistant Press Secretary (Domestic Affairs)	JOHN G. CARLSON
Assistant Press Secretary to the President	THOMAS P. DeCAIR
Associate Counsel	DUDLEY H. CHAPMAN
Personal Secretary to the President	DOROTHY E. DOWNTON ✚
Director, Correspondence Office	ROLAND L. ELLIOTT
Director, Office of White House Visitors	MICHAEL J. FARRELL
Deputy Editor, Editorial Office	MILTON A. FRIEDMAN ✚
Director, Office of Presidential Messages	ELISKA A. HASEK
Deputy Staff Secretary to the President	DAVID C. HOOPES
Personal Photographer to the President	DAVID HUME KENNERLY
Personal Assistant to the President	MILDRED V. LEONARD ✚
Special Assistant for Legislative Affairs (House)	CHARLES LEPPERT, JR.
Special Assistant for Legislative Affairs (Senate)	PATRICK E. O'DONNELL
Aide to the President	TERRENCE O'DONNELL
Assistant Press Secretary	JOHN W. ROBERTS ✚
Executive Assistant to the Counsellor to the President	RUSSELL A. ROURKE
Director, Scheduling Office	WARREN S. RUSTAND ✚
Assistant Press Secretary (Foreign Affairs)	EDWARD J. SAVAGE
Assistant Press Secretary	LARRY M. SPEAKES
Director, Research Office	AGNES M. WALDRON
Deputy Director, Office of Public Liaison	DONALD A. WEBSTER
Deputy Director, Presidential Personnel Office	M. ALAN WOODS
Social Secretary	NANCY RUWE
Press Secretary to the First Lady	SHELIA RABB WEIDENFELD
Physician to the President	REAR ADM. WILLIAM M. LUKASH, MC, USN
Chief Executive Clerk	ROBERT D. LINDER
Chief Usher	REX W. SCOUTEN

434

INDEX

★★————————★★

435